1995

This second volume of Chopin studies contains the most recent Chopin research of twelve leading scholars. Three main topics are addressed: reception history, aesthetics and criticism, and performance studies. The first four chapters investigate certain images associated with Chopin during his lifetime and after his death: Chopin as classical composer, as salon composer, as modernist, as 'otherworldly', as androgyne. The next four essays contextualise and define aspects of his musical language, including narrative structures, baroque affinities, progressive tendencies and functional ambiguity. The last four deal with analysis and source study in relation to performance, structure and expression, *tempo rubato* and 'authentic' interpretation. The book ends with a thumbnail sketch of Chopin as revealed in a newly discovered diary from 1847 to 1848.

Chopin Studies 2

Chopin Studies 2

edited by
JOHN RINK
Lecturer in Music, University of Surrey
and
JIM SAMSON
Professor of Music, University of Bristol

Published by the Press Syndicate of the University of Cambridge
The Pitt Building, Trumpington Street, Cambridge CB2 1RP
40 West 20th Street, New York, NY 10011–4211, USA
10 Stamford Road, Oakleigh, Melbourne 3166, Australia

First published 1994

Printed in Great Britain at the University Press, Cambridge

A catalogue record for this book is available from the British Library

Library of Congress cataloguing in publication data

Chopin Studies.
Edited by John Rink and Jim Samson (vol. 2).
Includes bibliographical references and index.
1. Chopin, Frédéric, 1810–1849 – Criticism and interpretation.
I. Rink, John.   II. Samson, Jim.
ML410.C54C48 1988 786.1'092'4 87–25614
ISBN 0 521 30365 6 (vol. 1)
ISBN 0 521 41647 7 (vol. 2)

ISBN 0 521 41647 7 hardback

Contents

Preface   page ix

1 JIM SAMSON   Chopin reception: theory, history, analysis   1
2 ANDREAS BALLSTAEDT   Chopin as 'salon composer' in
                                 nineteenth-century German criticism   18
3 ANNE SWARTZ   Chopin as modernist in nineteenth-century
                                 Russia   35
4 JEFFREY KALLBERG   Small fairy voices: sex, history and
                                 meaning in Chopin   50
5 KAROL BERGER   Chopin's Ballade Op. 23 and the
                                 revolution of the intellectuals   72
6 ANTHONY NEWCOMB   The Polonaise-Fantasy and issues of
                                 musical narrative   84
7 JEAN-JACQUES EIGELDINGER   Placing Chopin: reflections on a
                                 compositional aesthetic   102
8 EDWARD T. CONE   Ambiguity and reinterpretation in Chopin   140
9 CARL SCHACHTER   The Prelude in E minor Op. 28 No. 4:
                                 autograph sources and interpretation   161
10 L. HENRY SHAFFER   Performing the F♯ minor Prelude
                                 Op. 28 No. 8   183
11 DAVID ROWLAND   Chopin's tempo rubato in context   199
12 JOHN RINK   Authentic Chopin: history, analysis
                                 and intuition in performance   214

   Appendix
   JEREMY BARLOW   Encounters with Chopin: Fanny
                                 Erskine's Paris diary, 1847–8   245

Index   249

153, 187

Preface

It has been our intention in commissioning this book to complement the documentary and analytical focus of Cambridge University Press's first volume of Chopin studies, published in 1988. This new collection targets three main areas of research – reception history, aesthetics and criticism, and performance studies – although the boundaries between these are by no means tightly drawn.

The first chapter, by Jim Samson, constructs a conceptual framework for reception studies in general and in Chopin's case specifically, and it goes on to assess the position of historical and analytical enquiry within the 'new musicology'. Andreas Ballstaedt and Anne Swartz home in on particular strands in Chopin reception, investigating the images of Chopin as 'salon composer' in nineteenth-century Germany and Austria, and as 'modernist' in nineteenth-century Russia. Another approach is taken by Jeffrey Kallberg, who considers the implicit and explicit invocations of sexual ideology in connection with Chopin during the last century in the form of 'otherworldly' metaphors and such recurrent tropes as Chopin the androgyne.

Both Karol Berger and Anthony Newcomb offer insights into narrative process in Chopin, Newcomb looking inwards to the musical discourse itself, Berger looking outwards to the historical consciousness of the Polish émigré community in 1830s Paris. A rather different contextualisation is provided in Jean-Jacques Eigeldinger's essay, which demonstrates the composer's predilection for the musical past, rejection of the present and indifference to the future, despite his eventual influence on later composers. Edward Cone looks at one of the principal reasons for that influence: the enriching ambiguities of his musical language and its consequent susceptibility to multiple interpretation.

Interpretation again comes to the fore in the final chapters, specifically in the realm of performance. Carl Schachter brings together analytical and genetic insights in devising a strategy for performing the E minor Prelude Op. 28 No. 4, while Henry Shaffer uses computer-originated data drawn from recent performances of the F# minor Prelude Op. 28 No. 8 to investigate the relation between structure and expression. A more historically based account of performing traditions is offered in David Rowland's examination of *tempo rubato* as practised before and after Chopin and by the composer himself. The final chapter, by John Rink, assesses the role of such historical evidence as well as analytical insight and the performer's own artistic convictions in formulating an 'authentic' interpretation of Chopin's music. The book is rounded off with a brief appendix by Jeremy Barlow offering a thumbnail sketch of Chopin the man as revealed in a recently discovered diary from 1847–8 of a Paris acquaintance, Fanny Erskine.

We should like to thank in particular Lucy Passmore of the University of Surrey, who helped with correspondence and expertly prepared much of the typescript (especially the two translations); the staff of the Biblioteka Narodowa, Warsaw, for permission to reproduce the manuscript shown in Plate 2; the current owner of the Erskine diary for permission to publish excerpts; the Department of Music, University of Surrey for financial support; and Penny Souster at Cambridge University Press for her encouragement and assistance.

John Rink
Jim Samson

1   Chopin reception: theory, history, analysis

JIM SAMSON

Introduction

Reception studies can form a useful link between two themes of concern to the new musicology. I will put them in the form of two questions. (i) How can we theorise context? (ii) How can we understand music as text? The first expresses our concern not just to situate the musical work within a broad social and cultural setting – there is nothing 'new' in that – but to interpret its relationship to the social world. The second addresses the competence of analysis to salvage the musical work as a text, making its own statement in a world where texts are habitually recognised as partial and contingent.

I will approach Chopin reception initially by way of the first of these themes – music and the social world. There are three levels on which music's social content might be addressed, corresponding more or less to categories familiar to semiology. They are the social 'cause' of a musical work (the proper subject of a traditional social history of music), the social 'trace' imprinted on its materials (the notoriously complex and sensitive issue addressed by Adorno and some more recent cultural theorists) and the social production of its meanings (the subject of a reception history). My concern here is with the third level, but it is important to locate it within the larger field, and to reveal clearly its conceptual difference from the other levels.

The first two levels – social cause and social trace – invoke critical hermeneutics and analysis respectively, and their common concern with context already suggests some convergence of interests between these two contrasted perspectives. For my purposes, however, it is more important to emphasise that these two levels work together to congeal the musical composition into a stable configuration. The third level challenges this, proposing rather unstable, even receding or 'vanishing', meanings. Stanley Fish speaks of a 'disappearing text'.[1] And here my first theme meets my second. Because of its challenge to determinacy, a reception study raises in a particularly acute form the issue of identity – the identity of the musical work. So it bears very directly on the second of the two themes outlined above, the nature of music as text.

---

[1] Stanley Fish, *Is There a Text in This Class? The Authority of Interpretative Communities* (Cambridge, Massachusetts 1980).

Reception history: the late nineteenth century

In its afterlife a musical work threads its way through many different social and cultural formations, attaching itself to them in different ways, adapting its own semblance and in the process changing theirs. The work remains at least notionally the same object – at any rate it is the product of a singular creative act – but its manner of occupying the social landscape changes constantly. In tracing these multiple social existences a reception study can light up the ideology concealed in the corners of music history. And it can expose in the process some of the vested interests at work in the promotion, dissemination, influence and evaluation of musical works. In the course of such a study, we collect and examine multiple data – concert programmes and advertisements, critical notices, musicological and other writings, editions, recordings and even musical works by later composers. However, it seems to me essential to focus the examination of this data in clearly defined ways. Reception history should be more than just supposedly neutral opinion collecting.[2]

A helpful starting-point in the interpretation of such data for Chopin reception is to examine the dispersal of meanings in the second half of the nineteenth century, following the composer's death in 1849. I will try to do so by sketching four profiles of Chopin which emerge with reasonable consistency in the late nineteenth century.[3] They can be associated especially clearly with particular modes of reception and particular cultural communities, though there is nothing exclusive about this association. I will consider French critics, German publishers, Russian composers and English amateurs (I use the term with its original and literal meaning). And I need hardly say that my remarks will be reductive. I see no way of identifying large patterns in cultural history without doing some injustice to detail – to what is after all an infinite diversity of facts, unavailable to any single researcher. A reductive interpretation is offered so that it might be examined critically and adjusted accordingly.

French critics

Chopin's reputation was largely created in Paris, and it was preserved and enhanced by French journals after his death. Yet from the start a very particular view of Chopin was presented by French critics, one which highlighted the notion of expression. Not only do we have the rather novel idea that a musical work might be a fragment of autobiography ('it seems impossible to make a clear distinction between his music and his personality'[4]): we further learn that it might act as a channel between the inner emotional world of the creator and that of the listener – a form of communication. As one critic put it, '[the listener] will weep, believing that he really suffers with one who can weep so well'.[5]

---

2   See Carl Dahlhaus, *Analysis and Value Judgment*, trans. Siegmund Levarie (New York 1983; original German edn 1970), pp. 24–8.
3   Roman Ingarden uses the term 'profile' to describe particular 'concretions' of a work of art. *The Literary Work of Art: An Investigation on the Borderlines of Ontology, Logic, and Theory of Literature*, trans. George G. Grabowitz (Evanston, Illinois 1973).
4   Hippolyte Barbedette, *Chopin. Essai de critique musicale* (Paris 1869), p. 65. All translations in this chapter are mine unless otherwise stated.
5   Ibid., p. 71.

A cluster of images gathered around this central preoccupation with expression. Above all the metaphor of poetry was worked exhaustively in descriptions of Chopin's music. This extended beyond a generous allocation of poetic programmes to incorporate a more generalised category of the poetic,[6] suggestive of the sublime and mysterious, distilled to intimacy. Such ideas were already current in his lifetime. 'To listen to Chopin is to read a strophe of Lamartine';[7] 'Chopin is a poet, and above all a tender one';[8] 'he is an elegaic, profound and dreamy poet of tones';[9] 'it is poetry in translation, but a superior translation made through sounds alone'.[10] The implication of a hidden emotional content is clear, and it became part of the ambience of the music for later generations. It is no coincidence that one of the first French biographies was published under the title *Chopin ou le poète*.[11]

Two further connotations might be mentioned. The image of Chopin the consumptive, with 'the pallor of the grave', was given a kind of explanatory value by some French critics. This fused well with aspects of romantic thought, where suffering and creative inspiration were linked as parallel (Schopenhauerian) escapes from the commonplaces of the world. Through music he 'discloses his suffering'.[12] Then there is the feminine topos, which has been discussed at length by Jeffrey Kallberg.[13] That image was promoted in portraits, drawings and pictorial representations on French editions, as well as in critical writing. It could be disparaging: music 'for the drawing-room; for the ladies',[14] or flattering: music of nuance and refinement, written 'with a man's strength, but for a woman's sensitiveness of finger'.[15] The nocturne was a principal focus for such associations, and it is perhaps not surprising that the nocturne was the favoured Chopin genre in late-nineteenth-century France.[16] There is indeed an issue here for gender studies and it could usefully carry through to our century; Chopin and the cinema is one obvious theme. Now these images both fed upon and helped to create a kind of ideal Chopin biography in the late nineteenth century.[17] Few composers were quite so susceptible to apocrypha, designed it would seem to transform

6   See Dahlhaus, *Analysis and Value Judgment*, pp. 16–18.
7   *Le Ménestrel: Journal de musique*, 2 May 1841. Quoted in Olgierd Pisarenko, 'Chopin and His Contemporaries: Paris 1832–1860', in *Studies in Chopin*, ed. Dariusz Żebrowski, trans. Halina Oszczygieł (Warsaw 1973), p. 35.
8   Léon Escudier in *La France musicale*, 27 May 1842. Translation from William G. Atwood, *Fryderyk Chopin: Pianist from Warsaw* (New York 1987), p. 239.
9   *Revue et Gazette musicale de Paris*, 2 May 1841.
10 *Revue et Gazette musicale de Paris*, 27 February 1842.
11 Guy de Pourtalès, *Chopin ou le poète* (Paris 1927).
12 Barbedette, *Chopin*, p. 65. For a more radical interpretation, see Jeffrey Kallberg's chapter in the present volume.
13 'The Harmony of the Tea Table: Gender and Ideology in the Piano Nocturne', *Representations*, no. 39 (Summer 1992), pp. 102–33.
14 Chopin's own description of his Op. 3. See *Korespondencja Fryderyka Chopina*, ed. Bronisław Edward Sydow, 2 vols. (Warsaw 1955), vol. I, p. 112.
15 *Revue et Gazette musicale de Paris*, 2 January 1842.
16 For a discussion of such associations see Jeffrey Kallberg, 'Understanding Genre: A Reinterpretation of the Early Piano Nocturne', *Atti del XIV Congresso della Società Internazionale di Musicologia*, 3 vols. (Turin 1990), vol. III, pp. 775–9.
17 I have discussed this briefly in 'Myth and Reality: A Biographical Introduction', in *The Cambridge Companion to Chopin*, ed. Jim Samson (Cambridge 1992), pp. 1–8.

a figure of classical orientation into the archetype of a romantic artist. And this ideal biography in turn created the climate for particular readings of the music, embracing a manner of performance, listening and even editing.

It was indeed in French writing on Chopin that a central aspect of what we may call the romantic ideology was actively promoted. It has been resonantly described by Rose Subotnik as 'sensuous distinctiveness'.[18] This is premised on the assumption that value may reside in a personal identity, a personal style, or, as one critic said of Chopin, 'a mysterious language known only to himself',[19] and on the further assumption that within the musical work value may reside as much in the fragment – the 'arresting phrase' – as in the whole. It is still to French writers – novelists as well as critics – that we turn for the most telling accounts of that personal style and those 'arresting phrases'. Proust's description of the Chopin melody has yet to be bettered: those

long sinuous phrases . . . so free, so flexible, so tactile, which begin by reaching out and exploring far beyond the point which one might have expected their notes to reach, and which divert themselves in those byways of fantasy, only to return more deliberately – with a more premeditated reprise, with more precision, as on a crystal bowl that reverberates to the point of making you cry out – to strike at your heart.[20]

In assessing the portrayal of Chopin by French critics, we need of course to look behind the scenes, to examine contexts and motivations. Katharine Ellis has ably demonstrated that there were clear sub-texts underlying the promotion of some composers at the expense of others in the French press.[21] There are in short no neutral readings. A single but important example must suffice. The most influential of the journals was the *Revue et Gazette musicale*, and its promotion of Chopin contributed greatly to his high standing in France. It helps to know that its founder-editor Maurice Schlesinger was Chopin's principal French publisher. But beyond that, the image of Chopin as a composer of deep feeling and high seriousness – a romantic poet – suited the larger agenda of the *Gazette*. This was a journal committed to a sustained war against the trivia promoted by what we may call the piano industry, and against the journalistic support of that trivia elsewhere in Paris, especially by *La France musicale*. (Incidentally, in its very early stages that rivalry actually gave rise to a duel, and Chopin found himself testifying in court on Schlesinger's behalf.[22]) Chopin's avoidance of the public concert made him the *Gazette's* perfect candidate for a kind of alternative idol to the popular pianist-composers of the concert-hall. The careful construction of his image, then, was in very large measure a polemic against the shallow virtuosity of public pianism, and for some of the *Gazette's* critics, that included Liszt.

We should be in no doubt of the power of the nineteenth-century critic, whose rise to pre-eminence signified a major shift from functional to aesthetic judgements

---

[18]   Rose Rosengard Subotnik, 'On Grounding Chopin', in *Music and Society: The Politics of Composition, Performance and Reception*, ed. Richard Leppert and Susan McClary (Cambridge 1987), pp. 105–32.

[19]   *Revue et Gazette musicale de Paris*, 2 March 1843, in a review of a concert by Carl Filtsch.

[20]   Marcel Proust, *Remembrance of Things Past*, trans. C. K. Scott Moncrieff and Terence Kilmartin, 3 vols. (Harmondsworth 1983), vol. III, p. 361.

[21]   Katharine Ellis, '*La Revue et Gazette musicale de Paris* 1834–1880: The State of Music Criticism in Mid-Nineteenth-Century France' (Dissertation, University of Oxford 1991).

[22]   This took place on 29 April 1834.

in music as in the other arts.[23] Arguably more than any other single factor, it was the success of the *Gazette* which established the prevailing view of Chopin in late-nineteenth-century France – a composer detached from, even aloof from, society, with an unmistakable personal idiom which nevertheless avoided the more iconoclastic modernisms. He came to represent the survival of very particular values in French music, associated with salon culture at its best, with intimate performance contexts, with an art of nuance, sophistication and refinement. Conveniently appropriated by French culture, his music became the perfect bulwark against encroaching German influence in the late nineteenth century, against the pretension of a 'music of the future' on the one hand and the populism of a so-called *Trivialmusik* on the other. The concealed social energies in French Chopin criticism worked then to preserve a peculiarly French form of patronal culture, and increasingly to bolster this with style-historical interpretations. Chopin, in short, came to be viewed in France as a kind of vital missing link connecting the clavecinistes to the great pianist-composers of the *fin de siècle*, Fauré, Debussy and Ravel.[24] Something of that perception remains today.

German publishers

Chopin's acceptance in the canon of great composers owed much to the publication of the Breitkopf & Härtel collected edition in 1878–80. From the start his international reputation had been heavily dependent on his association with German publishers, initially Kistner and later Breitkopf & Härtel. During his lifetime his music was published simultaneously in France, Germany and England – for copyright reasons. But its wider dissemination was ensured by his contract with Breitkopf, who had agents and distributional networks throughout the world. Leipzig was after all the capital of music publishing, and Breitkopf & Härtel was the leading firm. For a pianist-composer who avoided the public concert, with its associated promotional apparatus, such patronage was vital. One English critic remarked that where other pianists would promote their music by 'announc[ing] a concert or see[ing] company at Erard's or Broadwood's . . . M. Chopin quietly publishes 2 [*sic*] *Waltzes*'.[25] Breitkopf was not the only publishing house to produce a collected edition following Chopin's death. Several appeared in France, Russia and Poland in the 1860s and 1870s, prepared in the main by his pupils. But whereas these editions had a limited circulation and impact – at least in the short term – the Breitkopf edition represented a major landmark in Chopin reception.

To understand the full significance of this, we need to be aware of the background to the edition. From 1850 onwards Breitkopf & Härtel embarked on an extended series of collected editions of major composers, completed only some forty years later. The series, described by one recent commentator as 'the first serious and systematic attempt

23 See Dahlhaus, *Analysis and Value Judgment*, pp. 10–15.
24 See Roy Howat, 'Chopin's Influence on the *Fin de siècle* and Beyond', in *The Cambridge Companion to Chopin*, ed. Jim Samson (Cambridge 1992), pp. 246–83; see also Jean-Jacques Eigeldinger's chapter in the present volume.
25 *The Athenaeum*, 22 January 1848. The reference is to the three Waltzes Op. 64.

to establish the works of musical authors in a canonic way',[26] was launched by editions of Bach and Handel, clearly viewed as the foundation stones of German music, and it went on to include Mozart, Beethoven, Schubert, Mendelssohn and Schumann. The whole project had obvious ideological significance. The formation of a musical canon and the development of the associated category 'classical music', with all its atemporal resonance, was largely a product of the nineteenth century. It can be traced most clearly in concert life, as the early-nineteenth-century salon and benefit concert gave way to the late-nineteenth-century recital and subscription concert, complete with a repertoire centred on the Viennese classics with a sprinkling of ambitious modern works. But it can also be traced through music criticism, and through publishing history. The Breitkopf editions were part and parcel of a development famously described as the invention of tradition.

Canon formation was not of course unique to Germany (indeed it began in England and France rather earlier),[27] but it was above all in Germany that the canon became associated with a dominant national culture, perceived as both specifically German and at the same time representative of universal values, a paradox well in tune with German classical art and the new philology. The Viennese classics became literally that, with all the Hellenistic connotations. The practical and ideological force of the German canon is well known. Practically it allowed the significant to push into obscurity the only marginally less significant (the Brahms symphony obscures the Bruch symphony). Ideologically it manipulated an innocent repertoire to confirm the social position of a dominant group in society. I should stress, of course, that to identify an ideological element in canon formation is not to deny the validity of the canon as a body of excellence, nor to propose its deconstruction. But it would be reasonable to probe the conditions of its formation, to question the rigidity of its boundaries and to consider the terms of its revisability.

None of these tasks will be undertaken here. My concern is simply to note that the inclusion of Chopin in the Breitkopf canon was tantamount to a form of adoption. Like Palestrina, also embraced by Breitkopf, he became a sort of honorary member of the German tradition. And it is no exaggeration to claim that the edition represented an almost symbolic moment of resolution in German Chopin reception, following a lengthy polemic which had begun in his lifetime with Schumann, Rellstab, Kahlert and many others, and continued through to the late nineteenth century. In a culture which was no longer willing to make an easy equation between the significant and the well-composed, Chopin's associations with the salon had proved a considerable obstacle to his public success in Germany. And it was above all the Breitkopf edition which changed that, conferring dignity on Chopin in the German world. The essay by Andreas Ballstaedt in this volume draws attention to the reclassifications of several of Chopin's works in the later editions of certain well-known German music guides, where they are in effect removed from the category 'salon piece'. Chopin, in short, became a classical composer.

[26] Philip Brett, 'Text, Context, and the Early Music Editor', in *Authenticity and Early Music*, ed. Nicholas Kenyon (Oxford 1988), p. 86.

[27] See William Weber, *The Rise of Musical Classics in Eighteenth-Century England: A Study in Canon, Ritual, and Ideology* (Oxford 1992).

Once this status had been achieved, it was secured by other means. A German translation of selected letters was published by Breitkopf,[28] together with serious biographies by Adolf Weissmann[29] and Bernard Scharlitt,[30] designed to dispel lingering associations with the ephemeral and the lightweight, though even they succumbed in part to these associations. A major Riemann-inspired analytical study by Hugo Leichtentritt followed shortly after, subjecting virtually every work of the published music to detailed analytical scrutiny.[31] This huge study by Leichtentritt was an astonishing venture for its time. Very few composers were granted such treatment. It was truly a monument to a recently established and increasingly specialised *Musikwissenschaft*. These early days of scientific musicology in Germany make for a fascinating study, especially as the values expounded there continue to influence Anglo-American scholarship. I will elaborate just a little on this. In keeping with its philological inspiration, the youthful science of music effectively distanced the unworthy art of the present from the perfection of the classical canon and at the same time reduced that classical canon to the conscientious typologies of the new science. Historicism and scientism met in this endeavour, and Leichtentritt's study, with its morphological analytical approach, was a characteristic product.

Yet powerful voices were raised in protest. Some time after Nietzsche railed against the narrowness of the new philology,[32] Heinrich Schenker likewise turned his back on the institutions and the developing orthodoxies of academic musicology, finding richer sustenance – again like Nietzsche – in the thought of Schopenhauer.[33] It is a telling paradox, then, that the Schenkerian canon, cultivated with no less chauvinism than that of academic musicology, should also have adopted Chopin as an honorary member of the great tradition. Schenker spells this out in the following extraordinary terms. 'If the writer elevates the name of Frederic Chopin for inclusion in the roll of great German masters, this is because, despite the fact that his masterworks do not stem directly from Germanity but are indirectly bound to it, he wishes them, too, to be accessible as a source of the highest operations of genius, and in this most exalted sense also to place them newly at the service of the German youth.' And again, 'For the profundity with which nature has endowed him, Chopin belongs more to Germany than to Poland.'[34]

28 *Friedrich Chopins gesammelte Briefe*, ed. Bernard Scharlitt (Leipzig 1911).
29 Adolf Weissmann, *Chopin* (Leipzig 1912).
30 Bernard Scharlitt, *Chopin* (Leipzig 1919).
31 Hugo Leichtentritt, *Analyse der Chopin'schen Klavierwerke*, 2 vols. (Berlin 1921–2). Those works that are excluded are just the ones that might condone the image of Chopin as salon composer. There is an earlier biographical study by Leichtentritt, *Frédéric Chopin* (Berlin 1905).
32 Friedrich Nietzsche, *Untimely Meditations* (see especially the second of these, 'On the Uses and Disadvantages of History for Life'), in *Basic Writings of Nietzsche*, trans. Walter Kaufmann (New York 1968).
33 This is not a point I can elaborate in the present essay. For a commentary on Schenker and Schopenhauer see Nicholas Cook, 'Schenker's Theory of Music as Ethics', *Journal of Musicology*, 7 (1989), pp. 415–39. But the most penetrating discussion of this subject is in Barbara Whittle, 'The Cultural Context of the Theories of Heinrich Schenker' (Dissertation, The Open University 1994).
34 These excerpts from *Der Tonwille* and *Das Meisterwerk in der Musik* are translated by Ian Bent in 'Heinrich Schenker, Chopin and Domenico Scarlatti', *Music Analysis*, 5/2–3 (1986), pp. 131–49.

There is a footnote. In one of the most fascinating journeys of modern intellectual history, Schenkerian thought was radically transformed in America, and above all stripped of its nineteenth-century philosophical content, before making its way back to central Europe in the guise of 'Schenkerian analysis', a construction which Schenker himself would not have recognised, still less approved. There is rich fare here for another reception study. However, my real point, parenthetical but important, is that it was largely thanks to Schenker's commitment to Chopin that English and American analysts, no less than German musicologists, placed his music centrally within their particular classical canon.

Russian composers

The larger pattern of Chopin reception in Russia is documented elsewhere in this volume, and I will refer here to just a single issue, his influence on Balakirev and his circle. The poetics of influence have engaged literary and musical theorists at length and need not be elaborated here,[35] beyond remarking that Balakirev's debt to Chopin might well be understood in terms described by Joseph Straus as 'analytical mis-reading'[36] and by Leonard B. Meyer as a 'deforming of prior meaning'.[37] The point here is that the perception of Chopin as a Slavonic composer – one of the first com-posers of significance to have promoted a form of cultural nationalism in music – was largely a matter of reception. It is true that he wrote at one point of his attempts 'to express the nature of our national music'.[38] It is also true that his approach to national dances changed profoundly at the end of his Warsaw period (partly I suspect under the influence of the writings of Kazimierz Brodziński),[39] moving some way towards the aesthetic promoted by late-nineteenth-century Russian nationalists. Yet on the level of intention Chopin cannot be confined within a nationalist aesthetic, however much he may have derived energy from it.

Increasingly Chopin's originality as a composer – and not just a composer of mazurkas – was given a nationalist interpretation by the Balakirev circle, naturally at the expense of other, no less vital, aspects of the music. For Balakirev the key point was that in Chopin, folk materials were integrated with the most advanced techniques of contemporary European art music. It was just such a fusion of nationalism and modernism that Balakirev himself tried to promote at the Free School of Music, and he acknowledged Chopin as a powerful inspiration in both respects. For him Chopin

---

[35]   There are several relevant texts by Harold Bloom, most famously *The Anxiety of Influence: A Theory of Poetry* (New Haven 1973). See also Göran Hermerén, *Influence in Art and Literature* (Princeton 1975). Specific to music are Charles Rosen, 'Influence, Plagiarism, and Inspiration', in *On Criticizing Music*, ed. Kingsley Price (Baltimore 1981); Susan Youens, 'Schubert, Mahler and the Weight of the Past', *Music & Letters*, 67 (July 1986), pp. 256–68; Kevin Korsyn, 'Towards a New Poetics of Musical Influence', *Music Analysis*, 10/1–2 (1991), pp. 2–72; Joseph Straus, *Remaking the Past: Musical Modernism and the Influence of the Tonal Tradition* (Cambridge, Massachusetts 1990).

[36]   Straus, *Remaking the Past*, p. 21.

[37]   Leonard B. Meyer, *Style and Music: Theory, History, Ideology* (Philadelphia 1989), p. 23.

[38]   *Korespondencja*, vol. I, p. 57.

[39]   Brodziński wrote about the deeper significance of Polish national dances in *Melitele* (Warsaw 1829), pp. 85–105. For a discussion see Tadeusz Frączyk, *Warszawa młodości Chopina* (Warsaw 1961), pp. 182–222.

was neither a salon composer nor a romantic composer, but a radical, progressive figure, and this view was widely shared by other members of the Balakirev circle and by Slavonic nationalists generally in the later nineteenth century.

Not surprisingly, then, his stylistic influence on progressive tendencies in Russian music was considerable, and it ranged from direct emulation through to transformation and recontextualisation. Technically Russian composers selected carefully from the fused whole of Chopin's musical style. In the harmonic sphere they focused on modalities and chromatic symmetries. Melodically they favoured elements which give priority to decoration and variation over dissection and development. And structurally they picked up on a subtle and prophetic change in the relative weighting of components in Chopin, and especially a promotion of texture. All are features which provided Russian composers with alternatives to the forms and methods of an Austro-German tradition, and that fact was to prove of enormous significance for the development of twentieth-century musical styles.

Anne Swartz has suggested elsewhere in this volume that the image of Chopin as nationalist and modernist declined significantly in Russia in the later nineteenth century. In the end it was kept alive principally by Balakirev himself, when his circle was no longer a unified and vital force in Russian music. Balakirev did, however, hand on the torch. Through a nice irony it was his initiative which helped Polish musical circles come to an adequate appreciation of their own composer. At the very end of his life Balakirev paid several visits to Warsaw, prodding the Warsaw Music Society into doing something to awaken public interest in Chopin. On 14 October 1894, at Balakirev's instigation, a Chopin monument was unveiled at the composer's birthplace in the tiny village of Żelazowa Wola, some thirty miles west of Warsaw, and three days later a celebration concert was given, with Balakirev himself performing the virtually unknown *Lento con gran espressione*.

This was just the beginning of a renaissance in Polish Chopin reception, following a period when little more than lip-service was paid to his genius. Two years after the Balakirev concert the young Karol Szymanowski wrote his earliest piano pieces, the first music by a Polish composer to take up Balakirev's challenge and establish genuine contact with Chopin. And it was Szymanowski more than anyone who went on to revitalise the image of Chopin as nationalist and modernist, holding him up to the world as an 'eternal example of what Polish music was capable of achieving – a symbol of Europeanised Poland, losing nothing of his national features but standing on the highest pinnacle of European culture'.[40] From there the story took intriguing new directions. The subsequent manipulation of Chopin by successive Polish authorities – through the communist era and beyond – would make a chapter in itself.

English amateurs

In his study of domestic music-making in eighteenth-century England, Richard Leppert illustrates the role of music as social regulation and status confirmation, a role which

---

[40]   Karol Szymanowski, *Z Pism*, ed. Teresa Chylińska (Cracow 1958), p. 185.

was strengthened through the early nineteenth century and the Victorian age.[41] Both religious and social values promoted music-making in the middle-class English home, and the rigid separation of this amateur arena from the professional concert platform served to underline other divisions within Victorian society. A whole complex of xenophobic, gender and class issues bears on this, and the matter clearly cannot be debated here. But it may be worth remarking that the public sphere matched the private in one particular, its conspicuous lack of resistance to the political and religious establishments. I have commented elsewhere on the historical reasons for this.[42] Nor is it appropriate here to analyse those Victorian attitudes which ensured that women were the main consumers and practitioners of an art firmly centred on the piano – the 'household orchestra'.

It is enough to highlight the outcome of all these influences. In the last quarter of the century there was a remarkable expansion in the sale of pianos in England. As one critic put it, 'The home art of the present day is summed up in the word "piano".'[43] The result was a flood of music suitable for performance by the Victorian woman, including short, manageable piano pieces – simple transcriptions, dance pieces, 'character' pieces. Stylistically this repertoire was modelled on the European art music of a half-century earlier. Derek Carew refers to a 'stylistic time-lock' and describes characteristic Victorian salon pieces as 'lacklustre reflections of the living, breathing art of their early-Romantic progenitors'.[44] Among the most prominent of those progenitors was Chopin, and the external features of his nocturnes and mazurkas proved especially vulnerable to imitation by Victorian composers. Technically this amounted to a reduction of Chopin's densely woven textures and delicately shaped phrases to a handful of easy gestures: it is tempting to resort to Matthew Arnold's word *kitsch*. The contrast with Chopin's influence on Russian composers could scarcely be more marked.

And in due course Chopin's own music was lumped together with this progeny. We find the nocturnes published in collections called 'drawing-room trifles'; we encounter the preludes described as 'pearls' and the etudes as 'tuneful gems'. We meet publications of simplified and shortened versions of some of the more technically demanding works, including the G minor Ballade. Compare this with the Breitkopf enterprise. There is some irony in Charles Hallé's remark that Chopin had become 'the property of every schoolgirl',[45] and in the observation of *The Musical Gazette* that 'the grand-daughters of the young ladies who trundled through *The Battle of Prague* now trundle through Chopin'.[46] Chopin, in short, was domesticated in England, as he was deified in Russia. And as his music was increasingly commodified, its unique

---

[41]   Richard Leppert, *Music and Image: Domesticity, Ideology and Socio-cultural Formation in Eighteenth-Century England* (Cambridge 1988).

[42]   Jim Samson, 'Music and Society', in *The Late Romantic Era: Man & Music*, vol. VII, ed. Jim Samson (London 1991), pp. 28–33.

[43]   *The Musical Standard*, December 1866.

[44]   Derek Carew, 'Victorian Attitudes to Chopin', in *The Cambridge Companion to Chopin*, ed. Jim Samson (Cambridge 1992), pp. 226–7.

[45]   *The Autobiography of Charles Hallé*, ed. Michael Kennedy (London 1972; first published 1896), p. 54.

[46]   *The Musical Gazette*, 4 December 1900. *The Battle of Prague* was a popular genre piece by Kotzwara, composed in the late eighteenth century.

features, well noted in early-nineteenth-century English criticism, were smoothed out by their association with the surrounding lowlands of mediocrity. They became indistinguishable from their environment in a way which rather anticipates some of the effects of today's culture industry.

Summary

It is worth reflecting for a moment on these four profiles. The picture I have painted is over-compartmentalised, without a doubt; I am well aware that there are dangers in thus drawing many strands into a single figure. Nevertheless it seems clear that Chopin's music was a kind of cultural battleground in the late nineteenth century, prey to appropriation. And it is perhaps relevant to point up a central paradox here. The more closely music approaches an autonomy character, the more susceptible it becomes to such appropriation. The Chopin work was an intimate communication; it was an icon; it was an agent of cultural and even political propaganda; it was a commodity.

It is rather as though Chopin held a mirror to the conflicting ideologies attending a critical period in music history, right on the cusp between classical and modernist notions of art. French critics sought to preserve him as the 'Ariel of the piano', an ideal romantic composer, a poet. English consumers tried to domesticate him, absorbing him easily into a musical culture which affirmed, with no significant critical element, the middle-class ascendancy. Russian composers turned him into a modernist, drawn into the orbit of a pioneering music responsive neither to the professional establishment nor to public taste. It is especially intriguing to see this polarity of response in two countries on the edge of Europe, an advanced industrialised nation and a backward feudal one. In these opposed perspectives we view separately, and with particular clarity, the two strands that were held in dialectical opposition in Germany, resolved only when Chopin was elevated to the canon, and thus absorbed by history – a classical composer.

Reception history: the challenge of formalism

Following this dispersal of meanings in the late nineteenth century, there was a discernible closure of meaning in twentieth-century Chopin reception. However, this new determinacy, characterised by what might be called the myth of the musical work, stood in a polarised relation to the perceptions of Chopin's own era. I claim no special credit for drawing attention to this polarity, which is well known in general terms. But I do want to reflect a little on it. So having looked at four aspects of reception within a single period, the late nineteenth century, I will now look briefly at two broad periods, Chopin's time and ours.

The contrast is apparent when we consider the relationship between performance and text. Chopin was shaped by the world of post-classical concert music, the so-called 'brilliant style', and within that world a hierarchy of values subordinated work to genre, and genre to performance. The work exemplified a genre (principally variations, fantasies and independent rondos) and the genre exemplified a performance –

a particular communicative act directed towards a specific audience. Chopin's early music belonged centrally to this repertoire. He went on to transcend it, of course, relocating its performance space, distilling originality from its stylistic conformity, promoting the work at the expense of the genre. He transcended it, but he also remembered it. His innovations arose from and were implied by the post-classical repertoire, and they were conditioned in every particular by its central assumption – that work and performance are inseparably fused. To his contemporaries Chopin remained a pianist-composer, writing 'pianists' music' rather than 'pianoforte music', as one highly influential critic put it.[47] There was even some suggestion, notably from Moscheles, that Chopin the performer held a sort of monopoly on Chopin the composer.[48] As Jeffrey Kallberg has convincingly argued, the endless variants in the manuscript and printed sources for Chopin's compositions reflected nothing so much as the fluidity of the very concept of the musical work for Chopin and his listeners.[49]

In later reception, on the other hand, performance and text were prised apart. The drama of separation was enacted on several fronts. Editors played their part. Initially we had the attempt by Chopin's pupils and their pupils to preserve a living Chopin tradition (one which gave precedence to his own practice as a performer), recreating in print memories of versions played by Chopin and his students, even where these depart from manuscript and printed sources.[50] By today's standards, this was a permissive society, though we should not rush to judgement. In any event this approach gave ground slowly before the growing concern of editors to investigate a manuscript tradition of great complexity in a paper chase for the definitive text, a text supposedly validated by final intentions – as though it might be so simple.

Pianists also played their part in the separation of performance and text, as that modern institution, the piano recital, likewise developed its two opposing cultures. It was above all Anton Rubinstein who acclimatised Chopin's music to the public concert in the later nineteenth century, forcing it into a new kind of performance arena, bending it to his will and in the process changing it utterly. As Hallé remarked, 'It is clever, but it is not Chopin.' This was no longer the pianist-composer playing to the gallery, proudly displaying his wares. Rather it was the public recitalist exerting control over someone else's music – a form of ownership, as Edward Said has suggested[51] – where the text is not just dominated, but may indeed be reshaped, culminating in the arrangements and transcriptions of pianist-composers such as Godowsky.

Yet this subjugation of the text ran parallel to a growing respect for its authority. The historically aware performance, aiming to recover the composer's intentions

---

47   From the famous review by Fétis of Chopin's first concert in Paris, *Revue musicale*, 3 March 1832.

48   Moscheles' remarks on Chopin are recorded in *Aus Moscheles' Leben*, a publication in two volumes (1872–3) prepared by his wife Charlotte. For a discussion of his views on Chopin see Emil F. Smidak, *Isaak-Ignaz Moscheles: The Life of the Composer and His Encounters with Beethoven, Liszt, Chopin and Mendelssohn* (Vienna 1988), pp. 120–2.

49   See Jeffrey Kallberg, 'Hearing Poland: Chopin and Nationalism', in *Nineteenth-Century Piano Music*, ed. R. Larry Todd (New York 1990), pp. 221–57. The relevant passage is on pp. 232–3.

50   For a discussion see the review by Zofia Chechlińska of the Polish National Edition of Chopin in *Chopin Studies*, 2 (1987), pp. 7–20.

51   Edward W. Said, *Musical Elaborations* (London 1991). See the chapter 'Performance as an Extreme Occasion', pp. 1–34.

through a careful examination of primary sources and a circumspect approach to performance conventions, was already a reality in the late nineteenth century, and I should add in passing that women pianists were active here. Women in general had to struggle to establish credibility on the concert platform, and it seems they could best do so by assuming traditional female roles of subservience (in this case to the composer and his text).[52] In due course historically aware performances were absorbed by a so-called authenticity movement which now offers us performances and recordings of Chopin on early-nineteenth-century fortepianos in a studied and notoriously problematic attempt to let the music speak as once it did.[53] This, ironically, is almost as far from the spirit of Chopin as Godowsky.

The contrast between Chopin's time and ours is of course made explicit in music criticism. It was common practice for Chopin's contemporaries to relate his music to real or imagined contexts. The work was understood to mediate larger realities, and of several kinds: it expressed an emotion; it told a story; it exemplified a genre; it articulated a style; it confirmed an institution. And its meaning was therefore contingent. Moreover the work was habitually described in sequential terms. It was not a structure but a succession of styles, even of genres – combination rather than integration, succession rather than synthesis. It was, in a sense, a narrative.

In contrast, our own century's criticism sought to de-contextualise the work, so that it might become a world in itself, laying claim to an ideal relationship of part to whole. We can trace the idea of a structural sense of form to the schemata of theorists such as Adolf Bernhard Marx.[54] But from these beginnings the idea gained unstoppable momentum, sweeping music theory before it, and in the end building on its premise the entire edifice of a newly independent discipline, music analysis. Unity and wholeness, whatever these may mean in a temporal art, were assumed *a priori* in the musical masterpiece, and the analytical act was their demonstration. The work became a structure, and in that lay its value. And just as the critic had replaced the patron, so the analyst replaced the critic as the ultimate arbiter of quality. The experience of listeners is another matter, no doubt influenced by, yet at the same time separate from, these organicist articulations. I doubt very much if listeners habitually experience musical works as closed and unified, excluding the world outside the work. Indeed the divergence of rhetoric and reality here has been seen by Nicholas Cook for one as culturally defining for our century.[55]

Let us then contrast Chopin's world and ours through an exercise in imaginative recreation. In the reprise of the fourth Ballade we may hear a triumphant synthesis of two very different surface styles – canon and ornamental *bel canto*, Bach and Italian opera. Chopin's world might have related the sequence to a conventional succession of contemporary improvisation, noted in just these terms in the method books, and it

---

52 There are parallels with twentieth-century women conductors. I am indebted to Jeanice Brooks, who is currently researching on Nadia Boulanger, for drawing my attention to this.
53 An alternative interpretation of 'authenticity' is offered in John Rink's chapter in the present volume.
54 See the remarks by Jeffrey Kallberg in 'Small "Forms": In Defence of the Prelude', *The Cambridge Companion to Chopin*, ed. Jim Samson (Cambridge 1992), pp. 124–44.
55 Nicholas Cook, *Music, Imagination, and Culture* (Oxford 1990).

might even have heard in the bravura coda a distant echo of the familiar applause-seeking perorations of popular concert pieces. In the second Ballade we may hear a dramatic confrontation of sharply contrasted materials, heightened by a two-key scheme which points daringly to Wagner and Mahler. Chopin's world might have related this to the classic formal ingredients of the brilliant style – bravura figuration squared off against popular melody, etude against siciliano. As for the two-key scheme, it would have remembered enough of these from the post-classical repertoire not to worry unduly.[56] In the introduction to the Fantasy Op. 49 we may hear a multi-sectional upbeat to the first tonal and thematic cycle. Chopin's world might rather have heard the stylisation of an operatic scena: slow march, recitative, grand chorus.

One could continue along these lines. We signally fail to notice generic features which would have struck Chopin's contemporaries – those gestures in the A minor Prelude that signal a funeral march; those features of the G minor Ballade that identify it as a lament; those sections of the B♭ minor Sonata that point to the nocturne and the etude; and above all those waltz and barcarolle markers that infuse extended works such as the scherzos and ballades.[57] And where we do notice this play of genres, we interpret it as an early fissure in the integrated world of a notionally unified period style, foreshadowing Mahler rather than echoing the topoi of post-classical traditions. The point here is that the analytical mode of our century has not just elevated the concept of structure, and with it the status of the musical work: it has also reduced the rich diversities of stylistic history to its own canon of competing and successive period styles. Not only is the work a unity in itself; it must belong to one of two unified style paradigms, 'classical' or 'romantic'. Its true origins are lost.

Reception aesthetics, music history and music analysis

It remains to discuss some of the implications of reception studies such as this for the more established disciplines of music history and music analysis, and I will do this in necessarily more abstract terms. I have traced here what I take to be a significant pattern in the reception history of one composer, a pattern of dispersal and closure. The presentation has been synoptic, but I hope it may at least have afforded glimpses into some dimensions of reception study – the effect of taste-creating institutions such as journals and publishing houses, the poetics of musical influence, and above all the shifting ideologies that underlie the way we write and think about music. Naturally I am not suggesting that such topics have been ignored by musicologists in the past. But by bringing them right into the foreground and giving them unprecedented explanatory value, reception studies issue a challenge to more traditional modes of enquiry. In the closing section of this chapter, I want briefly to consider that challenge, specifically in relation to music history and music analysis.

It seems to me that such investigations can play their part in extending the range and competence of historical enquiry, especially in relation to the first of the two themes I outlined at the beginning, music and the social world. Music historiography

---

[56]   See my remarks on this in *Chopin: The Four Ballades* (Cambridge 1992), p. 16.
[57]   I have discussed this in 'Chopin and Genre', *Music Analysis*, 8/3 (October 1989), pp. 213–31.

has traditionally tended either towards stylistic history, essentially a thread connecting certain highly valued composers, or towards so-called social history, an account of the role or function of music in society, usually in terms of production and immediate context. Both approaches construct narratives, and these narratives – as I argued at the outset – effectively stabilise the musical work, in that they view it either as a relational object or as the effect of a cause. Reception studies, on the other hand, construct a rather different history, a history of response, of people's involvements with musical works. By firming up those preconceptions and prejudices that condition response, reception studies offer an insight into the socially formative qualities of musical works, complementing existing investigations into their social causes. To my mind the story of late-nineteenth-century Chopin reception not only speaks volumes about how the apparently closed and highly specialised world of music can be appropriated by dominant ideologies for their own purposes: it also feeds back to compositional praxis. Specifically it grounds one interpretation of the rise of modernism.

What of the implications of reception studies for music analysis? They are of course more contentious. On one level reception studies help us to locate and situate music analysis, to expose some of its philosophical roots, to reveal its sub-texts. They promote in short a self-reflective analytical practice. On another level the challenge is more fundamental, reaching right through to the central premise of music analysis – the determinate musical work. And this of course brings us into the territory of my second theme, music as text. It is rather obvious that receding or vanishing meanings do indeed threaten music analysis by calling into question the stability of the work's identity. I offer no straightforward solutions to this problem, but I do want to argue that we need to construct both a listener-orientated and a work-orientated approach to identity – that neither alone will be adequate.

I suggest that a listener-orientated approach to identity requires us to rethink, rather than to reject, the analytical project. Our study of Chopin reception does, after all, reveal some degree of textual determinacy, qualifying substantially the notion of a receding work. There is a measure of consistency and conformity in the larger pattern described earlier which suggests that although determinacy recedes in the face of social mediation, it does so only to certain boundaries. Stanley Fish refers to 'the authority of interpretative communities', and although that concept is not without its problems, it conveys something of that legitimising of perspectives described in my four profiles of Chopin. The notion of a 'horizon of understanding', a 'horizon of expectations', borrowed from German reception aesthetics, is another useful way of expressing this, and especially the formulation 'fusion of horizons', where the work itself is viewed as a mediator between different horizons of understanding.[58]

This bears on analysis. By confronting our world with Chopin's, I already intended to suggest that analysis in the end tells us more about our world than Chopin's, since it effectively recreates his music – makes a representation of it – according to certain assumptions, assumptions which really reduce to the autonomy character of

---

[58] This stems from Hans-Georg Gadamer, *Truth and Method*, trans. Garrett Barden and John Cumming (New York 1975; original German edn 1960).

the musical work; indeed we exercise our power over Chopin by exploiting this non-identity or *différance*. Reception studies bring us, then, with some immediacy to a recognition of something we know rationally but may prefer to forget – that even as analysts we remain vulnerable perceiving subjects, constructing the *object* of our own analysis. Through our encounters with other subjects, including historical subjects, we are made aware that our knowledge is perspectival.[59] If any trace of objective knowledge is to be rescued from this, a knowledge separate from what we know, it can be located only as that which crosses the boundaries between perspectives, so to speak, and not predicated on some embarrassing assumption of absolutes. Jan Broeckx speaks of salvaging 'residual layers of receptional insight', and this in a sense is just what an historically aware analysis does.[60] In Hans–Georg Gadamer's terms, the historical horizons associated with my earlier profiles of Chopin would be projected and simultaneously removed, fused within, and embraced by our present analytical horizon.

Ironically, studies in ontology suggest that a work–orientated approach to identity, no less than a listener–orientated approach, imposes constraints on the analyst. In the first place such studies locate the work concept as a relatively recent one in music history,[61] and in the second place they remind us that the musical work embodies indeterminate areas of a kind not at all susceptible to analysis.[62] Within tonal traditions the persistence of the work's identity – always recognisable, never the same – may on one level protect the role of the analyst, as traditionally practised. Yet on another level it limits that role to something like the identification of schematic structures. In other words, what we analyse is a schematic structure and not a musical work.[63]

I will consider first the protection, then the limitation. The protection is made concrete in music theory. It should be obvious that there can be no sensible claims for music as a form of straightforward communication. There are no messages, just listeners constructing images of musical works. Yet within particular interpretative communities there will be a shared repertoire of images. And this repertoire has memorably included the powerful image of the stable text emerging as a kind of vision of immanence. This is where music theory comes in. Once powerfully prospective, music theory has for some time now functioned almost entirely retrospectively, formalising our shared knowledge, validating our analysis, and at the same time allowing some relativity as to its claims. The analysis will ring true, as it were, in the terms of a particular theory (it cannot be true, for analysis is ultimately unverifiable). Here we carve out some space for a traditional formalist enterprise, for the kind of analysis we all

---

[59]   Gadamer's position here has something in common on a larger philosophical plane with the thought of Habermas, since he too seeks a middle ground between the chimera of objective knowledge and the helpless relativism of perspectival knowledge. For a discussion, see Julian Roberts, *The Logic of Reflection: German Philosophy in the Twentieth Century* (New Haven 1992).

[60]   Jan L. Broeckx, *Contemporary Views on Musical Style and Aesthetics* (Antwerp 1979), p. 129.

[61]   See especially Lydia Goehr, *The Imaginary Museum of Musical Works: An Essay in the Philosophy of Music* (Oxford 1992).

[62]   See Roman Ingarden, *The Work of Music and the Problem of its Identity*, trans. Adam Czerniawski, ed. Jean G. Harrell (Berkeley and Los Angeles 1986; original Polish edn 1928); see also Zofia Lissa, 'Einige kritische Bemerkungen zur Ingardenschen Theorie des musikalischen Werkes', in her *Neue Aufsätze zur Musikästhetik* (Wilhelmshaven 1975), pp. 172–207.

[63]   See Ingarden, *The Work of Music*, for a refinement of this point.

used to undertake and some – very properly – still undertake. In making that space available, we recognise the value and potency of the myth of the musical work for our culture.[64]

Yet in the very act of recognising and locating that myth, the new musicology has professed the limitations of a traditional tandem of theory and analysis, preferring to draw both into a much larger network of realignments, one which calls into question the very possibility of structure. As analysis floats free of theory, it forms new alliances, not least with critical theory and the cognitive sciences, and these in turn have encouraged the analyst to step beyond descriptions of the schematic structures of musical works (by whatever sophisticated method) and to address instead, or as well, the larger mysteries of their musical materials. Reception studies have played their part in these developments. To the extent that they encourage us to deconstruct the musical work, allowing its edges to blur and dissolve, they force us to confront the social nature of musical materials and at the same time to explore the mechanisms involved in their realisation and perception. And it is precisely in these areas that the elusive meeting-point between listener-orientated and work-orientated approaches might be found, though there is a long way to go before this might be adequately formulated.

I will end with a shorter reception study. The journey from the earlier volume of Chopin studies to this collection is neatly symptomatic of some of the broader changes outlined here. Our first volume celebrated the musical work through genetic studies and analysis. The present volume engages rather with the listener and with the performer. And where it does focus on the work, it deals either with its dramaturgy (represented as narrative), or with the issue of what I called social trace at the beginning of this chapter. There are perhaps other differences arising from this. The first book rehearses familiar themes with confidence and assurance. This book is more exploratory and at the same time (I believe necessarily) more tentative. It is perhaps not surprising that the new musicology leaves many questions unanswered or partially answered. Cognitive studies seem too often in need of the informed musical insights of the well-trained analyst. Attempts to ground musical discourse in the social world often amount to little more than a crude juxtaposition of traditional analyses and social constructs in the hope of finding a 'good fit'; and many of them are performed in apparent innocence of those solidly theorised frameworks for the study of social mediation already proposed by Adorno and the Frankfurt critical theorists. Answers may be incomplete, then, but worthwhile and important questions are asked. Recent Chopin reception bears witness to a necessary and liberating process of renewal within the discipline.

---

[64] I need scarcely add that analysis has the further protection of its institutional infrastructure. In Britain alone it has its own journal, its own society and its own conference.

2   Chopin as 'salon composer' in nineteenth-century German criticism

ANDREAS BALLSTAEDT

Although aesthetic discourse on music in the nineteenth-century German-speaking world was dominated by absolute music and artistic autonomy, a simple question remained of compelling interest to the wider musical public: how is a composer's life related to his music? Eduard Hanslick, one of the most outspoken critics of the commonplace in art, noted this in an article on Chopin:

Who can resist drawing connections between the life and character of a poet or composer and his poetical works? We all like to read between the staves of an enthralling tone poem to discover which aspects of the composer's life might be interwoven in his music. The more suggestive, unusual and individual the composition sounds, the more pricked our curiosity. Tone poets with mysteriously captivating features such as Chopin stimulate our appetite for biographical explication almost more than those classical masters whose personality seemingly disappears behind their monumental works.[1]

In the case of a composer like Chopin, who shunned the limelight and who refrained from public propaganda about his compositions, one's imagination has unusually free rein to respond to both the music and the stories that surround his life. Chopin's notorious reluctance to explain his music almost invited the verbal interpretations of his contemporaries, and the complicated and often tendentious history of the documentary evidence about his life adds a further wrinkle.

In nineteenth-century German Chopin reception, two recurrent topoi can be identified. On the one hand, Chopin's work is often interpreted in terms of specific political messages (among others the Polish struggle for freedom); on the other hand, in apparent contradiction to the former,[2] there are countless emotional and sentimental descriptions of the music, which together define the topos of 'impassioned dreaming'. Robert Schumann, one of the first to champion Chopin's music in German (long before the two men actually met), may well be a source of both these topoi.[3] In an imaginary scene from 1837 in which Florestan and Eusebius attend an 'editor's ball',

---

[1] Eduard Hanslick, 'Das Leben Chopins [1877]', in his *Suite: Aufsätze über Musik und Musiker* (Vienna and Teschen n.d.), p. 243.

[2] See Andreas Ballstaedt, 'Frédéric Chopins "Revolutionsetüde" – ein Mythos?', *Musica*, 43 (1989), pp. 389–93.

[3] Neither topos features in one of the earliest monographs on Chopin to appear in German: Rudolf Hirsch, *Gallerie lebender Tondichter: Biographisch-kritischer Beitrag* (Gruens 1836).

both the music and the image of Chopin are enlisted by Florestan to woo Beda (i.e. Clara Wieck), the youngest daughter of the host. When the E♭ major Waltz Op. 18 is played and the two dance together for the first time, Chopin is the main topic of conversation. Florestan tells her

what an unforgettable sight it was to see him [Chopin] at the piano, like a dreaming visionary, and how, as he played, one became identified in one's own mind with his dream, and how he had an iniquitous habit, at the end of each piece, of running a finger from one end of the keyboard to the other in a disruptive glissando, as if to break the spell, and how he had to spare himself because of his delicate health, and so forth. She pressed herself ever more closely to me, seemingly prompted by a combination of anxiety and pleasure, and begged me to go on.[4]

When Beda later plays Chopin's Bolero Op. 19, Florestan comments to the reader: 'You know this tender, love-drenched composition, this image of Latin passion and shyness, of Latin abandon and reserve. And here, now, was Beda, pouring out her heart at the pianoforte, the picture of her beloved [Chopin] pressed to her bosom.'[5] In these few lines highly significant words are used: visionary; dream; spell; delicate; tender; Latin passion, shyness, abandon and reserve. At the same time, however, Schumann invokes the other topos mentioned above (neatly summarised in his dictum 'guns smothered in flowers')[6] when Beda shows Florestan 'the picture of her beloved' Chopin that she had painted; about this Florestan remarks, 'It was splendidly done, the head almost like Chopin's right down to the revolutionary curve of his mouth, the figure rather too big, but with the body bent backwards, the right eye covered by a hand, the other gazing boldly into the darkness. Lightning flashes in the background provided the illumination.'[7]

Although the topos of 'impassioned dreaming' could be understood as little more than a 'typically romantic' reaction to Chopin's music (Chopin was styled a 'romantic' in the literature from the very start, and even Schumann succumbed to this description), another provenance can be proposed which is probably more valid in terms of nineteenth-century German Chopin reception and which at the same time demonstrates some of the latter's specific characteristics: the phenomenon of the salon, or – to reformulate the topos – Chopin as 'salon composer'. Now whenever the term 'salon' is used, one must, strictly speaking, explain precisely what is meant, for 'salon' (and related compound forms such as 'salon atmosphere', 'salon music', 'salon culture', etc.) is an extraordinarily imprecise and permeable concept, employed in most cases not merely to describe but to impose a value judgement.[8] For the time being defining

---

4 Robert Schumann, *Gesammelte Schriften über Musik und Musiker*, 5th edn, ed. Martin Kreisig, 2 vols. (Leipzig 1914), vol. I, p. 258. Translation derived from Robert Schumann, *Schumann on Music*, trans. and ed. Henry Pleasants (London and New York 1965), p. 130.
5 *Gesammelte Schriften*, vol. I, p. 259; translation from *Schumann on Music*, p. 131.
6 *Gesammelte Schriften*, vol. I, p. 167.
7 *Gesammelte Schriften*, vol. I, p. 260; translation from *Schumann on Music*, p. 132.
8 For more detailed information about the history of the salon, the nature and social function of salon music, and related terminological problems, see Andreas Ballstaedt and Tobias Widmaier, *Salonmusik: Zur Geschichte und Funktion einer bürgerlichen Musikpraxis* (Stuttgart 1989); Peter Gradenwitz, *Literatur und Musik im geselligen Kreise: Geschmacksbildung, Gesprächsstoff und musikalische Unterhaltung in der bürgerlichen Salongesellschaft* (Stuttgart 1991); and Tobias Widmaier, 'Salonmusik', in *Handwörterbuch der musikalischen Terminologie*, ed. Hans Heinrich Eggebrecht, instalment 17 (Stuttgart 1990).

the salon simply as a room, one's meaning is entirely different if it is the Salon Pleyel under discussion (i.e. one of the smaller Paris concert-halls used for public performances), or the semi-public salon of a French aristocratic lady, opened once a week for representatives of the worlds of politics, business and culture, or the salon of a minister of commerce in the German *Kaiserreich*, which was put to use only a few times each year, otherwise left empty in splendid austerity and never entered by the family. But if one interprets 'salon' in a metaphorical sense, for instance referring to 'salon atmosphere', little is said about the character, make-up or disposition of an actual assembly of people. And the ubiquitous term 'salon music' is just as slippery and resistant to explanation, as we shall see. The fact that nineteenth-century Chopin reception in Germany and Austria was so closely bound up with various conceptions of the salon helped create a particular image of his life and music, which the following discussion will attempt to reconstruct in the light of contemporary sources. This study by no means represents the full spectrum of German Chopin criticism, but will attempt to shed light on an essential facet of how Chopin was viewed in the German-speaking states.

Two brief remarks on text selection and critical methodology should be made by way of introduction. Only two sorts of texts have been considered: monographs and extended essays exclusively on Chopin, and general piano-music guides (*Klaviermusikführer*), all published between 1830 and 1914. Smaller articles and reviews in journals and other periodicals, which would of course form part of a more comprehensive study, have not been included. The means of interpreting the chosen sources has been somewhat unusual and risks offending the historian seeking 'truth'. The excerpts referred to or quoted in the following study are *not* evaluated in terms of their accuracy or veracity, for deciding whether they are 'right' or 'wrong' is clearly less important than determining how they mould the image and establish the 'worth' of their subject. They are rather to be taken at face value in order to define and assess their place within a potentially coherent reception structure. This approach will not dissect each individual source with hermeneutical rigour, but will examine the texts to be considered in a comprehensive context, as if part of a single 'metatext', in an effort to search for recurrent stereotypes and to gauge how these are related.

Hardly a single monograph fails to highlight the importance of the salon (in the sense of venue) at each stage in Chopin's life. Thus we read about his youth: 'As a child of nine he felt very much at home in the aristocratic salons of Warsaw, and this early contact with the highest social echelons no doubt endowed him with the finest manners; the sophisticated elegance that characterised him all his life confirmed without question his innate aristocratic disposition.'[9] One author even goes so far as to claim that Chopin first discovered his love of music in the salon.[10] The willing reader of the following passage can vicariously experience the little Fryderyk's excitement in 'the large, bright rooms with their shimmering lights, where an exquisite circle of noble persons was assembled – princesses and countesses in silk gowns ornamented

⁹   Hugo Leichtentritt, *Frédéric Chopin* (Berlin 1905), pp. 9–10.
¹⁰   See Johann Schucht, *Friedrich Chopin und seine Werke* (Leipzig 1880), p. 7.

with pearls and glittering jewels, and tall, dark noblemen, who were to him the epitome of courage and gallantry'.[11] In Paris, after his first moderately successful concerts, Chopin penetrated deeper 'inside his own empire: the salon',[12] as if tailor-made for this milieu. 'In the wake of his all-important evening at the Rothschilds, *the Salon* forever remained the essential foundation of Chopin's triumphs.'[13] 'Indeed his natural habitat was not in the open spaces of the concert-hall, but rather in the salon; a tight circle of poets, artists, connoisseurs was his natural audience.'[14] Even Chopin's piano teaching seemed to be dominated by the salon, a putative focal point of his entire life: 'The music-lesson was thus transformed by him into a fashionable pastime, an extension of the salon. On this he built his pattern of existence.'[15] And, as one might expect, even the hour of death (which no account fails to mention) follows the very same path: 'It seems that he wanted to die as he had lived: in the salon.'[16]

Even on this level of mere statement and description, two characteristics of the nineteenth-century salon become evident. First of all, it concerns a distinguished and exalted circle of persons, clearly set apart from the masses. This exclusivity is one of the constants in the history of the salon: the room itself, whether in a villa or manor, had a special function, reserved for the reception of guests and strictly separated from the private living quarters. The exclusive nature of the assembling 'society' was one of its chief attractions, for here one had the opportunity, in a socially circumscribed and relatively liberal domain, whether private or semi-public, to pursue interests considered taboo by the general public. Although this very exclusivity regularly provoked hostility to the salon and its 'society' because it was thought to foster secret or subversive activities (as, for instance, in the case of eighteenth-century political salons), the second characteristic alluded to in the excerpts above more or less justified this quality. In one of the sources the connoisseur element is stressed as a fundamental feature of 'salon society'. This was of course a principal *raison d'être* of the salon, which originally was an assembly of like-minded persons interested in a given subject (politics, language, art, etc.), consciously shedding all social restraint in the salon.

Such a conception of the salon came increasingly under pressure in the nineteenth century, however. On the one hand, the journalistic public, becoming more powerful and influential, assumed some of the salon's main functions (for example, the forming of political and cultural opinion). On the other hand, as in many other domains, the values of a competitive bourgeois capitalist society came to prevail over the spirit of conviviality; thus the display of material wealth and possessions eventually assumed central importance. This meant that the concentration on a common theme in the salon receded into the background, overtaken by a fascination merely with the luxurious atmosphere. Whereas in the eighteenth century the salon was the province of the aristocratic classes, after 1800 the bourgeoisie, growing richer and competing more

---

11   Else Redenbacher, *François Frédéric Chopin* (Leipzig 1911), p. 13.
12   Ibid., p. 46.
13   Hanslick, 'Das Leben Chopins', p. 255.
14   La Mara, *Musikalische Studienköpfe, I: Romantiker*, 6th, rev. edn (Leipzig 1883), p. 260.
15   Adolf Weissmann, *Chopin*, 3rd/4th edn (Berlin 1919), p. 48.
16   Ibid., pp. 79–80.

concertedly for social prestige, aped many aristocratic habits, one of them the salon. By now the salon had become a mark of social status whose exclusive character helped distinguish higher ranks within the new money from the lower middle classes, i.e. the petite bourgeoisie. The appeal of such gatherings lay not so much in the conversation, as a contemporary report from Paris reveals, but 'in the glitter of the apartments, in the abundance of refreshments and delicacies and in the number of guests'.[17]

Naturally, the role of music was not the same in every salon. There remained salons where it was the centre of interest and was listened to intensely, for example in the concert rooms of Erard, Herz, Pape and Pleyel (which were referred to as salons), or in the private salons of Friedrich Kalkbrenner or Maurice Schlesinger, the influential Parisian publisher and editor. But the general trend to superficiality did not stop with convivial pleasantries: it radically altered the function of the music heard in the salon, as a German correspondent writes from Paris.

Every topic of conversation is of fleeting duration; everyone girds his loins with the sword of opinion, but without showing the cold steel, instead keeping it in its sheath. It is only a skirmish, a short armistice within the great struggle that will see so many more battles and will claim so many human hearts. But when the women take control or when triviality comes to prevail, there remain, in the end, three things to substitute for the flagging conversation: music, games and dancing.[18]

Another account, by two Germans writing in the middle of the 1860s, outlines the salon's development in France, especially in Paris:

People used to say that in Paris everything is decided in the salon, even politics. And this is true enough if you imagine only the salons of Madame Roland, de Staël, Tallien, Récamier, of the Countess Lieven and the Princesse de Vaudemont . . . not to mention the golden days of the salon in the eighteenth century, which represented all of France's finest names, ideas and things of beauty. But there are no longer any salons . . . 'society' has taken its place, 'le Monde' and – credit is due to the French for giving us this word so that one can say and write – 'le Demi-monde'.

In the *salons* music had its rightful place, it was at home in them; at the same time the salon was the protector of concert music and of concerts. '*Society*', on the other hand, throws sumptuous feasts, and, as a rule, during the soirées following these formal dinners (unless there was dinner beforehand no one would go to a soirée!) there are hired sopranos . . . Twenty-five years ago [1842] the situation was entirely different! Though starting to disappear as well, the last salons were still evident, and right up to the end the great virtuosos remained loyal to them and vice versa. It was from this seat of good company and good manners that the fame of their artistic successes . . . spread throughout the whole country, just as the literary correspondence of Baron Grimm emanated from the salons of the Espinasse and Du Deffand.[19]

Those composers named specifically in this report were Franz Liszt, Sigismund Thalberg and Chopin, 'the most inspired and sensitive of all salon poets': 'one could say that with Chopin the true musical salon of Paris closed down'.[20]

17   Ferdinand von Gall, *Paris und seine Salons*, 2 vols. (Oldenburg 1845), vol. II, p. 177.
18   Karl Gutzkow, *Säkularbilder* (Frankfurt am Main 1846), Part 2, p. 75.
19   Heinrich Ehrlich and Julius Rodenberg, 'Oper, Concert und – Thérésa', in Julius Rodenberg, *Paris bei Sonnenschein und Lampenlicht*, 2nd edn (Leipzig 1867), pp. 242–4.
20   Ibid., p. 244.

In the light of such comments, it is not difficult to understand why Chopin, in the view of so many contemporaries, was firmly wedded to the salon: for them he was among the last to represent the true salon, where connoisseurs and amateurs could freely intermingle. This account also reveals another important function of the salon during the reign of the French bourgeoisie: namely, its role as the essential springboard for every virtuoso career in Paris. Having conquered the salon audience, the budding star could proceed to give public concerts in Paris and to tour other European cities. Chopin too wanted to avail himself of this platform, even though from early on in Paris he had little stomach for a full-blown virtuoso career. Nevertheless, in the account above, his name is uttered in the same breath as Liszt and Thalberg, both market leaders in virtuoso music for the pianoforte. The reasons for including him with the other two were probably not musically or aesthetically valid. It was after all the famous virtuoso Liszt himself who, once perfectly at home in the salon milieu, wrote a scathing critique of this 'society' in his Chopin biography, a sort of reckoning with the court, aristocracy and bourgeoisie simultaneously justifying his own professional conversion and change of direction while allowing us to overlook the fact that he more than any other figure had thrived in this domain, and also revealing a great deal about Chopin's special position. Liszt's central criticism was that the circumscribed and exclusive salon audience, which played a key role in determining public success, lacked any authority whatsoever in artistic matters, not to mention a desire to know the arts in any real depth:

It is frightened by the eccentricities of genius, it recoils from the boldness of a great and superior individuality, soul and spirit, for it feels too unsure of itself to recognise those who are truly called to higher things because of the inner exigencies of an inspiration which goes its own way, leaving in its wake without hesitation all those who harbour only small passions, who are unexceptional, and who aspire to no loftier goal than amassing wealth in a lucrative career, at the end of which lies a comfortable bourgeois retirement.

The salon world is unable to see that these different personalities are polar opposites, for it makes no attempt to trust its own judgement, to form its opinions independent of the dictates of the *feuilletoniste* . . .[21]

The salon world lacks the competence to differentiate between authentic artistic expression and more fashionable, ingratiating superficiality:

It does not distinguish between the powerful sway, the tumultuous aspirations and emotions piling Pelion on Ossa to climb to the stars, and the overt display of lowly narcissism, selfish complacency and contemptible servility to the passions of the day, the noble vice of elegance, immoral fashion and all-powerful profligacy. It sees no difference between the simplicity of great ideas, which require no 'effects', and the outmoded conventions of a style whose time has come and gone and is now jealously guarded by old women who lack the vision and intelligence to follow the endless changes of art.

So that it can spare itself the effort of appreciating or understanding the ideas of the poet-artist, whose star is rising in the firmament of art; so that it can avoid serious contact with art, which allows one to judge the promises of youth and the qualities that help them fulfil these, the salon world avidly supports or, better, stubbornly patronises only fawning mediocrity . . .[22]

---

[21] Franz Liszt, *F. Chopin*, 3rd edn (Leipzig 1882; first published Paris 1852), pp. 122–3. Although published in Germany, this edition was in French; all passages quoted here are translated from French.
[22] Ibid., pp. 123–4.

The total absence of open-mindedness and serious engagement means finally that art and the salon are diametrically opposed:

The *beau-monde* seeks after superficial impressions of so transitory a nature that they seem more physical than moral, for it lacks the foundation of first-hand knowledge, aptitude, and sustained and genuine interest to guide them. The world of society, preoccupied with day-to-day concerns . . . expects from poetry and art nothing more than emotions lasting a few minutes, exhausted by the evening's end and forgotten the next morning . . . In the chambers hung with red damask, art, great art is ossifying; it is vanishing in the salon of mother-of-pearl and gold. Every true artist felt this was so, though not all were aware of it.[23]

Though Liszt cannot of course deny Chopin's presence in the Parisian salon world, he later emphasises that a much smaller circle of connoisseurs surrounded him, and this more discerning audience was spared his harsh verdict.

My short excursion to Liszt usefully reminds us that one should not interpret salon culture as a straight line descending from the highest social echelons of Paris to the petit bourgeois salon, which is what Ehrlich and Rodenberg tried to do. Rather, one has to consider each case individually in gauging the value of the arts at a particular niveau. At the same time, Liszt reveals that Chopin's position was unusual, and that only less informed observers could link him with Thalberg and Liszt himself. Needless to say, such subtle distinctions had little effect on Chopin reception in general: most authors failed to differentiate between Chopin and those around him, in part because Liszt's poetical, sentimental descriptions of Chopin's music meshed all too conveniently with the images of the composer evolving at this time, as we shall see.

It is interesting to note that Ehrlich and Rodenberg go on to qualify their statement about the development of the salon in a manner which proves prophetic of later attitudes towards the salon:

To be honest, however, one should acknowledge that the salons were an excellent training for a *certain* kind of elegant life, which contemplated even the loftiest philosophical and political questions about art in a lively conversation over a few cups of tea. In this way, unrefined, sensual natures can naturally be exposed to higher things, and there is no lack of stimulation for the artist as well; but, in general, truth and a superior perspective on life remain lost, and the most polished *manners*, which know how to shape and control even the noblest conversation, have the upper hand over simplicity, which only truth strives for, and which is loath to pass round to the entire salon the fruits of intensive and profound enquiry.[24]

Despite their fascination with the cosmopolitan, elegant and free-thinking salon society that they encountered in coming from the social and political provinces to 'the capital of the nineteenth century' (to use Walter Benjamin's phrase), these German observers nevertheless suspect the salon of superficiality and conceit.

The extent to which the concept of the 'salon' carried such negative associations in Germany becomes evident in examining the attitudes, roles and behaviour attributed to those persons associated with it, for the central place the salon was thought

---

[23]   Ibid., pp. 127–8. Schumann also believed that the true 'home of art . . . could not be found in the salons of the great and the rich' (Schumann, *Gesammelte Schriften*, vol. I, p. 409).

[24]   Ehrlich and Rodenberg, 'Oper, Concert und – Thérésa', pp. 244–5.

to hold in their lives inevitably influenced and determined how their outlook and character were described. Chopin is portrayed as a delicate, refined and distinguished person who belonged perfectly to the salon milieu: 'in this soft, gentle and yet intoxicating atmosphere of feminine adoration, the artist developed such an elegant character that he gave everyone the impression of being a *grand seigneur*, but at the same time his nature was so sensitive that he recoiled from each brutal encounter with the outside world, which he flew in terror'.[25] Two aspects of this portrayal are closely linked with the salon: first, the predominant feminine influence, which we shall discuss in more detail later, and second, the element of sensitivity and timidity, which led to the salon's becoming a place of retreat. This recourse to the sanctuary of an enclosed space inspired some authors to try to identify the very seat of Chopin's inspiration:

He [Chopin] can only be imagined indoors, never in the open air . . . His scenery is not the wood and the field, but the salon of sophisticated society. The rustling [in Chopin's music] comes from the gowns of beautiful women, the whispering from the conversation of lovers. No one knows better than he the enticement of social pleasures and beautiful proportions.[26]

In contrast to Beethoven and Schubert, whose most essential inspirations, as we know, came from direct contact with nature, we find no evidence in Chopin's case that he fled to the loneliness of the forest or plain or that he was moved to deeper impressions by looking at a landscape. A poetical description of nature had a much more profound effect on him than nature itself. It is for this reason that he had no love for the country, as George Sand indicated. When visiting Nohant, he enjoyed the appealing variety of country life for the first few days, but after that he felt like a fish out of water. He was a man of the salon through and through, and he longed for its atmosphere.[27]

Both of these comparisons are much more than pure descriptions, because they conceal latent reservations about the salon. First of all, it is obvious that nationalist sentiments play a central role in these accounts, as the 'German' Beethoven and Schubert are mentioned in opposition to the 'French' Chopin. The salon was rightly considered a French phenomenon, whose imitation and acceptance into German culture were disparaged by conservative nationalist groups: 'The salon, as its very name indicates, is a foreign growth grafted onto the German house.'[28] Just as the convivial French salon was thus deemed incompatible with cosy German family life, the comparison above of the composers is tantamount to a confrontation of aesthetic conceptions. According to both of these quotations, the salon is a totally artificial world, a contrived mode of existence. The salon's rustling does not originate from leaves but from elegant clothing, and the whispering has its source not in the wind but in the company itself. Whereas the German composer is inspired directly by nature, which for him is an inexhaustible source of ideas, the salon can in contrast offer only the 'enticement of social pleasures and beautiful proportions' as a substitute for man's original relationship to nature. The salon is a self-contained world, in which nature exists only in the form of secondhand copies (it is surely not insignificant that

25   Otto Lüning, *Friedrich Chopin: Ein Künstlerbildnis* (Zurich 1892), p. 9.
26   Louis Ehlert, 'Frédéric Chopin', in his *Aus der Tonwelt: Essays* (Berlin 1877), p. 286.
27   Bernard Scharlitt, *Chopin* (Leipzig 1919), p. 73.
28   Wilhelm Heinrich Riehl, *Die Familie* (Stuttgart 1861), p. 219.

the German salon of the *Kaiserreich* was normally decorated with dried flowers, the so-called *Makart-Bouquet*). And although Chopin's capacity for deeper impressions is not altogether denied, his reaction to the countryside is more or less limited to its 'appealing variety', which is of course the highest principle of the salon. This is part and parcel of the superficiality and inconsequentiality described earlier, which in the eyes of German contemporaries prevented profound understanding of or serious engagement with the arts. 'The musical world was perpetually divided in two antagonistic camps: the first comprises salon society, for whom music is little more than a cheap trinket or a kind of perfume for the mind; the other embraces the classics, who acknowledge only the strict, historically legitimate style.'[29] Although it is never explicitly stated that the former criticisms apply to Chopin, such implications can easily be inferred in Chopin reception. For some writers the artifice and sanctuary of the salon were the very essence of Chopin's being. One author, for instance, asked whether his

lack of any difficult experiences as a young man laid the foundation for the indulgence that characterised the master's entire life. That he was so little equal to the later storms of life can perhaps ultimately be explained by his untroubled youth. Such an upbringing does not as a rule forge a man. And in Chopin remained something of the spoilt child to the very end, as he himself aptly said shortly before his death.[30]

In thus referring to an absent masculinity and a fundamental immaturity, the image of the feminine is not far away in the nineteenth-century mind: in this light it was entirely logical to claim that Chopin's life was played out wholly in the salon, a place whose essential history was written by women.

Chopin, himself an aristocrat in lifestyle and inclination from his early childhood, thoroughly acquainted with the elegant style of the salon, gifted with the most sophisticated taste and an astonishing creativity, remains . . . the darling of these noble circles, on whom the women in particular generously bestow their favour, just as they prefer to become his pupils.[31]

Chopin's closeness to the female sex, widely exploited in the biographies in connection with his various disappointing love affairs, led in the eyes of some contemporaries to a sort of gender reversal: 'his inner being was distinguished by an almost female delicacy'.[32] Even his behaviour is frequently characterised as womanly:

The tone-poet does not at all care for her [George Sand] at their first meeting (as he writes to his family); rather, she repels him with her manly bearing. But she is *the* George Sand, the masculine woman [*das Mannweib*], and as such is superior to Chopin's female essence, which she has realised for a long time. The roles are reversed. She courts him, just like a man.[33]

29 Johanna Kinkel, 'Friedrich Chopin als Komponist: Geschrieben im Jahre 1855. Aus ihrem Nachlaß', *Deutsche Revue*, 27 (1902), p. 93.

30 Scharlitt, *Chopin*, p. 20. He continues (p. 21): 'So his years of travel, which strictly speaking were no such thing, are lacking in those heroic episodes that lend many of his brothers in Apollo their particular glory. They are much more like the years that a wealthy aristocratic scion devotes to his studies. The young Chopin does not "wander" to blaze a path for himself and his art, but rather he travels to expand his spiritual and musical horizons.'

31 La Mara, *Romantiker*, p. 259.

32 Scharlitt, *Chopin*, p. 85.

33 Ibid., p. 64.

In matters of dress he was so well-informed as to give advice even on women's clothing, and his acute eye [for fashion] was astounding.[34]

From this virtual transformation of Chopin into a woman and the belief that 'an almost feminine excitability and delicacy of feeling are vital to do justice to his music',[35] it requires only a short step to look at his works as a forthright expression of the feminine character, a sentiment expressed by Liszt, for example, in a passage referring to the preludes, nocturnes and impromptus:

Here are evoked one by one the passionate states of pure and spiritual souls: the lovely enticement of innocent flirtation, attractions unrecognised as such, capricious flights of fancy; the fatal crushing of a pale joy which is dying even as it is born, black roses, flowers for mourning; or perhaps winter roses, white as the surrounding snow, whose scent itself conveys sadness because the slightest breath of air makes the petals fall off. Sparks lacking in sparkle but illuminating worldly vanity like the gleam of rotting wood, which glows only in the dark; pleasures without past and future, arising from chance meetings like the fortuitous union of two distant stars; illusions, odd desires for adventure, like the sour taste of half-ripened fruits which delight us even as they dull our teeth. Hints of emotions whose range is infinite and which are transformed into true (often sober) poetry by the innate superiority, beauty, refinement and elegance of those feeling them, when one of those chords that seemed to be no more than a rapid arpeggio suddenly becomes a solemn theme, whose bold and fervent modulations take on the shape of an eternal passion in the heart of the exalted![36]

Once again the topos of impassioned dreaming surfaces, but now motivated in two ways – first of all, in terms of the allegedly feminine character of the composer, in whom 'a chaste spirituality and an inclination towards intensive, sensual effects are strangely joined together',[37] and whose 'feminine nature' is revealed 'in a dependence of thought upon the world of fantasy and feeling'[38] (Ignaz Moscheles wrote as early as 1839 that 'Chopin's appearance is absolutely identical with his music, both delicate and effusive'[39]). The other meaning of the topos in this context has to do with the salon, which was separated from the real world and whose atmosphere inspired the imagination and invited one to enter into a state of contemplation. In this sense we can understand a description of the Waltz in D♭ major Op. 64 No. 1 as a 'love poem': 'Like the flowing hair ribbons of one's beloved, the quaver passages of the principal section flutter here and there, while in the *sostenuto* section the sweet and tender melody is rocked by the silvery lilt of the rhythm, and in the repeat of this passage the light, graceful A♭ sounds like distant wedding bells.'[40]

---

34 Lüning, *Friedrich Chopin*, p. 28.
35 Ibid., p. 13.
36 Liszt, *F. Chopin*, pp. 108–9.
37 Louis Köhler, *Der Klavierunterricht: Studien, Erfahrungen, Rathschläge*, 5th, rev. edn (Leipzig 1886), p. 20.
38 Lüning, *Friedrich Chopin*, p. 29.
39 Quotation from Walter Dahms, *Chopin* (Munich 1924), p. 27. Moscheles expressed a less favourable opinion of Chopin's music: 'my fingers always stumble over certain difficult, inartistic, incomprehensible passages [*Modulationen*], as the whole often seems to me too sickly sweet, unworthy of a man and learned musician'. (Quotation from Arnold Niggli, 'Friedrich Chopin's Leben und Werke', in *Sammlung musikalischer Vorträge*, ed. Paul Graf Waldersee (Leipzig 1879), p. 301.)
40 Niggli, 'Chopin's Leben und Werke', p. 318.

Throughout the late nineteenth and early twentieth centuries, certain works and genres are again and again linked directly to the salon, above all the waltzes and nocturnes:

While Chopin's waltzes belong almost exclusively to the salon and an aristocratic character is predominant in the polonaises, a rural element, by way of contrast, is prominent in the mazurkas.[41]

Nocturne (serenade), intoned by *Field* in an innocent manner on the piano, transformed by *Chopin* into a salon piece of great virtuosity.[42]

Nowhere did Chopin pay homage to the salon in so noble a manner, at once unreserved and masterly, as in this [A♭ major] Ballade [Op. 47].[43]

Given the negative connotations that the salon had in Germany, it is hardly surprising that from very early on qualifying adjectives or explanations are attached to the term. For instance, Schumann writes about the *Grand Duo concertant* for piano and cello (without opus): 'A piece for the salon, in which the head of a famous artist can be seen now and then over the shoulders of a count; it is not meant for tea-parties, where the music merely accompanies the conversation, but for the most educated circles, who pay respect to the artist as his profession duly deserves.'[44] Schumann was obviously thinking not of the common salon, but of the exclusive gatherings described by Liszt. About the Waltz Op. 42 he comments: 'The waltz . . . is, like the earlier ones, a salon piece of the noblest sort. Florestan says that if he were to play it for dancing, at least half the females would have to be countesses. He is right, of course. The waltz is aristocratic through and through.'[45] Whenever Chopin's music was related to the salon, it was necessary to point out that the works in question were in some way *special*.

Explicit links between music and the salon in such terms as 'salon piece', 'salon genre' and 'salon music' originated in France in the mid 1830s and spread through the German-speaking world in tandem with the establishment of a salon tradition. It need hardly be said that the term 'salon music' is just as vague as 'salon' itself, for its meaning is often revealed only in a particular context. Salon music essentially means a repertoire for solo piano, first of all the 'brilliant' works of the keyboard lions from the 1830s French salons, and then, with increasing generality in the second half of the nineteenth century, all virtuosic piano music which sounds difficult to play but which technically lies within the grasp of the moderately skilled amateur. Such works were usually given poetical titles. Schumann aptly characterised the genre as a 'mixture of sentimentality and pianistic passagework'.[46] This music was specifically designed to achieve the greatest possible commercial success, and this inevitably had ramifications

---

[41]   Leichtentritt, *Frédéric Chopin*, pp. 107–8.
[42]   Köhler, *Klavierunterricht*, p. 233.
[43]   Weissmann, *Chopin*, p. 137. In this book even the Concertos Opp. 11 and 21 are called 'salon piano concertos' (p. 151).
[44]   Schumann, *Gesammelte Schriften*, vol. I, p. 180.
[45]   Ibid., vol. II, p. 32; translation derived from *Schumann on Music*, p. 179.
[46]   *Gesammelte Schriften*, vol. II, p. 240.

for its content and style as well as the way in which it was promoted. The essence of this repertoire was carefully tailored to the functions which it had to fulfil. By this time music was no longer the centre of the salon but was a means to certain ends: the young lady of the house was expected to show the invited guests her technical dexterity, obtained through assiduous effort; at the same time the music was required to transport the company to a cosy and harmonious state. For many contemporary critics this practice represented the nadir of musical culture. While the 'bad music' of the lower classes could be tolerated as an unavoidable social evil, salon music propagated a sort of 'non-music' in those very echelons which until then had been regarded as standard-bearers of goodness, truth and beauty. It was at this point that 'salon music' became a term of abuse.

A further conceptual difficulty arises from the then common practice of playing in the salon not only the salon music just defined but also certain works of the classic-romantic repertoire which had been embraced by the amateur public, music which satisfied its specific requirements although it had been composed with quite different aesthetic intentions. So Tekla Bądarzewska's notorious *Maiden's Prayer* (*Modlitwa dziewicy*) can be found in certain salon albums or series of volumes cheek by jowl with works of Mozart, Beethoven, Mendelssohn, Schubert and Schumann. For the salon public, aesthetic and stylistic clashes were of little or no concern, as long as the pieces served their purpose; furthermore, such juxtapositions at least provided some contact with the classical masters (in this respect, the great composers suffered the same fate as the poets: in many bourgeois salons one could find an edition of the works of Goethe or Schiller, even though the works themselves had never actually been read). Repertoire which was not composed expressly for salon use could be included in a broader category of salon music, that is, 'music in the salon'. In the salon more or less anything could be played, for the repertoire was as disparate as the various rooms that were called salons: chamber music, vocal music (in 1830s Paris, for instance, an epidemic of romances broke out), or solo instrumental music – and it did not matter whether the pieces were newly published or of older vintage. Even Chopin's music crops up in this salon repertoire next to pieces of the most trivial sort.[47] His position, however, is more precarious than that of other composers because of his actual associations with the world of the salon; for that reason, designating him a composer of salon music or a salon composer would not have been incorrect, even though it was potentially misleading. The difficulty of judging and 'situating' his oeuvre (this difficulty helps us understand the contemporary public's inconsistent critical outlook) can be seen by surveying the piano-music guides, or *Klaviermusikführer*, that prospered as a genre in the second half of the nineteenth century. Intended to help both piano teachers and pupils choose their repertoire, these guides were structured in several different ways, subdividing the music according to performance-related matters, stylistic criteria, or sometimes both. In some publications one can find in addition

---

[47] A survey of salon repertoire is given in Ballstaedt and Widmaier, *Salonmusik*, including the following works by Chopin: Nocturne Op. 9 No. 2, Waltz Op. 18, Polonaise Op. 26 No. 1, Impromptu Op. 29, Nocturne Op. 32 No. 1, Polonaise Op. 40 No. 1, Waltz Op. 42, Berceuse Op. 57, Barcarolle Op. 60, Waltz Op. 64 No. 1, Impromptu Op. 66 and an unidentified Mazurka in F♯ major (*sic*).

more or less detailed commentaries about composers or works. Although in most cases the criteria used to classify the repertoire are not clearly defined, these handbooks nevertheless offer a surprising amount of information about how individual composers or works were regarded by the general public. Some guides were of only passing significance, whereas others appeared in numerous editions right up to the 1920s.

As one might expect, Chopin falls between several stools here as well. Although there is not a single *Klaviermusikführer* which fails to mention his name, many do much more than simply gauge the level of difficulty of his works, in addition classifying them in great detail. Consider for example the guide of Louis Köhler (1820–86), one of the most famous German piano pedagogues in the nineteenth century who himself composed numerous piano works, edited several collections and wrote important essays on piano teaching. His piano-music guide was published in no less than nine editions within just thirty-five years.[48] The first edition of 1859 simply grouped the repertoire according to performing criteria (for two hands, four hands, etc.) or pedagogical considerations (for beginners, for sight-readers, etc.). Köhler's first remark about Chopin seems rather odd – 'all of *Chopin's* music is at least *relatively* worthy and thus merits being played'[49] – but the meaning of this 'relatively' becomes clearer in a later passage:

Polish ardour and social elegance with a touch of the hysterical, – in addition a melancholy tendency, which characterises the Slavs in general and the Poles specifically because of their grievous national fate: on this foundation rests Chopin's original and sensitive artistic soul, mourning for his native country far away in the finest intellectual and social circles of Paris, gifted with an impassioned soul and a sickly body, who feels every sort of pain and pleasure more sharply and more individually than others and expresses himself accordingly, often in strange ways, at other times piquant, eccentric, garish, wrapped in a mourning shroud: all this in intimate union created a *Chopin*, whose music is ardent, elegant, overwrought, elegiac, capricious, inspired, endearing, repulsive, delicate, fragrant, morbid, eccentric – these captivating spiritual qualities found in alternation with each other as well as blended together. The freedom of genius lives and breathes in this unique music, which is full of virtue and frailty organically wedded to one another to create what is clearly an original artistic nature of the high society.[50]

Despite all the homage paid to Chopin's unique character within these lines, hints of disapproval and rejection are nevertheless palpable, especially in the negative epithets interrupting the series of descriptive words: the music is ardent and elegant, but also overwrought; it is elegiac, capricious, inspired and endearing, but also repulsive; it is delicate and fragrant, but also morbid and eccentric. Moreover, the words of praise are qualified at the end when the composer is described as an original artist of the *high society*, a social echelon for which an overwhelming artistic sense was hardly necessary (recall Liszt's remarks). In another passage in the same guide, this time concerning Adolph Henselt, Chopin's name unexpectedly reappears, but now with a decidedly negative undertone:

---

48   Louis Köhler, *Führer durch den Clavierunterricht* (Leipzig, Hamburg and New York 1859). Of the later editions, the following can be verified: 2nd, 1860; 3rd, 1865; 5th, 1874; 6th, 1879; 7th, 1882; 8th, 1886; 9th, 1894 (reworked by Bernhard Vogel).
49   Köhler, *Führer* (1859), p. 47; latter emphasis added.
50   Ibid., pp. 47–8.

Henselt is a German *Chopin*. Whereas the latter sounds almost foreign, Henselt on the contrary sounds very much 'at home'; whereas Chopin has a hot-blooded southern temperament, Henselt's in contrast is agreeably moderate. Chopin's combined dissonances are often burning and piercing, but Henselt is warm and gentle even in the expression of pain. Chopin is the Latin, Henselt the Nordic piano bard; their music breathes a life of love in every respect – in Chopin's case there is a blistering, impetuous and all-consuming passion, in Henselt's milder, yearning devotion. Chopin can be coquettish with his rich and suggestive genius, Henselt is more reserved.[51]

In the third edition of this guide (1865), the classification according to performance considerations is replaced partly by stylistic categories, resulting in the following sections: didactic works; classical, romantic works, etc.; salon pieces; virtuoso pieces; and entertainment pieces. Chopin is placed in the third section (with the identical prefatory comment), along with well-known, even notorious early salon pieces like Friedrich Kalkbrenner's *La femme du marin* and Theodor Döhler's Nocturne in D♭ major. Although Köhler now seems to find salon music the most appropriate rubric, he nonetheless does not entirely lack pedagogical and artistic discretion in attaching this label, for he could have banished Chopin to the fifth section, which contains fatuous repertoire appealing to the broader salon public.

The equally distinguished Swiss piano pedagogue Carl Eschmann (1826–82) and his German colleague Adolf Ruthardt (1849–1934) proceed in precisely the opposite manner in their piano-music guide (the first and second editions of which were edited by Eschmann, the following by Ruthardt).[52] Up to the third edition (1888) Chopin's oeuvre is divided into two sections: most of his works are classified as 'Independent [*freie*] solo piano compositions', but the waltzes and nocturnes above all fall into the section 'Good, honest salon, entertainment and concert pieces, for the sake of diversion'.[53] Once again the editor feels obliged to clarify Chopin's relationship to the salon: 'Some of his compositions are salon music, but in the noblest sense of the word; one must call this *"classical salon music"*. Other works, certainly the bulk of his output, are much greater than salon music; these are independent, genuine and original tone poems of an inspired and highly poetical nature.'[54] From the fifth edition of 1900 onwards, none of Chopin's works is placed in the section 'Salon and showy concert pieces'; on the contrary, all the music is classed as independent compositions. Apparently the editor anticipated the public's confusion, for he felt it necessary to explain this grouping:

Chopin, F., as salon composer. Although I included Chopin in the chapter 'Independent compositions for the pianoforte', I could have done so here with equal justification, for if ever a composer was suited to the salon through and through, it was Chopin. The piano-playing world – naturally by this I do not mean mature, sensitive artists of a high standard – is labouring under a grave misapprehension in regarding Chopin merely as a first-class salon composer. So-

---

51   Ibid., p. 61.
52   The following editions can be verified: J. Carl Eschmann, *Wegweiser durch die Clavier-Literatur*, 2nd edn (Leipzig 1879); 3rd, 1888, revised and ed. by Adolf Ruthardt (likewise all subsequent editions); 4th, 1893; 5th, 1900; 6th, 1905; 7th, 1910; 8th, 1914; 9th, 1918; 10th, 1925.
53   In the third edition, this section is entitled 'Salon and showy [*effektvolle*] concert pieces'.
54   Eschmann, *Wegweiser* (1879), p. 87.

called salon music is subject to fashion, and the elegance defined by a certain vogue fades just as fast as the fashion itself and very soon seems ridiculous. Just as there exists a heartfelt courtesy which can be distinguished from conventional politeness (though the two are not entirely unrelated), an elegance of mind, of feeling, of imagination can equally be found here, all of these happily embodied within the most distinctive aristocratic forms. The deeper knowledge and decisive originality are in no way harmed but in contrast are refined and intensified by this embodiment. I believe I have indicated the nature of Chopin's elegance: it is an immortal, timeless one.[55]

If one thus wanted to classify or describe Chopin's music on the basis of his real or ostensible proximity to the Parisian salon, the salon music label was very much at hand to the late-nineteenth- and early-twentieth-century critic, even though it seems imprecise to us today. But, once again, qualifying adjectives had to be employed in order to avoid possible pejorative connotations:

The master's waltzes have become more high-spirited, more accessible and therefore even more popular, true salon pieces in the best sense of this widely misused word, full of perfect grace and elegance, their sparkling, animated rhythm magically conjuring up the image of a glittering ballroom, packed with dancers in full flight.[56]

His fantasies and impromptus, his variations and rondos and waltzes, all his works belonging to the most refined salon genre[s] contain much beauty and individuality; there is a new spirit throughout, permeating and inspiring the old forms with a breath of fresh air.[57]

In assuming that Chopin's contributions to the salon genre were true, perfect and refined, these authors follow the same strategy as Liszt in his discussion of the salon: Chopin was to be placed within the salon tradition (indeed, all the more emphatically, because of its increasing decline in the second half of the century), without however being burdened by the negative connotations associated with it. But even this strategy reveals an undercurrent of animosity towards the salon:

Most of his waltzes are brilliant, attractive, captivating offspring of the salon, which knows nothing of the misfortune and suffering of the person who only now and then timidly sets foot outside the door. His nocturnes, the best-known of his tone poems, are enormously sweet fruits and intoxicating blooms which rather remind one of a hothouse.[58]

While a dissociation from the comforts and artificiality of the salon can be sensed once again in the previous quotation, in the following description of Chopin it is hard to determine whether it is an aversion to the 'cosseted favourite' which prevails, or a fascination for the best salons, which remain inaccessible but whose inhabitants one can imagine through the music: 'The cosseted favourite of the aristocratic salons recreates in his waltzes this "great world" in transfigured outline. Its luxuriant splendour and elegance, its noble and exclusive character, its refined habits and polished manners are here . . . incomparably fixed in sound.'[59] Sometimes, however, the

55 Eschmann, ed. Ruthardt, *Wegweiser* (1900), pp. 186–7.
56 Niggli, 'Chopin's Leben und Werke', p. 318.
57 La Mara, *Romantiker*, p. 279.
58 Lüning, *Friedrich Chopin*, p. 24.
59 Scharlitt, *Chopin*, p. 162.

disparaging undertone surfaces to such an extent that it eclipses the music, despite the author's evident respect for the latter: 'But an art as exquisite as Chopin's is inseparable from luxury. Champagne and truffles go hand in hand with the Nocturne in F♯ major. It is a form of artistic dessert, a beautiful if perhaps non-essential treat, although valued by those who appreciate the more refined artistic delights.'[60]

Objections to such estimations of Chopin as a 'salon composer' arose from time to time after the 1850s, increasing in vehemence as the concept of salon music grew more negative. 'Chopin made only rare concessions to the salon audience, and even then he refined these shallow, fashionable forms with his cultivated taste. His *Duo concertant* for piano and violin [*sic*] on *Thèmes favoris* from *Robert le diable* (Op. 12) [*sic*] is one of the few exceptions where he lowered himself to the taste of *la mode*.'[61] Even the nocturnes were defended against the accusation of being salon music:

Most of them are lovely melodies, in the general sense of the word, from beginning to end; sometimes they are softish, sentimental, perhaps too sweet. Occasionally Chopin wrote these pieces for the ladies of the elegant Parisian salons. But on the whole the nocturnes are so artistically worthy that they must be considered a prized possession.[62]

Consider also the way in which hasty judgements about Chopin's waltzes are corrected: these 'are his most aristocratic and elegant compositions, also his most piquant, brilliant and lightweight. By this I do not mean to suggest superficiality, because Chopin is never superficial.'[63] Liszt, too, strongly defended the polonaises: 'They in no way recall the polonaises churned out by dance orchestras and virtuosos, the hackneyed repertoire of mannered and tasteless salon music, dainty and pomaded *à la Pompadour*.'[64] A few authors – for instance, Hugo Riemann, at the turn of the century – refused categorically to apply the salon music label to Chopin:

When some (for example, Louis Köhler in his *Führer durch die Klavierlitteratur*) number Chopin among the salon composers, they are guilty of a dreadful terminological muddle; it is much more correct to put Chopin's music in strict opposition to salon music, which is characterised by the illusion of virtuosity, whereas Chopin's music often seems easy but in fact requires advanced technical skill at all times. His preludes, nocturnes, mazurkas, polonaises and waltzes are separated by a deep gulf from the vapid fashion accessories of the time, and with good reason one could describe his dances as especially idealised.[65]

Such a volte-face, consciously severing the connection between Chopin and the salon in every respect, is understandable for two reasons. First, the status of the truly artistic salon had declined to such a degree in the second half of the century, even in France, that one could hardly continue to use the word 'salon' in its original, positive

---

60 Ehlert, 'Frédéric Chopin', p. 288.
61 Kinkel, 'Friedrich Chopin als Komponist', pp. 358–9. Schumann writes about this work: 'It seems to me to have been drafted wholly by Chopin, and Franchomme simply agreed to it all; for whatever Chopin touches takes on form and spirit, and even in this lesser salon style he expresses himself with grace and refinement, in comparison with which all the good manners and nice touches of other composers writing "brilliant" works disappear into thin air.' (*Gesammelte Schriften*, vol. I, pp. 180–1).
62 Leichtentritt, *Frédéric Chopin*, p. 98.
63 Redenbacher, *François Frédéric Chopin*, p. 87.
64 Liszt, *F. Chopin*, p. 27.
65 Hugo Riemann, *Geschichte der Musik seit Beethoven (1800–1900)* (Berlin and Stuttgart 1901), p. 318.

sense. Secondly, the musical practices of the bourgeois salon, especially in Germany, completely dominated the range of associations attached to the word 'salon'. The piano-playing 'well-bred daughter', perhaps inspired by the sensational fictions perpetrated in the Chopin literature, and wanting to appear sophisticated even while pouring out her adolescent feelings through his music, arranged his works according to her particular needs and abilities, but at the same time she changed their function and she trivialised them. A contemporary critic, who himself helped form the ubiquitous salon image of the composer, lamented salon practices in the German *Kaiserreich* as follows: 'Just think of the bungling superficiality, the embarrassing triviality of the bourgeois salon; of open windows which release scraps of melody disfigured by the pedal to a tonal mush.'[66] While this attack was limited to amateur performance practice, other pedagogues fuelled the reservations and misconceptions about Chopin's work by stamping the composer himself as a threat to the development of youth:

One of the most pernicious bad habits of today's piano-loving young ladies is the zealous cult of Chopin. Far be it from me to want to degrade the genius of this suffering man. But to consider his musical ideas (which are as wonderful and enchanting as they are overwrought, alternating irreverently between heaven and hell) as appropriate for the musical education of the young is one of the most incomprehensible perversions in the history of pedagogy.[67]

Such rantings may amuse us nowadays, but we should also interpret them in the context of a manifest prejudice against the salon and its public, as an indication of those aspects of Chopin's music that German critics, schooled in German musical traditions, found either inaccessible or disconcerting; in any case it is difficult to know whether pure ignorance, uneasiness, insecurity or even secret admiration was the most decisive factor in German Chopin reception. We can perhaps more safely observe that Riemann's dissenting cry in the wilderness produced hardly any effect: by the 1920s, writers again freely invoked Chopin's salon image.

In retrospect, recourse to the salon in the German reception of Chopin seems to have been a double-edged sword. On the one hand, it accurately reflects aspects of Chopin's life; but at the same time, the widespread antipathy and hostility to the salon expressed in the literature inevitably strike a hammer blow at Chopin's music, whether deliberately or not. Although the case should not be overstated, the formative effect of the salon concept on German Chopin reception seems to be one of the reasons why Chopin scholarship of a serious and wide-ranging nature has never thrived in Germany and Austria – in contrast to his unceasing popularity in the concert hall and the world of recording. It is obvious that Chopin cannot be fully understood without reference to the salon; but to avoid the manifold terminological and aesthetic traps surrounding the salon concept, one must reconstruct as realistically as possible the Parisian salon scene in which Chopin lived. Thus we arrive at a paradox: only when Chopin is freed from the stigma of the salon can one do justice to him in the salon.

---

[66] Weissmann, *Chopin*, p. 115.
[67] Hermann Kretzschmar, 'Die Klaviermusik seit Robert Schumann (1882)', in his *Gesammelte Aufsätze über Musik und Anderes aus dem Grenzboten* (Leipzig 1910), p. 97.

3   Chopin as modernist in nineteenth-century Russia

ANNE SWARTZ

> Fryderyk Chopin, famous pianist and composer of the mazurkas which are well known to the entire musical world, expired on the seventeenth of this month in the arms of his students and friends; he died of consumption . . . The art of music, to which the deceased lovingly and unselfishly devoted himself, sustained an irretrievable loss.   (*Sanktpeterburgskiia vedomosti*, 19 October 1849)

The question of Chopin's impact within the growing national consciousness of Nicholas I's Russia remains an intriguing one. In the decade following the composer's death in 1849, his music clearly satisfied the artistic demands of both the Slavophiles, a group of intellectuals whose beliefs essentially centred around the Orthodox Church and the Russian past, and the Westernisers, who looked to European romanticism and the earlier virtuoso tradition.[1] As Nicholas's views on Russification began to take effect in the arts, critical writings on music gradually reflected the ideals of the Slavophiles. Their perception of Chopin as a 'modern' (*noveishii*) national composer, rather than a

---

[1] The Slavophiles were particularly active in Russia during the 1840s and 1850s, i.e. the latter part of Nicholas's reign (1825–55). Leading members included Alexis Khomiakov, Ivan and Peter Kireevsky, Constantine and Ivan Aksakov, and George Samarin. Although primarily social and political thinkers, these men held views of mid-nineteenth-century Russian culture which, like those of certain key music critics to be investigated below, are of relevance to this study. For further discussion, see Nicholas V. Riasanovsky, *A History of Russia*, 4th edn (New York 1984), pp. 362–3, and James H. Billington, *The Icon and the Axe: An Interpretive History of Russian Culture* (New York 1970), pp. 320–1.

    It goes without saying that classifications such as 'Slavophiles' and 'Westernisers' greatly oversimplify the highly complex, contradictory critical environment in mid-1800s Russia. In fact, the views of the figures cited above were anything but uniform; furthermore, there is not always the close relationship between the thoughts of the Slavophiles and those of Nicholas I that I suggest in certain circumstances. Nevertheless, a number of important trends and shared attitudes can be discerned, and it is on these that my study is based. A great deal of information from the Russian-language press, as well as French- and German-language publications, cannot of course be adduced here for reasons of space; this includes the fascinating insights of such men as Odeyevsky, Cui and Laroche.

    I should like to thank the National Endowment for the Humanities Summer Stipend Program, the International Research and Exchanges Board and the City University of New York Research Award Program for supporting research trips to Russia to complete this chapter. For their assistance I also extend thanks to James Billington, Teresa Dalila Turło, Irena Poniatowska, Faina Davidovna Bartnovskaia, Natalia Ramazanova Vasil'evna, the staff of the M. E. Saltykov-Shchedrin State Public Library (now the National Library of Russia) and the staff of the music library of the St Petersburg N. A. Rimsky-Korsakov Conservatory (formerly the Leningrad Conservatory). Annie Hemmingway translated the French texts. The Russian translations are mine.

    Transliterations of the Cyrillic alphabet are based on the 1961 Harvard University system. The names of some nineteenth-century Russian composers, such as Tchaikovsky, have been spelled in the Western manner. Dates are given according to the Julian, or Russian, calendar, except where the author or editor employs Julian and Gregorian dates. In those instances both dates are provided as in the original source. During the nineteenth century the Julian calendar was twelve days behind the Gregorian calendar.

35

European romantic, paralleled Nicholas's vision of Russia as an independent modern state, particularly in the wake of the European revolutions of 1848. By 1850 Chopin's music had come to represent a distinctly 'modern' keyboard style, one which embraced melodic beauty, simplicity, restrained ornamentation and national expressiveness.

This study will present evidence of the artistic connections between Chopin and the Slavophiles and will show that Chopin's keyboard music functioned largely outside the previously established Western tradition in St Petersburg. This will help to explain why, unlike other frequently performed European composers in the capital, including Beethoven, Liszt, Bach and Mozart, Chopin alone captured the imagination of the Slavophiles. The investigation will also determine why Chopin's influence began to decline in Russia during the 1870s, as what had once been seen as 'modern' increasingly became linked to the romantic past.

The tradition of the Western virtuoso was established in St Petersburg during the reign of Alexander I (1801–25). Despite later opposition from the Slavophiles, official support for this tradition continued well into the rule of his successor, Nicholas I. Among the assemblage of pianists and composers in St Petersburg before 1830 were Maria Szymanowska (Court Pianist to the Empresses Marie Feodorovna and Elizaveta Alekseevna), Adolf von Henselt (Court Pianist to Nicholas I – an appointment made at least partly for political reasons), John Field and Charles Mayer. During the late 1830s, the expressive performance style associated with these musicians gave way to the more ostentatious pianistic display identified with such European virtuosos as Sigismond Thalberg and Alexander Dreyschock. Since the piano works of Chopin, Schubert and Liszt were, for the most part, not performed in St Petersburg until after 1840,[2] the compositions of Thalberg and Dreyschock represented, perhaps incorrectly, the ideals of Western romanticism.

Primarily due to opposition from the Slavophiles, the excessive ornamentation and lack of melodic and formal integrity exhibited in much of the repertoire of the Western virtuosos had become outmoded by the late 1840s. As Nicholas's views concerning a national 'cultural identity' gained support among literary figures and musical critics, the compositional merits of Liszt, Thalberg, Dreyschock and others were increasingly debated,[3] and critics began to reflect the 'official' attitude in journals and gazettes. Under Nicholas, the Slavophiles succeeded in establishing a new emphasis

[2]   According to Glinka, who studied in the capital with Charles Mayer, Liszt in 1842 was the first to play Chopin's music in St Petersburg – specifically, a number of unspecified 'fashionable [*modnyi*]' mazurkas, nocturnes and etudes. Not surprisingly, his pioneering performances generated considerable interest in Chopin's music. (M. I. Glinka, *Literaturnoe nasledie*, ed. B. Bogdanov-Berezovski, vol. I, 'Avtobiograficheskie i tvorcheskie materialy' (Leningrad 1952), p. 216.) The *Journal de St.-Pétersbourg*, 18/30 August 1842 describes an afternoon recital by Liszt in the Hall of the Assembly of the Nobility, where he performed 'five or six pieces' 'without the accompaniment of the orchestra, without the usual prestige of a concert' (pp. 1929–30). The author mentions unidentified concertos of Hummel and Beethoven, but offers no further information concerning the performance of Chopin's works.

[3]   The earlier musical achievements of Field and Mayer proved insufficient to discourage a harsh reaction to the virtuosity cultivated by both Thalberg and Dreyschock, who compensated for lack of expressivity and melodic inventiveness through displays of complicated keyboard pyrotechnics. According to the official *Journal de St.-Pétersbourg* (hereafter *JSP*), Thalberg and Dreyschock projected a 'relentless preoccupation' with difficult technical passages at 'the expense of musical meaning', during a period

on national expression in the arts. Unlike his predecessors, Alexander I and Catherine II (1762–96), who enthusiastically embraced a predominantly European culture, Nicholas sought an empire rooted in Slavic culture and scientific thought. In the musical realm, overtly nationalistic gestures began to replace the showy virtuosity associated with European romanticism.

Notwithstanding his commitment to nationalistic ideals, Nicholas did remarkably little to facilitate the availability of formal musical training in the Russian capital. Among the offerings of the St Petersburg Academy were religion, language and literature, statistics, history, physics and chemistry, classical studies, drawing, gymnastics, dancing and fencing,[4] but even as late as 1849 music was not a recognised subject. Nevertheless, several cultural and technological developments took place during Nicholas's reign which played significant roles in the dissemination of Chopin's keyboard music. Among these were the increasing availability of Russian and foreign single editions of Chopin's works and the growth of technologically advanced piano manufacturing firms in St Petersburg. As a result of both these and the sharp critical reaction of the Slavophiles against the 'romantic' Western virtuoso, Chopin's music came to be regarded as 'modern', and indeed retained this status in Russia at least until the late 1860s when Tchaikovsky heralded the rise of a new generation of conservatory-trained musicians.[5] Although Chopin never performed in Russia, his sphere of influence thus remained considerable.

The piano industry advanced Nicholas's vision concerning the modernisation of science and technology and paralleled the revitalisation of the Russian iron industry during the 1840s.[6] Accompanied by the expansion of the middle-class market, the renewed interest in piano manufacturing fell within the acceptable political and social boundaries of Nicholas's 'modern' Russia. The firms of Jakob Becker (1841–71) and Hermann Lichtenthal (1840–70) joined those of Theodore Diederichs (1810–1918)

when audiences no longer appeared interested in the 'endless arsenal of trills, turns, scales and staccatos' which these pianists executed, admittedly with 'remarkable dexterity' (*JSP*, 31 August/12 September 1839, p. 106). Such banal acrobatics not only ceased to captivate the public but also failed to inspire the next generation of Russian composers: Balakirev, Rimsky-Korsakov, Borodin, Cui and Musorgsky.
    In another early gesture of support for the Slavophiles and against the excesses of the Western virtuoso, *JSP* criticised Dreyschock's compositional style with its excessive ornamentation (*JSP*, 25 May/6 June 1840, p. 553). Although his 'tangled web' of 'chromatic scales in octaves' achieved a dramatic *tour de force*, Dreyschock nonetheless remained on the fringes of an antiquated style which lacked expression and musical substance. The same held true for Thalberg, whose attempts to imitate Liszt's compositional style proved 'futile'. Moreover, few of his works appeared to exhibit much compositional merit.

4 *JSP*, Supplement, 18/30 September 1849, pp. 2–3.
5 See *Muzykal'nyi svet'*, January 1861, p. 1; *Revalsche Zeitung*, January 1861, [p. 4]; and *JSP*, 8/20 March 1858, p. 2787. See also Igor Beľza, 'Tradycje uprawiania muzyki Chopina w Rosji i ZSRR', *Rocznik Chopinowski*, 1 (1956), pp. 263–81; Zofia Lissa, 'Der Einfluß Chopins auf die Russische Musik', in *Chopin-Almanach zur hundertsten Wiederkehr des Todesjahres von Fryderyk Chopin* (Leipzig 1949), pp. 88–108; 'Dva neizdannykh' pisma Fr. Shopena', *Russkaia Muzykal'naia Gazeta*, 28 February/7 March 1910, pp. 250–3; Ia. Mil'stein, 'K istorii izdaniia sochinenii Shopena', in *Friderik Shopen: Stat'i i issledovaniia sovetskikh muzykovedov*, ed. Georgii Edel'man (Moscow 1960), pp. 323–60; L. S. Sidel'nikov, 'Puti pazvitiia sovetskogo shopenovedeniia', in *Venok Shopenu*, ed. L. S. Sidel'nikov (Moscow 1989), pp. 5–29; and Irena Poniatowska, *Muzyka fortepianowa i pianistyka w wieku XIX* (Warsaw 1991), pp. 154–95.
6 See William L. Blackwell, *The Beginnings of Russian Industrialization: 1800–1860* (Princeton 1968), pp. 56–60.

and Johann Friedrich Schreder (1818–1917). These builders remained preoccupied with structural 'improvements' which increased the resonance and expressivity of the instrument, and they openly competed with the recognised European firms of Broadwood and Erard.[7] Unlike many of their European counterparts, however, St Petersburg manufacturers were able to offer a durable, inexpensive piano with a cast-iron frame. Russian-owned musical instrument factories, represented by the firms of Andrei Kulakov and Petr Rozmyslov, did not emerge in St Petersburg until the 1870s.[8]

As piano manufacturers adapted to the more expressive performance style that suited Chopin's works, Russian and imported foreign editions of his music proliferated. In the *Journal de St.-Pétersbourg* the St Petersburg music publishing firm of M. Bernard advertised a small collection of 'modern and brilliant pieces for the piano', among them an 'étude favorite' (Op. 10 No. 1) of Chopin.[9] Following the publication of Chopin's etudes, Bernard offered the composer's 'four new mazurkas for piano' Op. 41 in February 1841, for the price of 4 rubles 50 kopecks.[10] In April 1841 Bernard again drew public attention to his collection of etudes, which included, inter alia, works by Chopin, Theodor Döhler, Ferdinand Hiller, Henselt, Liszt, Mendelssohn, Ignaz Moscheles and Thalberg.[11]

Although official censorship of Western books and literary journals continued unabated throughout the 1840s, Chopin's music and articles about the composer appeared with some frequency in Russian musical journals. In 1840 Bernard founded the journal *Literaturnoe pribavlenie k Nuvelisty* (Literary supplement to the *Nuvelist*), publishing single editions of new musical works in addition to biographical profiles of Chopin and other contemporary Russian and European composers. In the year preceding Chopin's death Bernard advertised Chopin's Mazurkas Op. 63 and his E♭ major Waltz Op. 18.[12] Several years later, in August 1851, Chopin's 'Douze grandes études' Op. 10 were offered for 2 rubles and his 'Douze études' Op. 25 for 2 rubles 58 kopecks.[13] Furthermore, an advertisement in the *Journal de St.-Pétersbourg* revealed that the *Abeille musicale* intended to publish a 'beautiful waltz of Chopin' (Op. 18), which the 'visiting virtuoso Theodor Döhler successfully executed during a recent tour in St Petersburg'.[14] About this time, *Muzykal'nyi svet'* (Musical world), introduced by St Petersburg publisher V. Frackmann in 1847, printed lengthy posthumous essays on Chopin.[15]

---

7   See *JSP*, 24 May/5 June 1841, p. 1161; M. Bernard, 'Royali Bekkera', *Literaturnoe pribavlenie k Nuvelisty*, April 1849, p. 29; and *Kratkii istoricheskii ocherk' stareishei fortepiannom fabriki rossii Brat'ia R. i A. Diderikhs', osnovannaia v 1810 g.* (St Petersburg 1911), pp. 1–2.

8   See *Preis'-Kurant' torgovago doma Andrei Emel'ianovich Kulakov' v S. Peterburge. Fabrika muzykal'nykh instrumentov* (St Petersburg 1891), p. ii, and *Illiustrirovannyi Preis'-Kurant', muzykal'nykh instrumentov Petra Rozmyslova s Synov'iami* (St Petersburg 1895–6), p. 1.

9   *JSP*, 28 January/9 February 1841, p. 972.

10   *JSP*, 18 February/2 March 1841, p. 1008.

11   *JSP*, 10/22 April 1841, p. 1092.

12   *Literaturnoe pribavlenie k Nuvelisty*, December 1848, pp. 97–8.

13   *Literaturnoe pribavlenie k Nuvelisty*, Supplement, August 1851, p. 66.

14   *JSP*, 20 March/1 April 1845, p. 3526.

15   *Muzykal'nyi svet'* circulated in French until 1851 and thereafter in separate Russian and French editions. Its publication in Russian not only confirms the expanded market of amateur and professional musicians in St Petersburg, but also attests to the adaptability and willingness of music publishers to offer new journals in the Russian language, despite Nicholas's strict censorship laws which discouraged

In addition to the musical essays in the *Nuvelist* and *Muzykal'nyi svet'*, further criticism and commentary on Chopin appeared in the years following his death in *Teatral'nyi i muzykal'nyi vestnik* (Theatrical and musical herald), *Journal de St.-Pétersbourg, Messager de Saint-Pétersbourg, Sanktpeterburgskiia vedomosti* (St Petersburg gazette), *St. Peterburgische Zeitung, Illiustrirovannaia gazeta* (Illustrated gazette), *Moskovskiia vedomosti* (Moscow gazette), *Russkii invalid'* (Russian invalid), *Severnaia pchela, gazeta politicheskaia i literaturnaia* (The northern bee, a political and literary gazette), and *Nedelia. Gazeta politicheskaia i literaturnaia* (The week . . .). Because these journals maintained a large following among the Slavophiles, they remained the primary conduit for the dissemination of Chopin's 'modern' style.

In a particularly important early essay which appeared in 1841 in *Severnaia pchela*, Chopin was portrayed as a composer who successfully assimilated both Slavic and Western musical traditions, and who had attained stature not only as a composer but also as a 'poet' and 'genius' whose artistry remained unsurpassed, especially when he sat at the piano and 'began to improvise' (*improvizirovat'*).[16] This is noteworthy in that the Slavophiles associated Chopin's improvisations with imaginative evocations of Poland, thus partly satisfying their yearnings for a national style. The expressive vocabulary of his mazurkas in particular went well beyond stylised 'local colour' (*mestnost'*), transcending in importance the mere incorporation of national songs and dances in operas and character pieces as in the works of Stanisław Moniuszko.[17] Rather, Chopin's artistry allied itself more closely with Nicholas's broader principles concerning a Slavic national 'cultural identity' (*narodnost'*), however that might be defined.

After Chopin's death some composer-pianists began to imitate the style of his national dances in their own works. As a result, the music of such otherwise unremarkable virtuosos as Schulhoff held a certain appeal for the conservative critic Bertold Damke,[18] who wrote in March 1851 that, whereas he could not stomach the overblown 'romantic, lyrical, dramatic or diabolical [keyboard] fantasias' of 'our most illustrious virtuosos', nothing gave him more pleasure than listening to Schulhoff's simple mazurkas, primarily because they were so 'clearly reminiscent of Chopin's'.[19] Evidence in the *Nuvelist* and *Muzykal'nyi svet'* also attests to an increasing fascination with his national dances (both mazurkas and polonaises). During this period Bernard confirmed in the *Nuvelist* that, with these and other works, Chopin 'paved a new [*novyi*] path in the repertoire of the pianoforte'.[20]

the founding of new periodicals and attempted to reduce the circulation of less expensive journals. See S. V. Rozhdestvenskii, *Istoricheskii obzor deiatel'nosti Ministerstva narodnogo prosveshcheniia, 1802–1902* (St Petersburg 1902), pp. 334–5, cited in Alexander Vucinich, *Science in Russian Culture: A History to 1860*, 2 vols. (Stanford 1963), vol. I, pp. 249–50.

[16] 'Muzykant Shopen', *Severnaia pchela, gazeta politicheskaia i literaturnaia*, 15 July 1841, p. 618.
[17] See Alexander Serov's comments in *JSP*, 13/25 March 1870, p. 1.
[18] In 1845 Damke settled in St Petersburg and, as 'Damcke', began to write regularly for *JSP*. Damke remained a strong supporter of Nicholas I, upheld the artistic ideals of the Slavophiles and was an advocate of Chopin's music.
[19] *JSP*, 11/25 March 1851, p. 5448. In a further attempt to position himself against the excesses of Western European romanticism and gain the court's favour, Damke also launches into a passionate diatribe against unnamed 'over-ambitious orchestration pianists' who 'pound the keyboard thick and fast, transforming their wrists into flails, smashing the chords and dislocating the keys of their instrument', thereby creating a 'frightful racket'.
[20] *Nuvelist*, December 1852, p. 92.

Immediately after Chopin's death in October 1849, *Sanktpeterburgskiia vedomosti* published a brief tribute acknowledging his achievements as a 'famous pianist' and 'composer of the mazurkas which are well known to the entire musical world'.[21] The Slavophiles viewed Chopin's death as a great loss. The national style associated above all with his mazurkas reinforced the view of Chopin as representative of a restrained 'modern' idiom which had supplanted Western romanticism. Interest in Chopin's early composition studies in Warsaw with Józef Elsner surfaced in subsequent essays. In October 1849 *Sanktpeterburgskiia vedomosti* began a series of narratives on the composer's life which whetted the imagination of the Russian musical public. Of particular interest was the ostensible competition between Chopin and Liszt, which focused on the former's reputed distaste for large gatherings and public performances. Because Chopin only occasionally played in public, he could not rival Liszt's 'worshippers and fanatical followers'.[22] Unlike Liszt, who sought public acclaim, Chopin performed in public only when compelled by financial circumstances: unmoved by applause, he 'remained a profitless admirer of art', choosing to devote his life to its 'exclusive and tender service'.[23]

Chopin's affinity for performing before small groups of students and admirers enhanced his reputation in Russia as a composer whose works represented a new artistic path, 'art for art' (*iskusstvo dlia iskusstva*).[24] The concept 'art for art' was for the Slavophiles an achievement which went far beyond public acclaim and recognition. Like the contemporary literary figure Afanasy Fet (whose works foreshadowed the symbolists Konstantin Balmont and Aleksandr Blok), Chopin remained a spiritual visionary who devoted his entire life to his art. *Sanktpeterburgskiia vedomosti*, citing Berlioz, declared that Chopin's artistry formed the basis of a musical school in its own right. His works were characterised by a 'distinctive elegance' and by the 'unexpectedness of their melodic turns', 'boldness of their harmony' and 'independence of their rhythmic accents'.[25] More importantly, Chopin's approach to ornamentation was considered entirely without equal.

Details concerning Chopin's funeral in Paris appeared in *Moskovskiia vedomosti*, 29 November 1849 and *Sanktpeterburgskiia vedomosti*, 20 November 1849,[26] while *Russkii invalid*, 1 November 1849 focused retrospectively on Chopin's spiritual nature and his 'dreamy, poetic and tender soul' which could be invoked only through 'solitude and meditation'.[27] This view of Chopin as a spiritual and solitary composer whose works represented 'art for art' was echoed in a lengthy unsigned essay, 'Frédéric Chopin', which appeared in the *Messager de Saint-Pétersbourg* in November 1849.[28] A few years later *Moskovskiia vedomosti* hailed Chopin as 'one of the most original

---

21   See full quotation above. *Sanktpeterburgskiia vedomosti*, 19 October 1849, p. 937.
22   *Sanktpeterburgskiia vedomosti*, 29 October 1849, p. 913.
23   Ibid.
24   Ibid.
25   Ibid.
26   *Moskovskiia vedomosti*, 29 November 1849, p. 1509; *Sanktpeterburgskiia vedomosti*, 20 November 1849, p. 1047.
27   *Russkii invalid*, 1 November 1849, p. 933.
28   *Messager de Saint-Pétersbourg*, 11 November 1849, p. 1066.

phenomena of the artistic world'.[29] The portrayal of Chopin as a poetic composer continued through the late nineteenth century and even into this century: for instance, the 1903 edition of *Brokgaus-Efron* regarded him as a composer of 'graceful, grandiose and poetic music' and as a performer who conveyed a 'now radiant, now completely mysterious, tender, intermittent, rich *tempo rubato*'.[30]

After Nicholas's death in 1855, stories concerning Chopin's private life proliferated. Anecdotal evidence appeared in Russian gazettes and journals about the state of his health, his relationship with George Sand and his dislike of public performances, all of which actively engaged the public. Quoting from Sand's literary works, an essay in *Teatral'nyi i muzykal'nyi vestnik* focused on Chopin's romantic connection with the writer, rather than on his compositional legacy.[31] Another popular myth circulating in 1866 appeared in the political and literary gazette, *Nedelia*. According to this account, Chopin's health declined because he was compelled for financial reasons to give private performances 'in return for his dinner' in the homes of 'wealthy, unsympathetic, boorish patrons', in addition to his public concerts.[32] These narratives promulgated the romantic myths surrounding Chopin's life and works, but did little to add to his stature as a 'modern' composer, unlike the translations of essays by the American pianist Louis Moreau Gottschalk and the conservative Belgian musicologist François-Joseph Fétis which appeared during the early 1860s in *Muzykal'nyi svet'*. While the latter praised Chopin's music for its 'originality', 'imagination' and 'melancholy beauty',[33] the Russian version of Gottschalk's article employed the adjective 'modern' (*noveishii*) to describe Chopin's expressive style;[34] moreover, for the first time a clear distinction emerged between Chopin's 'modern' (*noveishii*) compositional style and the 'contemporary' (*sovremennyi*) practice of the European virtuoso, who by now was linked with the past.

This debate between 'contemporary', or Western, practice and 'modern', or national, tradition carried on throughout the 1860s, fuelled in part by the journalistic campaign some years earlier of Feofil Matveevich Tolstoi (1809–81), a crusty St Petersburg music critic and composer who after 1850 wrote under the pseudonym Rostislav for the *Journal de St.-Pétersbourg*. Rostislav deplored empty pianistic display, placing Chopin's keyboard music in contrast within the expressive domain of the modern national school. In an essay, 'Une réaction salutaire contre *la voltige transcendante du piano*', which appeared in the *Journal de St.-Pétersbourg*, 8/20 March 1858, he attempted to define Chopin's keyboard style. In his view, Chopin was the first modern pianist to rebel against the 'useless acrobatics' once *en vogue*: unlike others, Chopin did not demand that the instrument 'roar or make drum rolls'.[35] In addition, Chopin's music portrayed a melodic originality which expressed national sentiment, a broader view upheld earlier by the Slavophiles in the posthumous accounts of his

29 *Moskovskiia vedomosti*, 21 July 1856, p. 368.
30 'Shopen', *Brokgaus-Efron Entsiklopedicheskii Slovar'*, (St Petersburg 1903), vol. LXXVIII, p. 791.
31 *Teatral'nyi i muzykal'nyi vestnik*, 7 June 1859, pp. 225–6.
32 *Nedelia*, 24 June 1866, p. 318.
33 *Muzykal'nyi svet'*, November 1862, p. 76.
34 *Muzykal'nyi svet'*, February 1861, p. 13.
35 *JSP*, 8/20 March 1858, p. 2787.

life in *Sanktpeterburgskiia vedomosti*. By drawing these contrasts between pianistic pyrotechnics and a 'modern' national style, Rostislav presaged the clean break that would take place during the 1860s between the Slavophiles and Westernisers.

In the late 1850s, as Mily Balakirev and the *Moguchaia Kuchka* (Mighty Handful) sought with the assistance of the Slavophiles to create a national school, Grand Duchess Elena Pavlovna, sister-in-law of the late Nicholas I, threw her enthusiastic support behind Anton Rubinstein and the Westernisers. In 1862 Rubinstein founded the St Petersburg Conservatory, appointing Alexander Dreyschock as a piano teacher notwithstanding the critical attitude that the Slavophiles had earlier displayed towards his supposedly unimaginative performances. The *Kuchka*, reacting vociferously against this proliferation of Western values in the capital, established the Free School of Music at about the same time.[36]

It was not until after the founding of the St Petersburg Conservatory that the first attempt was made to place Chopin's art within a historical context, which in turn led to altogether new interpretative approaches to his music. *Illiustrirovannaia gazeta*, upholding Chopin's merits, hyperbolically declared that as early as 1830 he had become a well-known musical figure in Poland, Russia and Germany.[37] His Concertos in F minor Op. 21 and E minor Op. 11 had made a particularly strong impression, reflecting an individual compositional style which was at once 'pensive' and 'elevating'. Furthermore, although the author praised Liszt, Thalberg and Döhler for advancing *contemporary* performance practice, it was Chopin who had occupied 'one of the first places' in the *modern* art (*iskusstvo*) of composition, and who, some twenty years after his death, remained among the 'three or four' 'original' musicians of the epoch.[38] Entering into the controversy between the Slavophiles and the Westernisers was Alexander Serov, a gifted and outspoken critic who wrote for the *Journal de St.-Pétersbourg* and was largely responsible for increasing the public's awareness of both Chopin and Wagner during the late 1860s. Although Serov, himself a composer of operas, remained a strong supporter of Wagner's music dramas, he nevertheless included Chopin among the composers featured in an essay on 'the limits of very modern music' which appeared in the *Journal de St.-Pétersbourg*.[39]

---

[36]   See Leonid Sabaneyeff, *Modern Russian Composers*, trans. Judah A. Joffe (New York 1927), pp. 130–44. For further discussion of the *Kuchka* and the many musical rivalries surrounding the establishment of the Free School of Music, see Robert C. Ridenour, *Nationalism, Modernism, and Personal Rivalry in Nineteenth-Century Russian Music* (Ann Arbor 1981), pp. 65–109; also, Edward Garden, 'Balakirev: The Years of Crisis (1867–1876)', in *Russian and Soviet Music: Essays for Boris Schwarz*, ed. Malcolm Hamrick Brown (Ann Arbor 1984), pp. 147–55. Richard Taruskin's *Opera and Drama in Russia: As Preached and Practiced in the 1860s* (Ann Arbor 1981), pp. 348–400, outlines the many contradictions occurring within the broader context of the nineteenth-century Russian musical tradition. See also Taruskin's study, 'Glinka's Ambiguous Legacy and the Birth Pangs of Russian Opera', *19th-Century Music*, 1 (1977), pp. 142–62.

[37]   *Illiustrirovannaia gazeta*, 13 March 1869, p. 173.

[38]   Ibid., p. 174.

[39]   *JSP*, 9/21 November 1869, p. 1. This essay also contains an inspired and prolonged discourse on the 'most modern terrain' of symphonic, dramatic and keyboard music after the era of Beethoven and Weber. Serov embraced not only Chopin and Glinka, but, turning away from the Slavophiles, Wagner, Mendelssohn, Meyerbeer and (with reservation) Liszt as well. To the dissatisfaction of the Slavophiles he found only the promise of talent in the efforts of Balakirev and the *Kuchka*, because of their opposition to Wagner.

The emergence of conservatories in St Petersburg and Moscow during the 1860s contributed to renewed interest in the publication of a Russian edition of Chopin's complete works, which itself was part of a broader effort to secure the composer's place in music history. With the support of Nikolai Rubinstein and the Moscow Conservatory, Petr Jurgenson established a music publishing firm in Moscow in August 1861[40] and during the years 1873–6 brought out a six-volume edition of Chopin's piano works, *Fr. Chopin. Oeuvres complètes*.[41] Nikolai Albertovich Gubert (Hubert), a former student of Rubinstein at the St Petersburg Conservatory and by this time a professor of music theory at the Moscow Conservatory, provided the commentary for Jurgenson's edition; this represented the first step in Russia towards a systematic critical interpretation of Chopin's music. Karl Klindworth, a student of Liszt and an enthusiastic supporter of Wagner who in 1868 was appointed by Rubinstein as a teacher at his recently established Moscow Conservatory, edited Jurgenson's edition. Its availability proved particularly valuable in the dissemination in Russia of the composer's early works, as previously this repertoire had remained largely inaccessible to performers in Moscow and St Petersburg.

In the preface to the first volume of the *Oeuvres complètes*, published in 1873, Hubert distinguished the modern period, to which Chopin's music belonged, from the earlier classical tradition. With recent developments in musical practice and the expansion of critical thought, Hubert advocated judicious evaluation of the 'master works' not only of the 'classical period', but also of the 'modern'. This evaluation represented 'definite progress' towards the 'faithful interpretation of a work in the spirit and the style of its composer'.[42] Anticipating the technical difficulties that the performer might encounter in rendering Chopin's keyboard works, Hubert devoted considerable attention to specific problems, such as performance indications, fingering and the execution of melismatic ornaments, trills, appoggiaturas and unspecified *gruppetti*. He also established principles of expressive phrasing, comparing the art of phrasing to declamation in speech: according to Hubert, in a musical phrase, as in spoken language, smaller motifs (*motifs*) combine to express larger thoughts.[43] Hubert's observations on Chopin's music reflected an increased interest in Moscow and St Petersburg during the 1870s in the musical interpretation of 'historical' works.

Despite Serov's intense adoration of Chopin and Wagner, his biting criticism of Balakirev and Alexander Dargomizhsky created a less-than-enthusiastic response among the Slavophiles. When the task of writing Serov's obituary for *JSP* fell to the contentious, ailing Rostislav, the latter projected a narrowly veiled dislike of Serov in the opening statement of his biographical account: 'It is not through Serov's popularity that one can explain the enormous public crowds at the funeral of that eminent man' (*JSP*, 30 January/11 February 1871, p. 1). Rostislav, who earlier argued the case for Chopin and the Slavophiles, now criticised Serov's abstruse prose style, which he regarded as largely inaccessible to the general Russian public. Nonetheless, Rostislav revered Serov as a 'self-taught musician', whose operas, with their expressive melodies and restrained ornamentation, were 'national treasures'. Rostislav chose to focus on the emotional, subjective qualities of the music of both Chopin and Serov.

40 *Preis'-Kurant' sklada muzykal'nykh instrumentov i notopechatni P. Iurgensona v Moskve* (Moscow 1903), p. 5.
41 *Fr. Chopin. Oeuvres complètes, critiquement revues par Ch. Klindworth*, vol. I (Moscow 1873), p. 1. The titles of subsequent volumes vary. For detailed discussion of Jurgenson's first and significant subsequent editions, see Józef Michał Chomiński and Teresa Dalila Turło, *Katalog dzieł Fryderyka Chopina* (Cracow 1990), pp. 267–8.
42 *Oeuvres complètes*, vol. I, p. 1.
43 Ibid., p. 2.

Indeed, in the years following the founding of his firm, Jurgenson published the works of earlier European masters such as Mendelssohn, Schumann, Schubert and Liszt, as well as those of living composers like Tchaikovsky, Nikolai and Anton Rubinstein, Ippolitov-Ivanov, Borodin, Balakirev, Musorgsky, Rimsky-Korsakov, Napravnik and Rachmaninoff. In addition to the *Oeuvres complètes*, Jurgenson offered separate editions of Chopin's waltzes, mazurkas, variations and fantasies,[44] as did M. Bernard, whose *Fr. Chopin. Sämmtliche Pianoforte Werke. Kritisch repidirt [sic] und mit Fingersatz versehen. Walzer* was identical in editorial scope and content to Jurgenson's *F. Chopin Valses*.[45]

Although Hubert's commentary in the *Oeuvres complètes* was the first systematic study of Chopin in a Russian edition, the Nocturne Op. 72 No. 1, composed in the late 1820s and first published in Russia in the December 1855 musical appendix of *Muzykal'nyi svet'*, elicited a considerably earlier theoretical discussion of Chopin's imaginative harmonic language. After remarking on the 'delightful melody' of this nocturne, accompanied by a 'bass part in triplets which also forms a pleasant and soft melody', the *Journal de St.-Pétersbourg* criticised a 'spelling mistake' in the bass line (bar 21), 'where the triplet [on the first beat] is written: F♯, C♯, F♮, and the following triplet starts again with an F♯'.[46] The author maintained that since the 'right hand [interval] is a minor seventh', or, rather, a 'suspension which resolves to a major sixth', there should be an E♯ instead of the F♮ on the last quaver of beat 1 (and, by extension, of beat 3) as in the 'corrected' edition quoted in Example 3.1.[47] In the years following

Example 3.1   Nocturne Op. 72 No. 1, bars 20–2 (from *Complete Works*, vol. VII, ed. I. J. Paderewski, L. Bronarski and J. Turczyński)

the publication of Op. 72 No. 1, *Muzykal'nyi svet'* confirmed the wide acceptance of Chopin's music in St Petersburg, noting in particular the striking popularity of the E♭ major Waltz Op. 18, Mazurkas Op. 7, A minor Waltz Op. 34 No. 2, C♯ minor Waltz Op. 64 No. 2, D♭ major Waltz Op. 70 No. 3 and 'the Nocturnes dedicated to Madame Stirling [Op. 55], Madame Billing [Op. 32] and Madame Pleyel [Op. 9]'.[48]

44   *F. Chopin Valses (Ch. Klindworth). P. Jurgenson à Moscou.* (Moscow n.d.), pp. 2–68; *Edition Jurgenson. Variations et Fantaisies Op. 2, 12, 13, 49 pour le piano composées par Fr. Chopin. Édition revue et corrigée par Ch. Klindworth.* (Moscow n.d.), pp. 2–60; *F. Chopin. 52 Mazurkas. (Ch. Klindworth)* (Moscow n.d.), pp. 3–139.

45   *Fr. Chopin. Sämmtliche Pianoforte-Werke. Kritisch repidirt [sic] und mit Fingersatz versehen. Walzer* (St Petersburg n.d.), pp. 2–59.

46   *JSP*, 15/27 December 1855, p. 3733.

47   Ibid.

48   *Muzykal'nyi svet'*, October 1870, p. 37.

Interest in the interpretation of Chopin's works increased after Anton Rubinstein's return to St Petersburg in 1874. In *Razgovor o muzyke* (Conversations about music) Rubinstein painted a quite individual portrait of Chopin. For him, Chopin was the 'bard, rhapsodist, spirit and soul' of the piano; his style portrayed 'the tragic, the romantic, the lyric, the heroic, the dramatic, the fantastic . . . the dreamy, the majestic, the simple . . . every possible expression'.[49] In his 'Conversations' Rubinstein referred specifically to the mazurkas, preludes, etudes, nocturnes, polonaises (except for Op. 53), F minor Ballade Op. 52, Scherzos in B minor Op. 20 and D♭ major Op. 31, and Sonatas in B♭ minor Op. 35 and B minor Op. 58. In all these works Rubinstein heard narratives about Poland. Chopin's profoundly expressive style, with its 'beauty of creation', 'perfection of technique and form', and 'newness' (*novizna*) of harmony depicted 'tales and exultations' about the 'former greatness of Poland', as well as 'sighing, mourning and lamentation for her subsequent ruin'.[50] Ironically, Rubinstein's elegiac view was more closely tied to the older traditions of European romanticism than to the 'modern' values of the Slavophiles.

Upon his return to St Petersburg for the opening of the 1874 season, Rubinstein devoted a large portion of one recital programme to Chopin's Etudes Op. 10 and Op. 25 and the Preludes Op. 28, these works having been published by Jurgenson in 1873 in the first and third volumes of the *Oeuvres complètes*. As a gesture to the Slavophiles, Rubinstein concluded his programme with several of Chopin's mazurkas. Wilhelm von Lenz, a pianist and critic who was identified only as 'L' in the *Journal de St.-Pétersbourg* and who also wrote for the *St. Peterburgische Zeitung* and the *Deutsche Blätter für Rußland*, commented at length on Rubinstein's performance: virtually ignoring his interpretations of Schumann and Beethoven, Lenz instead focused his attention on the nostalgic recollections of Chopin's rubato and the composer's own expressive style.[51]

The appearance of Hans von Bülow in the hall of the Bol'shoy Theatre during the spring of 1874 generated considerable excitement in St Petersburg. Lenz praised Bülow in the *Journal de St.-Pétersbourg* for his thoughtful and skilful performances of Beethoven, Chopin and Liszt.[52] By the time Bülow arrived in St Petersburg he had already developed a reputation for presenting concert programmes dedicated to the works of a single composer, a practice which Rubinstein later adopted; Beethoven, Mendelssohn and Chopin supplied the material for Bülow's successive recitals in the capital. His interpretation of the Nocturne Op. 37 No. 2 represented its first performance in St Petersburg: although composed in 1839, the work had remained virtually unknown in the capital. Following Bülow's programme, however, music stores were

49   Anton Rubinstein, *Muzyka i eia predstaviteli. Razgovor o muzyke* (Moscow 1891), p. 96.
50   Ibid., p. 97. Incidentally, it is worth noting the uneasy relationship that existed between Poland and Russia in the mid 1800s. Poland (looking westward, especially to France, and Catholic) was often regarded as the Slav world's renegade rather than as part of a 'Slavic national cultural identity' such as I referred to earlier. (For instance, the Polish scenes in Glinka's *A Life for the Tsar* were sometimes booed.) In this light, Chopin's association with Polish nationalism, in revolt against Russian oppression, was something of an obstacle to his appreciation by nineteenth-century Russian critics and consumers.
51   *JSP*, 2/14 March 1874, p. 1.
52   *JSP*, 22 March/3 April 1874, p. 1.

unable to meet the demand for the work. The second of his 1874 concerts included Chopin's *Allegro de concert* Op. 46, composed in 1841.[53] Evincing little interest in Bülow's historical approach to Chopin's music, Lenz disapproved of the choice of this work, which, in his view, too closely resembled the outmoded style of Hummel and therefore did not deserve an airing in St Petersburg. Lenz maintained that the *Allegro de concert* would have received far more acclaim had it been performed during the early 1840s, when such virtuoso display dominated the concert hall.

Performances of Chopin's early works increased in St Petersburg during the mid 1870s, as music historians became preoccupied with the fertile cultural past and its relationship to Russian music of the 'modern' era. While the Slavophiles sought to define the history of Russian music, Rubinstein and the conservatory students continued with their performances of Chopin's little-known early-period works. Several conservatory students presented a concert which included Chopin's *Andante spianato and Grande Polonaise brillante* Op. 22 and his B♭ minor Nocturne Op. 9 No. 1. The E♭ major *Grande Polonaise*, composed in 1830–1, was rarely performed in St Petersburg before its appearance in the third volume of the *Oeuvres complètes*, published in 1873. Rostislav argued in the *Journal de St.-Pétersbourg* that the Polonaise represented a past tradition. Chopin composed the work during his youth, when, according to Rostislav, 'he was caught somewhere between the style of Hummel, then the fashion of the day, and his own genius, which was already quite great'.[54] In a further attempt to divorce Chopin's youthful style from that of his mature period, Rostislav pronounced Op. 9 No. 1 'an anachronism, not yet fully emancipated from Field's tradition'.[55]

The renewed preoccupation with virtuoso display coloured at least some of these performances. In the spring of 1875, one of Anton Rubinstein's conservatory students, a Miss Timanov, played Chopin's B♭ minor Nocturne Op. 9 No. 1 in the Concert Hall of the Imperial Court Kapella. Lenz faulted Timanov's interpretation. In the *Journal de St.-Pétersbourg* he cautioned against the excessive liveliness and passion that she exhibited in the rapid execution of the ornamentation.[56] Such technical excess was too closely associated with the romanticised style of the Western virtuoso of the 1840s and seriously detracted from the music's expressive message. The correct interpretation of Chopin's ornamentation remained a significant issue for Lenz, who entreated pianists to avoid imitating the virtuosity of Liszt.

In 1875 Nikolai Rubinstein presented a concert of Chopin and John Field in the Hall of the Assembly of the Nobility in St Petersburg, illustrating for Lenz the extent

---

53   Ibid.
54   *JSP*, 3/15 May 1873, p. 1.
55   Ibid. For the most part, Rostislav ignored the interest in musical and historical studies that began with Vladimir Stasov during the 1850s and continued with Vladimir Mikhnevich and Serov in the 1870s. See Vladimir Stasov, *Avtografy muzykantov v Imperatorskoi Publichnoi Biblioteke* (St Petersburg 1856), pp. 1–20; Vladimir Osipovich Mikhnevich, *Ocherk' istorii muzyki v rossii v kul'turno-obshchestvennom' otnoshenii* (St Petersburg 1879), pp. 274–91; and *JSP*, 23, 24 July/4, 5 August 1881, p. 1. See also Gerald Abraham, 'Vladimir Stasov: Man and Critic', in his *Essays on Russian and East European Music* (Oxford 1985), pp. 99–112, and T. N. Livanova, 'Stasov o shopene', in *Venok Shopenu*, ed. L. S. Sidel'nikov (Moscow 1989), pp. 92–104.
56   *JSP*, 21 March/2 April 1875, p. 1.

to which 'Chopin used Field as a model'.[57] Among Rubinstein's offerings were Field's Concerto in A♭ major, which he reclaimed from the piano archives of the Moscow Conservatory, and Chopin's B minor Sonata Op. 58.

Chopin's own piano concertos, in solo-piano format, appeared in 1873 in the first and second volumes of Jurgenson's *Oeuvres complètes* and were firmly established as part of the repertoire of the St Petersburg Conservatory by 1875. In an essay in the *Journal de St.-Pétersbourg*, Lenz once again upbraided conservatory students for their unstylistic interpretation of these works, an approach which favoured technique and ignored expressivity.[58] Lenz defended Chopin and the modern keyboard school of the 1850s, which essentially espoused the views of the Slavophiles and opposed the conservatory tradition. With respect to interpretation, mere execution of the notes of the Concerto Op. 11, without intelligent and expressive rendering of the 'cantilena-counterpoint sections', produced for Lenz a performance utterly devoid of musical meaning.[59] Lenz's disapproval of the bland, lacklustre performances of many of Rubinstein's students led him to question the ultimate value of conservatory training with respect to expressive interpretation of Chopin's music:

It is life, not a professor, which can teach Chopin. It is an entire artistic existence . . . One can sense [how to play] Chopin, one cannot learn it. He is not contained within the four walls of a classroom; he inhabits the great wide world; he is a rhapsody inspired by the vicissitudes of life. Chopin is to the piano what Balzac is to the novel, a supreme elegance, with the most passionate aspirations. One neither understands nor enjoys Chopin simply by *wishing* to, but by *being able* to. After completing formal studies [*l'école*], one can tackle Mozart, Hummel, even Beethoven's first three piano concertos, but never Chopin or Weber, because academic training never supplies the intelligence of the masters, but only, if even that, the means of acquiring it . . .[60]

After more than thirty years of exposure to Chopin's music in Russia, it became fashionable in St Petersburg to refer to Chopin's music as embodying masculine and feminine traits. Due in part to Rubinstein's emotive performance style and to the anecdotes circulating about the delicate nature of Chopin's health, qualities associated with masculinity and femininity soon became rife in the discourse surrounding his music and its interpretation. Lenz accordingly defined the two themes from the Allegro of the E minor Concerto Op. 11, maintaining in the *Journal de St.-Pétersbourg* that the 'first and main theme in E minor' presented a 'male character, proud and triumphant'.[61] His description of the second, or 'feminine', theme affirmed that 'the expression is passionate and is in harmony with the Italian dramatic musical style'.[62]

An increasing feminisation of Chopin's music continued into the late 1870s in Russia, as the emphasis shifted from the compositions themselves to interpretations of his music. Rostislav maintained in the *Journal de St.-Pétersbourg*, 23 April/5 May 1877

57 Ibid. Rubinstein's interest in Field, who was well known in Russia during the first third of the century, illustrates the increasingly important role of historical studies within the Moscow conservatory tradition.
58 'Conservatoire de Musique', *JSP*, 30 May/11 June 1875, p. 1.
59 Ibid.
60 Ibid.
61 Ibid.
62 Ibid.

that Chopin's works required a 'soft, elegant touch', and should only occasionally be performed with 'masculine force'.[63] In the *Journal de St.-Pétersbourg*, 19/31 March 1880, Rostislav offered an imaginative description of Anton Rubinstein's physical transformation during a performance of the Funeral March from Chopin's B♭ minor Sonata Op. 35 in the Hall of the Assembly of the Nobility:

The Olympian God Jupiter was, in his numerous metamorphoses, transformed in turn into a swan, a bull, even a shower of gold, but he never gave himself the pleasure of taking the characteristics and voice of a woman. The Jupiter of the piano [Rubinstein] allows himself this fantasy from time to time. After having rolled forth mountainous sounds, he sometimes plays intonations so sweet, so caressing, that he seems for a moment to have changed sexes. The way in which he phrases . . . Chopin's Funeral March, one could almost hear the strains and weepings of a young girl . . . I would not say if that represented part of the composer's intentions, but the voice that Rubinstein undoubtedly makes us hear during the Funeral March is that of a young girl.[64]

Rubinstein's highly individual interpretations, which emphasised both sentiment and virtuosity, gradually began to overshadow the simpler style in which Chopin's music had earlier been performed. As Rubinstein seduced the St Petersburg public, Chopin's more discreet national expressiveness no longer prevailed. Rather, Rubinstein's 'variety and richness of colouring' and his 'unbelievable *cantabile*' revealed Chopin's artistry in a different light.[65] By 1880 Rubinstein's dramatic and emotional readings symbolised a new era in which the performer as interpreter held sway. Whereas during the 1850s the simplicity of Chopin's music had represented a modern style for the Slavophiles, now Rubinstein's emotive virtuosity tempered melodic expressivity and determined an entirely different musical meaning.

Although Chopin thus provoked the imagination of both Slavophiles and Westernisers, of Glinka and Rimsky-Korsakov,[66] of Serov and Anton Rubinstein, a significant shift in critical thought occurring at this time would fundamentally alter the way in which the composer was perceived henceforth. In the *Journal de St.-Pétersbourg*, 11/23 February 1872, Rostislav announced that in recent years Tchaikovsky had inaugurated a 'new school' of Russian composers, primarily because he sought 'new forms in music' which conformed to principles drawn from his 'classical studies' at the St Petersburg Conservatory.[67] Tchaikovsky, who exploited 'Russian national themes', adopting their 'cadence, rhythm and expression', was the first Russian composer to combine compositional elements from the Western conservatory tradition and the Russian national school.[68] Thus it was Tchaikovsky, not Chopin, who, after 1870, represented 'modern' compositional practice in Russia.

63 *JSP*, 23 April/5 May 1877, p. 1.
64 *JSP*, 19/31 March 1880, p. 1.
65 *JSP*, 17/29 April 1880, p. 1.
66 Rimsky-Korsakov maintained in his 'Chronicles' that it was Chopin who influenced his decision to include national dances in his operas (N. A. Rimsky-Korsakov, *Letopis' moei muzykal'noi zhizni, 1844–1906* (Moscow 1926), p. 380), while for the new generation of conservatory musicians the combined artistry of Glinka and Chopin symbolised 'the highest expression of Slavic musical genius' (*JSP*, 14/26 January 1881, p. 2).
67 *JSP*, 11/23 February 1872, p. 1.
68 *JSP*, 20 April/2 May 1874, p. 1.

During the 1870s and 1880s, as critics and historians turned their attention to questions of originality within a native Russian musical tradition, the focus of their investigations differed from the Slavophilic vision of the 1850s. Whereas Chopin's melodies had once characterised the expressive simplicity of the emerging national style of Balakirev and the *Kuchka* and represented a 'modern' keyboard school for the Slavophiles, and whereas during the 1860s and 1870s the interpretation of Chopin's works had become associated with a renewed dedication to Western tradition, with the assassination of Alexander II on 2/14 March 1881, followed by the death of Nikolai Rubinstein in Paris later that month, Chopin's era as 'modernist' in Russia drew to a close. During the intense period of Russification that followed under Alexander III (1881–94), Chopin's keyboard works ironically recalled a romanticism which had earlier been considered diametrically opposed to the very qualities his music represented. The new musical consciousness looked to Russia itself for inspiration, to Glinka and Tchaikovsky, just as the previous generation had looked to both Chopin and the West.

4 Small fairy voices: sex, history and meaning in Chopin

JEFFREY KALLBERG

Ariel, Queen Mab, Trilby, a coterie of unnamed fairies, elves and angels: through much of Chopin's life and for generations after he died, his name and his art were styled metaphorically using these entwined terms and others like them. Manifestly a form of praise, a means of drawing attention to the ways in which Chopin transported the purveyor of the metaphor into transcendentally ethereal realms, these configurations performed another kind of cultural work as well: they enabled the subject of sex to figure into the understanding of Chopin.

Sexual meanings in music have lately concerned a number of musicologists.[1] But particularly when they have attempted interpretations which have to do with 'sexuality' and 'desire', the results of their studies have generally been disappointing. Three problematic suppositions derail them. First, they assume that the methodologies of formalist analysis allow unmediated access to the notions of 'sexuality' and 'desire' that are supposedly embedded in the works under discussion. That is, they equate desire for, say, harmonic closure with desire for, say, orgasm. Such historically and critically unfiltered homologies yield crudely literalistic readings of both sex and music. Secondly, they tend unreflectively to establish 'sexuality' and 'desire' as universalist discourses. In so doing, they risk imposing present-day structures of understanding on cultures in which these concepts, when they were deployed at all, may have been construed differently. And thirdly, they take as the point of departure for their interpretations of individual works the composer's presumed sexual orientation. They then read the composer's 'sexuality' as a text which is somehow composed out in a score, and thus discernible through formalist analysis. But this is to allow the figure of the composer to police interpretation in a way which (for the early nineteenth century at least) does not stand up to historical or hermeneutical scrutiny.

In this essay, I want to redress these methodological issues by restoring history to the critical matrix. The concern that motivates me is not how music 'speaks' sex,

[1] See, for example, Susan McClary, 'Sexual Politics in Classical Music', in her *Feminine Endings: Music, Gender, and Sexuality* (Minneapolis 1991), pp. 53–79; McClary, 'Schubert's Sexuality and His Music', *GLSG Newsletter*, 2/1 (1992), pp. 8–14 (expanded as 'Constructions of Subjectivity in Schubert's Music', in *Queering the Pitch: The New Gay and Lesbian Musicology*, ed. Philip Brett, Elizabeth Wood and Gary Thomas (New York and London 1994), pp. 205–33); and Robert Fink, 'Desire, Repression, and Brahms's First Symphony', *repercussions*, 2/1 (1993), pp. 75–103.

how the formal dimensions of the score articulate both a sexual orientation (presumably that of the composer) and sexual experiences. Rather, I want to investigate how sex 'spoke' music, how (and if) sex entered into the reception of music at a given historical moment.[2] In what follows, I will outline the history of the otherworldly metaphors that were applied to Chopin, trace the mechanics by which, through multiple deferrals and deflections of meaning, these metaphors were understood to invoke sex, and explore some of the images hazily limned through this unsteady historical process: Chopin as androgyne, Chopin as hermaphrodite, Chopin as sodomite.

Otherworldly metaphors

People who heard and saw Chopin play the piano, who encountered his music or who made his acquaintance repeatedly tried to share their experience by evoking various otherworldly beings, in particular fairies, elves, sylphs and angels. The metaphors first began to attach themselves to accounts of Chopin soon after his emigration to Paris, and continued to configure him not only for the rest of his life, but also through the nineteenth century and well into the twentieth.

Chopin's idiosyncratic manner of performing served as one of the most powerful stimuli to flights of otherworldly metaphor. Hector Berlioz, writing in *Le Rénovateur* in 1833 and himself no stranger to associating music with elves and fairies, offered one of the earliest such descriptions, moving beyond the general to compare Chopin to a particular sprite, the title character of Charles Nodier's *Trilby ou le lutin d'Argail* (1822):

There are unbelievable details in his Mazurkas; and he has found how to render them doubly interesting by playing them with the utmost degree of softness, *piano* to the extreme, the hammers merely brushing the strings, so much so that one is tempted to go close to the instrument and put one's ear to it as if to a concert of sylphs or elves. Chopin is the *Trilby* of pianists.[3]

In 1836, the young Charles Hallé, recently arrived in Paris, described his first hearing of Chopin in a letter to his parents. To the otherworldly menagerie of elves and fairies, Hallé adjoined angels, a particularly common displacement which would also be used to characterise Chopin's personality:

The same evening [30 November 1836] I went to dine with Baron Eichtal . . . where I heard – Chopin. That was beyond all words . . . Chopin! He is no man, he is an angel, a god (or what

---

[2] I do not mean to foreclose the possibility that knowledge of a composer's sexual orientation can affect the reception of a musical work. But I doubt that it would have been likely to do so before the latter part of the nineteenth century, when 'sexuality' became a generally conceivable phenomenon.

[3] Cited and translated in Jean-Jacques Eigeldinger, *Chopin: Pianist and Teacher as Seen by His Pupils* (hereafter *CPT*), trans. Naomi Shohet with Krysia Osostowicz and Roy Howat, ed. Roy Howat (Cambridge 1986), p. 272.
     Liszt (or Carolyne von Sayn-Wittgenstein, who may have written large portions of Liszt's biography of Chopin) also associated Chopin with Nodier when treating the composer's aversion to public performance: 'Chopin knew that his talent – in style and imagination recalling Nodier, through purity of delivery, through familiarity with *La Fée aux miettes* and *Les Lutins d'Argail* [*sic*], through echoes of *Séraphines* and *Dianes* whispering their most confidential laments and most secret dreams – Chopin knew, we insist, that he had no effect upon the multitude and could not strike the masses.' See Franz Liszt, *Frédéric Chopin*, trans. Edward N. Waters (New York 1963), p. 83.

can I say more?). Chopin's compositions played by Chopin! That is a joy never to be surpassed. I shall describe his playing another time . . . During Chopin's playing I could think of nothing but elves and fairy dances, such a wonderful impression do his compositions make. There is nothing to remind one that it is a human being who produces this music. It seems to descend from heaven – so pure, and clear, and spiritual.[4]

The journalist and founder of *La France musicale*, Léon Escudier, lit upon a particularly felicitous version of the trope in his review of Chopin's Paris recital of February 1842:

A poet, and a tender poet above all, Chopin makes poetry predominate. He creates prodigious difficulties of performance, but never to the detriment of his melody, which is always simple and original. Follow the pianist's hands, and see the marvellous ease with which he performs the most graceful runs, draws together the width of the keyboard, passes successively from *piano* to *forte* and from *forte* to *piano* . . . Listening to all these sounds, all these nuances – which follow each other, intermingle, separate and reunite to arrive at the same goal, melody – one might well believe one is hearing small fairy voices sighing under silver bells, or a rain of pearls falling on crystal tables. (Cited in *CPT*, pp. 293–4.)

Chopin's Paris recital of February 1848 occasioned an especially elaborate Shakespearean version of the otherworldly trope in a review printed in the *Revue et Gazette musicale de Paris*:

A concert by the *Ariel* of pianists is something much too rare to be treated like any other concert where the doors are open to anyone who wants in . . .

That being the case, it was only natural that Pleyel's rooms should have been filled on Wednesday with a select flowering of the most distinguished aristocratic ladies in the most elegant finery. In addition there was also present another aristocracy, that of artists and music lovers, all overjoyed to catch the flight of this musical sylph . . .

The sylph has kept his promise and with what success, what enthusiasm! It is easier to recount the reception he received and the delirium he aroused than to describe, analyze, and reveal the mysteries of a performance that has no equal in our earthly realm. Even if we possessed that pen which traced the delightful marvels of Queen Mab (hardly bigger than the agate which gleams on the finger of an alderman) and her chariot drawn by her diaphanous steeds, it would still be impossible to give an accurate impression of such a talent – one so ideal it hardly seems to belong to the crass world of material things . . .[5]

---

4 Cited in *CPT*, p. 271. Hallé used similar language when he recounted this scene in his autobiography (ca 1894–5): 'The same evening I heard him play, and was fascinated beyond expression. It seemed to me as if I had got into another world . . . I sat entranced, filled with wonderment, and if the room had suddenly been peopled with fairies, I should not have been astonished' (*CPT*, p. 271).

The angelic trope was later echoed in Balzac's letter of 28 May 1843 to Madame Hanska. Comparing Liszt and Chopin, Balzac wrote: 'You should judge Listz [*sic*] only once you have had the opportunity to hear Chopin. The Hungarian is a demon; the Pole is an angel' (*CPT*, p. 285).

5 Cited and translated by William G. Atwood, *Fryderyk Chopin: Pianist from Warsaw* (New York 1987), p. 244. The Marquis de Custine invoked similar language when he wrote to Chopin asking for tickets to the recital: 'What, the sylph of the piano is to be heard, and I am informed about it by the public?' Letter of February 1848 in Frédéric Chopin, *Correspondance de Frédéric Chopin*, ed. Bronislas Edouard Sydow, 3 vols. (Paris 1953–60), vol. III, p. 321 (here and henceforth, translations are mine unless otherwise indicated). This letter is mistakenly dated to 'before 5 March 1838' in Fryderyk Chopin, *Korespondencja Fryderyka Chopina*, ed. B. E. Sydow, 2 vols. (Warsaw 1955), vol. I, p. 310.

This vision of Chopin as the Ariel of the piano resonated strongly amongst cultural observers of the time, and touched a particular nerve upon the composer's death in 1849. The trope figured centrally in the recollections of his playing that were recounted in several obituaries:

Perhaps never has any artist more than he had a physique which corresponded to his talent. As frail as he was in body, was he delicate in style: a bit more, he evaporated into the impalpable and imperceptible. His manner of playing the piano resembled no one's: it necessarily disappeared in a vast hall; within reach of a confidant, it was something delicious. One nicknamed Chopin the Ariel of the piano. If Queen Mab had ever wanted to pass herself off as a pianist, it is assuredly Chopin she would have chosen, and only the divine pen that described the fantastic retinue of the dream fairy could analyse the complicated, infinite and yet as-light-as-lace tangle of that phrase charged with notes, in the folds of which the composer always enveloped his ideas.[6]

He has been styled the *Ariel* of the piano; but he was also its *Prospero* – a mighty magician, inventing imagery, flowing like an impetuous torrent, whilst his hands were a tornado aggregating the subjects and investing them with piquant and picturesque colouring, alternately pathetic and gay, as his fancy dictated.[7]

Jules Janin explicitly linked the appellation to Chopin's status as an exile, and moreover went on to suggest that this 'Ariel' was comprehended most acutely by women:

Only those who heard him could conceive an idea of this talent so fine, so delicate, so varied, who addressed that which the human soul holds most honest and most charming. He avoided, as others sought to, noise, fanfare and even fame. One called him the Ariel of the piano, and the comparison was just. He grew up in exile, he died there, surrounded by exiles like him, for whom he called to mind the absent country . . .

Of all of the artists of our day, it is Chopin who most took possession of the soul and spirit of women. His students, and he produced students worthy of him, loved him with a quasi-maternal tenderness; they surrounded him with an enthusiasm mixed with veneration, his music so spoke to them an honest and chaste language. Alas! they have lost him, and they cry! They have watched him pass away, they have closed his eyes . . .[8]

Other instances of otherworldly metaphors provoked by Chopin's pianism include Ignaz Moscheles referring to Chopin's 'delicate fingers' gliding with 'elfin lightness' over the 'harsh modulations' in his music (cited in *CPT*, p. 272); Elizavieta Cheriemietieff calling forth angels and ethereal realms upon hearing Chopin play in private (*CPT*, p. 162, 278); and Bohdan Zaleski hearing angels' voices in an elaborate improvisation by Chopin (*CPT*, pp. 283–4).

6   *Revue et Gazette musicale de Paris*, 21 October 1849, p. 334.
7   *The Illustrated London News*, 27 October 1849, as reproduced in *Chopin na obczyźnie*, ed. Maria Mirska and Władysław Hordyński (Cracow 1965), p. 325.
8   *Journal des Débats*, 22 October 1849. The notion that Chopin's creations were most deeply felt by women was also sounded by Henri Blanchard in his article about Chopin's funeral:

This talent was especially understood, profoundly felt by women, not by those nice little human bird-organs [*serinettes*] who only aspire to make heard a brilliant fantasy in a salon in order to inspire those to marry them, and to say soon after, in speaking about music and the piano: 'Since my marriage, I have neglected all of that'; but by ladies, if not of high, then at least of good society, where one always recognised an aristocracy, that of talent. Mmes de Belgiojoso, de Peruzzi, etc. were the disciples, the admirers, the friends of the poor melancholic artist, of vaporous, fine, delicate inspiration. They loved to follow him when he lulled his intimate auditor with his capricious melodic arabesques over an unforeseen harmony, strange, but distinguished, classic, pure and nevertheless sickly, which seemed a swan song, a hymn of death.

The imagery evoked in Chopin's obituaries continued to colour recollections of the Pole's remarkable pianism long after his death. Antoine-François Marmontel's discussion of Chopin is thoroughly suffused with otherworldly metaphors, the evocation of which leads effortlessly to the afterworld:

Fabulous [*romanesque*] and impressionable to an excess, Chopin's imagination loved to haunt the world of spirits, to evoke pale phantoms, frightful chimeras. The poet-musician delighted in improvising in a penumbra where the indecisive glimmers added a more thrilling element to his dreamy thoughts, elegiac plaints, sighs of the breeze, sombre terrors of the night.

Death, often so prompt to crush stronger organisations, took twelve years to destroy, fibre by fibre, the frail nature of Chopin.[9]

Chopin's compositions doubtless played a role in all these recollections, since he typically was heard performing his own works. Other writers more explicitly deployed otherworldly metaphors to describe Chopin's compositions. This occurred occasionally during the composer's lifetime, as in the following comments by J. W. Davison from 1843:

In taking up one of the works of Chopin, you are entering, as it were, a fairy land, untrodden by human footsteps, a path, hitherto unfrequented, but by the great composer himself . . .[10]

The habit of invoking otherworldly metaphors in order to explain characteristics of Chopin's compositions grew more common after his death. Thus Franz Liszt, in his 1852 monograph on the composer, depicted by means of the supernatural trope the airy fragility of many of Chopin's works – a fragility which, in his view, also embodied qualities of frustration and aversion:

In most of Chopin's *Ballades*, *Valses*, and *Etudes*, as well as in the pieces just mentioned [i.e. the mazurkas, preludes, nocturnes and impromptus], there lies embalmed the memory of an elusive poesy, and this he sometimes idealizes to the point of presenting its essence so diaphanous and fragile that it seems no longer to be of our world. It brings closer the realm of fairies and unveils to us unguarded secrets of the Peri, of Titanias or Ariels or Queen Mabs, of all the genii of water, air, and fire, who are also the victims of the most bitter frustrations and the most intolerable aversions.

At times these pieces [i.e. the mazurkas] are joyous and fanciful, like the gambolings of an amorous, mischievous sylph . . .[11]

See 'Obsèques de Frédéric Chopin', *Revue et Gazette musicale de Paris*, 4 November 1849, p. 348.

Two other obituaries are worth brief mention. Théophile Gautier, writing in *La Presse*, 22 October 1849, p. 1, began his memorial with a unique image: 'the Novalis of the piano, Frédéric Chopin, is dead'; I suggest how Novalis might fit in with angels and fairies in the next section. And Auguste Luchet, in *La Réforme*, 5 November 1849, p. 2, used more familiar imagery: 'They celebrated the funeral of that angel of the piano who is called F. Chopin.'

9   *Les pianistes célèbres: silhouettes et médaillons*, 2nd edn (Tours 1887), p. 11.
10   'Essay on the Works of Frederic Chopin', *Musical World*, as cited in Liszt, *Frederic Chopin*, p. 170.
11   Liszt, *Frederic Chopin*, p. 77. Liszt was not the only critic to associate the ballades with the supernatural trope. James Huneker subtitled his chapter on the ballades 'Faëry Dramas'; most of the fairy imagery that he adduced derived from what he understood to be the poetic bases of the individual ballades, namely, various poems by Mickiewicz. See *Chopin: The Man and His Music* (New York 1900; repr. edn New York 1966), pp. 155–64.

The otherworldly imagery was also at times mediated through visions of another party playing Chopin's music. The Reverend H. R. Haweis, after first touting music's function as a restorative outlet in the life of women, next turned to the dreams that music might arouse in them. In the following passage, just as remarkable as the embodiment of the 'angel of music' in a 'weird *nocturno* of Chopin' is the sensuous mood evoked by Haweis's prose style:

That poor lonely little sorrower, hardly more than a child, who sits dreaming at her piano, while her fingers, caressing the deliciously cool ivory keys, glide through a weird *nocturno* of Chopin, is playing no mere study or set piece. Ah! what heavy burden seems lifted up, and borne away in the dusk? Her eyes are half closed – her heart is far away; she dreams a dream as the long, yellow light fades in the west, and the wet vine-leaves tremble outside to the nestling birds; the angel of music has come down; she has poured into his ear the tale which she will confide to no one else, and the 'restless, unsatisfied longing' has passed; for one sweet moment the cup of life seems full – she raises it to her trembling lips.[12]

In the rich imagery of Haweis's rumination, we begin to sense that the angelic trope resonates in ways other than the religious. When angels come to mind, devils often linger at the edges of consciousness as well. This sensuous, sexual side of the supernatural metaphor was drawn upon by Thomas Mann in *Doctor Faustus*. The narrator, Serenus Zeitblom, quotes a youthful letter by the protagonist of the novel, the composer Adrian Leverkühn. Leverkühn turns in his last paragraph to the subject of Chopin:

Playing much Chopin, and reading about him. I love the angelic in his figure, which reminds me of Shelley: the peculiarly and very mysteriously veiled, unapproachable, withdrawing, unadventurous flavour of his being, that not wanting to know, that rejection of material experience, the sublime incest of his fantastically delicate and seductive art.[13]

That Leverkühn should first sense the angelic in Chopin's persona, and only later in the 'sublime incest' of his music, draws attention to another stimulus for the supernatural trope. Chopin's distinctive character occasionally led the composer's associates to employ otherworldly imagery, as for example when Astolphe de Custine signed off a letter with 'Farewell, terrible year 1839! and you, inconstant Sylph, allow me a better one!'[14]

---

12 H. R. Haweis, *Music and Morals* (New York 1875), pp. 103–4.
13 Thomas Mann, *Doctor Faustus: The Life of the German Composer Adrian Leverkühn as Told by a Friend*, trans. H. T. Lowe-Porter (New York 1948), p. 143. Leverkühn's pronouncement engages otherworldly themes both outside and within the novel. Looking externally, Shelley was often styled as an otherworldly spirit by his contemporaries. Indeed, he himself assumed the mantle of Ariel, in his 'With a Guitar. To Jane'. (For an interesting treatment of this poem in the context of a discussion of 'transitivity' in both Shelley and Chopin, see Lawrence Kramer, *Music and Poetry: The Nineteenth Century and After* (Berkeley and Los Angeles 1984), pp. 119, 121–3.) Within *Doctor Faustus*, Mann would return to the theme of supernatural sprites in the figure of the child Echo, Leverkühn's one true love, whose name resounds in the 'Ariel's Songs' that he composes before the child dies.
14 Chopin, *Korespondencja*, vol. I, p. 455. Custine's use of 'Sylph' to describe Chopin may originally have derived from encounters with his playing and composing. Writing to Sophie Gay in June 1837 from his home in Saint-Gratien, Custine described the pleasures of hearing Chopin improvise: 'I am still just being enchanted by the magician, by the sylph of Saint-Gratien. I had given him for themes the *ranz des vaches* and the *Marseillaise*. To tell you the use he made of this musical epic is impossible. One saw the shepherd people flee before the conquering people. It was sublime.' See Marquis de Luppé's excellently documented biography, *Astolphe de Custine* (Monaco 1957), p. 190.

But George Sand returned almost obsessively to supernatural and especially angelic configurations of Chopin in the early stages of her relationship with the composer.[15] Sand frequently deployed the metaphors in ways which linked Chopin's physical being to his spiritual sensitivities. Thus Sand's marvellous letter to Wojciech Grzymała in which she debates the merits and repercussions of entering into a physically intimate relationship with Chopin – a superb document which sheds real light on the personalities of both Sand and Chopin – is dotted with references to 'this angel' and 'poor angel'.[16] Later, after the two lovers arrived for their stay in Majorca, she wrote to her friend Charlotte Marliani about the tenuous state of Chopin's health, and noted, 'I care for him like my child. He is an angel of sweetness and kindness!'[17] Writing again to Marliani on 26 April 1839 about the progress of Chopin's recuperation in Marseilles from the illness that struck him in Majorca, Sand invoked the trope in a particularly moving and prescient context:

This Chopin is an angel. His kindness, his tenderness and his patience disquiet me sometimes, I imagine that this organisation is too fine, too exquisite and too perfect to exist long in our vulgar and heavy earthly life. Being sick to death at Majorca, he made music which fully smelled of paradise. But I am so used to seeing him in the heavens that it does not seem to me that his

---

[15] Marie-Paule Rambeau draws frequent attention to the trope in the first two chapters of *Chopin dans la vie et l'œuvre de George Sand* (Paris 1985), pp. 35–135.

[16] Letter dated end of May 1838, in George Sand, *Correspondance*, ed. Georges Lubin, 25 vols. (Paris 1964–91), vol. IV, pp. 428–39; references to angels occur on pp. 436–8.

    This letter has simultaneously fascinated and disgusted many a commentator on Chopin. To note just one example, Edouard Ganche, in *Souffrances de Frédéric Chopin: Essai de médecine et de psychologie* (Paris 1935), felt compelled to reprint the entire letter even while terming it, variously, 'nauseating', 'odious' and 'abominable' (pp. 32–57; especially pp. 32, 54 and 57). Indeed, he was particularly repelled by the angelic trope:

    In this abominable letter and in her correspondence, George Sand shows the gist of her coarse nature. She designates Chopin by the most humiliating appellations: 'poor angel, the little one, this poor little being, our child, my little sufferer, my dear cadaver [*mon cher cadavre*], the old dodderer [*le père gâteux*] . . .' This is the ogress of a fairy tale who sees a sickly human creature, laughs at his sickliness which she will crush with her robustness, she knows, but which she envies. In this truthful story, Chopin was like a nightingale in the talons of an eagle. It happened, by a singular phenomenon, that the eagle became inoffensive and even protecting in listening to the song of the nightingale and in touching his weakness. Miracle of genius and of art. (pp. 57–8)

    Need one observe that this 'fairy tale' tells us much more about Ganche than about Sand or Chopin? Indeed, two of his 'humiliating appellations' resulted from his misunderstanding or misreading of the Sand correspondence. If Sand ever referred to Chopin as 'mon cher cadavre', it surely was a jest shared by the composer. Sand joked with her son Maurice in just this way, even using a pleasantry from the Berry dialect which Ganche might have misapprehended: 'ne joue pas trop avec ton *ch'tit* et sec *calabre*', where '*ch'tit*' and '*calabre*' mean 'bad' and 'living body or carcass' respectively (see letter of 11 November 1843 to Maurice Sand; *Correspondance*, vol. VI, pp. 274–5, and in particular Lubin's commentary on p. 275). Sand did at least once call Chopin a cadaver, but in an angry letter written to Emmanuel Arago in the midst of her rupture with the composer: 'il y a neuf ans que pleine de vie, je suis liée à un cadavre' (letter of 18–26 July 1847; *Correspondance*, vol. VIII, p. 48). This is hardly the same as calling him 'mon cher cadavre'. And Sand nowhere called Chopin 'le père gâteux'. What she actually wrote was 'le père Gatiau', a variant form of 'Père-Gâteau' (meaning, roughly, 'sugar daddy'), which refers to Chopin's generosity with gifts to the children (see letter of 6 June 1843 to Maurice Sand; *Correspondance*, vol. VI, p. 156, and especially Lubin's commentary).

[17] Letter of 14 December 1838; Sand, *Correspondance*, vol. IV, p. 531. Sand used almost the identical words in writing to Marliani from Barcelona on 15 February 1839: 'He is an angel of sweetness, of patience and of kindness. I care for him like my child and he loves me like his mother'; *Correspondance*, vol. IV, pp. 569–70.

life or his death bears witness to anything for him. He himself does not rightly know on what planet he exists. He does not take any account of life as we conceive it and as we feel it.[18]

Sand did not entirely abandon the sobriquet 'un ange' as the years passed, although it gradually gave way to her favourite affectionate diminutive, 'le petit'. When she did refer to Chopin as an angel later in their romance, the term often continued to resonate with concern and sympathy about his health, only now it was modified with an adjective: 'pauvre ange'.[19]

What most strikingly, if perhaps enigmatically, emerges from Sand's reflections on Chopin's character is the way themes of the angelic and the heavenly are juxtaposed with the pathological and the diseased. To begin to understand what was at stake in the conjoining of these concepts, we need to shift our attention away from a chronicle of the trope, and explore the diverse and changing cultural significance of it.

The literary otherworld and the ambiguity of sex

At about the same time that otherworldly metaphors began to attach themselves to Chopin, many of the same symbols enjoyed a vogue in literary, philosophical and artistic circles throughout Europe, and especially in France. The chronological overlap is not coincidental, and goes a long way towards explaining some of the particular implications that these terms took on for Chopin. For metaphorical representations of him as an angel, sylph, fairy and elf did not function solely as 'otherworldly' or 'supernatural' figures of speech. These terms also engaged a complex of unstable meanings having to do with sex and gender, and so ultimately helped forge a changing image of Chopin as an androgynous, hermaphroditic, effeminate and/or pathological being.

The wide cultural dissemination of otherworldly and androgynous figures having been thoroughly rehearsed in a number of studies, we may forgo a detailed tour of their particular manifestations.[20] It will suffice here simply to recall some of the more

---

[18] Sand, *Correspondance*, vol. IV, p. 646.

[19] See letters to Ferdinand François, 12 or 13 November 1843 (Sand, *Correspondance*, vol. VI, p. 915) and to Wojciech Grzymała, 18 November 1843 (*Correspondance*, vol. VI, p. 286). The sense of 'poor angel' in the letter to Grzymała of late May 1838, cited above, is different: it is Sand's outcry in response to Chopin's prudishness, and to her questions, 'What wretched woman has left him with such impressions of physical love? He has thus had a mistress unworthy of him? Poor angel'; *Correspondance*, vol. IV, pp. 437–8. Arthur Hedley's translation of this letter (*Selected Correspondence of Fryderyk Chopin*, trans. and ed. Arthur Hedley (New York 1963), p. 159) omits the second sentence quoted, as well as a number of other sentences and clauses from this fascinating letter.

   Sand also turned the angelic trope against the composer in a passage which she penned in the manuscript of her *Histoire de ma vie*, but cancelled before publishing. In this passage, Sand portrayed Chopin as incapable of being satisfied with anyone outside his dream world; even a succession of angels could not withstand his demands. See George Sand, *Histoire de ma vie*, in *Oeuvres autobiographiques*, ed. Georges Lubin, 2 vols. (Paris 1970–1), vol. II, p. 1303.

[20] Still the most useful place to begin surveying the topic is A. J. L. Busst, 'The Image of the Androgyne in the Nineteenth Century', in *Romantic Mythologies*, ed. Ian Fletcher (London 1967), pp. 1–95. Also worth consulting are Fritz Giese, *Der romantische Charakter I: Die Entwicklung des Androgynenproblems in der Frühromantik* (Langensalza 1919); Mario Praz, *Romantic Agony*, trans. Angus Davidson, 2nd edn (London 1951), pp. 289–411; Carolyn G. Heilbrun, *Toward a Recognition of Androgyny* (New York 1973); Sara Friedrichsmeyer, *The Androgyne in Early German Romanticism: Friedrich Schlegel, Novalis and the Metaphysics of Love* (Bern 1983); *L'androgyne dans la littérature*, ed. Frédéric Monneyron (Paris 1990); Diane Long Hoeveler, *Romantic Androgyny: The Women Within* (University Park, Pennsylvania 1990); Camille Paglia,

consequential invocations of the tropes in two different spheres of activity. The first of these was a body of work, mostly philosophical and religious but also encompassing visual art as well as a handful of fictional writings, which deployed the androgyne in order symbolically to represent higher ideals of unity and integration. Although one can trace this line of thought at least as far back as Plato's *Symposium*, the more relevant tradition dates from the late eighteenth century, its German branch including such figures as Franz von Baader, Friedrich Schlegel (particularly in the novel *Lucinde*) and Novalis, and its French branch encompassing Antoine Fabre d'Olivet, Pierre-Simon Ballanche, Prosper Enfantin, Pierre Leroux, Honoré de Balzac (*Séraphîta*), Paul Chenavard and Gustave Moreau. As A. J. L. Busst notes, this religious–philosophical sphere of thought generally conceived the androgyne in optimistic terms, indeed as symbolic of human brotherhood and solidarity and the original goodness and purity of mankind.[21] Certainly these religious–philosophical connotations carried over into the metaphorical configurations of Chopin, particularly in their overt function as a means of praise.

But also conditioning the formulation of metaphors around the composer was a variety of literary constructions of otherworldly and sexually ambiguous characters, many of whom have already been signalled in the quotations gathered above. While some of these figures preserved the general sense of optimism that attached to the religious–philosophical androgyne, others offered a more tempered vision of sexual ambiguity.

These fantastic characters came from diverse sources. The works of Shakespeare, enjoying a newly heightened presence on the early-nineteenth-century stage, placed a host of airy sprites before the imaginations of *literati* throughout Europe. Charles Nodier did not admit to direct Shakespearean influence in crafting the eponymous elf of his *Trilby*, but he did allow in his preface that the initial inspirations for the story came from an unnamed work by Sir Walter Scott (an author not far removed from Shakespeare, either topically or geographically, in the minds of many nineteenth-century French), and a poem by Henri de Latouche entitled 'Ariel exilé' (the Shakespearean connection here being explicit).[22] Latouche in turn, through his 1829 novel *Fragoletta*, served as a point of departure for a number of French fictional works dating from the 1830s which treat themes of otherworldly and sexual ambiguity, including Balzac's *Sarrasine*, *La Fille aux yeux d'or* and *Séraphîta*, Théophile Gautier's *Mademoiselle de Maupin*, and George Sand's *Gabriel*.[23]

Sexual Personae: Art and Decadence from Nefertiti to Emily Dickinson (New York 1991), 389–421; and Kari Weil, *Androgyny and the Denial of Difference* (Charlottesville, Virginia and London 1992). Jessica R. Feldman's *Gender on the Divide: The Dandy in Modernist Literature* (Ithaca and London 1993), pp. 1–96, explores issues related to androgyny in the first part of the nineteenth century. A concise survey of 'romantic androgyny' as it might have served Richard Wagner's philosophical and musical needs is found in Jean-Jacques Nattiez, *Wagner Androgyne: A Study in Interpretation*, trans. Stewart Spencer (Princeton 1993), pp. 111–27.

21   'The Image of the Androgyne', p. 38. See also Busst's general discussion of the 'optimistic image of the androgyne', pp. 12–39, as well as Nattiez's treatment in *Wagner Androgyne*, pp. 111–27.

22   Charles Nodier, *Trilby; La fée aux miettes* (Paris 1989), p. 45; H[enri] de Latouche, *Adieux: Poésies* (Paris 1844), pp. 345–53. *Adieux* collects a number of poems actually written much earlier than its publication date. In a footnote to 'Ariel exilé' (p. 345), Latouche acknowledges with thanks Nodier's citation of the role of his poem in the genesis of *Trilby*.

23   Paglia traces the chain of influences further back, arguing that Mignon of Goethe's *Wilhelm Meister* served as the prototype for the French Romantic androgyne. See *Sexual Personae*, p. 252.

The Archangel Gabriel

It is worth lingering over the last of these titles. Not only is *Gabriel* less well known than any other work I have cited (none of the studies I have referred to so much as mentions it), but Sand drafted this *roman dialogué* in April 1839 in Marseilles during Chopin's recovery from their harrowing sojourn in Majorca, and hence precisely during the period when she was most inclined to style the composer as an angel.[24]

Gabriel tells the story of a young member of the nobility whose 'true' female sex has been disguised from her since birth. (Following Sand, I will refer to the title character as 'him' when 'he' plays a masculine role, and 'her' when 'she' plays a feminine role.) This extraordinary state of affairs has been orchestrated by Gabriel's grandfather, a renaissance prince. In order to ensure that the family inheritance devolves to his granddaughter's branch rather than to his grandson's (violation of the inheritance laws, which exclusively favour the masculine line), he takes steps to raise the girl as a boy and, moreover, to train 'him' to despise the trappings of the feminine sex. When Gabrielle discovers her biological sex, the Prince gives her the option of remaining male and living a princely life, or assuming a female identity and joining a convent. But Gabriel(le) rejects the Prince, instead staking out his/her own existence by posing alternatively as a man and a woman.

In leading the reader through these transformations, *Gabriel* insightfully critiques received notions about gender. It claims that the supposedly 'natural' qualities that society felt distinguished men from women were instead fabrications which society inculcated in its members from the earliest age.[25] And more specifically, with its abundance of imagery relating to angels and sexual ambiguity, it clarifies the routes by which metaphorical stylisations of Chopin as an angel could take on sexual connotations.

Two of the more striking invocations of angels in *Gabriel* (whose name already intimates the subject of angels) occur in passages charged with ideas of sexual ambiguity. The first takes place in the third scene of the Prologue, where Gabriel's preceptor is attempting to prepare his pupil for the meeting with the Prince, his grandfather, where his 'true' sex will be revealed. The early part of the scene revolves around a tension in the respective attitudes towards gender evinced by teacher and student. The preceptor takes care sharply to delineate qualities he presumes appropriate for the different genders (he remains keen to continue instilling a distaste for the feminine in Gabriel), whereas Gabriel seems more ambivalent (at one point he admits, 'I do not feel that my soul has a sex, as you often endeavour to demonstrate to me'[26]). Before

---

24   The modern fortunes of *Gabriel* may be in for a change, for in recent years there have appeared both an excellent edition (Paris 1988) by Janis Glasgow of the original French version (Paris 1840) and an English translation of an 1867 printing of *Gabriel* – somewhat different from the original version – by Gay Manifold (Westport, Connecticut and London 1992). Manifold also includes an appendix which outlines alterations made by Sand when she revised the work into a play entitled *Julia* in the 1850s. I am grateful to Jean-Jacques Eigeldinger for bringing *Gabriel* to my attention.

25   See the speech of Gabriel's preceptor to the grandfather, which begins, 'since his earliest childhood . . . he has been imbued with the grandeur of the masculine role, and the abject condition of the feminine role in nature and in society'. *Gabriel*, pp. 52–3; Manifold trans., p. 7.

26   *Gabriel*, p. 57; Manifold trans., p. 10. In all of my citations from Manifold's translation, I have slightly modified the English translation to conform more precisely to the French original as published by Glasgow.

the preceptor can tell Gabriel about the impending visit from the Prince, Gabriel relates a 'bizarre' dream he had the previous night:

Gabriel
. . . in my dream I was not an inhabitant of this world. I had wings, and could fly high enough to traverse other worlds, towards I don't know what ideal place. Sublime voices sang all around me; I saw not a soul, but some light and fluffy clouds, which passed through the ether, reflecting my image, and I was a young girl dressed in a long flowing gown and crowned with flowers.

The Preceptor
Then you were an angel, and not a woman.

Gabriel
I was a woman; because all of a sudden my wings became numb, the ether closed in around my head, like the vault of an impenetrable crystal, and I was falling, falling . . . and I had around my neck a heavy chain, the weight pulling me towards the abyss; and then I woke myself, overcome with sadness, weariness and fear . . .[27]

Gabriel's dream functions dramatically to foreshadow the tragic fate that awaits him as a result of assuming a female identity. But it also reveals some of the sexual uncertainty and confusion that surrounded the category of 'angel' in 1839. Sand draws on it while a young man (who is 'really' a young woman) narrates a dream of transvestism (though again, in 'reality' he is cross-dressed as he speaks). And its meaning proves unstable even to the two characters: the preceptor understands the transvestite Gabriel to be an angel (and thus implies that angels are not women, but rather men in drag), which interpretation Gabriel summarily dismisses (without clarifying what he understands an angel to be).

Gabriel's dream recurs later in a situation even more charged with sexual ambiguity, the remarkable 'mirror' scenes of Act II.[28] The scenes take place in Florence during Carnival; Gabriel has been persuaded by his cousin Astolphe to costume himself in women's clothes for the festivities. Posing in front of a mirror after dressing himself, Gabriel 'lets out a cry of surprise' and becomes utterly absorbed by the image he sees. When Astolphe, who as yet has no notion of Gabriel's 'real' sex, enters, he too is transfixed by the vision of Gabriel in a white silk dress. Astolphe tells Gabriel, 'if I were to see you for the first time, I would have no doubt as to your sex . . . In fact, I would fall head over heels in love with you . . . You would immediately become my mistress and my wife.'[29] (Indeed, this is precisely what happens after Astolphe learns that Gabriel is 'really' Gabrielle.) After telling Gabriel that he 'plays his role like an angel', Astolphe goes on to question Gabriel about his costume:

Astolphe
But who placed on your brow this crown of white roses? Do you know that you resemble the marble angels in our cathedrals? Who gave you the idea for such a costume, so simple and so refined at the same time?

27 *Gabriel*, p. 60; Manifold trans., p. 12.
28 Act II, scenes 4–5. *Gabriel*, pp. 107–13; Manifold trans., pp. 50–4.
29 *Gabriel*, p. 109; Manifold trans., p. 51.

Gabriel
A dream that I had . . . some time ago.

Astolphe
Ah-hah! You dream of angels, do you? Well! don't wake up, because you will only find women in real life![30]

The angel looms as a particularly vertiginous figure as we strain to grasp the dynamics of sex and gender in these scenes. In both instances, the men who interpret Gabriel's dream read into it a kind of transcendental transvestism: Gabriel garbed in a silky white dress represents an angel.[31] For Gabriel reporting his dream in the Prologue, the angel would seem to denote an apparently unattainable ideal female identity. But in Act II, it signifies in a different way. Gabriel is brought to a kind of crisis of identity precisely at the moment when his male gaze fixes upon her female image in the mirror: the moment seems to wrench him/her free of the moorings of gender, such that he/she can only cry out in surprise – surely the literary envoicing of Michel Poizat's sexually nondifferentiated, operatic 'angel's cry'.[32] And if the depth of Astolphe's reaction to the mirror-bound Gabriel indicates that he has already intimated the 'real' sex of the person in the dress, does the angel then somehow become doubly cross-dressed – a woman passing as a man passing as a woman?[33]

The play of interpretations can continue *ad infinitum*, which is precisely the point. Sand plainly meant the image of the angel in these scenes to act as a decentring device: it accentuates the wobbly basis of the edifice of gender, the critique of which serves as the principal message of the *roman dialogué*. As such, the angelic trope in *Gabriel* plumbs further reaches of sexual ambiguity than other literary angels from the period.[34] Sand's Gabriel(le) instead seems to anticipate in literary form aspects of Judith Butler's recent challenge to the foundational status of the categories of sex and

[30]   *Gabriel*, pp. 112–13; Manifold trans., p. 53.
[31]   Later, after Astolphe has discovered Gabrielle's 'true' sex and married her, his interpretation of her angelic form is further clarified. In a dialogue from Act III, scene 5 (in an earlier segment of which Gabrielle says, 'Look, Astolphe, you made me become a woman again, but I have not yet altogether given up being a man'), Astolphe tells Gabrielle, 'I know women, and you do not know them, you who are not half man and half woman as you think, but an angel in human form' (*Gabriel*, pp. 150–1; Manifold trans., pp. 78–9). Manifold's text differs in many significant respects from that printed in the original French version). If Gabrielle is in Astolphe's mind a kind of angel, then he does not view angels as androgynous or hermaphroditic beings ('half man and half woman'). Rather, harking back to his earlier invocation of the trope, to be an angel would appear to involve some kind of cross-dressing.
[32]   Michel Poizat, *The Angel's Cry: Beyond the Pleasure Principle in Opera*, trans. Arthur Denner (Ithaca and London 1992).
[33]   For an interesting discussion of themes of cross-dressing and mirror-gazing in a musical work, see Lawrence Kramer, '*Carnaval*, Cross-Dressing, and the Woman in the Mirror', in *Musicology and Difference: Gender and Sexuality in Music Scholarship*, ed. Ruth A. Solie (Berkeley, Los Angeles and London 1993), pp. 305–25. For all of the acuity of its cultural analysis, however, this article remains wedded to the very techniques of formalist analysis that it criticises in the hands of other interpreters of *Carnaval*.
[34]   Compare, for example, the angelic imagery in Balzac's *Séraphîta*. Séraphîtüs-Séraphîta, an androgynous angel derived from the mystic doctrines of Swedenborg, does not so much represent sexual ambiguity as sexual alternation (the character appears as male to Minna and female to Wilfrid) and synthesis (achieved through the loving union of Minna and Wilfrid). For a good discussion of angelic androgyny in Balzac, see Busst, 'The Image of the Androgyne', pp. 78–85.

gender.[35] In Butler's bracing thesis, sex and gender are both performative effects which enact the identities they claim to be. Summarising her arguments about gender in particular, Butler writes: 'gender ought not to be construed as a stable identity or locus of agency from which various acts follow; rather, gender is an identity tenuously constituted in time, instituted in an exterior space through a *stylized repetition of acts*'.[36] One might comprehend the 'mirror' scene as a performance of Butler's performative theory: it so thoroughly demonstrates the contingency of the notion of being 'in drag' as severely to undercut any fixed meaning that this term might have. *Gabriel*, much like *Mademoiselle de Maupin* before it, attacks the basis of commonly held distinctions between male and female by enacting the impossibility of locating any fixed essence in these categories.[37]

And the celebrated figure of the author herself must also have reinforced her challenge to sexual essence. As most readers surely grasped, Sand embodied some of the traits she ascribed to Gabriel(le). This reflexivity appears most obviously in connection with Sand's famous (and over-emphasised) penchant for bedecking herself in male haberdashery. But rather more interesting is the case made recently by Leyla Ezdinli for Sand's literary transvestism.[38] Ezdinli argues that Sand was much the exceptional female writer of her period, not by virtue of her male pseudonym (these were common coin among women writers), but instead because of the public perception of her double gender identity. Among the authorial signatures adopted by women, only 'George Sand' was recognised as female but categorised as male, in the sense that Sand possessed the social resources and cultural power of a man. And Sand regularly exploited the rhetoric of her double gender identity in her prefaces, constructing an elusive sense of her authorial persona. 'George Sand' itself stood as a fictive category: it was a construct whose very name and whose very societal function worked to undo the fetters of traditional distinctions of gender. Thus *Gabriel* and 'George Sand' reflexively frame one another, each buttressing the political and social message of the other.

Supernatural sprites

And how did Chopin's becoming attached metaphorically to various elves, fairies and airy sprites also bring with it implications of sexual ambiguity? At first glance the matter might seem more complex than for angels, since most literary elves, fairies and

---

[35]   *Gender Trouble: Feminism and the Subversion of Identity* (New York and London 1990).

[36]   *Gender Trouble*, p. 140. The italics are Butler's.

[37]   Gautier and Sand differed in the goals of their explorations of the indeterminacy of gender. Gautier's interests lay more in the realm of aesthetics (as is clear from the famous preface to *Mademoiselle de Maupin*): the contingent identities in the novel are bound up with ideas of an aesthetics of impersonality, of 'l'art pour l'art'. Sand's target was contemporary political and social life: in order to challenge the accepted status of women in society, she focused on the artifice that upheld the gender system.
        My understanding of *Mademoiselle de Maupin* is much indebted to Feldman's reading of it in *Gender on the Divide*, pp. 25–53.

[38]   'George Sand's Literary Transvestism: Pre-Texts and Contexts' (Dissertation, Princeton University 1988), especially pp. 199–235. See also Isabelle Hoog Naginski, *George Sand: Writing for Her Life* (New Brunswick and London 1991), pp. 16–34, for a discussion of the topos of androgyny in Sand's life and work, and Kristina Wingård Vareille, *Socialité, sexualité et les impasses de l'histoire: l'évolution de la thématique sandienne d'Indiana (1832) à Mauprat (1837)* (Uppsala 1987), which examines androgyny in a number of Sand's works from the period before *Gabriel*.

sprites have determinate sexual identities (Ariel and Trilby are males, Queen Mab and Titania females).[39] But the issue is not so much the sexual identities of the airy sprites themselves as how a metaphorical affiliation with them might be wielded in interpreting the sexual tendencies of a human being.

Briefly put, although the interactions of literary fairies and elves with other fairies, elves or even humans of the opposite sex (one of the first things we learn about Trilby is that he is in love with the brunette Jeannie) scarcely differ from those of literary humans, their small stature and high voices – their 'small fairy voices' – lead us to think of them as being akin not to adults, but rather to children.[40] Now if on the one hand children apparently inhabit a realm of innocence with respect to sex, it is also the case, as Michel Foucault has observed, that from the later eighteenth century onwards, childhood came to be increasingly sexualised.[41] Thus children occupied a vexed position with respect to reigning ideas about sex: they were thought at once to be pure of it (and hence to a degree asexual) and utterly possessed by it (and thus the object of fierce campaigns against masturbation and other forms of precocious sexual activity). Labelling an adult male a fairy or an elf in the 1830s and 1840s was to invoke, besides the obvious qualities of lightness, charm and magic, notions of a being at once removed from sex and possessed by a longing for it.[42] (It may well be through this dual construction that the English word 'fairy' came, towards the last decade of the nineteenth century, to stand for a male homosexual, and in particular a male homosexual prostitute – a figure who, although he stood outside the sexual matrix of the majority of society and was thus in a way inexplicable in its terms, was also clearly given over to a sexual way of life.[43]) To some degree, then, ambiguity for fairies and elves differs from that associated with angels: angels undermine an assured determination of sexual identity, whereas fairies and elves weaken a secure sense of the presence or absence of sexual appetite. Yet as with every other term under consideration here, these two forms of ambiguity cannot really be so neatly separated.[44] We will see that, as they cluster around Chopin, their distinctions readily blur.

[39] Recall, however, that we have seen one instance of straightforward cross-gendering in connection with fairies, by the writer of the obituary of Chopin published in the *Revue et Gazette musicale de Paris*. This critic rejected the nickname 'Ariel of the piano' for the deceased, and substituted in its place that of a female fairy, Queen Mab. Moreover, the determinate sexual identities of these sprites were not always treated determinately in the world of opera. Both Johann Friedrich Reichardt and Johann Rudolf Zumsteeg, in their 1798 settings of Friedrich Wilhelm Gotter's operatic libretto, *Der Geisterinsel* (based on *The Tempest*), followed Gotter's instructions and assigned the part of Ariel to a woman.

[40] I am indebted for this idea to Michel Poizat, who, in seeking to understand why the angel's voice is so often (and so mistakenly, in his opinion) thought to be only high, formulates a hypothesis around a perceived relationship between children and angels (even though Poizat ultimately rejects its application to the angel's voice). See *The Angel's Cry*, pp. 128–31.

[41] Michel Foucault, *The History of Sexuality, Volume I: An Introduction*, trans. Robert Hurley (New York 1978), pp. 104, 153.

[42] Busst notes that one of the principal 'vices' associated with the pessimistic symbol of the androgyne is what he calls 'cerebral lechery', a yearning which finds no object and no fulfilment in reality. Cerebral lechery may most often be detected in situations of total sexual abstinence. Busst offers an insightful reading of *Mademoiselle de Maupin* from this point of view: see 'The Image of the Androgyne', pp. 42–4.

[43] For a remarkable testimony of the 'fairy' as homosexual prostitute, see Earl Lind, *Autobiography of an Androgyne* (New York 1918; repr. edn New York 1975), passim.

[44] Indeed, Balzac brought the two terms together when he described how the finale of Beethoven's Fifth

Between androgyny and hermaphroditism

As we attempt to understand the perpetually shifting terrain of signification around Chopin and otherworldly images, we should examine one more curious bit of documentation from the composer's personal circle. This comes in a letter written in 1842 by the thirteen-year-old Solange Dudevant-Sand. Solange was responding to a missive from her mother, George Sand, who had reported news from their summer home in Nohant. In Solange's reply, after asking for correspondence from her brother, she added the odd request, 'also tell Sexless to write to me [*dis aussi à Sans-sexe de m'écrire*]' – 'Sans-sexe' seeming to refer jokingly to Chopin.[45] Apparently self-evident in intent, Solange's comment actually can be read in at least two ways. Most patently, her remark draws on idealised imagery in order to set up Chopin as an asexual being, an androgynous object for adolescent teasing. But 'Sans-sexe' invokes the category of sex even as it denies its presence: there do seem to be indications from a few years later that she entertained obsessively sexual feelings for the composer.[46] Since Solange's elliptical remark resists resolution to one interpretation or the other, 'Sans-sexe' would seem then to waver between two different characterisations of the composer's sexual ambiguity, the one veering towards asexual and ideal realms, the other bound to the earthily experiential and (given Solange's age and status as George Sand's daughter) the morally divisive. In its unresolvable semantic slippage, 'Sans-sexe' thus replicates the disorder that marks the relationship between the two key terms in nineteenth-century perceptions of sexual ambiguity, androgyny and hermaphroditism.

'Androgyne' and 'hermaphrodite' are typically understood to be synonyms.[47] But, as Kari Weil has persuasively contended, the terms have different histories and meanings with respect to the status of the body.[48] The conjoined female and male elements of the androgyne, according to Plato in the *Symposium*, stand for one of the harmoniously whole original states of human beings. The dual nature of the hermaphrodite, as told by Ovid in the *Metamorphoses*, represents the fall from grace of man. Having

Symphony allowed one to 'perceive beauties of an unknown kind, fairies of fantasy, these are the creatures who flutter with womanly beauty and the diaphanous wings of angels'. See letter of 7–14 November 1837, in Balzac, *Lettres à Madame Hanska*, ed. Roger Pierrot, 2 vols. (Paris 1990), vol. I, p. 419. The adjective 'womanly' can apply equally to men or women, and thus leaves open the sex of the fairies with angelic wings.

45 Letter of 20 July 1842; Sand, *Correspondance*, vol. V, p. 375 n. 1. Georges Lubin, the eminent editor of the *Correspondance*, also feels that 'Sans-sexe' designates Chopin.
    A line from Chopin's letter to Julian Fontana of 7 March 1839, written during his recovery in Marseilles, may be relevant to Solange's remark: 'I drink neither coffee nor wine – only milk; I keep myself warm and look like a young lady'. Chopin, *Korespondencja*, vol. I, p. 337.

46 For evidence to this effect, see Sand's letter of 18–26 July 1847 to Emmanuel Arago; Arago's reply; and a document from 1845 in Solange's hand with Chopin's name and initials repeated many times (suggesting, in Lubin's words, 'a certain obsession' on Solange's part), all in Sand, *Correspondance*, vol. VIII, pp. 46–50. For a perspicacious discussion of this evidence, see Rambeau, *Chopin dans la vie et l'œuvre de George Sand*, pp. 104–7. Gastone Belotti denied strenuously that Solange did anything more than flirt with Chopin, but he fails to discuss any of the materials presented in volume VIII of the Sand *Correspondance*; see *F. Chopin l'uomo*, 3 vols. (Milan and Rome 1974), vol. III, pp. 1183–5.

47 Busst begins his otherwise excellent article by stoutly proclaiming the distinctions between the two terms to be 'purely arbitrary' ('The Image of the Androgyne', p. 1).

48 *Androgyny and the Denial of Difference*, especially pp. 9–11.

different histories, however, does not mean that the ideas existed independently from one another. Rather, the two notions come to infect one another, the one present relationally to the other, whether this relation is spoken or silent. Already in Plato, at the very first invocation of the term 'androgynous' in Aristophanes' speech, after saying that once the word 'really meant something', Aristophanes admits that now it is 'only used as an insult'.[49] What once delineated an ideal balance and symmetry now derisively and divisively configures a physical body – that of a man interested in same-sex love. This ironical coupling of the androgyne and the hermaphrodite, intertwining an ideal sexual past with an original chaos of the sexes, haunts several of the central romantic portrayals of sexual ambiguity, as Weil demonstrates through readings of *Lucinde*, *Séraphîta* and *Mademoiselle de Maupin*.

Weil's analysis suggests that the metaphors linking Chopin to an idyllic androgyny ordinarily deflect silently towards fragmentary hermaphroditism as well. Occasionally, the traces of this refraction surface so that a plurality of sexual connotations loosely gathered around the androgyne/hermaphrodite becomes more explicit. Recall, for example, Liszt's evocation of the gauzy frailty of the essence of Chopin's art, an 'elusive poesy' which 'brings closer the realm of fairies . . . who are also the victims of the most bitter frustrations and the most intolerable aversions'. In this formulation, Chopin's music evokes a realm of airy sprites at once magical and quarrelsomely strained and factional. A mystically ideal existence also summons forth an earthy fractiousness.

More commonly, though, the disorderly hermaphrodite remains an absent presence within the androgynous metaphors.[50] Hence the overtly innocuous import of Astolphe de Custine's 'inconstant Sylph' was gently to implore more social contact with his distant friend, whose ethereal art and personality he enfolded under the rubric 'Sylph'. But Custine's imagery imparts another meaning, somewhat analogous to the dual sense of Solange's 'Sans-sexe': echoes of bodily frustration ring in his words. As a result of being the focus of one of the more infamous sexual scandals of the early nineteenth century, Custine himself occupied an ambiguous sexual space in the eyes of French society. In 1824 he suffered intense, public opprobrium (as well as a severe beating, which brought the matter to public attention) for apparently having made sexual advances to a young soldier.[51] Without making any suppositions about Custine's intent or Chopin's response (and, indeed, recognising the impossibility of discovering any essential position for either subject), 'inconstant' and 'Sylph' inevitably bear the trace of Custine's sexual history.

Between hermaphroditism and sodomy

Custine's brief remark draws attention to another significant deflection in the meanings associated with otherworldly metaphors. 'Hermaphrodites' were not just mythological

---

49 Plato, *Symposium,* trans. Alexander Nehamas and Paul Woodruff (Indianapolis and Cambridge 1989), p. 25.
50 For the notion of 'absent presence', I am indebted to Weil, *Androgyny and the Denial of Difference*, p. 11.
51 The 'affaire Custine' is amply documented in Luppé, *Custine*, pp. 96–101. See also Julien-Frédéric Tarn's monumental study, *Le Marquis de Custine* (Paris 1985), pp. 68–70.

representations of notions of an earthy disorder: they also existed in the 'real' world of Chopin's time. Indeed they came under intense scrutiny in various medical and medico-legal texts which explored the phenomenon of hermaphroditism in what were understood to be its various physical and psychical manifestations. And in this medico-legal discourse, one of the figures to embody these psychical symptoms was the sodomite or pederast.[52]

By describing this figure as the sodomite or pederast rather than the homosexual, I mean to suggest that the culture that gave rise to the otherworldly metaphors around Chopin differed from ours with respect to the ways in which it configured the relationship between sexual practice and identity.[53] In our modern view – which we may trace linguistically and conceptually back to the later nineteenth century – the categories of 'homosexuality', 'heterosexuality' and, indeed, 'sexuality' itself all ultimately read the genital proclivities of individuals as significant, if at times mysterious, determinants of their character, judgement, personality, taste and so forth.[54]

[52]   The two terms were often used synonymously in the early nineteenth century to refer to men who engaged in sexual relations with other men, though of course the latter term was at times reserved to describe men who pursued sexual relations with boys. On 'sodomite' and 'pederast' as synonyms, see Claude Courouve, *Vocabulaire de l'homosexualité masculine* (Paris 1985), pp. 169–78 and 191–8.
    I do not however mean to assert a stable identity for these terms. 'Sodomy' ('that utterly confused category', as Foucault termed it (*History of Sexuality*, p. 101)) encompasses in its multiple configurations a variety of sexual activity between members of the same sex, between males and females, and between humans and animals.

[53]   Much recent scholarship has addressed this issue. Most influential to my argument have been Foucault, *History of Sexuality*; Arnold I. Davidson, 'Sex and the Emergence of Sexuality', *Critical Inquiry*, 14 (1987), pp. 16–48; Ed Cohen, 'Legislating the Norm: From Sodomy to Gross Indecency', *South Atlantic Quarterly*, 88 (1989), pp. 182–217; Robert A. Nye, 'Sex Difference and Male Homosexuality in French Medical Discourse, 1830–1930', *Bulletin of the History of Medicine*, 63 (1989), pp. 32–51; David M. Halperin, 'One Hundred Years of Homosexuality', in his *One Hundred Years of Homosexuality and Other Essays on Greek Love* (New York and London 1990), pp. 15–40 and 154–68; and Klaus Müller, *Aber in meinem Herzen sprach eine Stimme so laut: Homosexuelle Autobiographien und medizinische Pathographien im neunzehnten Jahrhundert* (Berlin 1991). I have found the Halperin essay, which also appeared in an earlier version as 'Is There a History of Sexuality?', *History and Theory*, 28 (1989), pp. 257–74, particularly cogent and helpful.
    A number of writers firmly oppose the position I have espoused here, arguing strongly for something like a transhistorical concept of sexual identities. A collection of these writings may be found in *Forms of Desire: Sexual Orientation and the Social Constructionist Controversy*, ed. Edward Stein (New York 1990; repr. edn New York and London 1992).
    For an excellent survey of recent scholarship on sexuality, see Domna C. Stanton, 'Introduction: The Subject of Sexuality', in *Discourses of Sexuality: From Aristotle to AIDS*, ed. Domna C. Stanton (Ann Arbor 1992), pp. 1–46.

[54]   The *Oxford English Dictionary* cites early-nineteenth-century usages of 'sexuality'. But these construe the word as indicating 'the quality of being sexual or having sex' in the biological sense. As such, it was typically applied to plants or insects; it did not yet refer to a manner of constituting human identity.
    Not everyone would agree with my assertion that our modern conceptions of 'homosexuality' and 'sexuality' date from the later nineteenth century. The issue, particularly as it concerns homosexuality, has been debated intensely and complexly by historians of sexuality. Here I can only signal some of the more significant interventions. Foucault boldly announced that modern homosexuality began in 1870 (*History of Sexuality*, p. 43), a date – when generalised into something like the 'second half of the nineteenth century' – which is also accepted by Davidson ('Sex and the Emergence of Sexuality') and Jeffrey Weeks ('Discourse, Desire and Sexual Deviance: Some Problems in a History of Homosexuality', in his *Against Nature: Essays on History, Sexuality and Identity* (London 1991), pp. 10–45).
    Others, most prominently among them Randolph Trumbach, have argued that the modern homosexual role may be dated to the beginning of the eighteenth century. Among his many articles, see

The emergence of this modern view marked a significant and complex shift in ways of conceiving of human individuals. Foucault famously described the nature of this shift:

As defined by the ancient civil or canonical codes, sodomy was a category of forbidden acts; their perpetrator was nothing more than the juridical subject of them. The nineteenth-century homosexual became a personage, a past, a case history, and a childhood, in addition to being a type of life, a life form, and a morphology, with an indiscreet anatomy and possibly a mysterious physiology. Nothing that went into his total composition was unaffected by his sexuality . . . Homosexuality appeared as one of the forms of sexuality when it was transposed from the practice of sodomy onto a kind of interior androgyny, a hermaphrodism of the soul. The sodomite had been a temporary aberration; the homosexual was now a species.[55]

Before this shift, then, for someone of the dominant culture to label a man a sodomite or pederast was not to stake a claim about his fundamental mode of being. Rather, it was to identify (again, from the perspective of the dominant culture) and ultimately control a pathological symptom of criminal and amoral behaviour.[56]

The wish to subject hermaphrodites to juridical control animated Isidore Geoffroy Saint-Hilaire's influential text *Histoire générale et particulière des anomalies de l'organisation* (1832–7).[57] Geoffroy Saint-Hilaire erected an elaborate forensic apparatus to enable physicians properly to diagnose the many kinds of hermaphroditism that they might encounter (thus he divided hermaphrodites into two classes, 'without excess in the number of parts' and 'with excess in the number of parts', which he then subdivided into four and three different orders respectively). The point of these diagnoses was less

'Sodomitical Subcultures, Sodomitical Roles, and the Gender Revolution of the Eighteenth Century: The Recent Historiography', in *'Tis Nature's Fault: Unauthorized Sexuality during the Enlightenment*, ed. Robert Purks Maccubbin (Cambridge 1985), pp. 109–21; and 'London's Sapphists: From Three Sexes to Four Genders in the Making of Modern Culture', in *Body Guards: The Cultural Politics of Gender Ambiguity*, ed. Julia Epstein and Kristina Straub (New York and London 1991), pp. 112–41. But as Eve Kosofsky Sedgwick properly notes, all of these arguments blithely assume that there is such a thing as a modern homosexual role which 'we' are able to divine (they do so even as they articulate different versions of what they understand this role to be). Such an assumption not only wrongly distils an oversimplified unity from a plurality of sexual roles, but also incorrectly and dangerously presumes that 'we' may reach a consensus about the 'genuinely *unknown*' (Sedgwick's italics). See *Epistemology of the Closet* (Berkeley and Los Angeles 1990), pp. 44–8. To which I would add only that the same cautionary note needs to be sounded to those who would assert a singular, knowable 'homosexual' or 'sodomitical' role for any given culture of the past.

55 *History of Sexuality*, p. 43. See also Davidson's discussion of the rise of the 'psychiatric style of reasoning' that begins around the mid nineteenth century; 'Sex and the Emergence of Sexuality', pp. 20–2.

56 This negative construction was obviously not the only one available. Klaus Müller, drawing on a corpus of autobiographical testimony, has begun the project of reconstructing the self-images of nineteenth-century male proponents of same-sex love; see *Aber in meinem Herzen*, pp. 155–265. And Randolph Trumbach, in the studies cited above, has recovered some of the perspectives of sodomitical subcultures in eighteenth-century England.

57 The full title is *Histoire générale et particulière des anomalies de l'organisation chez l'homme et les animaux, ouvrage comprenant des recherches sur les caractères, la classification, l'influence physiologique et pathologique, les rapports généraux, les lois et les causes des monstruosités, des variétés et vices de conformation, ou Traité de Tératologie*, 3 vols. and atlas (Paris 1832–7).
    For a good discussion of Geoffroy Saint-Hilaire in view of the cultural reception of sexual ambiguity, see Julia Epstein, 'Either/Or – Neither/Both: Sexual Ambiguity and the Ideology of Gender', *Genders*, 7 (1990), pp. 99–142, and especially pp. 113–16.

for the physician to offer therapeutic care than to ordain the 'true' sex of the hermaphrodite for the sake of determining 'his' or 'her' civil status with respect to ownership or inheritance of property.[58] The mechanics of teratology (as the study of malformations and monstrosities is termed) thus served the same legal system that generated the ambiguities of Gabriel's sexual nature in Sand's *roman dialogué*. Gabriel's ambiguous status represented the kind of subterfuge against civic laws that Geoffroy Saint-Hilaire's teratological technology aimed to suppress.

Geoffroy Saint-Hilaire largely maintained a coolly objective tone throughout his scientific description and analysis. Only twice in the chapters on hermaphroditism did he give vent to moral outrage, and precisely when he considered the possibility that the abnormal construction of his subjects might lead to sodomitic practices. Under discussion is the second kind of feminine hermaphroditism, wherein the 'clitoris is of considerable volume, and simulates a man's penis'. According to Geoffroy Saint-Hilaire, this species of hermaphrodite was prone to a mode of behaviour whose name he could not bring himself to utter:

one knows only too well the compensation against nature that these women have sometimes sought in infamous pleasures. I will not soil this page by the picture of this depravation of morals, common enough in antiquity to have motivated the creation of a special word, by which some contemporaries have even wanted to soil our language. But I felt it necessary at least to recall here the facts which, attested by all the historians, are the unfortunately too authentic proof of the influence exercised by hermaphroditism on the propensities [*penchans*] as well as on the physical organisation.[59]

Geoffroy Saint-Hilaire here drew on a well-established specific tradition of labelling women who had sex with other women as hermaphrodites, as well as on a more general habit of referring to male sodomites by this term.[60] The difference in these traditions was that the women were often understood to be physical hermaphrodites, while the men were generally constructed as metaphorical hermaphrodites.

That any of these sodomitic or pederastic meanings would emerge overtly in the metaphorical stylisations of Chopin is unlikely, given the manifest wish of most writers who deployed these metaphors to praise Chopin.[61] At most we sense a hint of the possibility of such meanings in such formulations as Haweis's 'weird *nocturno*'.

---

58   Epstein, 'Either/Or', p. 119.
59   *Histoire générale et particulière des anomalies*, vol. II, p. 96. The second, briefer commentary on the potentially deleterious effects that this form of hermaphroditism might have on the morals is found on p. 101.
60   Trumbach, 'London's Sapphists', pp. 115–21, offers a number of examples of these usages from the seventeenth and eighteenth centuries. The latter kind of formulation remained common through the nineteenth century, as suggested by Auguste-Ambroise Tardieu in *Etude médico-légal sur les attentats aux mœurs*, 4th edn. (Paris 1862), p. 159: 'Casper [Johann Ludwig Casper, author of important treatises on juridical medicine] also noted this particular taste for licentious images; one of the pederasts whose history we knew had accumulated copies of all the models of hermaphrodites in their seductive pose, and of numerous portraits of young boys.'
61   Only someone with the notoriously coarse sensibilities of the infamous Otto Weininger would state the matter baldly. After describing George Sand as 'part bisexual, part exclusively homosexual', Weininger later observed: 'The most famous of the many "relationships" of George Sand were with Musset, the most effeminate lyric poet known to history, and with Chopin, whom one could even designate the only effeminate musician – so womanly is he.' Weininger added in a footnote: 'His portrait also shows this clearly.' See *Geschlecht und Charakter*, 8th edn (Vienna and Leipzig 1906), p. 82.

(Although momentarily taken aback by this adjective – how can a gently lyrical work be heard as 'weird'? – we might recall the long history of characterising the nocturne as 'effeminate'.[62]) Other allusions are barely audible, in suggestions of the composer's affinity with women (which could carry a presumption of effeminacy), and in phrases like Custine's 'inconstant Sylph', or Mann's 'the sublime incest of his fantastically delicate and seductive art'. And one more way, perhaps: in the repeated coupling of the otherworldly metaphors with ideas of sickness and disease.

Conclusion: between sodomy and pathology

The issue of sickness and disease moves us back from otherworldly meanings and confronts us directly with Chopin's physical body. For (in the minds of the dominant culture) to be affiliated with notions of hermaphroditism was also to be conjoined to ideas of pathology, particularly in the nineteenth-century sense whereby the 'pathological' and the 'normal' were understood to exist on a continuum, with the former distinguished from the latter only by quantitative variations.[63] Hermaphrodites differed in numerical ways from 'normal' humans (recall Geoffroy Saint-Hilaire's initial categorical division); their anomalies helped determine (through an often complex chain of reasoning) their pathological status.[64]

Viewed in the terms put forward in nineteenth-century treatises on pathology and juristic medicine, Chopin's very body could have reinforced a sodomitical interpretation of the metaphors of hermaphroditism that gathered around him. According to the forensic mode of reasoning that was then in place, if the sodomite/pederast was understood as a pathological figure, then physical symptoms of this pathology should be detectable to the practised eye: the body should 'tell' of its pathological defects.[65] As with all of the signs that we have been considering, instability reigned: the same symptom could tell of a number of different pathologies, depending upon what kind of explanatory narrative it was embedded within. Hence Chopin's weakness, pallor and slight build, explicable as resulting from pulmonary or cardiac causes, could also have been read as a sign of sodomitical inclinations. So, too, his smooth skin and lightly developed musculature, when understood as indications of 'effeminacy', were

Of course, references to sodomy need not have been construed only in negative terms; it would not be surprising to learn of a 'reverse discourse' amongst the sodomitical subcultures of the 1830s and 1840s which put the negative terminology of the dominant culture to affirmative use.

[62] Thus Ferdinand Hand claimed in 1841 that 'the representation of sentiment in the notturno runs the danger of falling into the effeminate and languishing, which displeases stronger souls'. Frederick Niecks, some half a century later, made a similar point: 'these dulcet, effeminate compositions illustrate only one side of the master's character, and by no means the best or most interesting'. For discussion and full bibliographical details, see my 'The Harmony of the Tea Table: Gender and Ideology in the Piano Nocturne', *Representations*, no. 39 (Summer 1992), pp. 105 and 111.

[63] See Georges Canguilhem, *The Normal and the Pathological*, trans. Carolyn R. Fawcett (Dordrecht and Boston 1978; repr. edn New York 1991), pp. 39–112. (The original French version dates from 1966.) Canguilhem notes that 'semantically, the pathological is designated as departing from the normal not so much by *a-* or *dys-* as by *hyper-* and *hypo-*' (p. 42). There is a good summary and discussion of Canguilhem's thesis in Müller, *Aber in meinem Herzen*, pp. 40–6.

[64] On the complex relationship between the concepts of 'anomaly' and 'pathological', with specific respect to Geoffroy Saint-Hilaire, see Canguilhem, *Normal and Pathological*, pp. 131–7.

[65] On the 'speaking body' in early-nineteenth-century medico-legal tracts, see Müller, *Aber in meinem Herzen*, pp. 91–8.

available as indices of sodomy. Even those who were led to read these symptoms as evidence of tuberculosis could not rule out sodomy. Tuberculosis was thought by many to be connected to the practice of masturbation, and at least from the time of the great anti-onanism tracts of the eighteenth century, masturbation and sodomy had been understood as closely related practices.[66] In outlining these details, my purpose (I hasten to stress) is neither to demonstrate the 'actual' conduct of sodomy, whatever that might have been, nor to foreclose such an investigation in the future. Rather, I hope to indicate the means by which Chopin's pathologised body could have physically spurred the metaphorical enactments of hermaphroditism that we have discussed.

The contiguity of ideas of hermaphroditism and pathology helps explain the conjunction of otherworldly metaphors and images of disease in accounts of Chopin. Of course, the composer's frail health patently contributed to this imagery. But the affiliation occurs often enough that it cannot be understood solely as a response to his physical status. The linked topoi reverberate through Chopin's obituaries (as would fully be expected), they frame Marmontel's reminiscences of his playing (Marmontel's very first sentence about Chopin describes 'this name . . . that has preserved over the years the double halo of poetry and suffering')[67] and they colour George Sand's vision of his music ('being sick to death at Majorca, he made music which fully smelled of paradise'). The worlds of angels and fairies evoked through the metaphorical substitutions applied to Chopin were, at the most obvious level of perception, magical and charmed places. But we would be missing a key element of their signifying power were we not to recognise the diseased and disorderly images that also inhabit there.

How then did sex 'speak' music – Chopin's music – in the 1830s and 1840s? I have suggested here that it did so through processes of linguistic deferral and deflection which took place around supernatural images repeatedly attaching themselves to Chopin. The 'sex' so constructed by these processes was messily contingent. The sexual meanings, unstably concerned with notions of ambiguity and pathology rather than with ideas of identity and desire, often stood as shadowy presences beyond the foreground of awareness. At the same time, these meanings touched a 'Chopin' writ large: they inseparably configured the performer, his music, his character and his body.

---

[66] J. Morel de Rubempré, discussing the 'ills occasioned by onanism', includes 'dorsal consumption' and 'pulmonary phthisis'; see *Code de la génération universelle, ou les amours des fleurs, des animaux, et particulièrement de l'homme et de la femme, suivi de l'art de guérir l'impuissance ou faiblesse en amour, terminé par un traité de l'onanisme ou masturbation dans les deux sexes*, 2nd edn (Paris 1833), p. 399. For a more general discussion of tuberculosis and masturbation, see Thomas Laqueur, *Making Sex: Body and Gender from the Greeks to Freud* (Cambridge, Massachusetts and London 1990), pp. 227–30. On the perceived relationship between masturbation and sodomy, see George L. Mosse, *Nationalism and Sexuality: Middle-Class Morality and Sexual Norms in Modern Europe* (New York 1985; repr. edn Madison 1985), pp. 11–12.

[67] Marmontel, *Les pianistes célèbres*, p. 7. One might also include in this connection John Field's adage that Chopin was 'a sickroom talent', and Auber's or Berlioz's epithet (it has been ascribed to both) that 'he was dying all his life' (the French original is variously reported as 'il se meurt toute sa vie' or 'il se mourait toute sa vie'). The problem is that we have no evidence that either dictum was ever uttered. The supposed remark of Auber or Berlioz sounds suspiciously like a misconstrued reminiscence of a line from Berlioz's obituary of Chopin: 'Alas! Chopin was lost to music for quite a long time' ('Hélas! Chopin était perdu pour la musique depuis assez longtemps'). The obituary is reproduced in *Chopin na obczyźnie*, ed. Mirska and Hordyński, p. 325.

We might readily continue to pursue the multiple refractions of the supernatural trope. We might hear distant echoes of the 'pathological angel/fairy' in the occasional associations of Chopin's music with disease that took place in the 1830s and 1840s.[68] And we might also, as I have suggested elsewhere, investigate how the otherworldly, androgynous trope interacts with aspects of Chopin's musical productions: the perceived 'feminine' nature of his nocturnes or the generic uncertainty occasioned by his 'concert' preludes.[69] (Such an investigation would require a deft interpretative touch if it would hope to parse specific musical texts and procedures. For many of our analytical techniques, valuable as they might be in other present-day intellectual contexts, remain imbued with formalist ideals which firmly took root only towards the latter half of the nineteenth century, and thus would seem of questionable significance to an effort to elucidate values and modes of understanding of the early nineteenth century having to do with sex and music.[70]) These suggestions only begin to frame the possibilities for further research.

Yet we should not expect that such pursuits, or this pursuit for that matter, will lead to a mastery of the systems of thought that gave rise to the supernatural trope. Instead, we find ourselves confronting unresolvable limits to our knowledge similar to those described by Gary Tomlinson in his superb account of renaissance musical magic.[71] We can partially construe that segment of a musical culture whose strategies for making sense of Chopin included invoking images of otherworldly figures of a sexually unstable nature. But in some ways the epistemological premises that permitted the unsteady mapping of sex onto music in the first part of the nineteenth century remain foreign to our understanding: we cannot hope to experience images of Chopin as hermaphrodite or sodomite as his contemporaries in the 1830s and 1840s did. Far from leading to an appropriative control of the subject, then, following the refractive course of the otherworldly trope should suggest that we cannot continue blithely to enfold Chopin's musical culture into our own. Residues of difference and dislocation must surely remain as we strain to hear its voices – its small fairy voices – in some of their faintness, disorder and strangeness.

[68]   Examples include Ludwig Rellstab's feeling that the 'debaucheries' (*Ausschweifungen*) and 'trivial effeminacy' (*Weichlichkeit*) of the Concerto Op. 11, when juxtaposed against its finer qualities, could put one into a sick and miserable mood (review of Op. 11, in *Iris im Gebiete der Tonkunst*, 6 June 1834, p. 90); August Kahlert's characterisation of Chopin and Paganini as 'pathological' (*krankhaft*) representatives of the new musical romanticism ('Die Genrebilder in der modernen Musik', *Neue Zeitschrift für Musik*, 12 June 1835, p. 191); and two different British critics' perception of 'sickliness' in the Scherzo Op. 20 and in the melodies of the Mazurkas Op. 41 (for the reference to 'sickliness' in Op. 20, see Jim Samson, *Chopin: The Four Ballades* (Cambridge 1992), p. 5; as for Op. 41, see Frederick Niecks, *Frederick Chopin as a Man and Musician*, 2 vols. (London 1902; repr. edn New York 1973), vol. II, p. 279).

[69]   For discussions of the nocturnes, see my 'The Harmony of the Tea Table', p. 131; I examine the preludes in 'Small "Forms": In Defence of the Prelude', in *The Cambridge Companion to Chopin*, ed. Jim Samson (Cambridge 1992), p. 143.
     Something like these kinds of investigations has been undertaken in literary studies. For example, Weil discusses the possibility that Gautier's interest in fusing genres replicates his attempts to transgress boundaries of gender (*Androgyny and the Denial of Difference*, pp. 122–33).

[70]   For cogent analyses of the historiographical difficulties occasioned by formal description, see David Summers, '"Form", Nineteenth-Century Metaphysics, and the Problem of Art Historical Description', *Critical Inquiry*, 15 (1989), pp. 372–406; and Summers, 'Form and Gender', *New Literary History*, 24 (1993), pp. 243–71.

[71]   *Music in Renaissance Magic: Toward a Historiography of Others* (Chicago 1993), pp. 247–52.

5   Chopin's Ballade Op. 23 and the revolution of the intellectuals

KAROL BERGER

It goes crescendo, just as I like.[1]

The Ballade in G minor Op. 23, completed in 1835, was Chopin's first large-scale one-movement composition not based directly on classical formal models, and his most ambitious extended work to date, one in which he tried to create a new genre based on a new kind of compositional technique, arguably the first artistically significant result in a series of nineteenth-century attempts to provide a viable alternative to the classical sonata. The narrative continuity in the work depends primarily on the threads provided by a single sigh motif which with astonishing economy generates the essential motivic substance of the work, and by the obsessive focusing on a single pitch, C, which maintains its identity even through the changes of underlying keys, and which, as the opening pitch of the *Urmotiv* C–B♭, generates the expectation of the structural melodic descent from the fourth to the first scale degree of the main key. The expectation is repeatedly frustrated, and the work concludes instead with a climactic, catastrophic-heroic reversal of the structural melody's direction, that is, with an *ascent* from the fourth to the first scale degree in bars 234–50.

In a work of art, formal logic and expressive significance are inseparable. While describing the musical logic of the Ballade, we have also identified the leading poetic idea of the work. It is a narrative which proceeds from a weak and open, soft and moderate beginning, through successive waves of nervous intensification and acceleration, to an exceptionally strong and conclusive, frantic and fiery ending, with the final goal reached in an act of desperation, rather than by means of a logical and orderly progression, as the expected direction of the structural melodic line is 'catastrophically' reversed. The ending, while singularly emphatic, is clearly not triumphant, but heroic and tragic, and – appropriately – it is marked by traces of a funeral march which allude to Beethoven's two celebrated funeral marches for the fallen revolutionary hero, those in Opp. 26 and 55.

Chopin's predilection for the contemporary Italian opera comes across clearly in his correspondence, and the ubiquitous cavatina–cabaletta progression with its vocalistic fireworks at the end is likely to be one of the very general formal models that lie behind

[1] Chopin's comment on the success of his Viennese concerts, in a letter from Vienna to his family in Warsaw, 19 August 1829, in Fryderyk Chopin, *Korespondencja Fryderyka Chopina*, ed. Bronisław Edward Sydow, 2 vols. (Warsaw 1955), vol. I, p. 96. (All translations in this essay are mine unless otherwise indicated.)

72

the Ballade, as is the closely related wish of the virtuoso pianist for a dazzling finish. But the tragic quality of the final conflagration (Presto con fuoco) goes so far beyond the vulgar desire for applause that it forces us to look elsewhere for appropriate contexts for Chopin's creation, beyond the world of vocal and instrumental virtuosity.

The aim of the present essay is to explore the structural homology between the musical form of Chopin's work and the historical consciousness of the Polish émigré community in Paris between the revolutions of 1830 and 1848, the milieu of which the composer was a member. Needless to say, one can posit and explore such a homology only if the structures to be considered are in some way comparable. The common ground between musical forms and forms of historical consciousness can be established, I believe, on the basis of the concept of narrative as it is understood here, that is, as the temporal form in which parts succeed one another in a determined order, their succession being governed by the relationships of causing and resulting by necessity or probability. It is this common ground that will allow a comparison between the temporal structure of Chopin's musical narrative and the temporal structure of the kind of stories the composer's fellow émigrés would tell to identify themselves, to find out who they individually and collectively were.

In his celebrated Raleigh Lecture on History (British Academy, 1944), Lewis Namier presented a penetrating (and, from a post-1989 perspective, prophetic) interpretation of the revolution of 1848 as 'the revolution of the intellectuals (*la révolution des clercs*)'. 'The revolution of 1848', Namier argued,

was universally expected, and it was super-national as none before or after . . . The European Continent responded to the impulses and trends of the revolution with a remarkable uniformity, despite the differences of language and race, and in the political, social, and economic level of the countries concerned: but then the common denominator was ideological, and even literary, and there was a basic unity and cohesion in the intellectual world of the European Continent, such as usually asserts itself in the peak periods of its spiritual development.[2]

The European intellectuals of the pre-1848 period expected that the future revolution would complete the unfinished business of 1789 and universally replace the principle of dynastic property in certain countries with that of national sovereignty (hence the centrality of the German, Italian and Polish 'questions'). 'To the men of 1848 the dynastic principle stood for arbitrary rule and autocracy, that of popular sovereignty for human rights and national self-government . . .'[3] The principle of national sovereignty implied as its corollaries the right of self-government (that is, parliamentary democracy) and the right of self-determination (that is, nationalism), the former fostering unity and constitutional growth, the latter civil and international strife. 'In the interplay between constitutional and national movements on the European Continent, which opens in 1848, it is the latter that win . . .'[4] 'Thus in the *Völkerfrühling*, "nationality", the passionate creed of the intellectuals, invades the politics of central and east-central Europe, and with 1848 starts the Great European War of

2 Lewis Namier, *1848: The Revolution of the Intellectuals* (London 1946), pp. 3–4.
3 Ibid., p. 24.
4 Ibid., p. 31.

every nation against its neighbours.'[5] (It was no wonder, one might add to Namier's interpretation, that the creed of nationalism was embraced by the intellectuals with so much passion. Nationalism is a peculiarly modern way of legitimising political power as exercised in the name of a nation which, in east-central Europe at least, was usually defined in terms of its culture. Since culture is the intellectuals' domain, nationalism confers on this group the enviable role of the legitimising priesthood, the successors of earlier priesthoods which legitimised the God-derived powers of pre-modern rulers.)

The Polish question, the question of the future of a nation which did not want to accept the dismantling of its state by the three partitioning powers of Russia, Prussia and Austria at the end of the eighteenth century, played a central role in the pre-1848 ideological ferment and modulated it in an individual way. The great mass of the Polish emigration that assembled in Paris in the aftermath of the failed anti-Russian insurrection of 1830–1 commonly

saw that Poland's resurrection could only come through a war between the Partitioning Powers, or the defeat of all three (as happened in 1918); that this presupposed a general upheaval, a world war or a world revolution; that the July Monarchy, which was steadily moving to the Right, offered no base against the Powers of the Holy Alliance; and that a new revolution was needed, to mobilize popular forces in France and give the signal to Europe. They waited for 1848.[6]

The ideology of the Polish emigration was, of course, far from monolithic, as different factions envisaged different scenarios which would bring about the desired liberation and different political and social systems for the resurrected state. A particularly characteristic and influential version of the revolutionary ideology of the 1830s and 1840s was Polish romantic messianism, a belief widespread among the defeated émigrés that the suffering of the Polish nation would prepare it for the role of Europe's collective redeemer, one that would bring a salvation and regeneration of mankind's life on earth, rather than in heaven, by provoking a pan-European social revolution.[7] Adam Mickiewicz, the greatest Polish poet of the period and a figure of considerable consequence in Parisian intellectual circles, gave expression to this collective messianism in *Księgi narodu polskiego i pielgrzymstwa polskiego* (*The Books of the Polish Nation and of the Polish Pilgrims*), written in Paris at the very beginning of the Great Emigration in 1832. In the words of Andrzej Walicki, a perceptive student of Polish messianism, Mickiewicz's was 'a catastrophic vision of history' in which 'the unilinear Enlightenment conception of progress was replaced . . . by . . . a series of descents, followed by sudden upward surges which were achieved by means of sacrifice and regenerative grace'.[8] The messianic mission 'was to be fulfilled by the sword, by means of a revolutionary crusade against the corrupt old world'.[9] Indeed, *The Books* conclude with a 'Litania pielgrzymska' ('Pilgrims' Litany') which begins: 'O wojnę powszechną za Wolność Ludów! / Prosimy Cię Panie' ('For the universal war for the

---

5 Ibid., p. 33.
6 Ibid., pp. 47–8.
7 On Polish romantic messianism, see in particular Andrzej Walicki, *Philosophy and Romantic Nationalism: The Case of Poland* (Oxford 1982).
8 Ibid., p. 248.
9 Ibid., p. 249.

freedom of nations, we beseech thee, O Lord!'); and ends: 'O niepodległość całość i wolność Ojczyzny naszej. / Prosimy Cię Panie' ('For the independence, integrity and freedom of our Fatherland, we beseech thee, O Lord!').[10]

Needless to say, not every Pole in Paris in the 1830s and 1840s was a messianist. Chopin himself, much as he respected Mickiewicz, was too *mondain* and simply too sober a realist to be able to accept wilder aspects of the poet's messianism, in particular his involvement in the Towiański circle, without considerable scepticism. The composer's letters show that he observed Mickiewicz's participation in the circle with interest but also an entirely clear head. Thus, on 11 September 1841, he wrote from Nohant to his friend and copyist Julian Fontana in Paris: 'Are we still returning to the country [Poland]!! Have they completely lost their minds?! I do not fear for Mickiewicz and Sobański, they have strong heads and can survive another few emigrations, without losing their reason or their energy.'[11] A week later, perhaps in reaction to Fontana's more detailed report on the goings-on in the capital, Chopin wrote (Nohant, 18 September 1841 to Julian Fontana in Paris): 'Mickiewicz will come to a bad end, unless he is leading you on.'[12] As late as 23 March 1845, he reported on quarrels in the Towiański circle and on Mickiewicz's withdrawal therefrom in a letter from Paris to Stefan Witwicki in Freiwaldau.[13] Chopin clearly kept his distance from the more feverish manifestations of messianism and probably felt most comfortable with the conservative Hôtel Lambert wing of the émigré community led by Prince Adam Czartoryski, with whose family he was linked by ties of friendship (Princess Marcelina Czartoryska being one of his most gifted students).[14] Liszt's 1852 description of Chopin's political inclinations rings true:

Democracy never won his sympathies, as it presented in his view an agglomeration of elements too heterogeneous, too restless, and wielding too much brute power. The entrance of social and political questions into the realm of popular discussion was many years ago compared to a new and bold incursion of barbarians; and the terror which this comparison awakened in Chopin's mind made upon him a peculiar and most painful impression. He despaired of defending the safety of Rome from these modern Attilas; he dreaded the destruction of Art and its monuments, its refinements, and its civilisation – in a word, he dreaded the loss of the elegant and cultivated though somewhat indolent ease so well described by Horace.[15]

But it is important to realise that even the politically and socially conservative wing of the Polish emigration waited for a pan-European conflagration as the only plausible road to their country's liberation. The historical situation of the Polish émigrés in Paris in the 1830s and 1840s turned the great majority of them into natural revolutionaries, regardless of whether their political and social convictions were of the right or left. They all shared with the European revolutionary intellectuals of the period a common

---

10 Adam Mickiewicz, *Dzieła poetyckie*, 4 vols. (Warsaw 1979), vol. II, p. 265.
11 Chopin, *Korespondencja*, vol. II, p. 36.
12 Ibid., vol. II, p. 37.
13 Ibid., vol. II, p. 130.
14 See Jean-Jacques Eigeldinger, *Chopin: Pianist and Teacher as Seen by His Pupils* (hereafter *CPT*), trans. Naomi Shohet with Krysia Osostowicz and Roy Howat, ed. Roy Howat (Cambridge 1986).
15 Franz Liszt, *Chopin*, trans. John Broadhouse (London 1901; first published Paris 1852), p. 136.

vision of history and of their place in it, a vision – driven by the ideology of national sovereignty – of the coming pan-European revolution and war.

Thus it is not surprising to find Chopin writing from Paris in January 1833 to his friend Dominik Dziewanowski in Berlin: 'I love the Carlists, I cannot stand the Philippists, and as for myself I am a revolutionary . . .'[16] A most striking and thought-provoking example of how people of very different temperaments, interests and convictions could react similarly to their common historical predicament is provided by the astonishing affinity of thought and imagery in Chopin's and Mickiewicz's responses to the tragedy of the failed insurrection of 1830–1. Writing in a private diary in Stuttgart shortly after hearing of the fall of Warsaw to Russian troops on 8 September 1831, Chopin made a despairing and blasphemous entry: 'Oh God, Thou art! Thou art and avengest Thyself not! Thou hast still not enough of the Muscovite crimes; or, or Thou art Thyself a Muscovite!'[17] This entry in a private diary not destined for anyone's eyes could not have been known to Mickiewicz when he led Konrad, the revolutionary hero of the third part of his drama, *Dziady (The Forefathers' Eve)*, published in Paris in 1832, to the edge of blasphemy. At the end of his 'Improvisation', Konrad addresses God: 'I shall scream that Thou art not the father of the world, but . . .', with the voice of the devil completing the thought: 'the Tsar!'[18]

It would be a mistake to think that these extreme pronouncements of the composer belong only to the period of despair immediately following the failed insurrection. Towards the end of his life and at the beginning of the new revolutionary period, Chopin, the sober conservative at home in the most exclusive salons of the Faubourg Saint-Germain, wrote to Fontana (now in New York) about the prospects of revolution and war in Europe and their implications for Poland: 'this [revolution and war] will not happen without horrors, but at the end of it all there is Poland, magnificent, great; in a word, Poland'.[19] Namier's conclusion stands: in Paris, Poles of most political persuasions waited for 1848, for a catastrophic pan-European conflagration, so that Poland and other sovereign nations could be resurrected and regenerated from the ashes of the old order.

My claim now is this. Personal and collective identities always have narrative structure: we identify ourselves by means of the stories we tell about ourselves, stories about where we have come from, and where we are going.[20] The narrative that provided the community Chopin identified with most closely, the Polish emigration in Paris in the 1830s and 1840s, with their sense of who they were was the story of 'Exodus', its fundamental structure of past enslavement, present exile and future

16 Chopin, *Korespondencja*, vol. I, p. 223.
17 Ibid., vol. I, p. 185.
18 Mickiewicz, *Dzieła poetyckie*, vol. III, p. 163. The intriguing similarity between the Stuttgart diary and the 'Great Improvisation' of Konrad is discussed by Ludwik Bronarski, 'Chopin et la littérature', in his *Etudes sur Chopin*, 2 vols. (Lausanne 1944), vol. I, pp. 19–76, especially pp. 38–9.
19 Letter from Paris, 4 April 1848. Chopin, *Korespondencja*, vol. II, p. 239.
20 On the role narrative plays in the establishment of personal and collective identity, see in particular Paul Ricoeur, *Time and Narrative*, trans. Kathleen McLaughlin and David Pellauer, 3 vols. (Chicago 1984–8); David Carr, *Time, Narrative, and History* (Bloomington 1986); Paul Ricoeur, *Soi-même comme un autre* (Paris 1990).

rebirth preserved but modulated to stress the dimension of the future. Like the European intellectuals of the period who expected a revolution to complete the project started in 1789, these Poles waited for a universal catastrophe which would bring the old order down to make room for a new one, and, like Chopin himself, considered the violence and horrors attendant on revolution and war a heroic price worth paying. Chopin's G minor Ballade (and, incidentally, most of his major narrative works, in particular the ballades and the Polonaise-Fantasy) is, as we have seen, a musical narrative which, from a weak beginning, accelerates to a strong and fiery ending, with the goal reached in an act of desperation and experienced as a tragedy rather than a triumph. The homology that I am positing between the temporal structures of Chopin's musical narrative and the historical narrative in terms of which the composer's contemporaries established their identity is based on the fact that both are future- or end-orientated, and in both the envisaged ending is fiery and tragic.

In interpreting this homology, we should first clarify what it is not, namely, a case of programme music. Chopin's distaste for music which illustrates is well documented.[21] He gave his works fastidiously neutral generic titles, and was more than annoyed by the absurd 'poetic' headings under which they appeared in London (Op. 23, for instance, was given the title of 'La Favorite').[22] Thus, on 9 October 1841, Chopin writes from Nohant to Fontana in Paris: 'if he [Chopin's London publisher, Wessel] lost [money] on my compositions, this is surely because of the stupid titles he gave them in spite of my prohibition . . .'[23] What the Ballade Op. 23 certainly is not is a musical illustration of a programme for a future liberation of Poland. But for the 1830s and 1840s the distinction between programme and absolute music should not be drawn too sharply. Rather, some of the most innovative music of the period is located somewhere between these two extremes,[24] and it is in this 'in-between' region that a place for the Ballade must be found.

It would be good to know how Chopin himself understood the relationship between music and other expressive media, or, even more generally, between music and the world. However, unlike so many of his most interesting musical contemporaries, Chopin did not publicise his aesthetic views, and the best we can do is to catch glimpses of those as reported by Eugène Delacroix and George Sand, who seem to have been the composer's preferred partners for serious conversations on general artistic issues. Perhaps the most revealing of those glimpses is offered in Sand's masterly *impression* or *souvenir*, dated Paris, January 1841, though published much later,[25] in which she describes a half-day spent with Delacroix discussing, or rather

[21] See, e.g., Bronarski, 'Chopin et la littérature'.
[22] In Wessel's 1836 edition, according to the 'Critical Notes' (p. xxi) to Jan Ekier's 1986 Wiener Urtext Edition of the Ballades.
[23] Chopin, *Korespondencja*, vol. II, p. 42.
[24] See Walter Wiora, 'Zwischen absoluter und Programmusik', in *Festschrift Friedrich Blume*, ed. A. A. Abert and W. Pfankuch (Kassel 1963), pp. 381–8; Ludwig Finscher, '"Zwischen absoluter und Programmusik": Zur Interpretation der deutschen romantischen Symphonie', in *Über Symphonien: Festschrift Walter Wiora*, ed. Ch. H. Mahling (Tutzing 1979), pp. 103–15; and Anthony Newcomb, 'Once More "Between Absolute and Program Music": Schumann's Second Symphony', *19th-Century Music*, 7 (1984), pp. 233–50.
[25] George Sand, *Impressions et souvenirs* (Paris 1873), pp. 72–90.

listening to him discourse on, his theory of the interdependence of drawing (*dessin*) and colour (*couleur*), as opposed to the theory of their mutual independence, and the superiority of drawing, professed by the followers of Ingres (a late echo of the sixteenth-century dispute on the relative merits of the Florentine *disegno* and the Venetian *colorito*). The discussion continues at the dinner table *chez* Sand in the presence of her son, Maurice, and Chopin. After dinner, Chopin stops listening, sits at the piano and improvises. It is at this point that Sand makes a comment which, in spite of its length, deserves to be quoted in full:

The master [Chopin] knows very well what he is doing. He laughs at those who claim to make beings and things speak by means of imitative harmony. This silliness is not for him. He knows that music is a human impression and human manifestation. It is a human mind that thinks, it is a human voice that expresses itself. It is man in the presence of the emotions he experiences, translating them by the feeling he has of them, without trying to reproduce their causes by the sound. Music would not know how to specify these causes; it should not attempt to do it. There is its greatness, it would not be able to speak in prose.

When the nightingale sings in the starry night, the master will not make you guess or sense by a ridiculous notation the warbling of the bird. He will make the human voice sing in a particular feeling which one experiences listening to the nightingale, and if you do not dream of the nightingale while listening to the man, that matters hardly at all. You will, nevertheless, derive from it an impression of delight which will put your mind in the disposition where it will be, if you fall into a sweet ecstasy for a beautiful summer night, cradled by all the harmonies of the happy and meditative nature.

It will be so with all the musical thoughts whose design stands out against the effects of harmony. Sung word is needed to specify their intention. Where the instruments alone take charge of translating it, the musical drama flies on its own wings and does not claim to be translated by the listener. It expresses itself by a state of mind it induces in you by force or gently. When Beethoven unchains the storm, he does not strive to paint the pallid glimmer of lightning and to make us hear the crash of thunder. He renders the shiver, the feeling of wonder, the terror of nature of which man is aware and which he shares in experiencing it. The symphonies of Mozart are masterpieces of feeling which every moved mind interprets as it pleases without risking losing its way in a formal opposition with the nature of the subject. The beauty of musical language consists in taking hold of the heart or imagination, without being condemned to pedestrian reasoning. It maintains itself in an ideal sphere where the listener who is not musically educated still delights in the vagueness, while the musician savours this great logic that presides over the masters' magnificent issue of thought.

Chopin talks little and rarely of his art; but, when he does talk about it, it is with an admirable clearness and a soundness of judgement and of intentions which would reduce to nothing plenty of heresies if he wanted to profess with open heart.

But, even in private, he holds back and pours out his heart only at his piano. He promises us, however, to write a method in which he will discuss not only the skills of the profession, but also the doctrine. Will he keep his word?[26]

It is difficult to decide how much here represents Chopin's own views: the skilfully ambiguous passage might be read either as Sand's own interpretation of the relationship between music and the world, or as her report of the composer's 'doctrine'.

---

[26]   Ibid., pp. 86ff.

I believe, however, that the views presented may well preserve something of Chopin's own. For one thing, they agree with what we have learned elsewhere about the composer's distaste for musical illustration. For another, the reference to the musician who 'savours this great logic that presides over the masters' magnificent issue of thought' brings to mind Delacroix's report of his conversation of 7 April 1849 with Chopin: 'I asked him what establishes logic in music. He made me feel what counterpoint and harmony are; how the fugue is like pure logic in music, and that to know the fugue deeply is to be acquainted with the element of all reason and all consistency in music.'[27] In any case, Sand's essay gets us as close to the composer's own position on the matter at hand as we are ever likely to get.

Here is the central point of the 'doctrine'. It is silly to use music to imitate the sounds of the world, to make the world speak through music; only a human being should speak through music. Music expresses human emotions, states of mind, and induces them in the listener, without specifying their worldly causes, and it does not matter whether the listener discovers these causes or not. The causes may be specified only in language, when the music is combined with sung words.

The doctrine is reminiscent of, and seems to make reference to, Beethoven's celebrated remark on his 'Pastoral' Symphony: 'a matter more of feeling than of painting in sounds'.[28] In its claim that music is incapable of specifying the causes of the emotions it expresses, the Chopin–Sand theory also strikingly anticipates an aspect of Eduard Hanslick's argument in *Vom Musikalisch-Schönen* of 1854 to the effect that, since every emotion must have an intentional object (a fear is the fear of a lion, say), emotions can be expressed only when their objects are represented, and since music is incapable of representation, it is also incapable of expression. Kendall L. Walton takes Hanslick's point to be that music can portray only indefinite emotions, not definite ones.[29] An emotion has a cognitive component (a thought which involves the intentional object) and a component of sensation (a feeling which does not involve the intentional object). Different emotions may have the sensation in common, while differing in the cognitive component. Music may be unable to specify the cognitive component, while being able to portray the sensation. Thus, for instance, it may portray what fear and anger have in common, without being able to distinguish between them. Roger Scruton answers Hanslick differently.[30] Following Richard Wollheim's distinction between the transitive and intransitive senses in which we may understand an expression,[31] Scruton reminds us that an expression may be understood intransitively, that we may experience a musical expression in an act of spontaneous sympathy, without being able to say what is expressed.[32] In a song or an opera, the

[27] Eugène Delacroix, *The Journal of Eugene Delacroix*, trans. Walter Pach (New York 1937), p. 194.
[28] Alexander Wheelock Thayer, *Life of Beethoven*, rev. and ed. Elliot Forbes (Princeton 1967), p. 436.
[29] Kendall L. Walton, 'What is Abstract about the Art of Music?', *The Journal of Aesthetics and Art Criticism*, 46 (1988), pp. 351–64, especially pp. 356–8.
[30] Roger Scruton, 'Analytic Philosophy and the Meaning of Music', in *Analytic Aesthetics*, ed. R. Shusterman (Oxford 1989), pp. 85–96.
[31] Richard Wollheim, *Art and Its Objects*, 2nd edn (Cambridge 1980), pp. 41 and 48. Wollheim derives the distinction from Ludwig Wittgenstein's discussion of the words 'particular' and 'peculiar' in *The Blue and Brown Books* (Oxford 1958), pp. 158–60.
[32] Scruton, 'Analytic Philosophy', p. 92.

specific intentional object of the emotion is represented. In purely instrumental music, it is the listener's, or critic's, task to connect the music with an appropriate context of human values and interests.

The Chopin–Sand theory seems very close to these modern readings of Hanslick. The intentional objects (or 'causes', as Sand calls them) of the expressive gestures enacted in instrumental music may, and should, remain unspecified by the composer. The gestures have sufficient generality to allow for a number of such objects or causes, though the range of possible causes is never unlimited. The listeners or critics, in so far as they want the music to be more than a purely formal game and want to make a connection between the music's significance and their own deep concerns, will propose appropriate causes, that is, the intentional objects that fall within the range of the possible ones. (As Schumann said about Chopin's ballades: 'a poet could easily find words to set to his music'.[33]) But they will remember that the causes or objects they propose, even if plausible, are no more than exemplifications chosen from a number of possibilities.

An instrumental narrative, then, is not a piece of programme music; it does not illustrate a specific, particular story. But neither must it remain completely unconnected with non-musical human concerns. Its temporal form can be expressive of a general sense of 'how things hang together', of how life is likely to turn out. An individual biography or a collective history would then serve as no more than appropriate exemplifications, the kind of stories this music might illustrate if it were to illustrate any particular story at all. In short, the Chopin–Sand theory authorises the view of a musical narrative as an utterance in which individuals or nations may choose to read the general shape of their own destiny, the kind of prophetic utterance Ernst Bloch had in mind when, in his 1918 *Geist der Utopie*, he spoke of the great work of art as anticipating the homeward journey,[34] and of music as the first settlement in the holy land.[35]

It follows that the context of human concern that I have proposed for the G minor Ballade, the future-orientated revolutionary narrative that provided many European intellectuals, and in particular many Polish émigrés, of the period with a self-image and self-understanding, should not be taken as a 'private programme' which Chopin actually had in mind while composing but subsequently chose to suppress. It should, rather, be understood as one of those contexts the composer might recognise as relevant to his work.

And not only the composer, but also some of his listeners. Chopin is reported by Wilhelm von Lenz to have described his own aims as a performer thus: 'I indicate, . . . it's up to the listener to complete the picture.'[36] This is precisely what many listeners of the period did, with various degrees of skill and empathy, adducing contexts of greater or lesser relevance. The *Revue et Gazette musicale de Paris* of 9 September 1838 published an open letter 'To Mr F. Chopin, on his Polish ballad' ('A M. F. Chopin,

---

[33]   Robert Schumann, *Gesammelte Schriften über Musik und Musiker*, 5th edn, ed. Martin Kreisig, 2 vols. (Leipzig 1914), vol. II, p. 32.

[34]   Ernst Bloch, *Essays on the Philosophy of Music* (Cambridge 1985), p. 90.

[35]   Ibid., p. 139.

[36]   Quoted from *CPT*, p. 278.

sur sa ballade polonaise') by a minor French poet Félicien Mallefille (who, incidentally, was the man George Sand was shortly to drop in Chopin's favour).[37] In his letter, Mallefille describes a recent soirée for selected friends where Chopin played 'this Polish ballad we love so much' ('cette ballade polonaise que nous aimons tant'), the expression suggesting that this was not the first time his friends had heard the piece. It is not entirely clear whether the work in question was the first or the second Ballade. The Ballade Op. 38 was completed only in January 1839, that is, after the evening described by Mallefille. However, since Chopin performed an early version of the work for Schumann during their meeting in Leipzig in September 1836,[38] he might easily have played something less than the final version for his Parisian friends in 1838. In his excellent study of how Chopin's works were published, Jeffrey Kallberg quotes a letter from Heinrich Albert Probst, Breitkopf & Härtel's Parisian agent, to his firm in Leipzig, in which Op. 38 is referred to as 'a Pilgrim's Ballade [*eine Ballade des Pèlerins*]' and asks whether this could be the same work as the 'Polish ballad' of Mallefille.[39] (In a most perceptive aside, Kallberg mentions how important the image of the pilgrim was to the Polish émigré community in Paris in the 1830s, promoted especially by Mickiewicz.) Given that, as we shall see, Mallefille explicitly connects his *ballade polonaise* with the theme of the Polish exiles and their peregrination, the identification of the work with Probst's *Ballade des Pèlerins* seems plausible. For the purposes of the present discussion, however, the question of which ballade was actually played is relatively unimportant. The basic shape leading from a comparatively inconspicuous and tentative, private, domestic or pastoral beginning to a fiery, heroic, tragic and public ending is, as stated earlier, shared by many of Chopin's major one-movement narrative works, and the context of the ideology of Polish emigration is equally relevant to all of them. What is interesting about Mallefille's letter is that it gives us an insight into the sort of hearing which must have been quite widespread among the literary circles that formed one kind of Chopin's audience.

On hearing him play, Mallefille writes to Chopin,

we all fell into a profound daydream . . . What did we thus dream about, then, all together . . .? I cannot say it; since everyone sees in the music, as in the clouds, different things. But seeing our friend the Sceptic [Delacroix?], . . . I have imagined that he must have daydreamed of murmuring streams and of gloomy farewells exchanged in dark tree-lined paths; while the old Believer [Mickiewicz?], whose evangelical words we listen to with such respectful admiration, . . . seemed to interrogate Dante, his grandfather, about the secrets of heaven and the destinies of the world. As for me, . . . I wept following in thought the distressing images that you have made appear before me. On coming back home, I have attempted to render them in my own fashion in the following lines. Read them with indulgence, and, even if I have interpreted your ballad badly in them, accept their offering as a proof of my affection for you and of my sympathy for your heroic fatherland.[40]

---

37 *Revue et Gazette musicale de Paris*, 5/36 (1838), pp. 562–4.
38 See Gastone Belotti, *F. Chopin l'uomo*, 3 vols. (Milan and Rome 1974), vol. I, pp. 571–4.
39 Jeffrey Kallberg, 'Chopin in the Marketplace: Aspects of the International Music Publishing Industry in the First Half of the Nineteenth Century', *Notes*, 39 (1982–3), pp. 812–13.
40 Mallefille, 'A M. F. Chopin', p. 562. The probable identification of the 'Sceptic' as Delacroix and the 'Believer' as Mickiewicz has been made in Chopin, *Korespondencja*, vol. I, p. 558.

There follows a little piece of dramatic prose entitled 'The Exiles. – A Path' ('Les exilés. – Un chemin') in which the Chorus bids farewell to Poland, 'tomb of our fore-fathers, cradle of our children';[41] a Young Man asks his fellow exiles why they should continue to carry swords which had not succeeded in defending their fatherland from the enslavement; and an Old Man explains: 'We keep our weapons for the day of the resurrection.'[42] The Young Man answers: 'Hope is dead and God is sleeping',[43] but the Old Man asks the young ones to keep their arms and hope: 'The future is rich; it gives to those who know how to wait.'[44] The Young Man, in his despair, wants to kill himself. The Exiles leave him alone. A Passer-by tells him: 'Let them go; everyone for himself in this world. But you would be silly to kill yourself now . . .',[45] and he urges him to go to a great city, to enrich himself promptly and to enjoy the pleasures of life, good table, beautiful women, horses, travel. The encounter is salutary. The Young Man, shocked to discover that anyone might want to leave his fatherland and paternal home of his own free will, realises now where his duty lies and goes on to rejoin his fellow exiles in their common fate, so that they can sing together: 'To you, Poland! Saint Poland! tomb of our forefathers! cradle of our children, to you always!'[46]

In a recent analysis of the manner in which Chopin experienced his own exis-tence, Maria Janion and Maria Żmigrodzka demonstrated the extent to which the composer's sense of life was analogous to the experience of existence articulated by the major poets of Polish romanticism, and fellow Parisian exiles, Adam Mickiewicz, Juliusz Słowacki and Zygmunt Krasiński.[47] A central shared motif in their self-image was that of the 'orphan', a motif clearly resulting from the trauma of separation from the native realm after the insurrection of 1830–1, but also transcending this particular historical and political dimension to embrace a more universal condition of existential uprootedness and homelessness. 'In the biographies of many representatives of Polish romanticism . . . the historical drama of the November [1830] insurrection was profoundly internalised and it was decisive for their attempts at self-definition and for the understanding of their own fate',[48] write Janion and Żmigrodzka. (It should be recalled here that the G minor Ballade was completed in Paris in 1835, but, if we are to believe some Chopin scholars, it may have been sketched in Vienna as early as May and June of 1831.[49]) The trauma induced by history often led the Polish romantics to

41   Mallefille, 'A M. F. Chopin', p. 563.
42   Ibid., p. 563.
43   Ibid., p. 563.
44   Ibid., p. 563.
45   Ibid., p. 563.
46   Ibid., p. 564.
47   Maria Janion and Maria Żmigrodzka, 'Frédéric Chopin parmi les héros de l'existence du romantisme polonais', Chopin Studies, 3 (1990), pp. 35–51.
48   Ibid., p. 37.
49   See the literature listed in Krystyna Kobylańska, Rękopisy utworów Chopina: Katalog, 2 vols. (Cracow 1977), vol. I, p. 125. Jeffrey Kallberg's scepticism concerning this matter is noted in Anselm Gerhard, 'Ballade und Drama. Frédéric Chopins Ballade opus 38 und die französische Oper um 1830', Archiv für Musikwissenschaft, 48 (1991), p. 111 n. 1. Jim Samson argues that the first Ballade was probably not begun before 1833 and that it is most likely to have been drafted not long before its publication in 1835 (Chopin: The Four Ballades (Cambridge 1992), pp. 1, 21 and 88 n. 1).

extremes of morbid alienation, to what Krasiński termed 'a monomania of death'.[50] 'Thus it may happen that despair, the feeling of defeat and of imprisonment in an existence which tends inevitably towards self-destruction, dominate . . . Nevertheless, our romantics make their heroes exit, more and more resolutely, from the nightmare of imprisoned existence . . . Much more often one rediscovers salvation in the sphere of the values of collective life, in the union with the destiny of the nation . . .'[51] The widespread scenario, then, led from the collective trauma, through the solipsistic *delectatio morosa*, to the rediscovery of hope in collectively shared values.

Mallefille may not have been a great writer, but he understood this mechanism remarkably well. It is all there: the trauma of exile; the self-destructive solipsism of morbid alienation, a twin brother of the extreme alienation from collectively shared values bred by the conditions of life in the modern metropolis of the 1830s; and the return to the national community as the source of hope. Even the blasphemous despair of Konrad finds its echo here ('God is sleeping'). If it was Op. 23 that Mallefille heard, the spectre of the thoroughly modern Parisian bourgeois must have been raised in the poet's mind by the frenetically animated waltz of the *scherzando* episode (bars 138–66).[52] (From Berlioz and Schumann to Mahler and Richard Strauss, the waltz served as the emblem of urban sophistication.) The association of the modern metropolis with the condition of the essential homelessness of contemporary European man is telling (recall that Paris was the hub of nineteenth-century modernity, 'the capital of the nineteenth century', in Walter Benjamin's phrase[53]). But it is the master-image of the little drama, the image of the exiles on the path that would eventually lead to armed resurrection, that is of central importance here, since it encapsulates the self-understanding of the Polish emigration. Mallefille's text shows that a liberal Parisian intellectual could accept this Polish self-image and hear it expressed in Chopin's music just as easily as those generations of insurrectionist Poles whose sense of identity this music helped to mould, for better or worse, for about a century. It is a promise of return from exile which Chopin's listeners, nationalist Poles and cosmopolitan Parisians alike, heard in his music.

---

50 Quoted in Janion and Żmigrodzka, 'Frédéric Chopin', p. 45.
51 Ibid., pp. 49–50.
52 Jim Samson writes about the episode (*The Music of Chopin* (London 1985), pp. 178–9): 'Waltz elements were already implicit in the accompaniment to the main theme . . . and now they are extended into a fully characterised dance episode whose phraseology is the *moto perpetuo* arabesque so typical of the independent waltzes.'
53 'Paris, die Hauptstadt des XIX. Jahrhunderts', in *Das Passagen-Werk, Gesammelte Schriften*, vol. V (Frankfurt am Main 1989).

6 The Polonaise-Fantasy and issues of musical narrative

ANTHONY NEWCOMB

Chopin's Polonaise-Fantasy Op. 61 has attracted considerable critical and analytical attention in recent years, and much of this has engaged either directly or indirectly the issue of what I call narrativity in textless instrumental music.[1] Why might this be so? This essay will formulate an answer to that question, before proposing its own interpretation of narrative elements in Chopin's illusive and allusive piece.

Why the Polonaise-Fantasy? In its briefest form, my answer would be that the piece challenges one's sense of why one thing might plausibly follow from another in a series of events understood as a coherent human action. This understanding and organising of events as a comprehensible series of intentional acts is a principal ingredient of the narrative mode of understanding, as understood by psychologists such as Jerome Bruner and philosophers of history such as Paul Ricoeur.[2]

This view of narrativity, unlike many based in literary theory, is not tied to the presence of a narrator's voice (as with the mimesis/diegesis dichotomy), or even to verbal formulations of narrative, but can include non-verbal formulations, such as silent film, dance and even textless music. I say 'even' textless music, because such music is unique among those media that can carry narrative meaning in lacking what I call a human simulacrum – that is, there is nothing in music which must or can be described as human, in terms of physiognomy, height, gait, clothing and so on.

---

[1] Eero Tarasti, 'Pour une narratologie de Chopin', *International Review of the Aesthetics and Sociology of Music*, 15 (1984), pp. 53–75; Jeffrey Kallberg, 'Chopin's Last Style', *Journal of the American Musicological Society*, 38 (1985), pp. 264–315; Nicholas Cook, *A Guide to Musical Analysis* (New York 1987), pp. 335–43; John Rink, 'Schenker and Improvisation', *Journal of Music Theory*, 37/1 (1993), pp. 1–54. More generally on the issue of narrative elements in Chopin, see also Jim Samson, 'The Composition-Draft of the Polonaise-Fantasy: The Issue of Tonality', in *Chopin Studies*, ed. Jim Samson (Cambridge 1988), pp. 41–58; Samson, *Chopin: The Four Ballades* (Cambridge 1992); James Parakilas, *Ballads without Words: Chopin and the Tradition of the Instrumental Ballade* (Portland, Oregon 1992).

[2] My definition of intentional acts is drawn from Donald Davidson, *Essays on Actions and Events* (Oxford 1980), esp. pp. 43–63. For this sense of narrative and the narrative mode of understanding, see Jerome Bruner, *Actual Minds, Possible Worlds* (Cambridge, Massachusetts 1986), esp. chapters 2 and 3; Bruner, 'The Narrative Construction of Reality', *Critical Inquiry*, 18 (1991), pp. 1–21; Paul Ricoeur, 'Narrative Time', *Critical Inquiry*, 7 (1980), pp. 169–90; Ricoeur, *Time and Narrative*, trans. Kathleen McLaughlin and David Pellauer, 3 vols. (Chicago 1984–8). Ricoeur calls the narrative mode of understanding on the part of the listener/reader/viewer the 'narrative activity'.

As I discuss narrativity in instrumental music, I shall want to keep separate two distinct elements in the compound subject. The first comprises those aspects or characteristics *within the music itself* that suggest or stimulate a narrative interpretation. In this sense narrativity is a quality or property internal to the music. The second comes *from the listener or reader* and constitutes the set of criteria and strategies by which the listener identifies, locates and interprets narrative aspects in music. In this sense narrativity is brought to the music by the listener. A subheading within this second element is more general and less important to my present thesis: namely, the tendency or willingness to hear and interpret music as narrative, which will vary from culture to culture, from listener to listener and even from listening occasion to listening occasion.

Nineteenth-century Western culture witnessed a tremendous outpouring of narrative creativity in all media, and the tendency to narrative understanding was deeply rooted in most of its citizens. Those educated in that culture (including many living in this century) were thus more than ready to identify the first of the elements mentioned above: those aspects within the music itself that suggest a narrative interpretation. Without referring to (and probably without knowing about) the theories of philosophers, psychologists, historians or literary theorists, many musicians across the past century and a half have identified a narrative quality or flavour in Chopin's music, especially in the large pieces, including the Fantasy Op. 49 and the four ballades, in addition to the Polonaise-Fantasy, whose form is comparatively unschematic. For example, in an early review of a German edition of the first Ballade, which called the piece *Ballade ohne Worte*, Gottfried Wilhelm Fink, editor of the *Allgemeine musikalische Zeitung*, remarked that 'the newer music loves to compose stories in sound'.[3] This cultural tendency to narrative understanding led, of course, to finding narrative elements in music other than Chopin's. The young Henry Chorley, writing in *The Athenaeum* in 1834, remarked that 'we have always valued instrumental music as it has *spoken to us*, and can never listen to the delightful works of Beethoven, Mozart, Haydn, Ries, Onslow, and some others, without having their sentiment – nay, when we are in a fanciful humour – their *story*, as clearly impressed upon our minds as if it had been told in words.'[4] Schumann encouraged the tendency with titles, captions and expressive indications in his own music (for example, *Im Legendenton* from the Fantasy Op. 17), and revealed the tendency in his discussion of, among others, Chopin's music by trying to find a specific literary model for the second Ballade.[5] I would be tempted to

---

3 *Allgemeine musikalische Zeitung*, 39/2 (1837), pp. 25–6. 'Das erste musikalische Stück [in the collection under review – *Album Musical. Sammlung der neuesten Original-Compositionen für Piano u. Gesang*] ist eine Ballade ohne Worte für's Pianof. von Chopin. Hat man Lieder ohne Worte, warum soll man nicht auch Balladen ohne Worte haben? Ueberhaupt liebt es die neuere Musik Geschichten in Tönen zu dichten.' Fink commented on how difficult the piece was to understand. He had worked through it five times, with increasing comprehension and appreciation each time. At the end of the paragraph Fink comments, 'Es bliebe nichts übrig, als eine dichterische Auslegung des Gedichts zu geben, die, nicht schwierig, Jeder sich selbst am Besten gibt.'

4 *The Athenaeum*, 15 March 1834 (Chorley's italics). Quoted in Samson, *Chopin: The Four Ballades*, p. 11.

5 *Neue Zeitschrift für Musik*, 15/36 (1841), pp. 141–2; also Robert Schumann, *Gesammelte Schriften über Musik und Musiker*, 5th edn, ed. Martin Kreisig, 2 vols. (Leipzig 1914), vol. II, p. 32. Nicholas Marston (*Schumann: Fantasie, Op. 17* (Cambridge 1992), p. 17; see also plate 2, opposite p. 33) points out that Schumann's autograph of the first movement labels the slower central section *Romanza*, not *Im Legendenton*, as it becomes in the non-autograph *Stichvorlage*.

attribute Liszt's initial puzzlement and even revulsion before the Polonaise-Fantasy (which 'brings the mind to a pitch of irritability bordering on delirium . . . pitiable manifestations that the artist can usefully incorporate in his work only with extreme caution'[6]) to his inability to interpret the succession of musical events as a coherent series of human (musical) actions, which is my root definition of the listener's 'narrative activity'.

The tendency to hear music as narrative was repressed during and after the First World War, at least by those who considered themselves among the more advanced critics and analysts. Modernists vigorously rejected this and many other characteristic aspects of nineteenth-century culture. But the tendency to hear music narratively has begun to bubble up again as part of the current post-modernism.[7] Even the theorist's theorist Carl Schachter remarked in 1988 (concerning the Fantasy Op. 49 and the ballades): 'Among the musical values of all these works is their narrative quality, but the narrative is a musical one, carried out by tonal structure, texture, form, and motivic design.'[8]

My own view of this first element of musical narrative – those aspects within the music itself that suggest a narrative interpretation – is in almost complete accord with what Schachter says here. *The narrative aspects within music may occasionally make direct reference to the world outside music (especially via direct imitation of sounds), but they are themselves purely musical.* In other words, musical narrativity is not an extra-musical matter. It is suggested and developed by purely musical means, and it can achieve narrative effects which are different from and unobtainable by narratives in other media. I should stress in this connection that musical narrative is not necessarily attached to a specific story – though Beethoven, Mahler, Wagner and composers of symphonic poems do sometimes relate it to one.

The second element of musical narrative mentioned above – the narrative mode of understanding, or narrative activity, on the part of the listener – is stimulated by the challenge involved in patterning events into a series which is coherent and comprehensible as an intentional human action.[9] The series might well outline some archetypal plot, but this plot need not be fleshed out with specific details.[10]

---

6   Quoted from Franz Liszt, *Frederic Chopin*, trans. Edward N. Waters (New York 1963), pp. 62–3. Some twenty-five years later, a Liszt more accustomed to dealing with unconventional series of musical events recanted his judgement in a letter of 1 January 1876 to Carolyne Sayn-Wittgenstein: 'En 1849, je ne comprenais pas encore l'intime beauté des dernières œuvres de Chopin: Polonaise-Fantaisie, Barcarole – et gardais quelque réserve à l'endroit de leur ton maladif. Maintenant je les admire tout à fait – nonobstant la pédanterie de quelques critiques de courte ouïe qui les méconnaît.' *Franz Liszt's Briefe*, ed. La Mara (Leipzig 1893–1902), vol. VII, pp. 122–3.

7   The music critic of the *New York Times*, Edward Rothstein, writing about even as severe a musician as Elliott Carter, observes, 'Mr. Carter, I believe, writes . . . music with a plot. But the quartets, instead of being pictorial or imagistic, are plays, dramatic narratives constructed of dialogue and gesture.' (*New York Times* (27 October 1991), 'Arts and Leisure', p. 25.)

8   Carl Schachter, 'Chopin's Fantasy Op. 49: The Two-Key Scheme', in *Chopin Studies*, ed. Jim Samson (Cambridge 1988), p. 253. Schachter gives no specific example of how he might develop such an interpretation.

9   Again, I use 'intentional' in Donald Davidson's sense (see note 2 above): namely, whenever a person sets out to do something, that act is intentional, as opposed to, say, natural or accidental acts. To take musical examples, the rhythms of multiple cicadas on a hot summer day or the periodicity produced by a scratch on a record are natural or accidental, not intentional musical acts.

10   I have explored this distinctive aspect of musical narrative in 'Narrative Archetypes and Mahler's Ninth Symphony', in *Music and Text: Critical Inquiries*, ed. Steven Paul Scher (Cambridge 1992), pp. 118–36.

Chopin's larger forms are a particularly fortunate locus for the examination of the first element of narrative – the internal musical stimuli to narrative understanding – since Chopin, unlike many of his colleagues in the 1830s and 1840s, seems studiously to have avoided adding referential verbal elements to his musical narratives. His music thus discourages the listener's dependence on verbal/visual analogues, of which the music might then be understood as a secondary 'translation'. In fact, the opposite is true: the verbal/visual is a translation, via metaphor, of the musical characteristics of the musical series of events – which is not to say that such translations are not valuable. Though they are secondary, not primary, sources, they are a necessary and valuable means of commenting on and communicating about music as a part of culture.[11]

A heightened degree of narrative activity on the part of the listener – my second element in musical narrative, and an important component of narrative for Bruner, Ricoeur or a literary theorist such as Todorov – is stimulated by *a heightened sense of contingency* within the series of events itself, a greater uncertainty about where one is in what kind of series of events, about what will happen next.[12] 'How will this turn out?', one verbal formulation of what I mean, is itself a strange locution embodying in the phrase 'turn out' (or 'detour'; compare the French '*détour, détournement de route*') the idea of unpredictability and deviation. To arouse one's narrative interest and sensibilities, a story must be in some way unpredictable, must pose some conundrum.[13]

Chopin's Polonaise-Fantasy is constantly making detours. This is but the first of several *internal musical aspects* (the components of my first element of musical narrative above) which give the piece its strongly narrative quality or flavour. This first is the aspect of *formal segmentation* and *formal function of the segments* in the Polonaise-Fantasy, which offers puzzles that have baffled analysts since Leichtentritt attempted a formal segmentation of the piece in 1921.[14] A second such aspect is the rich patterning of *thematic transformation, interrelation and derivation* that stretches across the piece.[15] A

11 I have tried to make this point most particularly in 'Sound and Feeling', *Critical Inquiry*, 10/4 (1984), pp. 614–43.
12 One can, of course, carry this too far, as Chopin seems to have done for the Liszt of ca 1850, causing the listener to lose interest and turn away. An early review of the Polonaise-Fantasy in the *Allgemeine musikalische Zeitung* (49/7 (1847), cols. 115–16) makes a similar objection: 'Mancher wird nach zwei Seiten dieser Polonaise muthlos weglassen . . . Der Gedanke, den [Chopin] hinwirft, ist fast immer glücklich, warum verschmäht er nun so schwer sein feste Gestaltung, besonnene Entwicklung?' The review is signed A. K., whom I take to be Adolph Kullak, then a twenty-three-year-old pupil of A. B. Marx and later the author of the influential *Aesthetik des Klavierspiels* (Berlin 1861).
13 See Bruner, 'Narrative Construction', pp. 11–13 and Tzvetan Todorov, *The Poetics of Prose*, trans. Richard Howard (Ithaca 1977), esp. 'Structure of Narrative', pp. 130–7. Thus for Bruner and Todorov, eternally repeating series – rituals, liturgies, myths – do not stimulate the narrative activity. They progress by ritual logic rather than narrative logic (Todorov, p. 132). Samson makes a similar point concerning music in *Chopin: The Four Ballades*, p. 84.
14 Hugo Leichtentritt, *Analyse der Chopin'schen Klavierwerke*, 2 vols. (Berlin 1921–2), vol. I, pp. 110–21. See also Gerald Abraham, *Chopin's Musical Style* (London 1939), pp. 106–7; Tarasti, 'Pour une narratologie'; and Cook, *A Guide to Musical Analysis*.
15 This musical aspect is the principal locus of another important characteristic of series of events which have what I call a narrative flavour. Not all series have this flavour. Narrative series are transformational series, as opposed to circular, static or highly symmetrical series. Elements in narrative series emerge at the end recognisable but changed. See Todorov, 'Narrative Transformations', in *Poetics of Prose*, esp.

third such aspect involves the various *generic and formal signals* transmitted at different moments in the piece, which evoke the moods, cultural worlds and implied continuations associated with these generic and formal types. A fourth aspect is the rather *directly referential sounds* of the bardic opening of the piece, a feature which brings the Polonaise-Fantasy closer to the ballades than to any of Chopin's other works.

I am by no means the first to emphasise the matter of formal hybridisation, mixed generic signals and thematic transformation in the Polonaise-Fantasy,[16] but my method of trying to interpret the formal conundrums, conflicting generic signals and thematic interrelations that present themselves as the piece unfolds is distinct from conventional formal analysis. Formally, for example, what is essential in my view is not deciding *what* something is – what label to give it, where the sectional boundary falls – but interpreting the meaning of *how* a particular thing becomes or replaces another particular thing. Essential and distinctive, in other words, is not the assigning of a generic label to a given event (slower central section, closing section, transition, V^7 chord, structural downbeat) in order to locate it at a higher level of abstraction, but rather the use of such higher-level abstractions to interpret the character and meaning of the particular individual occurrence as a human action. The musical detours, ambiguities and challenges-to-sense that invite this interpretative activity constitute the first element – the internal musical element – of what I mean by musical narrativity. These detours, ambiguities and challenges are then complemented by the second element, contributed by the individual listener, to produce the narrative itself, which, as I have stated, may vary widely according to the listener, the listening occasion and the cultural context.

As I locate these detours and ambiguities in the music and propose interpretations of them, I am interested in what some theorists of narrative call breach of canonicity. 'To be worth telling, a tale must be about how an implicit canonical script has been breached, violated, or deviated from in a manner to do violence to what Hayden White calls the "legitimacy" of the canonical script.'[17] The canonical script into which the

---

pp. 230–3, and my article (cited above) on Mahler's Ninth Symphony. Lewis Rowell's 'Stasis in Music' (*Semiotica*, 66 (1987), pp. 181–95) in effect explores the various ways of frustrating narrative transformation in music.

Many readers will associate thematic transformation with Rudolf Réti and his followers; in published analyses of the Polonaise-Fantasy this approach is particularly evident in Paul Hamburger, 'Mazurkas, Waltzes, Polonaises', in *Frédéric Chopin: Profiles of the Man and the Musician*, ed. Alan Walker (London 1966), pp. 73–113. But most analysts who follow this path (what German analysts call *Substanzgemeinschaft*) tend not to focus on how the connections or transformations are presented to us as the piece unfolds in time or on the order in which the various transformations appear. Their concern is not with a diachronic narrative unfolding, but with a demonstration of synchronic unity.

[16] Leichtentritt (*Analyse*, vol. I, p. 110) groups the work with the Fantasy Op. 49, the Barcarolle Op. 60 and the Cello Sonata Op. 65 in its 'tendency to the dissolution of firmly outlined form' (my translation). He remarks that 'it is difficult to find a simple schema [*einfache Formel*] for the overall shape [*Gestaltung*] of the piece'. See also Zofia Lissa, 'Die Formenkreuzung bei Chopin', in *The Book of the First International Musicological Congress Devoted to the Works of Frederick Chopin*, ed. Zofia Lissa (Warsaw 1963), pp. 207–12.

[17] Bruner, 'Narrative Construction', p. 11, citing Hayden White, 'The Value of Narrativity in the Representations of Reality', *Critical Inquiry*, 7 (1980), pp. 5–28 (repr. in *On Narrative*, ed. W. J. T. Mitchell (Chicago 1981), pp. 1–23). Examples of canonical scripts adduced by Bruner include: boy woos girl, bully gets his comeuppance (p. 6), the betrayed wife, the fleeced innocent (p. 12). See also Todorov's *Poetics of Prose* for another version of the same assertion.

listener, following subtle generic and stylistic signs, fits the action places some limits on what is permissible in that kind of action. The breaches challenge the listener's ability to bring this succession into harmony with these limits in order to produce what I have called a 'coherent' series, which means one whose parts can be accommodated to this whole. Bruner calls this last 'hermeneutic composability', locating it, together with 'breach of canonicity', as one of the primary features of narrative: 'the best hope of hermeneutic analysis is to provide an intuitively convincing account of the meaning of the text as a whole in the light of the constituent parts that make it up.'[18]

I will propose an account which locates the meaning of the Polonaise-Fantasy in a shifting series of 'canonical scripts', whose transformation across time is conveyed to the listener by what I call 'functional puns' – that is, by a phrase or passage whose function as part of a series we thought would be one thing as we entered it, but whose function as the section continues turns out to be another.[19] The result threatens the stability of the canonical script, and may even cause one radically to readjust one's interpretation of the function of everything one has heard so far and to project anew the various possibilities of what might subsequently happen.

Let me return now to my opening question: why the Polonaise-Fantasy? Of the four internal musical aspects suggesting narrative interpretation that I listed above, the last – direct reference to the extra-musical world via imitation of sounds – is both the simplest and the one with the highest degree of semantic content. No other piece by Chopin opens with such mysterious, mist-shrouded strumming as Op. 61.[20] The closest to the Polonaise-Fantasy in its evocation of bardic fingers wandering across the strings of harp or lyre is the opening of the G minor Ballade.[21] But the strumming opening of the Polonaise-Fantasy is longer, wider in range and more harmonically labyrinthine than that of the Ballade. In this last sense it embodies one internal musical means of stimulating the narrative activity on the listener's part: the gradual emergence of coherence and pattern from a sense-challenging series of events, the first of the musical aspects listed above.

But what interests me at the moment about this opening involves the third of the musical aspects outlined above, in this case the fairly straightforward generic reference to the literary ballad. The importance of this literary genre for the early nineteenth century – in both its purely verbal forms and its musical settings – is traced in James

---

[18]   Bruner, 'Narrative Construction', p. 7.

[19]   I explore this aspect of musical narrative most thoroughly in 'Schumann and Late Eighteenth-Century Narrative Strategies', *19th-Century Music*, 11/2 (1987), pp. 164–74. My initial stimulus to this kind of thought was Frank Kermode's *The Sense of an Ending* (Oxford 1966).

[20]   A large, preludial introduction can also be found in the A♭ Polonaise Op. 53 (bars 1–16), but it is fanfare-like, militant and affirmative, not bardic and meditative.

   Incidentally, I note, without pretending to understand them, the strange discrepancies between the tempo markings of the introduction to the Polonaise-Fantasy in the sketch (Lento) and in the auto-graph (All[egr]o Maestoso), and between the latter and the tempos taken in most performances.

[21]   Carl Dahlhaus writes: 'The opening of Chopin's G-minor Ballade . . . was immediately recognizable as a musical rendering of a "narrative posture".' According to Arthur Hedley, 'the legendary atmosphere [of Op. 23] is created in the first bars: it is as though the bard were collecting his thoughts and hesitating before beginning his tale'. Dahlhaus, *Nineteenth-Century Music*, trans. J. Bradford Robinson (Berkeley 1989), p. 105; Hedley, *Chopin* (London 1963), p. 173.

Parakilas's recent book.[22] One of the characteristic elements of the literary ballad was the narrative frame given by an introductory and closing stanza or stanzas delivered by the narrator (for example, in Goethe's 'Erlkönig'). The opening of the Polonaise-Fantasy gives one not only the image of the bard's preludial strumming as the singer/improviser descends into his material, but also a formal framing gesture for the piece itself. I hear this framing gesture as being taken up in true balladic fashion at the end of the Polonaise-Fantasy as well. The last seven bars of the piece return not only to the quiet and slow motion of the opening but to the same descending aeolian tetrachord (Ab–Gb–Fb–Eb) that, in more elaborated form, had structured the opening of the piece. These bars have the flavour of a narrator/singer's emerging from the turbulent story and looking back on it with reflective distance: 'thus went the story of . . .'[23]

In addition to the striking of an explicitly narrative posture in the opening of the Polonaise-Fantasy, with its concomitant reference to a literary genre, I would posit that this opening also sends out *musical-generic signals* which say 'musical ballade'. Chopin's ballades, then as now, have been the touchstone for considering textless instrumental music as narrative. Indeed, some of the formulations closest to my own views of what musical narrative entails come from studies of Chopin's ballades.[24] In the instance of the Polonaise-Fantasy, I hear Chopin as conveying strong musical signals towards narrative interpretation with his balladic opening.

Yet the Polonaise-Fantasy is not called Ballade. Chopin's indecision about what to name the piece is recounted by Kallberg[25] in a study defining the generic characteristics of polonaise and fantasy in the previous polonaises and the Fantasy Op. 49 of Chopin and in the works of his predecessors. Common to the two genres were a lengthy motivic introduction and a slower central section. As Kallberg also points out, Op. 49's sections, including the slower middle section, are relatively closed, self-contained and tonally stable within themselves. The same cannot be said for the sections of the Polonaise-Fantasy, where instability has penetrated much more deeply into the structure, thus adding to what I would call the internally musical narrative element in the work, according to the first of the aspects listed above.

Not all slow introductions evoke 'ballade'. To compare the motivic introductions of Op. 49 and Op. 61, moreover, is to realise that the ballade-like elements – ruminative

22   *Ballads without Words*, esp. chapters 1 and 2.
23   The recurrence of this narrator/singer's voice in the centre of the piece raises issues of narrative meaning to which I shall return in discussing the unfolding of the events themselves.
     I note upon reading Leichtentritt's study of Op. 61 (*Analyse*, vol. I, pp. 110–21) that my interpretation of the opening and closing bars has a unique ancestor. He calls the introduction 'romantische, aeolsharfenmäßige' (p. 112), and characterises the 'shadowy harmonies [*dämmerigen Harmonien*]' of the closing bars as 'suggesting Irish, Scandinavian old folksongs' (p. 120; my translation).
24   For example, see Samson, *Chopin: The Four Ballades*, pp. 12–18 and 81–7, although I obviously do not agree that narrative can occur only when there exists a narrator's voice separable from that of individual agents or characters and from that of the implied author. See also Parakilas, *Ballads without Words*: '[Chopin's] method was to chart the unfolding [of a story] rather than to depict what is unfolded; it was to represent the story as a structure of utterances' (p. 56). 'He would thus be representing what was most universal in the ballad theme rather than what was peculiar, and perhaps incidental, to a single ballad story' (p. 39).
25   In a letter to his family of 12–26 December 1845 Chopin wrote, 'Now I would like to finish the Sonata for violoncello, the Barcarolle, and something else that I do not know how to name'; quoted in Kallberg, 'Chopin's Last Style', p. 267.

bardic strumming descending gradually into the material of the tale – that I have attributed to the introduction of the Polonaise-Fantasy are quite absent from that of Op. 49, which is march-like, metrically regular and well structured, much more tuneful than that of Op. 61, and firmly closed (at bars 36–43[1]). What the openings of the two pieces do share, incidentally, is the descending aeolian tetrachord, which returns in transformed fashion at the end of both pieces as a kind of framing device. Once again, the difference between the two outward forms that this structural device takes in the two pieces is symptomatic: directly stated in pitches, metrically and tonally clearly situated in Op. 49; melodically stretched out and camouflaged, almost non-pulsatile, harmonically/tonally riddling, and flowing gradually into and out of the main thematic material in the Polonaise-Fantasy. This blurring of boundaries and formal functions arouses one's sense of narrative contingency and stimulates questions about coherence, pattern and direction: 'what kind of event is this, where are its boundaries, of what kind of series might it form part?' This is the first and most important internal musical aspect suggesting narrative interpretation, and I shall return to it shortly, after mentioning a few more of the generic signals conveyed by the piece.

In his analysis of the sketches and drafts for the Polonaise-Fantasy, Kallberg points out that 'nowhere in any original layer in the sketches does the characteristic polonaise rhythmic figure occur; its rare appearances are always as additions or revisions to first thoughts'.[26] This and the near disappearance of the polonaise rhythm from the piece after the initial thematic exposition strongly suggest to me that the generic reference to the polonaise was added less for reasons intrinsic to the overall series of events (what music analysts call the formal design) in the piece than for extrinsic/ referential reasons – that is, to contribute to character or setting, if I may return to the metaphor based in verbal/visual narrative. Several generic types offered the ternary design with slower central section that is one of the formal backgrounds to the Polonaise-Fantasy. Only the polonaise offered the referential element of national pride and perhaps the triumphant military attitude that Chopin had introduced into Op. 40 No. 1 and Op. 53 in particular. This element is part of the meaning of the final outcome of the piece as I interpret it.

The slower central section of the Polonaise-Fantasy (*poco più lento*) has been characterised generically by both Tarasti and Kallberg as nocturne-like.[27] Kallberg in separate studies has thoroughly developed the generic associations of the nocturne, and these generic associations contribute to what I interpret as the narrative of the Polonaise-Fantasy.[28] Even more important for this narrative is the atypicality of bars 152–213 as a nocturne. This atypicality resides in the particular nature of the succession of the superficially nocturne-like musical events, and it extends to the material that surrounds this slower central section. It also leads directly back to my first aspect of musical narrative as listed above – *formal segmentation and function* – which is where the heart of the matter lies, in the Polonaise-Fantasy as in most other pieces.

---

[26] Kallberg, 'Chopin's Last Style', p. 282.
[27] 'Pour une narratologie' and 'Chopin's Last Style'.
[28] Jeffrey Kallberg, 'The Rhetoric of Genre: Chopin's Nocturne in G minor', *19th-Century Music*, 11 (1988), pp. 238–61 and 'The Harmony of the Tea Table: Gender and Ideology in the Piano Nocturne', *Representations*, no. 39 (1992), pp. 102–33.

Put in the most general terms, the formal conundrum is this. While in an important sense the kernel of the formal schema of the Polonaise-Fantasy is the ABA ternary form typical of Chopin's larger polonaises (and of many other small and large piano pieces from the nineteenth century), both the way the central section is introduced and proceeds and the way the reprise happens are not proper for a ternary form. The manner in which the entire series of musical events is handled destabilises one's sense that a symmetrical and stable ABA schema is governing the series. This brings the attentive listener, as the piece unfolds, to ask repeatedly where he or she is in what kind of series and how it will continue. This is the first and most basic question to arise once the narrative mode of understanding has been stimulated.

Before considering the central section itself, I want to approach it as it is approached in the piece, tracing this series of musical events as I understand them. This will also allow me to present some aspects of yet another formal/generic principle operating at times in the rich hybrid of the Polonaise-Fantasy: the sonata form. To do this I want to go as far back in the piece as the presentation of the first distinct thematic unit (Theme A) in bars 24ff., and to begin to trace the unfolding of the musical happening.

First we hear the initial statement of the four-bar phrase and its sequential restatement up a step. After this, the register of the piece expands and the harmonic and rhythmic activity picks up, towards what would seem to be a climactic pair of four-bar phrases rounding off the initial thematic statement with a cadence to the tonic.[29] But no such thing happens. At bar 34 the phrase bumps up against a premature, weak cadence of sorts after only three bars, the tune disintegrates into motivic fragments and the tonality is deflected momentarily to C minor, then F minor (bars 36–41). As a result the initial thematic statement is left without its closure and its customary local structural solidity. (Compare the four solid four-bar phrases of the main theme in Op. 53.) In my interpretation, this initial destabilisation and ensuing opening towards F minor are a first stimulus to narrative understanding and a premonition of events later in the tale. We have here, if you like, an initial and subtle breach of canonicity, which comes at a crucial structural moment – the first statement of the main thematic material. Then, for the time being, equilibrium is regained with the return of the initial theme and its sequential restatement (bars 44ff.), now over a dominant pedal and introducing a prolongation of V which lasts until the emphatic cadence on the tonic at bars 64–6.

What happens subsequently is the first big formal pun of the piece. Analysts since Leichtentritt (1921) and Abraham (1939) have simply labelled this Theme or Section B without further comment. But what happens here is not a theme: it is at best a brief bit of motivic figuration, derived from what I call the 'active' cell of the main theme.[30] (See Example 6.1.)

---

[29] One might imagine bar 34 as a dominant harmony, with the motivic sequence of bars 32–3 continuing through that bar to an evaded cadence on bar 35, followed perhaps by a varied repetition of the phrase to a firm tonic cadence four bars later.

[30] My division of the theme into two parts – a 'static' and an 'active' cell – is a variation on the division pointed out by Tarasti ('Pour une narratologie', pp. 64–5). The 'static' cell is the strange vacillation between B♭ and C in bars 24–5².

Example 6.1   Chopin Op. 61: thematic-motivic interrelations

Most distinctively, the section liquidates harmonic and rhythmic energy by repeating the same one-bar motivic unit over V–I cadences (bars 67–71). What does this sound like as it happens? To my ears, it is an unmistakable closing gesture, although it is not clear to what[31] – we might initially think to the A section of a ternary form. What we hear next, however, is not a clearly contrasting B section but one which sounds like a sonata-form development, with modulatory sequencing of motivic material, derived (as shown in Example 6.1) from the opening theme via its variant as closing theme (bars 72–93).[32] As we proceed into this section, the cadential figuration of bars 66–71 – in its local context at least, if not within an overall tonal scheme – sounds as if it functioned as a closing section of a sonata exposition. Perhaps, then, some sonata-like series is implied by the process of unfolding.

The arrival of a variant of Theme A in bars 94ff. reinforces rather than contradicts this interpretation. The whole section following bar 66 might so far be understood as proceeding along the lines of the sonata-like developmental procedures of the

Two fragments, bars 25³–7¹ and 66–72, appear side by side on an independent sketch sheet (KK 816), possibly suggesting that this related pair was the germinal idea for the piece. This may also imply that at the time of this initial conception Chopin had thought of firm closure to an A section and a more conventional ternary form. For reference to and brief description of this sketch sheet, see Kallberg, 'Chopin's Last Style', Table 1 (pp. 280–1, no. 18 in the manuscript numeration). Kallberg is unable to date the sketch sheet precisely by means of paper type (see Table 2, p. 306). Incidentally, Kallberg informs me in a personal communication that his Table 1 incorrectly states that the sketch sheet contains bars 24–5 (as well as 66–72): it should read bars 25–7 as I have it above, what I call the 'active' cell of the main theme. I have not seen this sheet, which, in contrast to other sketch material for Op. 61, is not reproduced in *The Worksheets to Chopin's Violoncello Sonata*, ed. Ferdinand Gajewski (New York 1988).

31   Similar gestures with analogous closing functions (in different kinds of forms) occur in, for example, the Barcarolle, bars 15–16; the F minor Ballade, bars 121–5; and the E major Nocturne Op. 62 No. 2, bars 32ff. The main difference between the positioning of this section in Op. 61 and that in the F minor Ballade (of the three, the closest to Op. 61 in scope and style) is that in the latter it comes at the end of a full three-key exposition, while in Op. 61 there has been as yet no other theme or key.

32   Here again, as at bars 38–41, the initial deflection away from A♭ is towards F minor via its dominant (bars 72–9).

A♭ major or F minor Ballades. The thematic versions of bars 94–115 gain in rhythmic and harmonic intensity, just as Parakilas points out that they tend to do in the largely uni-directional mounting towards climax and release of Chopin's ballade form.[33]

At this point comes one of the least striking (when it happens) and most puzzling (as one tries to interpret it in retrospect) of the functional puns of the piece. The passage that begins at bar 116 follows smoothly out of this developmental section with scarcely a hint of articulation, as Kallberg points out.[34] Diastematically the phrase of bars 116–19 traces the same outline as the two four-bar phrases of the main theme directly preceding, while continuing their stepwise rising sequence. (See the circled notes in Example 6.2.) Harmonically, its opening bars are, like theirs, a prolongation of the local dominant (of B♭ major). Thus it is introduced as a subtle variation of the main theme.

But other changes start at this point to alter the direction and function of the developmental section begun in bar 72. The textural agitation of bars 94–115 is subtly pulled back, as the range becomes narrower and more centred and the rhythmic activity slower. And the second four-bar phrase of the new section (bars 120ff.) is considerably different from the sequential continuation in the second phrase of the main theme, thus pulling away further from the original material. The following bars continue the progressive disintegration of the thematic material into the figurational material of what Jim Samson calls the brilliant style. By bar 128 we are in what is clearly a new and transitional section.[35]

One would in fact be tempted to understand all of bars 116–51 simply as a transition, were it not for the fact that, for me as for most interpreters of the piece, the initial material of the section returns twice as an independent (albeit varied) thematic unit later in the work, thus seeming to signal that it was not just a transitional stage in the developmental disintegration of the main theme but a functional thematic unit in its own right. This section and its recurrences become the primary functional riddle of the piece, challenging one's understanding of where one is in what kind of series of events. In a purely formal and thematic sense – the first two internal musical aspects of narrativity to which I referred above – it is an important factor in giving the piece its narrative flavour.[36]

---

[33]   Parakilas, *Ballads without Words*, chapter 3. In support of this uni-directional mounting towards a climax across this section, I might also point out the more active figuration of the left hand in bars 94ff., the omitting of the 'static' opening thematic cell in bar 98, the canonic complexity of 105ff., and the harmonic intensity and convoluted left-hand figuration (and *agitato* marking) of 108ff. I cannot hear this last phrase as a move towards closure in A♭ as does Kallberg ('Chopin's Last Style', pp. 291–3), both because of this agitation and increasing complexity and because the A♭ minor statement of the main theme is the first of what is always (as here) a sequential pair, moving away from the tonic rather than closing on and affirming it.

[34]   'Chopin gave no clue that the shift to a new section would occur: he avoided tonic closure and dropped no other hints that a formal divide was imminent. The earlier procedure [i.e. Chopin's earlier style] would highlight the section break either through harmonic closure or by an alteration of tempo, dynamics, or texture.' ('Chopin's Last Style', p. 293.)

[35]   See Samson, 'The Composition-Draft', pp. 41–58, esp. 56–8.

[36]   Bars 116ff. have also proved something of a riddle in the generic sense, and hence in my third musical aspect, the vague sort of referentiality connected with genres. Leichtentritt and Abraham simply give the section a letter without comment (Theme C); Samson calls it the 'first nocturne' ('The Composition-

Example 6.2   Chopin Op. 61: thematic-motivic interrelations

The formal function and even the generic implications of bars 152ff. would seem to be much clearer. Here we have the middle section of a large-scale ABA piece, like the middle sections of Op. 40 No. 2 or Op. 44, of the Fantasy Op. 49, or of the E major Scherzo Op. 54. Kallberg characterises the function of these slower central sections as forming an anchor of stability and repose in the centre of more agitated pieces. One might also speculate (with Kallberg) that the nocturne as a genre conveyed subtle signals of 'femininity' and all that the nineteenth century associated with the feminine, including gentleness, passivity, stability and the home.[37]

Here again, however, formal function and generic implication are belied by succeeding events. Although rhythmically, metrically and texturally placid, the section is

Draft', p. 52); Tarasti ('Pour une narratologie', pp. 67–8) calls it a mazurka, perhaps because it accents the second beat of the bar and is faster and rhythmically less placid than 151ff., which most generic labellers call a nocturne; Kallberg, a particular student of both the nocturne and the mazurka as genres, abstains.

[37]   See Kallberg, 'Chopin's Last Style', p. 271; 'The Rhetoric of Genre', p. 246; and (especially) 'The Harmony of the Tea Table', passim.

harmonically and tonally radically unstable: a sixteen-bar period modulating from B major to 'B♭' (literally A♯) major and back again. The semitone between leading note and tonic acquires a deeply unsettling instability, always threatening to slide down rather than push up. The modulation from 'B♭' back to B (bar 167) is forced and non-functional, and involves a wrenching set of thinly camouflaged parallel fifths. The section as a whole (bars 152–81) never finds a firm closing cadence in its supposed tonic, but evaporates through chromatically downward-sliding secondary dominants. This 'breach of canonicity', more than any other so far, challenges conventional interpretation and stimulates narrative interpretation. There is no repose and discharge of tension here. Why should the music behave like this? The section is like the centre of a storm, filled with inappropriately troubling behaviour and tense, whispered oppositions.

What happens next is a transformed return of the material of bars 116ff.[38] Thematic material in this piece customarily returns in continually evolving transformations – the second of my internal musical aspects suggesting musical narrativity. No thematic section in Op. 61 is repeated literally. In bars 182ff., the defining characteristics that make clear the connection with bars 116ff. are those that set the material apart when it first appeared: mainly texture and rhythm. The diastematic contours that had joined bars 116ff. to the main theme are cast aside in bars 182ff. (although a subtle melodic link to the 'active' kernel of the main theme still remains in the flourish at the beginning of the second bar of each subunit, especially bar 185). Kallberg ('Chopin's Last Style', p. 266) draws attention to Chopin's use of elements other than pitch as form-defining elements in his late music (or, I would say, as elements making formal interconnections, since I see 'defining' as too strong a word, given my argument concerning formal ambiguity). The formal interconnection between bars 116ff. and 182ff. is a striking example of this innovative technique.

Even if the listener accepts this connection, the question remains, where is he or she in what sequence of events? Has the end of a relatively small (compare the Fantasy Op. 49) and very unstable central section been reached? Or is the middle subsection of a larger, slow central section (the b section of an aba-shaped B section) just beginning? As the piece unfolds, the material dissolves, as it did before, into transitional, modulating figuration (bars 193ff.).[39] But instead of pursuing the transitional path of the previous analogous section (bars 124ff.) from main section to slower central section, the section coalesces on the dominant of B major and the extraordinarily effortful (to my ears at least) succession of double, triple, then quadruple trills that finally leads to a cadence in B major and tonic closure for the slower central section of the piece.

---

[38] Here I part company with Kallberg, who is at pains to deny the relationship between the two passages ('Chopin's Last Style', pp. 294–5 n. 34), principally, I think, because he feels that it threatens his argument of asymmetry and lack of clear articulation in the sectional joints of a large ternary form. As is clear from my ensuing discussion, I do not believe that to hear a transformational identity between these passages does threaten that argument.

[39] Samson ('The Composition-Draft', pp. 53–7) studies the sketches for this transition as the locus of the changing tonal conception of the piece. Might it also be a changing formal conception? Certainly the 'return' of the B major 'nocturne' material in bars 206ff. is formally unusual – not really a return at all, but a struggle for a cadence. Again, most commentators have simply subsumed this as part of the section beginning in bar 182, or have called it a return of the material of 151ff., without comment on the effect of its happening this way in this series of events.

As I have said, this moment is not, as some formal parsings of the piece would have it, a return of the opening material of the slow central section, but only a cadence to the section, accompanied by its initial rolling left-hand figuration. And the tonal instability of the original material remains unresolved as well: in the trills themselves with their wavering around the notes of the tonic chord, in the alto's A♯–B motion in the cadential chords at bars 209 and 212, and in the pronounced iii⁶–I progressions that go with these chords.[40] The sense of effort and instability remains.

This moment of seemingly exhausted, and at best inconclusive, stasis is succeeded by the bardic strumming from the beginning of the piece, but with this important difference: here the strumming enters *pp* instead of *f*, as at the beginning. As will be clear by now, I am not concerned here with the tonal function of this return of the introduction – this has been well and thoroughly discussed, by Kallberg, Samson and Rink in particular – or even with its formal segmentation, a subject of no disagreement from Leichtentritt through Samson. I am concerned with what it might mean in the overall narrative of the piece – in other words, why this gesture happens here and in this way.[41]

I might, atypically, be tempted to a semantic interpretation, somewhat in Tarasti's mode. Is this moment in the unfolding piece a voice heard *wie aus der Ferne* (as in Schumann or Mahler), which gains strength as it grows to *forte* in the second iteration? Following the parallels to literary ballads suggested by Parakilas, one might also understand the appearance of the introductory narrator's voice at this point in the same terms as those interruptions in the dialogue of the protagonists in a number of early-nineteenth-century poetic ballads – as a sign of peripety, or a change in the course of the action, and of the passage of time.[42]

This change in the course of action and this possible passage of time bring us once more to the material of bars 116ff. and 182ff. – the material that I have proposed as the primary functional riddle of the piece. Once more the material dissolves into transitional figuration, but not before it has moved strongly towards a return to A♭ major. (By the model of the previous occurrence (bar 187), the D♭ chord of bar 221 would be a subdominant of A♭.) The deflection here also reinvokes, to my understanding, the two previous deflections to F minor of the main A♭ major material (bars 38–41 and 72–9) and, as in those occurrences, starts to lead back to that main material.

---

40 The internal instability of the section, and hence its meaning in the overall series of events, is largely the same whether it is in B major or the original C major. I find some support for the view that this overall series was of primary importance to Chopin as he drafted the piece, in that the series itself did not change even though the tonal placement of the introduction and the middle section did.

41 One of the several similarities between Op. 61 and Op. 52 is that Chopin uses a return to the introductory material in a foreign key to unleash the sequential mechanism that will bring the piece back to the original key. In Op. 52, however, the return is much less strongly articulated, because of the similarity of the introductory passage to what follows the closing material of bars 121–4. Another difference arises as the return leads soon after to a reprise of the successive themes of the 'exposition' of the piece (bars 135ff.), followed by a fiery cabaletta/coda (bars 211ff.) which is separate from the thematic reprise (as in the first Ballade). In Op. 61, by contrast, the return of the introductory gesture is highly dramatised, comes at a moment of stasis and loss of direction, and does not lead directly to a reprise but to interrupted gestures towards one, culminating in a section which is both thematic reprise and fiery coda. This gives a wholly different meaning to the return of the introduction in the series of events.

42 See, for example, lines 149–74 of 'The Lilies' of Adam Mickiewicz, trans. Dorothea Prall Radin in *Poems by Adam Mickiewicz*, ed. George Rapall Noyes (New York 1944), p. 83.

There is a strong suggestion of reprise/return in all of this. But that suggestion is once again muted or deflected, this time by what is to me the principal narrative and compositional puzzle of the entire piece: the figurational transition of bars 226–41. Most commentators have been content to label this section 'transition' or perhaps to assign it a letter, and then to pass on without additional comment. Here Bruner's criterion of particularity in the narrative mode of understanding is especially relevant.[43] What is crucial is not only the abstract function of a passage in the series of events, but also how the function is carried out in the particular instance.

Nicholas Cook is, to my knowledge, the only analyst to call attention to the curious nature of this passage.[44] One way of hearing and performing this part of the piece is, he points out, as 'an unconvincing transition to the return of the main tune', after which 'the work ends in an orgy of tub-thumping rhetoric'. The main problem, as he sees it, is 'where does the B♭ at bar 242 come from? It seems completely unprepared both tonally and registrally; and the effect of all this will be that the whole "transition" passage is played in a hurried, breathless manner, with the return of the main tune and key at bar 242 being blurted out without any warning.' Cook's solution is to propose that the B♮ of bar 226 becomes the C♭ of the D♭ seventh chord in bars 227–8, which acts as a IV$^{♭7}$ in A♭ major and leads to the structural V of bar 242.

This is not, however, the way in which the D♭ seventh chord arrives or proceeds. As it is introduced (bar 226), it implies an augmented sixth chord in the local tonic of F minor. But it subsequently leads by expansion outward (bars 230–1, D♭ to D, F to F♭) to an inverted E^7 chord, which could in turn function as an augmented sixth harmony in A♭ major.[45] So far so good: the F minor/A♭ nexus is home base for the piece. This then is changed, by moving the E back to F, into a diminished seventh chord initially with a dominant function in C major (bar 234), this diminished seventh chord returning in bar 236 after a sequence, to be prolonged for two more bars (236–7).

This chord could potentially be made to function as V/V in A♭ major, giving at least a moderately strong preparation for the dominant arrival in bar 242. But the sudden scales of bars 238–41 challenge this interpretation. They seem to outline a chordal shift between the E♭–G–B♭–D♭ seventh chord and the F♭–G–B♭–D♭ diminished seventh chord – a very strange approach to an emphatic arrival on an E♭ dominant seventh chord, since the function and most of the pitches of that chord are already present in the implied chord of the preparatory scales, removing almost all sense of harmonic arrival at bar 242. Cook produces a voice-leading graph for the whole piece which incorporates his above-stated view of the transition (p. 340), but he admits (p. 342) that 'it is very difficult to produce convincing foreground graphs linking the middleground of [his graph] with the actual music Chopin wrote'. How are we to understand this reprise and its preparation?

Edward Cone has characterised the reprises in Chopin's late large forms as 'apotheoses',[46] and those of, for example, the F minor Ballade or the Barcarolle are convincing

---

[43]   See Bruner, 'Narrative Construction', pp. 6–7.
[44]   *A Guide to Musical Analysis*, pp. 339–41. Herbert Weinstock (*Chopin* (New York 1949), quoted in Hamburger, 'Mazurkas', p. 112) objects to it as 'fragmentary'.
[45]   As it could also have done at what I hear as a harmonically similar moment in bars 88–91.
[46]   *Musical Form and Musical Performance* (New York 1968), pp. 83–4.

as such. In them the thematic return lives up to the structural weight placed upon it because of several factors, among them harmonic intensification, thematic combination, contrapuntal/textural enrichment, and emphatic harmonic and linear preparation. In the Polonaise-Fantasy, however, not only are the first two present in small measure, but it should be clear from the preceding discussion that harmonic and linear preparation is virtually nil. (Compare the similar conflation of thematic and tonal return, also to A♭ major, in bars 183–212 of the Ballade Op. 47, where the harmonic and linear preparation, especially the long chromatic move from B up to E♭ in the bass, is extensive and emphatic.)

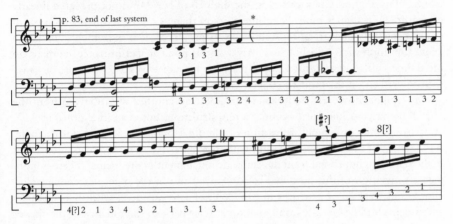

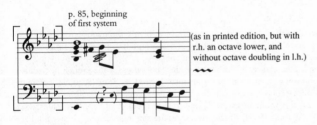

*Very faint sketching continues in the bracketed area of the upper staff, apparently experimentation with figuration.

Example 6.3   Chopin Op. 61: draft of bars 238–42. Transcribed from *The Worksheets to Chopin's Violoncello Sonata*, ed. Ferdinand Gajewski (New York 1988).

One aspect of the puzzle here is that Chopin in his initial draft gave a more emphatic pre-dominant preparation to the arrival at bar 242 (see Example 6.3, which I understand as a prolongation/decoration of V/V in A♭ major).[47] Jim Samson has pointed to the characteristic deferral of the structural dominant to an increasingly late point in the piece, after the recurrence of the main theme, as a marker of Chopin's

---

[47]   That is, if I have correctly deciphered the sketches.

later style.[48] Is it perhaps the intention behind the elliptical transition that appears in the printed editions and the autograph *Stichvorlage* to aim past the arrival at bars 242–5 towards an emphatically prepared structural dominant at bar 254, which would then be resolved by the cadence at bar 268? A number of indications might point this way. First, dynamics: in the French first edition at least,[49] bar 242 is marked *forte assai*, which progresses to *ff* at bar 250, followed by a hairpin crescendo across bar 253 to a *sempre ff* in bar 254. Secondly, as I pointed out above, the main theme had always acted as a point of departure, not of arrival. Thirdly, the cadence to A♭ in bar 245 is immediately destabilised by an upward rushing chromatic sequence in both hands.[50] Fourthly, as Cook observes, the high B♭ of bar 242 is not prepared linearly or registrally: it comes more as an interruption than as a goal. Nonetheless, even if one accepts this interpretation[51] and tries to project it, it is extremely difficult to avoid the impression of a botched arrival at this point in performance. Perhaps on the thinner-scaled pianos that Chopin played, a less noisy bars 242–5 would be easier to achieve than on the modern concert grand.

One might, however, understand bars 238ff. in another way, derived from the overall narrative of the piece – not as a miscalculation, but as an intentional backing away from, and consequent ironisation of, the final 'apotheosis'. Why, for example, is the return of the polonaise rhythm, with its fanfare-like rhythmic snap, prophesied in the transition but absent from the climactic restatement of the theme? There is more than a suggestion of this proposed backing away also in the quiet descending tetrachords and weak iii⁶–I cadences in bars 280ff. These cadences, with their unstable, ambivalent, leading-note-to-tonic semitone, refer back to the cadence of the slower central section, which, instead of offering the expected island of stability and repose,

---

[48]　*Chopin: The Four Ballades*, pp. 78–9. 'This is an important dimension of the "plot" of the works in that the thematic reprise is not yet a synthesis, nor indeed a means of resolving the major tensions built up during the piece.' The exception to this is the third Ballade, as Samson points out, whose similarities to and differences from the Polonaise-Fantasy I have mentioned above.

[49]　Of the two surviving autographs, the earlier, which served as the *Stichvorlage* for the French first edition (Brandus 1846), has been published in facsimile with an introduction by Jean-Jacques Eigeldinger (Areuse 1986). The marking in that source is a simple *f*, as it is in the German and English first editions. No *notae variorum* are given on this moment in the *Complete Works*, vol. VIII, ed. I. J. Paderewski, L. Bronarski and J. Turczyński (Warsaw 1949), which reproduces the *forte assai* marking. I have not been able to consult Chopin's *Handexemplar*.

[50]　Both extant autographs have the hairpin beginning with this bar, not the one before, as in the 'Paderewski' edition.

[51]　Leichtentritt (*Analyse*, vol. I, pp. 119–20) clearly understands the moment this way. There is, to my mind, a similarly ambiguous structural arrival at the other major articulation of the piece. The ambiguity revolves around the function of bars 148–52. Is the structural downbeat at bar 148 or 152? To me it should be at bar 152; this is the arrival of the thematic material and the fully confirmed tonic. Bars 148–51 function as a chordal passage preparing the cadence, rather like 64–5 earlier in the piece at the cadence to the main thematic exposition. Here again, Chopin's indications in the Brandus *Stichvorlage* differ from those in the French first edition. (The *Stichvorlage* has *più lento* at bar 148 and *poco più* [*lento*? – illegible, heavily crossed out] at bar 152; the published edition has *poco più lento* at bar 148 and no further marking in 152.) Even with this progressive slowing and in spite of the *pp* dynamic at bar 148, the impression of premature arrival is extremely hard to avoid in performance, because of the richly scored root-position B major chords in bars 148–9. The sketch reveals that bars 148–52 were an afterthought, added only when the slower section had been drafted through bar 181, although still in C major. Bars 144–7 were added even later, after the tonal setting had changed to B major.

had been unable to find either stability or closure in its thematic material, and had come finally to a tense, effortful, unstable standstill. Might this illusionary central repose and ironised apotheosis – calling into question two stylistic characteristics of Liszt's larger forms of the 1830s and 1840s – be what Liszt himself would later find so disturbing about the piece?

In closing I want to recall Chopin's uncertainty about what to name the piece, an uncertainty which Kallberg tells us was very rare for Chopin. I would claim that his hesitation had strong cause in the succession of events that was unfolding in his mind and in the sketches. Elements of fantasy, of ballade, of nocturne, of sonata and of polonaise were all present. The freedom of formal unfolding characteristic of the fantasy was basic, and this was the first title by which Chopin referred to the piece. In my interpretation the continuous narrative (or drama) of the ballade was also strong, abetted by some of the developmental habits and sectional articulations of the sonata. Both of these were diverted by the schematic form typical of Chopin's interpretation of the larger dance types, the polonaise and the scherzo: an ABA with a slower central section of repose (here a nocturne, although a curiously unstable one). The uni-directionally mounting excitement and activity towards a final climax characteristic of the ballades is broken by a gentler but unstable moment, from which the military, triumphant, assertive character of the polonaise does not fully succeed in freeing itself.

A summary look at the overall sequence of events, with its frequently shifting formal and generic implications, suggests first an unstable repose, implied but not achieved, and then a hollow triumph. This is not a defective but rather a highly characteristic succession of events, and one with considerable resonance in the world of the 1840s and in Chopin's life in particular. The whole ends in the shivering trills and iii^6–I cadences of bars 199–212 and the distanced, bardic descending tetrachords of the framing narrator: 'thus went the story of . . .'

7 Placing Chopin: reflections on a compositional aesthetic

JEAN-JACQUES EIGELDINGER

One of Chopin's most striking traits was an utter fidelity to the impressions of his adolescence and early manhood. His attachment to his native soil, family, childhood friends, teachers and fellow students only intensified after 1830, when he left Poland and began a life 'in exile'. This engendered a particular nostalgia in the retrospective outlook he consistently maintained:[1] the future held little or no interest for Chopin.

Liszt comments as follows on his friend's rather restricted musical tastes:

Chopin was thoroughly imbued with certain unique sentiments, the most lofty of which he felt he had acquired in his youth; these were the only ones he wished to express in his art. His view of that art was so unvaryingly the same that his artistic predilections could not fail to be influenced by it. From the great exemplars and masterpieces of art he sought only what corresponded to his own nature.[2]

It is this devotion to the artistic canons of his early years (he was exceptionally mature in recognising them as such) that lies behind his aesthetic preferences. The cultural and musical milieus that he frequented in Warsaw between 1822 and 1830 exerted a decisive influence on the whole of his artistic outlook. In this respect his two teachers played a central role: Wojciech Żywny (1756–1842), of Bohemian origin, came from the pre-classical school in Prague, while Józef Elsner (1769–1854) was a Silesian of German parentage who had studied in Vienna between 1789 and 1791.

---

[1] Note for instance Chopin's declaration in a pathetic letter to Wojciech Grzymała (30 October 1848) concerning the rumour of his possible marriage to Jane Stirling: 'and so I am not thinking at all of a wife, but of those at home, my mother and sisters' (*Korespondencja Fryderyka Chopina*, ed. Bronisław Edward Sydow, 2 vols. (Warsaw 1955), vol. II, p. 285; translation from *Selected Correspondence of Fryderyk Chopin* (hereafter *SCFC*), trans. and ed. Arthur Hedley (London 1962), p. 349). Without necessarily inviting a Freudian interpretation, note also the following from the pen of George Sand: 'He used to tell me about a romantic love affair [Konstancja Gładkowska] which he had had in Poland . . . and above all about his mother, who was the single passion of his life, even though he had become accustomed to the idea of living far away from her' (*Histoire de ma vie*, in *Oeuvres autobiographiques*, ed. Georges Lubin, 2 vols. (Paris 1970–1), vol. II, pp. 433–4).

As for Konstancja Gładkowska, it is interesting that Chopin, who had been in love with her for a year when he composed the Romance of the Concerto Op. 11, comments that this movement gives 'the impression of someone looking gently towards a spot which calls to mind a thousand happy memories' (*Korespondencja*, vol. I, p. 126, letter to Tytus Woyciechowski, 15 May 1830; translation from *SCFC*, p. 45). Already his feelings of passion are expressed through the prism of reminiscence.

[2] Franz Liszt, *F. Chopin*, 2nd edn (Leipzig 1876), p. 193.

Chopin declared to his occasional pupil Wilhelm von Lenz: 'There is but *one School,* the German'[3] – a remark limited, of course, to instrumental composition. Żywny, himself a violinist, generally supervised Fryderyk's training at the piano (Chopin largely taught himself to play) and was responsible for forming the 'taste' of his brilliant pupil: as a 'passionate admirer of the works of Bach',[4] he inculcated in him an abiding worship of the Cantor, basing his teaching on the *Wohltemperirtes Clavier.* There was nothing exceptional in this (compare Beethoven and Neefe), but what is extraordinary is the specific repercussion this worship had on Chopin. Clear indication of Chopin's devotion is an inventory made by his elder sister of the objects found in his apartment after his death, which mentions among other things 'two volumes of Bach and Cherubini'.[5] As for Elsner, Fryderyk's teacher of harmony and counterpoint first privately, then at the Conservatory, he was an adherent of both Haydn[6] and (above all) Mozart, who occupied a special place in his teaching. Note the fundamental similarity between the following reminiscences concerning Chopin's predilections in the years of his full maturity:

Mozart was his God, Seb. Bach one of his favourite masters whom he recommended to all his pupils.[7]

[Chopin] had all the great and beautiful works of the piano literature in his memory – a memory as highly developed as it was reliable. Above all he prized Bach, and between Bach and Mozart it is hard to say whom he loved more.[8]

Also recall the last words that Chopin addressed to his cellist friend Franchomme and to Princess Marcelina Czartoryska: 'You are to play Mozart in my memory.'[9]

Elsner, a man of the Enlightenment,[10] cultivated his pupils according to the views of that movement, and during the last months of his life Chopin had passages from Voltaire's *Dictionnaire philosophique* read out to him, especially the article on

---

[3] Wilhelm von Lenz, *The Great Piano Virtuosos of Our Time from Personal Acquaintance,* trans. Madeleine R. Baker (New York 1899; repr. edn New York 1973), p. 59.

[4] François-Joseph Fétis, 'Chopin', in *Biographie universelle des musiciens,* 2nd edn, 8 vols. (Paris 1860–5), vol. II, p. 283. The expression, which does not appear in the first edition (1835–44, vol. III, p. 128), is taken from Liszt (*F. Chopin,* p. 215), who uses it in the first version of his monograph (1852). It was also borrowed by Adalbert Sowiński, *Les musiciens polonais et slaves: dictionnaire biographique* (Paris 1857; repr. 1971), p. 115.

[5] Hanna Wróblewska-Straus, 'Nowe pamiątki Chopinowskie w zbiorach TiFC', *Ruch muzyczny,* 22/25 (3 December 1978), pp. 3–5.

[6] It is possible that Chopin sang on a few occasions (25 December 1824; 22 May 1825) in the choruses of Haydn's *Creation* in the evangelical church in Warsaw. See Eugeniusz Szulc, 'Nieznana karta warszawskiego okresu życia Chopina', *Rocznik Chopinowski,* 18 (1989), pp. 125–50, in particular pp. 132–6.

[7] Antoine Marmontel, *Les pianistes célèbres* (Paris 1878), p. 7.

[8] *Fr. Chopin's Pianoforte-Werke,* ed. Karol Mikuli, 17 vols. (Leipzig [1880]), *Vorwort,* vol. I, p. 3, col. i. Translation from Jean-Jacques Eigeldinger, *Chopin: Pianist and Teacher as Seen by His Pupils* (hereafter *CPT),* trans. Naomi Shohet with Krysia Osostowicz and Roy Howat, ed. Roy Howat (Cambridge 1986), p. 27.

[9] Frederick Niecks, *Frederick Chopin as a Man and Musician,* 3rd edn, 2 vols. (London 1902), vol. II, p. 317 n. 14.

[10] See Alina Nowak-Romanowicz, 'Poglądy estetyczno-muzyczne Józefa Elsnera', in Tadeusz Strumiłło, Alina Nowak-Romanowicz and Teresa Kuryłowicz, *Poglądy na muzykę kompozytorów polskich doby przedchopinowskiej* (Cracow 1960), pp. 51–99.

'Taste', attributed to Voltaire himself.[11] Elsner was, with Kamieński and Kurpiński, the founder of Polish national opera, and he was concerned to introduce into high art stylised elements of folklore; he also continually exhorted his pupil to work in an operatic domain. Chopin's contribution to a 'national' tradition was in quite another direction, however: it is found above all in the mazurkas scattered throughout his output, even though these were ultimately 'tainted' by imitative writing. The contrapuntal approach evident in Opp. 50, 56, 59 and 63 is characteristic of his late style in general, in which Bach's influence is revisited through Cherubini's *Cours de contrepoint et de fugue*.[12] Chopin's last composition was probably a mazurka, possibly Op. 67 No. 2 (Op. 68 No. 4's claim to that status has been quashed by Wojciech Nowik[13] and, especially, Jeffrey Kallberg[14]).

The National Opera had strong Italianate tendencies under Kurpiński's direction, and in the socio-cultural context of 1820s Warsaw it played a crucial role in feeding Chopin's enthusiasm for Rossini – and no less for the budding singer Konstancja Gładkowska, a pupil in Carlo Soliva's Conservatory singing class. It is probable that Fryderyk, serious connoisseur as he was in the matter of *bel canto*, was overwhelmed as much by Mlle Gładkowska's singing voice as by her appearance; his later devotion to the countess Delfina Potocka, who was celebrated for her soprano voice as well as her beauty, may have been motivated by similar reasons. Chopin's predilection for Rossinian *bel canto* was eventually to be catered for at the Théâtre-Italien in Paris, where the unique revelation of Bellini's cantilena awaited him as the logical development of his Warsaw passion for Rossini. The last music that Chopin heard was an aria sung at his bedside by Delfina Potocka. Its identity has not been definitely established: if not by Bellini, it might have been by Pergolesi, or perhaps a hymn by Stradella, a psalm by Marcello, or even a fragment of Handel's 'Dettingen' *Te Deum*.[15] Regardless, all these composers are significant to my argument.

For it is these composers, along with other eighteenth-century masters (J. S. Bach, Mozart), certain representatives of the *stile brillante* and *bel canto* (Clementi, Hummel, Weber, Moscheles, Rossini, Bellini), and his lingering impressions of Polish folk music, that constitute the essential foundation of Chopin's aesthetic orientation, laid down at an early stage, and more or less immutably.

The exile and his contemporary world

What major nineteenth-century composer had so little interest in contemporary music as Chopin after 1831? Although well aware of the musical trends of his time, he seems

---

11   It was the young Charles Gavard, the brother of Elise (a pupil of Chopin and dedicatee of the Berceuse Op. 57), who was the reader; he left reminiscences which were reproduced by Niecks (*Frederick Chopin*, vol. II, p. 314).

12   A number of musicologists have related Chopin's study of Cherubini's *Cours* (which began in the summer of 1841) to the emergence of his late style. See notably Gerald Abraham, *Chopin's Musical Style* (London 1939), p. 102, and Jeffrey Kallberg, 'Chopin's Last Style', *Journal of the American Musicological Society*, 38 (1985), pp. 264–315, in particular p. 266.

13   'Chopin's Mazurka F moll, Op. 68, Nr. 4: "Die letzte Inspiration des Meisters"', *Archiv für Musikwissenschaft*, 30 (1973), pp. 109–27.

14   'Chopin's Last Style', pp. 296–313.

15   Niecks, *Frederick Chopin*, vol. II, pp. 316–17.

to have turned a deliberately deaf ear to most of what was new. The one exception, his enthusiasm for Bellini, stands out all the more for its singular importance. After his initial excitement upon arriving in Paris and a few later sparks of interest which were soon stifled, Chopin seems to have attended many performances purely out of obligation, even against his will, seized as he was by a sceptical disenchantment. His aesthetic needs found little nourishment in the rather hollow glitter of Parisian musical life under Louis-Philippe.

'Everything *modern* escapes my brain', he wrote in his second letter from Paris to Tytus Woyciechowski (25 December 1831);[16] by this time he had recovered from his initial admiration for the playing of Kalkbrenner (to whom he paid homage as a disciple of Clementi) and for *Robert le diable*. His horror of vulgarity was equalled only by his disgust for the banal and the eccentric. Hence this facetious 'prescription' in a letter to Julian Fontana: 'If Moscheles is in Paris, have him administer an enema containing the oratorios of Neukomm, seasoned with [Berlioz's] *Cellini* and Döhler's Concerto. He will beat a hasty retreat to the *garde-robe*.'[17] Moscheles was a link between post-classicism and the generation of 1830, and his Etudes Op. 70 had some influence on Chopin's Op. 10. Even though Chopin found Moscheles' playing 'terribly baroque' in 1837, he regarded him as practically the only pianist of interest in the 1840s. We do not know what he thought of Alkan or Henselt. In a letter to Auguste Léo (who was, admittedly, a close friend of Moscheles), Chopin expresses regret at not being able to attend one of the latter's concerts: 'I should have been slightly revived, and rescued from the great barren tracts of the *modern school, which is in general undistinguished*.'[18] Whether this remark also refers to Liszt is uncertain. But the fact remains that Liszt's piano paraphrases were not at all to Chopin's taste: 'as regards the themes from his compositions, they will remain buried in the newspapers'.[19] It was already some time since Chopin had been captivated by Liszt's playing of his own Etudes Op. 10 in 1833, and the personal and artistic distance between the two composers had considerably widened.

Chopin did not attend Liszt's pioneering recital in Paris on 20 April 1840, but he received an account from one of his pupils who was greatly impressed by Liszt's sober mastery. Chopin responded by improvising this confession of artistic faith:

Simplicity is everything. After having overcome all the difficulties, after having played immense quantities of notes and more notes, then simplicity emerges with all its charm, like art's final seal. Whoever wants to obtain this immediately will never achieve it: you cannot begin with the end. One has to have studied a lot, tremendously, to reach this goal; it is no easy matter.[20]

Quite apart from its general import, this smacks of a lesson aimed indirectly at Liszt, who had not yet committed himself solely to composition.

16 *Korespondencja*, vol. I, p. 210. The French word *moderne* is used in Chopin's Polish original.
17 Ibid., vol. I, p. 359, letter to Julian Fontana, [29 September 1839].
18 Ibid., vol. II, p. 362 (15 October 1843); italicised words underlined in Chopin's manuscript.
19 Ibid., vol. II, p. 34, letter to Julian Fontana, [11 September 1841] (translation from *SCFC*, p. 204).
20 This statement was recorded by Chopin's pupil Friederike Müller. See 'Madame Streicher's (*née* Friederike Müller) Recollections', Appendix IX in Niecks, *Frederick Chopin*, vol. II, p. 342. (Translation based on *CPT*, p. 54.)

Chopin's view of the various operatic factions in Paris in the 1840s is distilled in a witty remark to George Sand's daughter, Solange, which was passed on to Princess Czartoryska:

One day I asked him to pronounce on the merit of five fashionable celebrities, and he replied: 'Rossini has genius, Meyerbeer talent, Auber grace, Halévy know-how, Donizetti a barrel organ.'[21]

This assessment reveals just how disillusioned Chopin was about the evolution of *bel canto* after Bellini. Verdi's Paris debuts are noted laconically in a neutral tone: 'we have not been to the Italian Opera [Théâtre-Italien] where they are giving Verdi [*Nabucco*].'[22] But Delacroix, Chopin's kindred spirit in aesthetic and operatic matters, tells us in a letter to George Sand:

Yesterday I saw the opera of the famous Merdi . . . ; Verdi or Merdi is all the rage at the moment; it's a rehash using all Rossini's cast-offs, without the ideas: nothing but noise . . . Where is Chopin, where is Mozart, where are the priests of the living God . . . ? Prepare poor Chopin for the uncouth music he'll find here.[23]

As for the all-powerful and unavoidable Meyerbeer, Chopin could not but feel revulsion at his massive effects and the realism of a grand opera conceived for the *juste milieu*. If he was momentarily dazzled by the scenic effects (but not by the music) in *Robert le diable* (1831), he was sceptical about the echoes of that production in *Le prophète* (1849).[24] Delacroix's journal confirms this: 'He had dragged himself to the first performance of *Le prophète*. His horror at that rhapsody . . .',[25] this last term referring to the trivial admixture of every style and atmosphere. After his first years in Paris, Chopin distanced himself from Berlioz,[26] whose outrageous attitudinising and programmatic manifestos were no more congenial to him than his orchestral gigantism. He was at the opposite extreme from the hot-headed Frenchman's symphonic and melodramatic conceptions: 'I believe that Chopin, who detested him, detested even more music which is nothing without the assistance of trombones fighting against flutes and oboes, or else all playing together', notes Delacroix[27] once more in a context to which we shall return. On the same topic, Solange Clésinger relates: 'I see Berlioz being admired. Chopin used to run away with his hands over his ears when he was forced to listen to that stuff.'[28] Finally, the oriental *couleur locale* of Félicien David's ode-symphony *Le désert*, which made a great impact at its first performance in 1844,

21 Fragment of an undated autograph letter (place also unspecified) to Princess Marcelina Czartoryska: Paris, Bibliothèque Nationale, Manuscripts Department (*n.a.f. 24.811*, fol. 254).
22 *Korespondencja*, vol. II, p. 155, letter to his family, 12 December [1845] (translation from SCFC, p. 258).
23 Ibid., vol. II, p. 423 (20 November [1845?]).
24 Ibid., vol. II, p. 451, letter to Solange Clésinger, 13 April [1849].
25 *Journal 1822–1863*, 22 April 1849 (Paris 1981), p. 193. Translation from *The Journal of Eugene Delacroix*, trans. Walter Pach (New York 1937), p. 196.
26 Nevertheless, on 25 January 1836 Berlioz wrote to Liszt: 'Richaut [*sic*] had asked me a month ago to arrange the *Francs-Juges* overture for piano duet. I did this with Chopin's advice' (*Correspondance générale*, ed. Pierre Citron, 5 vols. (Paris 1973–89), vol. II, p. 281).
27 *Journal 1822–1863*, 13 April 1860 (with reference to an entry from May 1855 or, possibly, 16 May 1857), p. 779.
28 This hitherto unpublished reminiscence was reported to Marcelina Czartoryska. See note 21 above.

could not meet with the approval of Chopin, who was scrupulous about the use of folk materials: 'Apart from some *real* Arab songs, the remainder only *works* because of the orchestration', to which the exiled composer added: 'It was when they heard that [music] at the first concert given here that the Algerian Arabs nodded their heads with smiles of pleasure.'[29]

This survey of Chopin's reactions to the innovations and dominant musical trends of Louis-Philippe's Paris has not been intended to demonstrate the composer's antagonism as much as his neutrality towards these, for it was not the present that essentially moulded his aesthetic perspective, rather the past.

Chopin and the musical past

The supreme maturity of Chopin's aesthetic outlook was evident at the time of his first visit abroad, in September 1828, when he became acquainted with the musical life of Berlin:

I have already heard one oratorio at the Singakademie and also, with great satisfaction, [Spontini's] *Cortez*, Cimarosa's *Il matrimonio segreto* and Onslow's *Le Colporteur*. However, Handel's oratorio *St Cecilia* came nearest to the ideal which I had formed of great music.[30]

This spontaneous declaration carries the weight of a first artistic credo. It is supported, after a second journey to Vienna, Prague and Dresden in the summer of 1829, by the following remarks about a pupil of Clementi:

Klengel is, of all my pianistic acquaintances, the one who pleases me most. I met him at Pixis's in Prague. He played me his fugues – one might say that they form a sequel to Bach's: there are forty-eight of them, and as many canons. The difference between him and Czerny is obvious.[31]

By 1828 Chopin had already completed the first two of his large-scale compositions destined for publication outside Poland: the Variations on 'Là ci darem la mano' Op. 2 and the Sonata Op. 4 (published posthumously in 1851 after various fruitless attempts). Written in the *stile brillante*, the Variations Op. 2 (which, though betraying a debt to his predecessors, are stylistically advanced) contain many of his pianistic innovations, and while Chopin's choice of 'Là ci darem' as the basis of variations was not original, it was nevertheless this very duet that Elsner cited in one of his treatises as an example of compositional *logic*.[32] The Sonata Op. 4, dedicated to Elsner, is a 'serious' work, intended to show what Chopin had learnt by the end of his studies.

---

[29] *Korespondencja*, vol. II, p. 147, letter to Kalasanty Jędrzejewicz, 1 August [1845].
[30] Ibid., vol. I, p. 83, letter to his family, 20 September 1828 (translation from *SCFC*, p. 17).
[31] Ibid., vol. I, p. 105, letter to Tytus Woyciechowski, 12 September 1829 (translation from *SCFC*, pp. 33–4).
    Chopin's interest in Klengel's forty-eight *Canons and Fugues* can also be compared with his study of the *stile osservato* pieces from Clementi's *Gradus ad Parnassum*. Another relevant document is the inscription by Aloys Fuchs in Chopin's album (Vienna, 1 May 1831) of the beginning of a 'Canon alla rovescia' from the *Musical Offering*, which indicates a joint admiration for the strict counterpoint of J. S. Bach (facsimile in Jaroslav Procházka, *Frédéric Chopin et la Bohême*, trans. Yvette Joye (Prague 1969), p. 108).
[32] See Alina Nowak-Romanowicz, 'Ideologia Józefa Elsnera a Chopin', in *The Book of the First International Congress Devoted to the Works of Frederick Chopin*, ed. Zofia Lissa (Warsaw 1963), pp. 713–17, especially p. 715.

Ludwik Bronarski has drawn attention to the almost exact reminiscence of Bach's second *Inventio* (BWV 773) at the start of the Sonata, where the figuration, key and imitative texture are strikingly similar (see Example 7.1). Furthermore, he notes, this quotation appears 'in Chopin's work like a motto at its head, like a symbol. It is as though the young composer, here attempting a large classical form for the first time, intended to launch his career under the banner of the great Leipzig cantor; it is as though he were invoking the name of this powerful "patron" of music, to whom he was all his life to show a reverence which had been inculcated in him from childhood.'[33]

Example 7.1   Sonata Op. 4, I, bars 1–12

[33] Ludwik Bronarski, *Etudes sur Chopin*, 2 vols. (Lausanne 1944–6), vol. II, p. 49.

Example 7.2   Ballade Op. 47, bars 1–8

One example of Bach's imprint on Chopin's later works can be found at the start of
the third Ballade Op. 47 (see Example 7.2). The four-part writing of this opening,
the contrary motion between parts (bars 1–2), the sharing of the melody between
upper part (bars 1–2) and bass (bars 3–4), the octave imitation of this same upper part
by the bass (bars 5–7) and finally the progression in bars 41–5 – all these derive from
Bach, while functioning simultaneously in a narrative vein. The same can be said of
Op. 56 No. 3, one of the most developed of the mazurkas, in which similar elements
achieve an ultimate stylisation of the dance (note in Example 7.3 the undisguised
resemblance of bar 12 to the opening of Op. 4 – even the mordent is preserved).

To return to the Allegro maestoso of Op. 4, observe the Tristanesque harmonies[34]
of bars 9–11 (see Example 7.1 above), produced by the simultaneous chromaticisms

[. . .]

Example 7.3   Mazurka Op. 56 No. 3, bars 1–6 and 12–14

[34] Concerning Chopin's anticipations of the Tristan chord, see Ernst Kurth, *Romantische Harmonik und
ihre Krise in Wagners 'Tristan'* (Bern and Leipzig 1920), pp. 365–466; Hugo Leichtentritt, *Analyse der*

in the bass and the treble line – just as the augmented sixth chord in bar 4 results from a contrapuntal tension culminating in the Ab of the bass against the F# of the alto. Note in comparison the (related) pitches with which Chopin first abandons his model, F#, G and Ab (see Example 7.4). The fundamental similarity between the opening of this Bach *Inventio* and Chopin's early Sonata suggests that the thought process behind the pre-Wagnerian audacities of bars 9–11 of Op. 4 is a linear one. As for the later music, even if there is no imitative writing in the forward-looking E minor Prelude Op. 28 No. 4, the whole piece is governed by chromatic lines, as in the approach to the first beat of bar 15 (see Example 7.5). An analogous process underlies the Mazurka Op. 68 No. 4; note especially the resolution (via the evocative A# appoggiatura) of the Tristanesque harmony on the third beat of bar 14 (see Example 7.6).[35]

Example 7.4   (a) J. S. Bach, *Inventio* No. 2, bar 1
             (b) Sonata Op. 4, I, bars 1–2

After bar 2's imitation at the octave, the Allegro maestoso from Op. 4 embarks on a chromatic descent in the bass spanning a fourth, which is then taken up by the alto in bars 8–11, where the Tristanesque harmonies also occur (Example 7.1). This is clearly a baroque *lamento* which has skirted the classical era to arrive at this late 1820s sonata: even though the introduction to the 'Dissonance' Quartet K. 465 is based on this formula (as are other minor-key pieces by Mozart as well as Gluck, Haydn and even

Chopin'schen Klavierwerke, 2 vols. (Berlin 1921–2), passim; Zdislas Jachimecki, *Frédéric Chopin et son œuvre* (Paris 1930), pp. 168–9; Ludwik Bronarski, *Harmonika Chopina* (Warsaw 1935), passim; Józef M. Chomiński, *Sonaty Chopina* (Cracow 1960), pp. 11 and 79–80; Maciej Gołąb, 'Über den Tristan-Akkord bei Chopin', *Chopin Studies*, 3 (1990), pp. 246–56.

[35] This innovative linear approach, born of Chopin's knowledge of Bach, also calls to mind the musical arabesque – i.e. the superimposed lines, the delicate 'contrapuntal' tracery – of such significance in the works of Debussy, who defined this notion specifically with regard to Bach and the sixteenth-century polyphonists (see Jean-Jacques Eigeldinger, 'Debussy et l'idée d'arabesque musicale', *Cahiers Debussy*, 12–13 (1988–9), pp. 5–14). As we shall observe later, Chopin – whose music Debussy worshipped – serves in this respect as an important bridge between the late baroque master and the principal representative of French musical symbolism.

Example 7.5   Prelude Op. 28 No. 4, bars 13–15

Example 7.6   Mazurka Op. 68 No. 4, bars 9–15

Beethoven), Chopin takes the pattern not so much from his classical forebears as directly from Bach himself.[36] Although in a major key, the orchestral introduction to the 'Là ci darem' Variations is tinged with melancholy through the use of the same

[36]   A good example of Bach's use of this pattern can be found in the bass of his ninth *Sinfonia* (BWV 795 – see Example 7.7), and the relation between the pattern and the affect of lamentation is made abundantly clear in the Adagissimo (in F minor) of Bach's *Capriccio on the Departure of His Most Beloved Brother* (BWV 992), the chorus in Cantata 12 (*Weinen, Klagen, Sorgen, Zagen* – also in F minor) and the Crucifixus of the B minor Mass, a transposition of the preceding chorus into the lamentational key of E minor (compare the opening chorus of the *St Matthew Passion*). Other examples of descending chromaticism in Bach's instrumental music include the subject of the F minor Fugue from *WTC* I and the A minor Prelude from *WTC* II (the texture of which might invite a crossing of fingers like that in Chopin's Etude Op. 10 No. 2, also in A minor).

Example 7.7   J. S. Bach, *Sinfonia* No. 9, bars 1–2

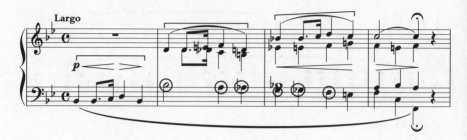

Example 7.8   Variations on 'Là ci darem la mano' Op. 2, introduction, bars 1–4

(a)

(b)

Example 7.9   (a) Concerto Op. 21, I, bars 1–4
                    (b) Concerto Op. 11, I, bars 1–4

Example 7.10   Sonata Op. 58, IV, bars 24–7

chromatic pattern in the bass (see Example 7.8). By counterpointing the original theme against a *basso ostinato* borrowed directly from the time of Bach, this rather 'scholastic' opening symbolically pays homage to the teaching of both Żywny and Elsner. The first themes of the Concertos Opp. 21 and 11, in F minor and E minor respectively, again employ the descending-bass pattern, which imbues the opening movements (marked Maestoso in Op. 21 and Allegro maestoso in Op. 11, as in Op. 4), with a heroic, funereal tone (see Example 7.9).

Example 7.11   Sonata Op. 58, IV, bars 1–9

Example 7.12   Sonata Op. 65, IV, bars 1–4

Example 7.13   Prelude Op. 28 No. 20, bars 5–8

It is almost as if Chopin was applying an obligatory formula in his large-scale works. As further proof, note his use of the pattern within the main theme of the finale of the Sonata Op. 58 (see Example 7.10). Here the enormous energy accumulated in the introductory bars drives the falling chromatics of the theme (see Example 7.11). As for the finale of the last sonata, Op. 65 for piano and cello, the first theme has the pattern at its centre, and this determines the chromatic character of the complete opening statement (see Example 7.12). Thus we see the generative power of this motif in Chopin's sonata forms, and the same formula recurs in the etudes[37] and preludes; in many cases, even the augmented sixth harmony and C minor tonality from the Sonata Op. 4 are preserved (see Example 7.13).

The most accomplished of Chopin's late lyrical pieces, such as the Berceuse Op. 57, the Barcarolle Op. 60[38] and the Nocturne Op. 62 No. 1, overflow with pianistic figurations characteristic of his early *stile brillante* compositions, especially the introductions to the Variations Op. 2 and the *Fantasy on Polish Airs* Op. 13, and, above all, the middle movements of the two concertos, which are pure nocturnes with orchestral accompaniment.[39] Hence Ravel's opinion of Chopin: 'If there is no evolution with him, there is a splendid efflorescence.'[40] In Opp. 57, 60 and 62 Chopin's style approaches that of musical symbolism/impressionism (the full implications of these terms cannot of course be explored here) through the use of formulas which derive principally from Hummel and Field and which partake of both purely pianistic writing and the stylised *bel canto* idiom inspired by Rossini and his circle. The excerpts shown in Example 7.14 provide convincing evidence of how the *stile brillante* and *bel canto* left their mark on Chopin's later style. Even the principle of melismatic diminution is transferred from the Romance of Op. 11 into the Berceuse and the Nocturne Op. 62 No. 1 (see Example 7.15). In both the Op. 11 passage and the Nocturne (see the transition between bars 21–5, as well as the coda, quoted in Example 7.15b), the melismatic figuration comes after an important cadence, whereas in the Berceuse it enters before the close but precisely at the turning point in the harmonic structure, namely the unique inflection to G♭ major, which (to use Marcel Proust's expression) 'enshadows the moonlight [*bémolise le clair de lune*]'. The Berceuse, initially called 'Variantes' (the term 'variations' was perhaps too scholastic for Chopin), elevates ornamentation to a

---

[37] See the Etudes Op. 10 No. 6 (bars 1–8, etc.) and Op. 10 No. 12 (bars 14–17, etc.).

[38] Mme Gérard de Romilly recounts in 'Debussy professeur par l'une de ses élèves (1898–1908)', *Cahiers Debussy*, nouvelle série 2 (1978), p. 6: 'Chopin's Barcarolle was one of his favourite pieces, and it was the cause of violent scenes between us! I played Chopin very badly, and particularly the Barcarolle, which I had taken a dislike to ever since Debussy insisted on my repeating it a considerable number of times: "You will work at it until you can play it well", he said, "for years if necessary." The way in which he explained and analysed the piece was admirable.'

[39] Chopin offers an excellent definition of the genre in his verbal paraphrase of the Romance from Op. 11: 'The *Adagio* of my new concerto is in E major. It is not meant to create a powerful effect; it is rather a Romance, calm and melancholy, giving the impression of someone looking gently towards a spot which calls to mind a thousand happy memories. It is a kind of reverie in the moonlight on a beautiful spring evening. Hence the accompaniment is muted' (*Korespondencja*, vol. I, p. 125; translation from *SCFC*, p. 45. Compare note 1 above.).

[40] Maurice Ravel, 'Les Polonaises, les Nocturnes, les Impromptus, la Barcarolle. Impressions', *Le courrier musical* (1 January 1910), p. 32, trans. Arbie Orenstein in *A Ravel Reader*, ed. A. Orenstein (New York 1990), pp. 336–7.

Example 7.14   (a) Variations on 'Là ci darem la mano' Op. 2, introduction, bar 19

Example 7.14   (b) Berceuse Op. 57, bars 31–2

Example 7.14   (c) Concerto Op. 11, II, bar 40

Example 7.14   (d) Berceuse Op. 57, bar 23

Example 7.14   (e) Barcarolle Op. 60, bar 27

Example 7.14   (f) *Fantasy on Polish Airs* Op. 13, introduction, bar 47

Example 7.14   (g) Berceuse Op. 57, bar 41

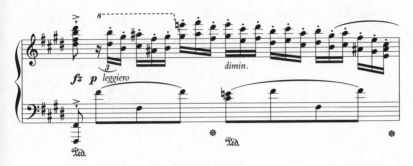

Example 7.14   (h) Concerto Op. 11, II, bar 45

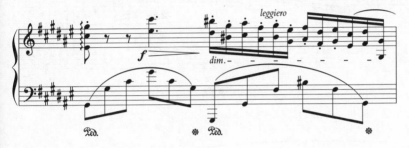

Example 7.14   (i) Barcarolle Op. 60, bar 14

Example 7.15   (a) Concerto Op. 11, II, bars 46–9

Example 7.15   (b) Nocturne Op. 62 No. 1, bars 81–5

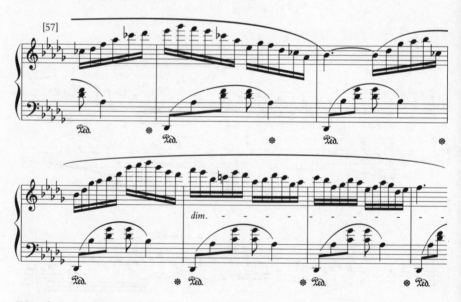

Example 7.15   (c) Berceuse Op. 57, bars 57–63

structural principle. Above a diatonic ostinato outlining the most basic tonal progression, the chromatic filigree in the right hand blends different styles (this notion of blurred outlines and colours is also implicit in the title 'Brouillards' of Debussy's first Prelude in Book II and one of the movements in his two-piano suite *En blanc et noir*).

The ornamented *melos*, in diminution, develops a life of its own and explores musical space through alternately descending and ascending contours; the dynamic is a constant *piano* subject to gradation and nuance, while the sustaining pedal subtly acts as a sonorous *sfumato*. Over the ostinato foundation, register, dynamics and timbre contribute so directly to the compositional process that the Berceuse can be seen as an early embodiment of Debussy's aesthetic.[41]

The Sonata Op. 4 (Allegro maestoso), the Variations Op. 2 (introduction) and the two Concertos Opp. 21 and 11 (first and second movements), all composed between 1827 and 1830, therefore contain more than embryonic manifestations of the 'splendid efflorescence' of Chopin's last works. At the same time, these early pieces are like a two-faced Janus looking backward to the heritage of Bach and, as we shall see, forward to the future of Liszt/Wagner and Debussy (almost despite the composer's own intentions). Chopin's immersion in a contrapuntal, Bach-inspired mode of thought is thus both a stimulus and an anchor.

Let us now review the documentary evidence of Chopin's veneration for Bach and his contemporaries, and for Mozart and the Viennese classical composers.

When George Sand, in *Consuelo*, writes of Bach: 'he is a genius who embraces, sums up and gives life to all the knowledge [*science*] of the past and the present',[42] who is guiding her pen if not Chopin? It is revealing that Bach's art is regarded as a vital part of the present, as the alpha and omega of music. In fact, Bach never ceased to inform Chopin's threefold activity as composer, pianist and teacher.[43] The *Wohltemperirtes Clavier* was apparently the only score he took to Majorca, which was just at the time he was completing the Preludes Op. 28.[44] Some months later, at Nohant, Chopin mentions that he is correcting for his own use the printing and editorial errors in his 'Paris edition of Bach'[45] (which must have been the same copy of the work, as he had not yet returned to Paris and by 1839 there was still no French edition of Bach's *Oeuvres complètes* for keyboard); these corrections were made intuitively, which speaks volumes about his love and knowledge of the work. Furthermore, Lenz states:

---

41 The piece composed by Chopin in 1829 and entitled *Souvenir de Paganini* in the first posthumous edition (1881) anticipates in a less subtle and inspired way the Berceuse Op. 57, whose sustained pianistic melisma is without equal.

42 George Sand, *Consuelo*, ed. L. Cellier and L. Guichard, 2 vols. (Paris 1959), vol. II, p. 242.

43 Among the various works on this subject, see Józef M. Chomiński, *Preludia Chopina* (Cracow 1950), passim; Walter Wiora, 'Chopins Preludes und Etudes und Bachs Wohltemperiertes Klavier', in *The Book of the First International Congress Devoted to the Works of Frederick Chopin*, ed. Zofia Lissa (Warsaw 1963), pp. 73–81; Jean-Jacques Eigeldinger, 'Chopin et l'héritage baroque', *Schweizer Beiträge zur Musikwissenschaft*, series III, vol. 2 (1974), pp. 51–74; *CPT*, pp. 60–1 and 135–6 nn. 136–7; Karol Hławicka, 'Chopin a Jan Sebastian Bach', in *Chopin a muzyka europejska*, ed. K. Musioł (Katowice 1977), pp. 3–17; Helmuth Rudloff, 'Notate zur Wirkungsgeschichte des Klavierwerkes Johann Sebastian Bachs in der ersten Hälfte des 19. Jahrhunderts', *Muzyka fortepianowa*, 6/37 (Gdańsk 1985), pp. 67–89; Jim Samson, *The Music of Chopin* (London 1985), pp. 142–58; Hartmuth Kinzler, '"Cela ne s'oublie jamais" oder das erste Präludium aus Bachs Wohltemperiertem Klavier als Modell für Chopins große C-Dur-Etüde', *Zeitschrift für Musikpädagogik*, 12/40 (1987), pp. 11–21; Carl Dahlhaus, 'Bach und der romantische Kontrapunkt', *Musica*, 43 (1989), pp. 10–22; Giorgio Pestelli, 'Sul Preludio di Chopin op. 28 n. 1', *Acta musicologica*, 63/1 (1991), pp. 98–114; Jean-Jacques Eigeldinger, 'Un exemplaire du *Clavier bien tempéré I* annoté par Chopin', *Revue de musicologie*, forthcoming.

44 *Korespondencja*, vol. I, p. 332, letter to Julian Fontana, 28 December 1838.

45 Ibid., vol. I, p. 353, letter to Julian Fontana, [8 August 1839].

'For himself and himself alone, he would play nothing but Bach, whose influence was absorbed in many places into his own compositions.'[46] Elsewhere Lenz notes that for the fortnight before a concert Chopin would shut himself up and play Bach: it was his way of preparing himself, as he never practised his own compositions.[47] Another pupil, Friederike Müller, tells how, during a lesson, her teacher played her fourteen of the preludes and fugues one after the other, declaring: 'It is impossible to forget them.'[48] The sources all agree that the 'Forty-Eight' was the basis of Chopin's teaching and was used to build piano technique and to develop polyphonic thinking.[49] On taking leave of an excellent female pupil, he advised her '*to practise Bach continually*, adding that that was the best means of making progress'.[50]

Without the necessary documentary evidence, it is difficult to establish what parts of Bach's output Chopin was familiar with. He could have had access to the complete keyboard works in Czerny's edition (1837–51) and, after 1843, the French version of this edition reissued by the Widow Launer under the title: *Collection complète pour le piano, avec et sans accompagnement, des œuvres de J.-S. Bach* (ten volumes containing the *Art of Fugue* and the six sonatas for violin and keyboard as well as the main harpsichord works). In addition, in December 1843 Maurice Schlesinger published the vocal score of the *St Matthew Passion* (with French text by Maurice Bourges), of which the editor offered Chopin an inscribed copy.[51] Although there is no proof, Clementi's English anthologies (of works by Bach, Handel and Domenico Scarlatti)[52] may have reached him; and, as Brahms was later to do with the annual publications of the Bach-Gesellschaft, one can imagine Chopin eagerly seizing upon each new volume, anxious to discover the delights contained therein.

The history of Chopin's relations with the devotees of 'ancient music' in Paris is a chapter of his artistic biography which remains to be written. A number of his musical links between 1831 and 1849 provide highly significant clues. Baillot, with whom he made contact as soon as he arrived in the capital and who supported his first concert (on 26 February 1832) through the participation of his quintet, finds room for Bach beside Corelli, Tartini, Viotti and the Viennese classics in his *Art du violon* (1834). Among Baillot's circle, his son-in-law Sauzay[53] and the violinists Chrétien Urhan and

---

[46] Wilhelm von Lenz, 'Die großen Pianoforte-Virtuosen unserer Zeit aus persönlicher Bekanntschaft', *Neue Berliner Musikzeitung*, 23 September 1868, p. 302.

[47] *The Great Piano Virtuosos*, p. 52.

[48] Niecks, *Frederick Chopin*, vol. II, p. 341.

[49] A hitherto unknown copy, which belonged to one of Chopin's female pupils, contains, in addition to practical annotations, analytical indications in his own hand for some of the fugues (nos. 8, 12, 16, 17, 18, 19, 22, 23 and 24), specifically, symbols marking the subject, countersubject, answer, augmented and retrograde entries, etc. See Eigeldinger, 'Un exemplaire du *Clavier bien tempéré I*'.

[50] Niecks, *Frederick Chopin*, vol. II, p. 107.

[51] See Ferdynand Hoesick, *Słowacki i Chopin*, 2 vols. (Warsaw 1932), vol. II, p. 249. Professor Mieczysław Tomaszewski kindly drew this reference to my attention.

[52] See Stephen Daw, 'Muzio Clementi as an Original Advocate, Collector and Performer, in Particular of J. S. Bach and D. Scarlatti', in *Bach, Handel, Scarlatti: Tercentenary Essays*, ed. Peter Williams (Cambridge 1985), pp. 61–74.

[53] See Félix Raugel, 'Autour de Sauzay, de Boëly et de Reber', *Recherches sur la musique française classique: Mélanges Norbert Dufourcq*, 15 (1975), pp. 146–52; see also Brigitte François-Sappey, 'La vie musicale à Paris à travers les *Mémoires* d'Eugène Sauzay (1809–1901)', *Revue de musicologie*, 60 (1974), pp. 159–210 and *Alexandre P. F. Boëly 1785–1858* (Paris 1989), passim.

Delphin Alard openly proclaimed the same preferences. Auguste Franchomme, Chopin's closest French friend from the start, could not ignore Bach's suites for his instrument, the cello. Ferdinand Hiller (a pupil of Hummel) was an ardent supporter of Bach and in 1833 played an Allegro from the Concerto for three keyboards (BWV 1063) together with Chopin and Liszt. Charles-Valentin Alkan, a faithful admirer of Chopin, shared his love of Bach, Handel and the French clavecinistes. Moscheles, whom Chopin met in Paris in 1839, had already founded his 'Concerts historiques' in collaboration with Fétis, in which the main focus was on Bach and his sons, Handel and Scarlatti (200 of the latter's sonatas were available in Czerny's 1839 edition, published in Vienna). Although not one of Chopin's intimates, the 'musical anti-quary' Jean-Joseph-Bonaventure Laurens, who was a French Bach enthusiast and editor of an anthology of thirty-eight of the best of Couperin's *Pièces de clavecin* (Paris 1841), would write to George Sand: 'I greet Mr Chopin in the person of Sebastian Bach.'[54] As for the young Pauline Viardot-Garcia, she entered the lives of both composer and novelist in 1839–40, and Sand noted two years later: 'Pauline and Chopin read whole scores together at the piano.'[55] Apart from playing piano-duet reductions, Chopin doubtless accompanied the singer in numerous arias by Italian and Italianate composers of the eighteenth century, of the schools of Marcello, Pergolesi, Handel and Gluck, all of whom figured in her repertoire. Marcello's *Psalms* were published in their entirety in Paris in 1842: No. 18, 'I cieli immensi narrano', was at that time one of Pauline's great successes, and Delacroix claims that 'Juda vainqueur' was 'Chopin's favourite psalm'.[56] As for Handel, there is this remark in a letter of Mendelssohn's (Leipzig, 6 October 1836): 'just before he left, my copies of Handel's works arrived, in which Chopin took a truly childish delight; but they are indeed so beautiful that I get inexhaustible pleasure from them; twenty-three large volumes'.[57] A small edition of Pergolesi's *Stabat mater* was always by Chopin's side, along with Mozart's Requiem.[58]

Chopin held Henri Reber in great esteem as a theoretician, and about 1845 he bequeathed to him two of his best professional pupils, Mikuli and Tellefsen. Reber, with his classical tendencies, command of technique and friendship with figures like the violinist Sauzay and the singer Delsarte (a pioneer in the restoration of the art of singing more or less as practised in the time of Lully and Rameau), could easily have been taken for a man of the eighteenth century who had erroneously strayed into the romantic era.[59] Tellefsen, who had been raised in a Nordic cantoral tradition, came to Chopin already steeped in Bach: he owned a pedal keyboard, gave performances at his house (after 1850) on an ancient harpsichord and edited various pieces by Bach's sons, Kirnberger and others, as well as some of Rameau's *Pièces de clavecin en concerts*. Another artist respected by Chopin was the pianist and teacher Pierre Zimmermann,

54 *Correspondance de George Sand*, ed. Georges Lubin, 25 vols. (Paris 1964–91), vol. V, p. 194.
55 Ibid., vol. V, p. 401, letter to Carlotta Marliani (13 August 1841).
56 *Journal 1822–1863*, 7 July 1850, p. 245.
57 Felix Mendelssohn-Bartholdy, *Briefe aus den Jahren 1830 bis 1847*, 9th edn, 2 vols. (Leipzig 1882), vol. II, p. 100, letter to his family.
58 *Korespondencja*, vol. II, p. 396, letter to Marie de Rozières, Pentecost 1846.
59 See the memorial article by Camille Saint-Saëns devoted to Reber, reprinted in *Harmonie et mélodie* (Paris 1885), pp. 283–4.

who held an important salon in Chopin's immediate neighbourhood, in the Square d'Orléans; his *Encyclopédie du pianiste compositeur* (1840) contains examples of fugues from Domenico Scarlatti, Eberlin, Mozart and Cherubini. Finally, there was Alfred J. Hipkins, who was Chopin's tuner in London in 1848. Thirty years later he became known as a clavichord and harpsichord specialist, playing a crucial role in the revival of these instruments in England. Hipkins was fascinated by Chopin's playing, and stressed his links with the aesthetic of the late baroque and *Empfindsamkeit.*[60]

Chopin regularly frequented the Concerts du Conservatoire in Paris, renowned for the seriousness of their repertoire and for the quality of their performances under Habeneck.[61] From 1832 to 1836 he assiduously attended the concerts given by Baillot, the *ne plus ultra* of chamber music with a repertoire almost exclusively based on Mozart, Haydn and Boccherini.[62] In this context, his friendship with Camille Pleyel (the son of Ignace, himself a pupil of Haydn) assumes particular importance: 'There is only one person left today who knows how to play Mozart, and that's Pleyel, and when he is good enough to play a piano-duet sonata with me I learn from the experience', Chopin often used to say.[63] His attraction to the purity of the classical tradition is a well-documented fact. His sketches for a piano method contain this word of praise: 'You have learnt to love Mozart, Haydn and B[eethoven]. You sightread the great masters',[64] which is echoed by the following passage in a letter to the pianist Caroline Oury de Belleville, who had heard Beethoven in Vienna: 'You interpret so marvellously the masters we all recognise, all the great composers like Mozart, Beethoven and Hummel.'[65] This reveals that, for Chopin, the Viennese classics continued to compete with J. S. Bach and the principal late baroque and pre-classical composers for first place in his affections.

The comparisons between Mozart and Haydn and between Mozart and Beethoven scattered throughout Delacroix's journal, almost always in favour of the former, stemmed for the most part from the conversations on aesthetics that the painter had with Chopin. When Chopin writes of his friend: 'He adores Mozart – knows all his operas by heart',[66] he is awarding him the highest artistic accolade. He included 'as a curiosity' a Mozart trio (K. 542?) in the programme of his last Paris concert (in collaboration with Alard and Franchomme), and in London at the home of the Duchess of Sutherland he played the Andante and Variations for piano duet K. 501

---

[60] See Edith J. Hipkins, *How Chopin Played: From Contemporary Impressions Collected from the Diaries and Notebooks of the Late A. J. Hipkins* (London 1937).

[61] For details of the programmes, see Antoine Elwart, *Histoire de la Société des Concerts du Conservatoire* (Paris 1860). Chopin's correspondence and that of George Sand allow us to determine the dates of various concerts which they attended.

[62] See Joël-M. Fauquet, *Les sociétés de musique de chambre à Paris de la Restauration à 1870* (Paris 1986), pp. 41–113 and 251–62.

[63] Ernest Legouvé, *Soixante ans de souvenirs*, 2 vols. (Paris 1886–7), vol. I, p. 375. Legouvé's reminiscences are confirmed by Antoine Marmontel in his *Virtuoses contemporains* (Paris 1882), p. 141: 'Camille Pleyel had acquired a truly extraordinary knowledge of the traditions, style and techniques belonging to every celebrated master . . . [He] used to give his artist friends invaluable advice.'

[64] Frédéric Chopin, *Esquisses pour une Méthode de Piano*, ed. Jean-Jacques Eigeldinger (Paris 1993), p. 42.

[65] *Korespondencja*, vol. II, p. 356 ([10 December 1842]) (translation from *SCFC*, p. 225).

[66] Ibid., vol. II, p. 398, letter to Auguste Franchomme, 30 August [1846] (translation from *SCFC*, p. 265).

with Julius Benedict – this was his Mozartian swansong. The injunction quoted above, 'to play Mozart in my memory', issued to Franchomme and Princess Czartoryska, was taken literally by the habitués of the Hôtel Lambert: the 'Club des Mozaristes' founded by the Princess in the 1850s included Delacroix among its members, together with Franchomme, Alard, Tellefsen, Mme Dubois-O'Meara and the young Gounod. The Viennese classics and, from time to time, Cimarosa, Rossini and Weber were most often performed at the Hôtel Lambert, which was infused with the serious spirit of chamber music. Chopin too was represented, notably through repeated performances by Franchomme of the difficult Sonata Op. 65, the composer's last published work, which was premiered (minus the first movement) at his last Paris concert. Afflicted with a somewhat earnest piety, Marcelina Czartoryska's coterie tended towards a formalism from which Delacroix wished to distance himself: 'The Princess's *note-munchers*, who swear only by Mozart, understand Mozart no better than they do Rossini. That vital element, that secret power which is throughout Shakespeare, does not exist for them. They must have their alexandrines and counterpoint: all they admire in Mozart is regularity.'[67]

The friendship between Chopin and Delacroix, based on similar aristocratic temperaments and (by extension) artistic tastes, is an important one from an historical viewpoint. Their mutual admiration[68] is inseparable from their respective groundings in the art of the great masters of the past, and from their shared reaction to a certain dull mediocrity, not to say vulgarity, in a world where industrial progress was directly proportional to the disintegration of artistic values. Their dilemma as modern creative artists, placed between a recent past which they cherished and an immediate future which they regarded with some apprehension, is reflected in their common love for the composer of *Don Giovanni*, who 'is a modern also, which is to say one who does not fear to touch upon the melancholy side of things'.[69] On the question of Chopin's musical inspiration George Sand observed: 'Although he had a horror of the incomprehensible, his overwhelming emotions carried him despite himself into regions which he alone could know.'[70] This sense of constraint, this struggle between the

---

[67] Delacroix expressed serious reservations in his journal about Franchomme's playing, and came to prefer that of Alexandre Batta: 'Today, Tuesday, excellent music in the evening, from the Princess and Batta. I am enthusiastic about the latter. I was glad to see that the Princess was struck, or at least I thought she was by the way she played. Franchomme seems to me cold and restricted by comparison' (*Journal*, 23 May 1854, pp. 425–6); 'She [Princess Czartoryska] prefers her Franchomme to Batta; I told her I disagreed. What she regards as expansive, solid and precise in Franchomme, I see as cold and dry. With Batta, I am less aware that someone is scraping on wood: the artist is not so obtrusive. Franchomme is a little like those painters who say to you: "See how strictly I observe the ancient rules, how this hand is exactly the hand I saw before my eyes"' (25 May 1854, p. 427). Interesting!

[68] Many commentators, following a passage in George Sand's *Impressions et souvenirs* (Paris 1873), pp. 80–1, insist that Chopin neither understood nor liked Delacroix's painting, given his presumed aesthetic sympathy with Ingres. The matter is not well documented, however (see Juliusz Starzyński, *Delacroix et Chopin* (Warsaw 1962)). If nothing else, Delacroix taught Chopin how to interpret some of his favourite paintings: note for instance Chopin's allusion to Veronese and his astute description of the staircase of Stafford House in London, in a letter to his family dated 19 August 1848 (*Korespondencja*, vol. II, p. 264).

[69] *Journal 1822–1863*, 29 June 1853, p. 358 (Pach trans., p. 321). This comment was made by Delacroix after hearing a fantasy (K. 475?) by Mozart.

[70] *Histoire de ma vie*, vol. II, p. 422.

savage power of an inspirational élan and its embodiment in forms civilised by a tradition of 'good taste' could be taken as characteristic of a large part of Chopin's output, as of Delacroix's. The painter quotes on more than one occasion Mozart's declaration – which Chopin could apply to himself:

Violent passions should never be expressed to the point where they arouse disgust; even in situations of horror, music should never offend the ear and cease to be music.[71]

The private conversations between the two artists, at Nohant and in Paris, leave a long trail in Delacroix's journal – and Chopin's opinions seem to be responsible for many of the points Delacroix develops in it after the composer's death. In this well-known passage the distinguished dilettante (he was unversed in musical theory) records the explanations of the expert:

During the day, he talked music with me, and that gave him new animation. I asked him what establishes logic in music. He made me feel what counterpoint and harmony are; how the fugue is like pure logic in music, and that to know the fugue deeply is to be acquainted with the element of all reason and all consistency in music. I thought how happy I should have been to learn about all this – which is the despair of the common run of musicians. That feeling gave me an idea of the pleasure in science that is experienced by philosophers worthy of the name. The thing is that true science is not what is ordinarily understood under that term, that is to say, a department of knowledge which differs from art. No, science, looked upon in the way I mean, demonstrated by a man like Chopin, is art itself, and, obversely, art is no longer what the vulgar think it to be, that is, some sort of inspiration which comes from nowhere, which proceeds by chance, and presents no more than the picturesque externals of things. It is reason itself, adorned by genius, but following a necessary course and encompassed by higher laws. This brings me back to the difference between Mozart and Beethoven. As he said to me, 'Where the latter is obscure and seems lacking in unity, the cause is not to be sought in what people look upon as a rather wild originality, the thing they honor him for; the reason is that he turns his back on eternal principles; Mozart never. Each of the parts has its own movement which, while still according with the others, keeps on with its own song and follows it perfectly; there is your counterpoint, *"punto contrapunto"*.' He told me that the custom was to learn the harmonies before coming to counterpoint, that is to say, the succession of the notes which leads to the harmonies. The harmonies in the music of Berlioz are laid on as a veneer; he fills in the intervals as best he can.[72]

Here we see Chopin's continuing commitment to the ideals of his early education under Elsner (as also expressed in his reactions in the late 1820s to Handel's *Ode for St Cecilia's Day* and Klengel's *Canons and Fugues*): here we discover his view of the fundamentals of musical logic and his belief in the supremacy of linear counterpoint, culminating in the art of fugue.

Insufficient attention has been given to the unusual figure that Mozart cuts in this context. It could be that in this discussion he merely stood in for Bach: Chopin was trying to explain himself to a friend who knew hardly any of Bach's work – like most

[71] *Journal 1822–1863*, 23 April 1849, pp. 193–4 (Pach trans., p. 198); see also the entry for 12 December 1856, p. 600.
[72] Ibid., 7 April 1849, pp. 189–90 (Pach trans., pp. 194–5).

Frenchmen of the period, with few and very special exceptions.[73] If Mozart's name was to be quoted for its own sake, it would have been as the composer of the Requiem (which Delacroix knew well) and other works written after 1781–2, that is, after the revelation of Bach had exerted its profound effect on his textures and syntax – again suggesting an implied link in Chopin's mind between Bach and Mozart. Mention of the Viennese master in this context has the added advantage of resurrecting a recurrent motif ('This brings me back') in the conversations between the two: the opposition of Mozart to Beethoven (who 'turns his back on eternal principles; Mozart never'). In this classical/romantic antinomy, the name of Beethoven is used to introduce that of his misguided successor, Berlioz, who 'lays on' the harmonies 'as a veneer' and 'fills in the intervals as best he can'.

On three occasions Delacroix returns to the central problem that haunts him as an innovator in the domain of colour: that of 'sonority, which Chopin would not admit as a legitimate source of sensation'.[74] The most extended passage on the subject is this:

> My dear little Chopin was waxing very indignant against the school of thought which attaches an important part of the effect of music to the particular sound of the instruments. It cannot be denied that certain men, Berlioz among others, are like that . . . A musical motif can speak to the imagination on an instrument confined to its own sounds, like the piano, for example, and which therefore has only one means of moving the senses; but even so it must be said that the assembling of various instruments, each of which has a different sound, produces a more powerful and charming sensation . . . On the piano itself, why alternate between veiled and brilliant sounds, if not to emphasise the idea to be expressed? Sonority in place of the idea is to be condemned, yet it must be admitted that there is in certain sounds, independent of the expression that speaks to the soul, a pleasure received by the senses.[75]

The seductiveness of timbre (and colour) in and of itself is precisely the point at which Delacroix's classically orientated position begins to shift towards the modern world. Whether the painter was more of a sensualist than his musical friend is a moot point. But for both, the musical idea in essence prevails independent of its instrumental embodiment. Hence their condemnation of Berlioz for his arrogant emancipation of the instrumentation, which allows the sound material to take 'the place of the idea'. Moreover, Chopin not only refuses to grant timbre the autonomous status it has enjoyed in this century since Debussy and Schoenberg, but he also regards the seductive powers of timbre as *corrupting*, as detrimental to the listener's grasp of the musical work as a whole, this Jansenist aesthetic representing a kind of defence against the potential dangers of excess. Hence the apparent contradiction recorded by a pupil: 'Chopin did not want [me to use the] pedal, yet he himself used it, particularly the soft pedal – without however indicating this to his pupils, in order not to exaggerate or overstep its resources.'[76]

[73] To the names mentioned above (pp. 120–2) may be added those of Alexandre P. F. Boëly, Félix Danjou, Aristide and Louise Farrenc, and Amédée Méreaux. See François-Sappey, *Alexandre P. F. Boëly*, especially pp. 177–90.

[74] *Journal 1822–1863*, 25 January 1857, p. 634 (Pach trans., p. 567).

[75] Ibid., 13 April 1860, pp. 779–80.

[76] Reminiscence of Mme Courty, reproduced in Louis Aguettant, *La musique de piano des origines à Ravel* (Paris 1954), p. 196 (translation from *CPT*, p. 58).

This recalls Delacroix's comment about the piano – 'why alternate between veiled and brilliant sounds, if not to emphasise the idea to be expressed?' – taste always being the arbiter between the exaggerated and the understated.

So by inferring the name of J. S. Bach from the reference to Mozart in Delacroix's journal and by interpreting the critique of Berlioz as an attack primarily on the emancipation of timbre (Boris de Schloezer said that 'he harmonised with timbres'[77]), I discern the *Art of Fugue* and the 'Forty-Eight' (in both of which the instrument is left unspecified) acting as a sort of paradigm for Chopin when he defines the spirit and technique of counterpoint: 'each of the parts has its own movement which, while still according with the others, keeps on with its own song and follows it perfectly'.

Just as Delacroix (whose spiritual masters were Raphael, Michelangelo, Veronese, Rubens and Poussin) was rightly considered by the painter and theoretician Paul Signac[78] as the immediate precursor of the impressionist movement, the pianist Raoul Koczalski (a pupil of Mikuli) suggested in 1910 that Chopin should be seen as 'the first *lyrical impressionist*'.[79] Whether or not this label is justified ('pre-symbolist'[80] might be preferable), there are undeniable links which can be shown between Chopin and Debussy, especially a shared linear conception of music deriving in each case from a latter-day reinterpretation of Bach. The use of timbre and dynamics in Chopin must also be considered from a pre–Debussyan perspective.

Chopin and Debussy

In 1913, towards the end of his career, Debussy published an article 'On Taste' in music, in which he wrote:

Geniuses can evidently do without taste: take the case of Beethoven, for example. But on the other hand there was Mozart, to whose genius was added a measure of the most delicate 'good taste'. And if we look at the works of J. S. Bach – a benevolent God to whom all composers should offer a prayer before commencing work, to defend themselves from mediocrity – on each new page of his innumerable works we discover things we thought were born only yesterday – from delightful arabesques to an overflowing of religious feeling greater than anything we have since discovered. And in his works we will search in vain for anything the least lacking in 'good taste'.[81]

Debussy had an unceasing veneration for the music of Bach, whose name is once again linked here with the arabesque, which was close to Debussy's heart and the source of his most fruitful innovations. The sixteenth-century polyphonists (Palestrina, Victoria, Lassus) and the Javanese gamelan (notable for its superimposed rhythms and percussive timbres) unveiled at the Exposition Universelle in 1889 also shaped his arabesque, the subtlety of which is by no means captured in the two innocent piano pieces of his that bear this title. It was above all in Bach that Debussy encountered a mastery of

---

[77] Cited in Stefan Jarociński, *Debussy: Impressionism and Symbolism*, trans. Rollo Myers (London 1976), p. 137.
[78] *D'Eugène Delacroix au néo-impressionnisme* (Paris 1899).
[79] *Frédéric Chopin: quatre conférences analytiques* (Paris [1910]), pp. 23 and 28.
[80] See Jarociński, *Debussy*.
[81] *Debussy on Music*, coll. François Lesure, trans. and ed. Richard Langham Smith (New York 1977), p. 277.

melodic contour and shape, and he duly pays homage as follows at the time of the first performance of *Pelléas*:

In reworking the arabesque [of the polyphonists], Bach made it more flexible, more fluid, and despite the fact that the Great Master always imposed a rigorous discipline on beauty, he imbued it with a wealth of free fantasy so limitless that it still astonishes us today. In Bach's music it is not the character of the melody that affects us but rather the curve. More often still it is the parallel movement of several lines whose fusion stirs our emotions – whether fortuitous or contrived. Based on this conception of the ornamental, the music will impress the public as regularly as clockwork, and it will fill their imaginations with pictures.[82]

It is astonishing that these words should so closely echo Chopin's explanations to Delacroix about the fertile logic of counterpoint; likewise the following quotation, in which Debussy invokes the art of Bach as if to argue his own case regarding super-imposed timbres:

We can be sure that old Bach, the essence of all music, scorned harmonic formulae. He pre-ferred the free play of sonorities whose curves, whether flowing in parallel or contrary motion, would result in an undreamed of flowering, so that even the least of his countless manuscripts bears an indelible stamp of beauty. That was the age of the 'wonderful arabesque' . . .[83]

Example 7.16   (a) Prelude Op. 28 No. 21, bars 1–4

Example 7.16   (b) Prelude Op. 28 No. 21, bars 41–4

[82] Ibid., p. 27.
[83] Ibid., p. 84.

Example 7.17 C. Debussy, 'Nuages', *Nocturnes* I, bars 1–4

Example 7.18   C. Debussy, 'Et la lune descend sur le temple qui fut', *Images* II No. 2, bars 31–3

Example 7.19   C. Debussy, 'Et la lune descend', bars 1–3

Example 7.20   *Rondo à la Krakowiak* Op. 14, introduction, bars 1–8

Although the historical and stylistic context of Debussy's *adorable arabesque* differs from that of Chopin's music, the ultimate reference is the same for both composers: a 'polylinear' mode of thought derived from Bach. Many examples could be offered of the bridge that Chopin provides between Bach and Debussy, but the following comparisons should suffice (see Example 7.16). In the Preludes Op. 28 (the chronological centre of Chopin's oeuvre), No. 21 is governed from the start by an underlying four-part texture, the alto and tenor progressing by contrary motion between longer bass and soprano notes. At bar 33, this contrary motion is found in both hands over a dominant pedal, and tension builds towards the cadence, the whole passage acting at once as an allusive recapitulation and a conclusion. Here the shape of the figuration prevails over the actual motivic substance; the expressive effect is indescribable. This passage is not unlike the skeletal introduction of 'Nuages', the first of Debussy's *Nocturnes* for orchestra, which is built on an arabesque in which contrary and similar motion alternate, beginning from the initial open fifth (see Example 7.17). A further stage is reached in the middle of 'Et la lune descend sur le temple qui fut' (*Images* II No. 2), where parallel, contrary and similar motion are combined (see Example 7.18), while parallel motion exclusively operates in the opening motif, which is built on a three-note aggregate (see Example 7.19). If Debussy pushes to an extreme the use of parallel voices, whose modal possibilities had been brought home to him by Satie's *Ogives*, it is the last step in a logical process which begins, as in Chopin's case, with Bach. One notable difference is that in the Debussyan aesthetic pure sonority forms an integral part of the composition.

Despite Delacroix's repeated assertions in his journal, however, Chopin attended constantly to the role of sonority in his music, from his first major works right up to the final compositions, in which sonority assumes an almost structural function. For instance, the introduction to the *Rondo à la Krakowiak* Op. 14 is based on a folkloric motif, delicately sounded in a high register with the hands two octaves apart, over a sustained horn and string 'pedal' (see Example 7.20). The manipulation of register and timbre[84] plays a large part in generating the pastoral atmosphere here, and Chopin himself was aware of the innovative nature of the passage,[85] which cleverly uses a mazurka idea (in 3/4) to start a krakowiak (in 2/4). In the Concertos Opp. 21 and 11 the fleeting 'cadenzas' of the central movements (bars 72–4 and 101–3 respectively) likewise exploit colouristic effects unrelated to the thematic material, the diminished arpeggios in Op. 11 sounding almost like a glass harmonica[86] (see Example 7.21). Chopin takes a similar approach in the cadenza (marked *a piacere* in the original Viennese edition) of the Prelude Op. 45, which is based on a chromatic progression in a lower register, falling and rising in turn, and which might even contain the secret

[84] References in the literature to Chopin's ostensible indifference to instrumental timbres can easily be refuted simply by adducing the finale of the Concerto Op. 21, with its striking *col legno* effect (bars 141ff.) and *cor de signal* (bars 406ff.). Berlioz himself refers to the former in his *Grand traité d'instrumentation et d'orchestration* (Paris 1843).

[85] 'The introduction is original – more so than I look in my felt greatcoat.' *Korespondencja*, vol. I, p. 86, letter to Tytus Woyciechowski, 27 December 1828 (translation from *SCFC*, p. 19).

[86] Abraham refers to similar passages in Op. 2, Op. 13 and Op. 14 as 'coruscating shower[s] of chromatic particles' (*Chopin's Musical Style*, p. 18).

Example 7.21   Concerto Op. 11, II, bars 101–3

of the entire composition. At the orchestral recapitulation of the opening theme in bars 105–14 of the Romance from Op. 11, the piano accompanies with mysterious chromatic figurations initially in parallel sixths, drifting into pure timbral ecstasy as it moves towards the coda. An analogous principle governs the reprise in the Nocturne Op. 55 No. 1, in which a varied repeat of the theme's first notes (bars 75–6) gives way to an oscillating chromatic figuration in the upper register (*molto legato e stretto*, bars 77–84), which is essentially based on two-part counterpoint before it dissolves into swirling arpeggios, an accelerando extending through the coda[87] (see Example 7.22).

In his playing Chopin achieved timbral effects of the ultimate refinement by means of the pedals. The pianist Marmontel, who heard him often, reports:

Chopin used the pedals with marvellous discretion. He often coupled them to obtain a soft and veiled sonority, but more often still he would use them separately for brilliant passages, for sustained harmonies, for deep bass notes, and for loud ringing chords. Or he would use the soft pedal alone for those light murmurings which seem to create a transparent vapour round the arabesques that embellish the melody and envelop it like fine lace. The timbre produced by the pedals on Pleyel pianos has a perfect sonority, and the dampers work with a precision very useful for chromatic and modulating passages; this quality is precious and absolutely indispensable.[88]

That mechanical precision was of vast importance to the composer-pianist, and thus it helped pave the way for Debussy. Chopin specified pedal markings (as well as dynamics and phrasing) with the most meticulous care in his manuscripts and insisted on inserting these himself in the *Stichvorlagen* prepared by copyists; ironically, it is these very markings which have been most frequently altered by editors.[89] Even though he

---

[87] It would be interesting to study the evolution of cadenzas and codas in the nocturnes, an evolution extending from the colouristic figurations of Op. 9 Nos. 2 and 3, through the more meditative codas in Op. 27 Nos. 1 and 2, Op. 48 No. 2 and Op. 55 No. 2, to the rocking motion concluding Op. 62 No. 1 (bars 81 to the end; see Example 7.15b). Such a study would show how ornamental material of a 'parenthetical' nature (as in Op. 9 Nos. 2 and 3) becomes structurally essential in a development which would culminate in the Berceuse. It would also investigate the close connection between the final phase of this evolution and Debussy's arabesque – the latter not in the sense of superimposed lines but as embodying 'the principle of the "ornament", which is at the root of all kinds of art (the word "ornament" here has nothing to do with the ornaments one finds in musical dictionaries)' (*Debussy on Music*, p. 27).

[88] Antoine Marmontel, *Histoire du piano et de ses origines* (Paris 1885), pp. 256–7 (translation from *CPT*, p. 58).

[89] In this respect, the best modern *Urtext* editions are Jan Ekier's: *Wiener Urtext Edition* – Ballades, Impromptus, Nocturnes, Scherzos; *Polish National Edition* (still being compiled) – Ballades, Concerto Op. 21, Etudes, Impromptus, Preludes, Scherzos and Miscellaneous Pieces.

Example 7.22   Nocturne Op. 55 No. 1, bars 73–9

warned his pupils against overuse of the sustaining pedal as well as the soft pedal, he employed them abundantly, if subtly, to exploit the colouristic properties of the Pleyel pianos of his time.

Register, dynamics, articulation and rhythm together produce a unique effect in the fleeting final bars of the Etude Op. 10 No. 9 (see Example 7.23). At the start of the Ballade Op. 38, the first harmony, in bar 3, emerges from the floating, vibrating unisons of the opening. A no less seamless connection joins the initially tentative second theme in the Ballade Op. 47 to the still resonating final chord from the opening section (see Example 7.24). By these means Chopin anticipates one of Verlaine's principles (stated in the symbolist manifesto *Art poétique*): 'Nothing is more precious than the grey song [*la chanson grise*] / In which the Indefinite is united with the Precise.'[90] In both the ritornello of the *Andante spianato* from Op. 22 (bars 53–66 and 97–110) and the conclusion of the Fantasy Op. 49, generous use of the pedal produces a mist of sound not unlike certain effects of light, at once blurred and distinct, in the paintings of Monet. The same effect is achieved in the Etude Op. 25 No. 1 in A♭ major, Chopin's playing of which inspired Schumann's famous evocation:

Imagine an Aeolian harp capable of all sonorous levels, and an artist's hand animating it, adding here and there all kinds of fantastic embellishments, always, however, with a strong bass audible and, in the treble, a softly flowing cantilena, and you have some idea of his playing. No wonder, then, that we most enjoyed the pieces we heard him play himself, and above all the

---

[90] Paul Verlaine, *Jadis et Naguère*, in *Oeuvres poétiques complètes*, ed. Yves-Gérard Le Dantec and Jacques Borel (Paris 1962), pp. 326–7. See also p. 138 below.

first [Etude] in A♭ major, which is more a poem than an étude. It would be a mistake to suppose that he made all the small notes individually audible: it was more an undulation of the A♭ major chord, lifted here and there high up on the keyboard, with the help of the pedal. But, exquisitely entangled in the harmony, one perceived the wonderful, deep-toned melody . . .[91]

Example 7.23   Etude Op. 10 No. 9, bars 65–7

Example 7.24   Ballade Op. 47, bars 48–53

Similar means produce quite the opposite effect at the start of the vertiginous Prelude Op. 28 No. 16, the autograph manuscript of which reveals a noteworthy change of heart: the original pedal marking on each minim has been crossed out and replaced by two continuous pedals, each three bars long (bars 2–4, 5–7: see Example 7.25). Pedalling also plays an essential colouristic role throughout the Barcarolle Op. 60, especially in the figuration at the end. Such examples could of course be abundantly added to in a more specialised study, which would propose a detailed taxonomy of Chopin's pedalling techniques.

Chopin never specified the *una corda* in editions of his works, no doubt 'in order not to exaggerate or overstep its resources' (Mme Courty, quoted above). On the other hand, his autograph annotations in Jane Stirling's score indicate soft pedal as well as the sustaining pedal in two ornamental passages and in the coda of the Nocturne Op. 15 No. 2 (bars 18, 20 and 58ff.).[92] Kleczyński[93] adduces other examples of Chopin's use

---

[91]   Robert Schumann, '12 Etüden für Pianoforte von Friedrich Chopin. Werk 25', *Gesammelte Schriften über Musik und Musiker*, ed. F. Gustav Jansen, 2 vols. (Leipzig 1891), vol. II, p. 73. (Translation derived from *CPT*, pp. 68–9.)

[92]   Jean-Jacques Eigeldinger and Jean-Michel Nectoux, *Frédéric Chopin: Oeuvres pour piano. Fac-similé de l'exemplaire de Jane W. Stirling avec annotations et corrections de l'auteur* (Paris 1982), pp. 70 and 72.

[93]   See *CPT*, p. 58.

Example 7.25   Prelude Op. 28 No. 16, bars 1–4

of the *una corda* by itself, in particular to bring out enharmonic relationships, thus showing that it had a timbral function for Chopin.

Debussy's works follow the very same path, and Marguerite Long – who studied his music with him – recalls:

Like Chopin, Debussy was preoccupied with the role of the pedal and wrote to his publisher on 1st September 1915: 'The truth is that an abuse of the pedal is one way of covering up a lack of technique and so one has to make a lot of noise to prevent the music one is mutilating being heard! In theory there should be some means of indicating the "breathing space" graphically: it is not impossible.' The publisher remembered hearing Debussy's marvellous way of treating the pedal at a *ff* followed directly by a *pp*.[94]

Debussy's almost categorical refusal to specify the use of the pedals in his scores (the few exceptions are all the more significant for this reason) thus stems from apprehensions identical to Chopin's. His piano-roll recordings of his own works confirm the close links between his conception of sound and that of his predecessor.

Because of these shared affinities, both composers treat the piano as essentially an instrument of the most intimate expression. Chopin's aversion for loud noise and for the public platform (which in his view fuelled a lust for display and lacked any relation to the essence of music) is well known. From the mid 1830s onwards he kept his distance from the concert arena, openly avowing that concerts 'are never real music; you have to give up the idea of hearing in them the most beautiful things of art'.[95]

---

[94] Marguerite Long, *At the Piano with Debussy*, trans. Olive Senior-Ellis (London 1972), p. 45.
[95] See Maria von Grewingk, *Eine Tochter Alt-Rigas Schülerin Chopins* (Riga 1928), p. 19. (Translation from *CPT*, p. 5.)

His approach was that of a musician *da camera* who happened to find himself in the Paris salons of Louis-Philippe, in which he became something of an idol. Debussy, who in his younger days graced many a salon of the Belle Epoque, also loved the piano for what he called 'conversations between the piano and oneself'[96] – 'For it is Nuance we seek, / Not Colour, but Nuance!', again in the words of Verlaine's *Art poétique*. Debussy was clearly Chopin's successor in the experimental use of dynamics, these ranging in his music from *piano* to triple (even quadruple) *piano* through subtle intermediate stages. Jarociński[97] has calculated that 80 per cent of Debussy's output varies between *piano* and *pianissimo*: in accordance with the symbolist aesthetic, music emerges from silence and returns to it. Emma Debussy-Bardac notes that

Debussy like Chopin nearly always played in a perpetual *demi-teinte*, but nevertheless with a full, deep sonority without any hardness in the attack. The scale of nuances must go from triple *piano* to *forte*, without ever producing confused sounds where the subtlety of the harmonies is lost.[98]

These points are confirmed by Debussy's own recordings, and by the reminiscences of others.[99]

Long before illness had taken its toll on his frail constitution, Chopin's aesthetic needs had dictated his preferences in the sphere of dynamics, as well as his choice of pianos (Graf, Pleyel). He was actually flattered to hear the reservations of certain Viennese listeners concerning the extreme delicacy of his playing,[100] and the waspish Paris journalist who criticised the 'vaporous nuances [of his] microscopic playing' by no means offended him. Charles Hallé notes the effect of Chopin's experiments in dynamics (and of his unique rhetoric of performance) when pushed to their logical conclusion:

at the last public concert he gave in Paris, at the . . . beginning of 1848, he played the latter part of his 'Barcarolle', from the point it demands the utmost energy, in the most opposite style, pianissimo, but with such wonderful nuances, that one remained in doubt if this new reading were not preferable to the accustomed one. Nobody but Chopin could have accomplished such a feat.[101]

In the same vein, the Scherzo Op. 54 – a piece which, as its title implies, thrives on a certain pianistic bravura – remains within *piano* for three-quarters of its duration. The gradations of Chopin's legendary *mezza voce* find a later counterpart in the '*lointain*' markings scattered through Debussy's scores, not to mention the analogous indications *atténué*, *estompé* and *presque rien*. What composer before Chopin so painstakingly indicated the extinction of sound by means of expressive and dynamic markings (which are particularly abundant before the mid 1830s)? Note for instance the coda of the Mazurka Op. 24 No. 4, where the following are found within just thirty bars:

---

[96] As a preface to his *Images oubliées* for piano (composed in 1894 and published posthumously with this title in 1977), Debussy notes: 'These pieces would not suit "the brilliantly lit salons" which normally bring together people who do not like music. They are rather "Conversations" between the Piano and Oneself . . .'

[97] Jarociński, *Debussy*, p. 139.

[98] Quoted in Janine-Weill, *Marguerite Long. Une vie fascinante* (Paris 1969), p. 87. (Translation from *CPT*, p. 128 n. 120.)

[99] See especially Alfredo Casella, *Il pianoforte* (Milan 1954), pp. 110–11.

[100] *Korespondencja*, vol. I, p. 93, letter to his family, 12 August 1829.

[101] *Life and Letters of Sir Charles Hallé*, ed. C. E. Hallé and Marie Hallé (London 1896), p. 36.

p – *ritenuto* – *dim* – *pp calando* – *pp* – *pp mancando* – *sempre rallentando* – *smorzando*. This exquisite detail would of course be achieved by Debussy as well: it was not only the extraordinarily evocative *dolce sfogato* (in bar 78 of the Barcarolle) which would find an echo in the later composer's music, as in the *rapide et fuyant* of his Prelude 'Les Fées sont d'exquises danseuses' (Book II No. 11).

A full sonority, a remarkable delicacy, a perfect mastery of nuance, an impeccable finish, an imperceptible rubato always framed within the beat, an astounding use of pedal: all this was what defined Debussy's playing.[102]

Jacques Durand's description could almost apply to Chopin's playing, were it not for the name of Debussy at the end. The term rubato, used constantly by Debussy, no doubt should be understood in only one of the meanings that Chopin attached to it.[103] This practice of slightly altering the basic tempo, which demanded a controlled agogic freedom, was a natural outgrowth of the essentially improvisatory nature of both composers. Nothing was further from their temperaments than the routine, the immutably fixed: under their fingers music was continually reborn, with a generous spontaneity akin to the impressionist painters' wish to capture the effect of the light at any given moment.

The close relation between the sound palettes of the two composers can be seen (or, better, heard) by juxtaposing the coda of the Nocturne Op. 27 No. 1 with the opening bars of 'Clair de lune' from the *Suite Bergamasque* (see Example 7.26). The enharmonically equivalent keys in these passages make the affinity of the two composers even more palpable: the kinship of their tactile and auditory response is there for all to hear. It is almost as if Debussy had the sound of the Nocturne in his inner ear and under his fingers, simply 'omitting' the bass at the start but introducing it later (bars 29–30), at which point it becomes a true nocturne – uncannily similar to Chopin's Op. 27 No. 2, in D♭ major. The writing in thirds and sixths is but one of many points of contact between the two composers (compare their respective etudes), allowing us to realise the extent of Chopin's enduring influence on his successor.[104] Debussy not only declared that 'he wore out his fingers'[105] on the A♭ Etude from the *Trois Nouvelles Etudes*, but he also wrote in an unpublished note of 19 February 1910 (contemporary with the completion of Book I of the Preludes): 'I loved Chopin almost as soon as I began to love music, and I have continued to do so!',[106] an allusion to his first piano

102 Jacques Durand, *Quelques souvenirs d'un éditeur de musique*, 2 vols. (Paris 1925), vol. II, p. 21. (Translation from *CPT*, p. 128 n. 120.)
103 On the problem of Chopin's rubato, see *CPT*, pp. 49–52 and corresponding notes. [See also David Rowland's chapter in the present volume. *Eds.*]
104 For discussion of the relationship between Chopin's and Debussy's music, see Robert Godet, 'Chopin – Debussy' [1918], *Cahiers Debussy*, 3 (1976), pp. 11–13; Casella, *Il pianoforte*, passim; Paul Badura-Skoda, 'Chopin's Influence', in *Frédéric Chopin: Profiles of the Man and the Musician*, ed. Alan Walker (London 1966), pp. 269–72; Zofia Chechlińska, 'Chopin a impresjonizm', in *Szkice o kulturze muzycznej XIX wieku*, vol. II (Warsaw 1973), pp. 21–34; C. Palmer, *Impressionism in Music* (London 1973), passim; Edward Lockspeiser, *Debussy: His Life and Mind*, 2 vols. (Cambridge 1978), passim; Samson, *The Music of Chopin*, pp. 216–17; *CPT*, pp. 127–30 nn. 120–2; Roy Howat, 'Chopin's Influence on the Fin-de-siècle and Beyond', in *The Cambridge Companion to Chopin*, ed. Jim Samson (Cambridge 1992), pp. 246–83.
105 Long, *At the Piano with Debussy*, p. 19.
106 Private collection, Urbana, Illinois, USA. The unidentified addressee of the note was the editor of a music periodical who was asking Debussy for an article to celebrate the centenary of Chopin's birth. Debussy never wrote this because of his poor state of health.

Andante très expressif

Example 7.26   (a) C. Debussy, 'Clair de lune', *Suite Bergamasque* No. 3, bars 1–4

Example 7.26   (b) Nocturne Op. 27 No. 1, bars 96–8

teacher, Mme Mauté, who ostensibly studied with Chopin.[107] The dedication of the *Douze Etudes* (1915) 'à la mémoire de Frédéric Chopin' represents the final expression of a devotion also evident in the Chopin edition that he prepared for Jacques Durand.

Final perspectives

By way of conclusion, let us consider the significance of Chopin's deep affection for Beethoven's Sonata Op. 26, in his beloved key of A♭ major and noteworthy for its *Marcia funebre*. He would often play the first movement, a set of variations, the last of which evokes an almost Chopinesque atmosphere. Lenz, a Beethovenian, left this striking testimony of Chopin's interpretation:

He played it well, but not so well as his own compositions; neatly, but with no contrasts – not like a *romance*, mounting from variation to variation. His *mezza voce* was a whisper, but he was unapproachable in his *cantilena*, endlessly finished in coherency of construction – ideally beautiful, but *womanish!* Beethoven is a *man*, and never ceases to be a man! Chopin played on a Pleyel – at one time he would never give a lesson on any other instrument; one *had* to have a Pleyel! Every one was charmed; I, too, was charmed – but only by his *tone*, by his *touch*, by his elegance and grace, by his absolutely *pure style*. As we drove back together, I was quite sincere when he asked my opinion. '*I indicate*', he remarked, without any touchiness, – 'the listeners must finish the picture.'[108]

---

[107] At present this link can be neither confirmed nor denied: see *CPT*, p. 129 n. 121.
[108] Lenz, *The Great Piano Virtuosos*, pp. 56–7.

This text tells us a great deal, despite the fact that Lenz's assessment of Beethoven is blatantly gendered. Chopin's performance, he says, is notable for its flexible yet logical phrasing, for exploring the full range of timbre possible on a Pleyel. Whereas Lenz craves a 'rhetorical' progression from variation to variation, Chopin, instead of stressing the structural outline, emphasises 'values' (in the painterly sense), responding in aristocratic fashion to Lenz's critique with the key remark: '*I indicate*, the listeners must finish the picture.' It is an aesthetic of suggestion which shapes his interpretation, with the emphasis placed on what is left unsaid. This amounts to an essential principle of symbolist poetics, as expressed in Mallarmé's declaration: 'To *name* an object is to stifle three-quarters of the enjoyment of the poem, which comes from divining bit by bit: to *suggest* it, that is one's dream.'[109] It goes without saying that the Variations from Beethoven's Op. 26 are no Mallarmé poem; nevertheless, in allowing them to be 'divined bit by bit' while still treating them with the utmost stylistic purity, Chopin avails himself of a *pre-symbolist aesthetic of suggestion* which, as I have shown throughout this essay, lies at the heart of his sound world from the Romance of the Concerto Op. 11 up to his final, lyrical pieces. In these few bars of the Nocturne Op. 62 No. 1 (see Example 7.27), Chopin, carried along in the reverie of his 'espaces imaginaires',[110] enters the domain of musical symbolism as it would later be embodied by Debussy, by the time of his first maturity.

Example 7.27   Nocturne Op. 62 No. 1, bars 62–7

---

[109] Response to Jules Huret, *Sur l'évolution littéraire* (Paris 1891), cited in Jarociński, *Debussy*, p. 31.
[110] Chopin's expression (in French in the Polish original) in a letter to his family, [18–20 July 1845] (*Korespondencja*, vol. II, p. 137).

But the real stylistic miracle of this passage is that it can co-exist with the contrapuntal arabesque in bars 76–80, whose strength of outline markedly contrasts with its suppleness (the two passages having been separated by a recapitulation of the opening idea, enveloped in trills – a trembling 'in which the Indefinite is united with the Precise. /. . . It is, in the faded autumn sky, The blue disorder of the bright stars!'). In this setting, the descending chromatic line in the bass (bar 76 – see Example 7.28) should no longer be interpreted as an obbligato pattern deriving from the rhetoric of J. S. Bach, but as a suggestive device with its own expressive and aesthetic significance.

Example 7.28 Nocturne Op. 62 No. 1, bars 76–80

A revealing text from January 1841 in George Sand's *Impressions et souvenirs* relates a conversation with Delacroix on Ingres's *Stratonice* in the presence of a fascinated Chopin (who feigns a lack of expertise in artistic matters during the discussion). After a brief survey of the composer's dislikes in the visual arts, Sand reaches the following generalisations about Chopin:

Everything that he regarded as eccentric offended him. He locked himself up in the narrowest of conventions. Strange anomaly! His genius is the most original and the most individual that exists. But he does not want anyone to say this to his face. It is [also] true that Delacroix's literary tastes are limited to the most classical and the most formalist.[111]

[111] See reference in note 68.

In highlighting the apparent contradiction shared by both artists[112] (and defining this in terms of their respective tastes in an art which they themselves did not practise), the novelist offers, in my view, a key insight into what unites Chopin and Delacroix in their aesthetic outlooks, as well as the position that posterity has assigned to them in the history of art. Possessed of a singular psychic energy, these two physically frail beings had to harness a forceful, ardent temperament in both their social demeanour and their artistic creation. Chopin managed this by exerting a constant check on himself, 'by striving to submit these feelings to what he thought *had to be* in order *to be right* [*devoir être* pour *être bien*]', in the words of Liszt.[113] Translating this moral trait into aesthetic terms, one can say that his art seems the result of a supremely controlled catharsis, his classicistic beliefs being the essential condition of this catharsis. This is why his marked individuality and futuristic tendencies could not be recognised as such by him: it was essential for Chopin – the Exile Incarnate – to belong to his ideal artistic tradition. This ideal made him shun the present and immerse himself in the music of J. S. Bach and Mozart, which, as we have seen, was both a stimulus and an anchor. The direction taken by Chopin's last works (from about Op. 47 onwards) joins together a solid foundation rooted in Bach with unmistakable anticipations of Debussy. What could be regarded by the historian and the analyst as two separate strands is of course one and the same compositional reality, whose result is a creative output in which Chopin's retrospective vision opens up a new path to the future. If Chopin arrives almost in spite of himself at the frontiers of musical symbolism (the same could be said of Delacroix and impressionism), he does so only by grounding himself in the heritage of late baroque and classical music, which he assimilates and moulds in his own image. This is precisely the conclusion reached in Charles Rosen's *The Classical Style*: 'The true inheritors of the classical style were not those who maintained its traditions, but those, from Chopin to Debussy, who preserved its freedom as they gradually altered and finally destroyed the musical language which had made the creation of the style possible.'[114]

To claim that Chopin was unaware of his innovations in musical syntax would be absurd. On the contrary, it could well be that he deliberately practised a *politique de l'autruche*, confining himself 'in the narrowest of conventions', in order to cope with his painful awareness of the consequences that his innovations might hold for later generations. But this is an *argumentum ex silentio*, as he could not bring himself to pronounce on the music of the future. Even if he had been able to do so, no doubt he would have chosen not to.

---

112 In *Histoire de ma vie*, vol. II, p. 250, George Sand devotes a passage to Delacroix which exactly corresponds to the one on Chopin in her *Impressions et souvenirs*: 'although, because of a sharp and unusual contradiction in his character, he incessantly attacks the present and rails against the future, although he contents himself with knowing, feeling, understanding, cherishing exclusively the works and often the ideas of the past, he is, in his art, the audacious innovator *par excellence.*'

113 *F. Chopin*, p. 181 (the italics are Liszt's).

114 Charles Rosen, *The Classical Style* (New York 1972), p. 460.

8   Ambiguity and reinterpretation in Chopin

EDWARD T. CONE

I

We know our Chopin too well. We experience every event in his music with unperturbed equanimity. We acknowledge each unusual turn of phrase, each unique progression, with a wise nod, as if to say, 'Yes, we were expecting that.' To be sure, the music of every well-known composer suffers from the effects of over-exposure, but Chopin's case is an exacerbated one. Familiarity has dulled our appreciation – has sometimes even blocked our recognition – of one of the primary characteristics of his style: the ambiguity that permeates every level of his musical thought.

Of course some degree of ambiguity is present in all music beyond the complexity of a bugle-call. What Empson said of poetry, that 'the machinations of ambiguity are among [its] very roots',[1] is true of music, especially if one accepts Empson's broad definition of the concept, which, *mutatis mutandis*, includes 'any [musical] nuance, however slight, which gives room for alternative reactions to the same piece of [music]'.[2] But the combination of persistence (in musical time) and penetration (of musical texture) that characterises Chopin's ambiguity is rare in pre-romantic usage.

One such musical nuance was almost a cliché throughout much of the eighteenth century and even the nineteenth: the addition of a seventh to an opening major triad, suggesting that the sonority might be a dominant instead of a tonic. The resulting ambiguity was typically resolved by a formula which presented the progression I–V^7/IV–IV–V^7–I or some variant thereof, often over a tonic pedal. Instances are numerous – for example, the opening movements of Mozart's Piano Quartet No. 2, Beethoven's Trio Op. 1 No. 1 and Schumann's Piano Quintet. In all these cases, the ambiguity is no sooner presented than resolved: the apparent dominant seventh is reinterpreted, once and for all, as a tonic in disguise. All doubts are dispelled early and definitively.

Chopin, too, employs the standard pattern, for instance in his A♭ Mazurka Op. 41 No. 3; but in the introduction to the fourth Ballade he adapts it – or subverts it – for his own purposes. An apparent V^7–I in F turns out to be a member of a rounded

---

[1]   William Empson, *Seven Types of Ambiguity* (New York 1955), p. 5.
[2]   Ibid., p. 3.

I^6–V^7/IV–IV–ii^9–V^7–I in C, but Chopin's tonic lacks the stability of its models. Far from being underpinned by a pedal, it is developed only gradually. The lonely octave G tentatively initiates the passage. Its chordal function is slowly revealed as the fifth of C when that triad emerges, at first as an unstable inversion. By the time the chord achieves root position, a seventh has already been added; so we are ready to accept F as the tonic. Not so: the continuing progression treats F as IV, leading through V^7 back to I, as in the old formula. But Chopin's deception is more fundamental, to be disclosed only after the passage has been repeated, cadentially confirmed and closed by a fermata. For the theme that now enters proclaims that C is not the tonic but the dominant it once seemed to be. F, which briefly sounded like a tonic but apparently turned out to be a subdominant, is revealed as the tonic after all!

Example 8.1   Ballade Op. 52, bars 1–8, alternative reductions

The entire progression can be approximately summarised as in Example 8.1a or 8.1b. But the monotonality of such sketches, based on syntactic analysis, reflects our failure – perhaps our inability – to savour the tonal ambiguity of the passage. That is partly due to the over-familiarity mentioned at the outset. But in addition, our present-day desire to demonstrate tonal unity wherever possible prompts us to describe the structure as the prolongation of a single harmony, whose function must not be in doubt. As a result, we do not hear the music as I believe it was intended to be heard. That is why I have resorted to what I call 'intentional analysis', which seeks to ascertain, as far as possible, how the composer wished us to hear his music. I suggest that Chopin was here being deliberately ambiguous, and that a convincing analysis of the passage must reveal that intention. I therefore offer, as a supplement to the syntactic analyses of Example 8.1, the following sketch, which tries to capture our experience of the successive reinterpretations required by the introduction.[3]

---

[3]   What I call 'intentional analysis' is closely related to the 'third-hearing analysis' of my essay 'Three Ways of Reading a Detective Story – or a Brahms Intermezzo', in Edward T. Cone, *Music: A View from Delft* (Chicago 1989), pp. 77–93. I now use the term 'intentional analysis' partly for polemical reasons, to indicate my opposition to certain voguish aesthetic (particularly literary) theories which insist on the inaccessibility of textual meaning and the irrelevance of authorial intent.

$$G(?) \rightarrow \begin{bmatrix} \text{5th of} \\ C \\ \underbrace{V^7 - I} \end{bmatrix}$$

$$\begin{bmatrix} F \\ \underbrace{IV - ii^9 - V^7 - I} \end{bmatrix}$$

$$\begin{bmatrix} C \\ \underbrace{V - i} \\ f \end{bmatrix}$$

Ambivalence of the same kind can also affect the stability of an entire thematic section within an otherwise well-established tonal framework. No doubt coincidentally, the second theme of the third Ballade (bars 52–115), like the introduction to the fourth, offers a choice between the keys of C and F, embodied in a variant of the same progression. Do we hear its first phrase as F:V^7–I–vi^7–V^7/V–V, or as C:V^7/IV–IV–ii^7–V^7–I? And if, as the music proceeds, the tonality vacillates, at what points does its orientation switch? The climax of bar 81 and the cadence of 98–9 are in F minor, and bars 103–4 effect a return to C – but to C as dominant or as tonic? Since the entire theme recommences here, its initial ambiguity again confronts us.

The entire subject, framed as it is by the global tonic A♭, can be described as (I)–III♮–vi–III♮–(I). But syntactic analysis cannot resolve the fundamental problem: whether V♮–i–V♮ (Example 8.2a) or I–iv♭–I (Example 8.2b) is represented locally. Here Chopin creates an unresolved ambiguity between alternatives presented simultaneously rather than successively. True, the reprise does resolve an analogous vacillation between A♭ and D♭ (C♯) in favour of the former; but that denouement, which triumphantly recovers the global tonic, cannot relevantly influence our retrospective comprehension of the theme in a different context.

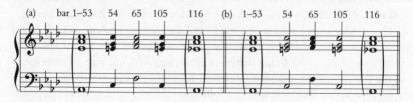

(a)   bar 1–53   54   65   105   116   (b)   1–53   54   65   105   116

Example 8.2   Ballade Op. 47, bars 49–116, alternative reductions

Another version of the same formula initiates a tonal problem which embraces the whole of the E minor Mazurka Op. 41 No. 1. Like Beethoven's First Symphony, the Mazurka begins directly with an apparent V^7–I. Like its notable predecessor it immediately reinterprets that cadence, for we can understand the first four bars as V^7/iv–iv–V^7–i in E minor. But if we try to listen to the opening afresh, suppressing what we 'know' of the piece, we hear two perfect cadences, the first in A minor and the second in E minor. Which is to be given precedence? One can argue that the downward transposition strengthens the second cadence, and that the minor mode vitiates any dominant tendency. But the same strictures apply to the Mazurka Op. 56 No. 3, in which the key of the transposed phrase does turn out to be the (minor) dominant. In the present instance an immediate repetition of the A minor cadence is continued by a melodic descent (g^1–f^1–e^1) which reverts to the harmony of E minor, but by utilising that most ambiguous of modes, the phrygian – hardly a strong tonal confirmation. E might well be a minor dominant. True, the central contrasting section expands B major as V of E minor; and the eventual reprise is effected through polyphonic motion from B major's own iii, D♯ minor. Here, at least, the root-position E minor cadence prevails over the inversion that represents A minor. Yet the final extension of the phrygian cadence, with its alternation of the two competing tonics, undermines E minor's pretensions. Indeed, after the solitary A minor of bar 66 it is possible to imagine Example 8.3 as a substitute ending – not as a tierce de Picardie, but as a frank admission of the dominant tinge of the phrygian cadence. So even if the Mazurka can be analysed as the prolongation of a single triad, that triad is hardly a strongly confirmed tonic. Unlike minor ambiguities which yield to immediate reinterpretations or other proximate resolutions, the tonal ambivalence of the Mazurka is fundamental to its meaning.

Example 8.3   Mazurka Op. 41 No. 1, hypothetical ending

Vacillation assumes a different form in the introduction to the third Scherzo, where the composer's approach to the tonic is unusually oblique. Again there are two candidates for tonic, a fifth apart. Here, however, the winner hardly seems to be in the running until its startling last-moment victory. The opening of the Scherzo can be heard as the elaboration of successive first inversions (Example 8.4a). An initially tentative adumbration of F♯ minor (VI^6–V^6) is reinforced when the sustained B major that punctuates bars 6–8 is succeeded by a similarly sustained, enharmonically respelled diminished seventh on B♯ in bars 14–16, pointing towards a dominant C♯. Those two versions of the subdominant are joined by a third in the inverted German sixth evolved by bars 18–24 (Example 8.4b). The expected C♯ at last arrives with the octaves that proclaim the principal theme – but it is C♯ minor not major. When, on the last beat of bar 27, E♮ replaces the expected E♯, that detail shockingly but effectively alters the entire perspective. At one stroke C♯ is converted from dominant to tonic. Now, postponement of an expected tonic certainly occurs in the music of Chopin's predecessors. But this one, uniquely, is both expected and unexpected: expected as a

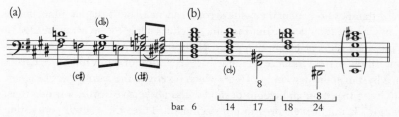

Example 8.4   (a) Scherzo Op. 39, bars 1–7, reduction
                (b) Scherzo Op. 39, introduction (bars 1–24) with hypothetical resolution (the
                bracketed pitches indicate Chopin's own notation)

major chord, unexpected as a minor tonic. Its function is established as it were by fiat, not by tonal necessity.

The first-inversion gambit of the Scherzo is employed by Chopin in many guises. It can be tentative, yielding only gradually to clarity in the Prelude Op. 45; or peremptory, resolving swiftly but unexpectedly in the introduction of the B♭ minor Sonata. Even the sustained octave, that stalwart herald of the key in so many classical symphonies, can be subverted in its favour. Thus the initial C of the first Ballade turns out to be, not the root of a tonic or dominant, but the bass of a first inversion, an elaborately arpeggiated A♭ chord. Its function is defined only when the G minor of the Moderato retrospectively identifies the opening harmony as a Neapolitan sixth.

The oblique approach to the tonic need not be purely introductory. It invades the first theme of the Mazurka Op. 17 No. 4. That takes off from a vaguely defined sixth chord whose role as VI[6] in A minor is only gradually revealed.[4] And although that most mysterious of all Chopin's movements, the finale of the B♭ minor Sonata, lacks a formal introduction, it requires four searching bars of the theme itself to locate a tonic.[5]

II

One should not conclude from the foregoing examples that Chopin's harmonic ambiguity depends on tonal instability, nor that it requires an entire theme or section – much less a whole composition – as its locus. On the contrary, it is typical of the composer to embed, within a stable key, a short passage which teasingly plays with 'alternative reactions' to a harmonic or polyphonic detail. Each passage involves a contrast, however brief, between possible interpretations, or between one interpretation and a subsequent reinterpretation. Three main types can be distinguished: those in which a harmony implies more than one function, those subject to divergent chordal and linear interpretations, and those involving what I call cadential reorientation.

---

4   See William Thomson, 'Functional Ambiguity in Tonal Structures', *Music Perception*, 1 (1983), pp. 17–27.
5   Although Beethoven's approaches to the tonic can be more complex and more extended than Chopin's (as in the introductions to the Quartet Op. 59 No. 3 and to the *Leonora* Overture No. 3), even the most devious will eventually signal the expected keynote in such a way as to make its arrival seem inevitable. Closer in spirit to Chopin's openings are those of some of Schubert's songs. See, for example, Walter Frisch, 'Schubert's *Nähe des Geliebten*', in *Schubert, Critical and Analytical Studies*, ed. Walter Frisch (Lincoln, Nebraska and London 1986), pp. 175–99, especially 188–9. But then, Schubert's ambiguities, particularly as they relate to his song texts, deserve an essay for themselves.

The first type was well known to earlier composers, who frequently exploited the multiple meanings of the diminished seventh; but then, that chord manifestly signals its own equivocation. More to the point is the familiar pun on the enharmonic identity of primary seventh and German sixth. Chopin exploits it in the Polonaise Op. 40 No. 2. At bars 73–7 (bar numbers as in the Henle *Urtext* edition) he introduces the German sixth (inverted) as a neighbour between two second-inversion tonics (A♭), then reinterprets it (in normal position) as the dominant seventh of a Neapolitan. That chord is celebrated as a temporary tonic before a return through vi to an extended cadence in the tonic A♭ (Example 8.5a). So far Chopin is close to classical models, but he has not finished. When the passage is repeated, the ambivalent chord bypasses its alternation with I and proceeds directly to the Neapolitan sixth (bars 81–2; Example 8.5b). Now the implied new key, A♮, produces its own punning chord, a semitone higher than its predecessor. Again, is it a German sixth or the dominant seventh of a new Neapolitan? After a moment of doubt it proves to be the latter (bar 83). This time the return requires two stages. First the B♭ Neapolitan must be resolved to its tonic A♮ by the progression utilised earlier (bar 84). In the further descent from A♮ (B♭♭) to A♭, the original punning chord seems impatient to pledge its allegiance to the true tonic rather than to the upstart Neapolitan. Hence bars 84–5 telescope bars 75–7, and the subsequent authentic cadence offers not only the return to the tonic but also the hitherto thwarted resolution of the German sixth.

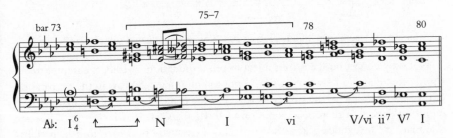

Example 8.5   (a) Polonaise Op. 40 No. 2, bars 73–80, reduction

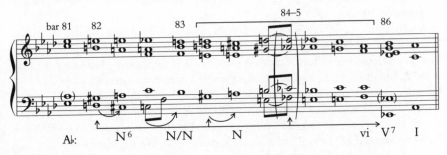

Example 8.5   (b) Polonaise Op. 40 No. 2, bars 81–6, reduction

One form of the augmented sixth, built on the tonic, is identical with V⁷/IV. In the Mazurka Op. 56 No. 1 Chopin exploits the equivalence at bar 44 to modulate from the B major of the opening to the E♭ (D♯) of the first Poco più mosso. There is little opportunity to savour the brief ambiguity. Besides, the composer has conspicuously employed another augmented sixth in bar 12, not to create a prolonged ambiguity but to resolve the one produced by the tentative, shifting harmonies of the opening phrase. By stating and repeating that progression he has, so to speak, attuned our ears to expect augmented sixths at crucial moments. That is why he can deceive us the next time around, at bar 102. When the cadence of the recapitulated first theme (again in B major) moves to a new dominant seventh, this time on D♮, we expect the usual pun – probably effecting a modulation to F♯. But no: the chord really is a dominant seventh, resolving to a new tonic, G (Example 8.6). Such double use of a single harmony to effect a modulation is of course well known to every music student. In the Mazurka, Chopin, by defeating the expectations he has previously encouraged, adds a layer of duplicity.

Example 8.6   Mazurka Op. 56 No. 1, bars 102–3, with hypothetical substitution

Not only chords but keys are subject to reinterpretation; indeed, the reinterpreted chord often entails a new key. A simple but telling instance occurs in the preparation of the second theme of the first Ballade. From the tonic G minor of the first theme a transition leads to a rhetorical extension of V/III (bars 64–7), which sounds like the dominant of an expected key. But that chord, reduced to a bare fourth, is transformed by a new bass into a member of V⁹/VI. Which is to be the new key, III (B♭) or VI (E♭)? The second theme teasingly vacillates between the two until its cadence confirms the latter.

Much more complex is the apparently false recapitulation of the A minor Mazurka Op. 59 No. 1. It is in the key of the leading-note, G♯ minor (bars 79–90). That key is approached from a cadence on V/V, B. That is to say, ♯vii functions here as iii/V. But after the first period of the principal theme has been stated in that key, ♯vii undergoes a remarkable transformation. Although the enharmonic identity is not specifically indicated, G♯ minor must be reheard as A♭ minor, for it takes its part in a iv♭–V⁷–I cadence in E♭. E♭ in its turn is revealed as the Neapolitan of D – which is the subdominant of the original tonic (Example 8.7a). By this time we realise that we are in the midst of a true reprise: from bar 91 the music follows the course laid down by bar 15 and its successors. But what has happened to the first two bars of that passage, 13–14? In the exposition they initiated a sequence by descending semitones, inviting a complex of reinterpretations:

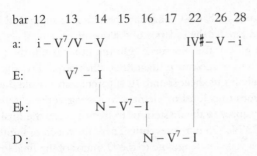

Example 8.7 (a) Mazurka Op. 59 No. 1, bars 74–103, reduction
(b) Mazurka Op. 59 No. 1, bars 13–16, reduction

A comparison of Example 8.7a with Example 8.7b reveals that the V^7/V of bar 13 is represented in the reprise by the cadential B major of bar 74, and that the period in G♯ minor replaces the V of bar 14 by iii/V. Whereas that earlier V became N of E♭, which was in turn N of IV, the substitute G♯ minor now becomes iv of that same E♭, again N of IV. The 'false' reprise thus has a doubly double meaning: the passage not only refers thematically to bars 1–12 but also serves as an expanded replacement of bars 13–14!

Passages which invite contrasting chordal and linear interpretations constitute the second type of local ambiguity. In the simplest of these a dissonant note is given sufficient rhythmic weight for it to be heard as a functioning chord member; yet it turns out to be only a melodic elaboration. The central section of the B♭ minor Nocturne Op. 9 No. 1 exhibits a seventh chord expanded at great length; yet its dissonant member turns out to be only a passing note. That pitch, C♭, descending from the temporary D♭ tonic of the preceding passage, is explicit in bars 51–8. Although it is dropped from the chord in bars 59–69, its continuing shadowy presence may be implied by the *sempre Ped.* of bar 57. At any rate, its resolution as a passing note can be heard in the B♭ minor tonic of bar 70. That interpretation is supported by the flattened second that, *con forza*, marks the cadence of the opening theme (bars 17–18) and returns, fourfold, at the end of the Nocturne. On the other hand, the prolongation of the C♭ followed by its evanescence suggests another possibility: the chord may be used impressionistically for its sheer sound. Its apparent status could then shift twice – from functional seventh to colouristic element to passing note.

A similar explanation may apply to the mysterious E♭ that converts the final chord of the F major Prelude Op. 28 No. 23 into a seventh. There the touch of impressionistic colour may also serve as a veiled passing note to the D minor of the final Prelude.

Typically Chopinesque is the treatment of the dissonant A♮ in bar 5 of the D♭ Nocturne Op. 27 No. 2. Filling the entire melodic space of the bar, that note could well be a chordal B♭♭ in a ii$^{6♭♭}_{4}$ aiming towards a V$^6_5$ (Example 8.8a); but it resolves upward as an appoggiatura to B♭ in the next bar (Example 8.8b). The same treatment, slightly varied, recurs in bars 29–30; so when the A♮ is replaced by a C♭ in bar 49 we expect a similar procedure. The new arrival, however, belongs to the V⁷/IV whose four-bar expansion (bars 49–52) leads us to suspect that the chord may really be functional. Subtly, Chopin resolves it functionally but deceptively to ii (vi/IV), passing on its way through an applied dominant (Example 8.8c). At the same time another interpretation is possible. The applied dominant, V$^6_5$/ii, can be construed as the functional harmony, to which the extended sonority of bars 49–52 acts as a huge appoggiatura chord (Example 8.8d).

Example 8.8   (a) Nocturne Op. 27 No. 2, bars 5–6, hypothetical resolution
(b) Nocturne Op. 27 No. 2, bars 5–6, actual resolution
(c), (d) Nocturne Op. 27 No. 2, bars 49–54, alternative reductions

Example 8.9   Polonaise Op. 26 No. 1, bars 66–73, alternative reductions

Sometimes the composer plays with such possibilities in passages which persistently vacillate between two chords, either of which can be considered as subordinate to the other. In the trio of the C♯ minor Polonaise Op. 26 No. 1, bars 66–73 can be read as governed either by a sequence of diminished sevenths preceded by appoggiaturas

(Example 8.9a), or by a sequence of half-diminished sevenths punctuated by neigh-bouring and passing notes (Example 8.9b).

In other cases a wider perspective enjoins a choice between two interpretations. Again in the C♯ minor Polonaise, a cadence on the dominant in bar 33 is succeeded by a lengthy elaboration of V^7/III; yet in bars 41–2 that chord returns to the tonic C♯ minor by way of the dominant from which it sprang. From the point of view of III, the progression could be construed as an interrupted cadence; but the broader view understands the apparent V^7/III as a linear detail – a neighbouring chord between two dominants (Example 8.10). A similar relationship, whereby $V^2/\flat III$ proves to be a neighbour between V^7 and $V^{9\natural}$, governs the Doppio movimento section of the Nocturne Op. 15 No. 2.

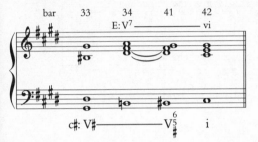

Example 8.10 Polonaise Op. 26 No. 1, bars 33–42, alternative interpretations

Example 8.11 Polonaise Op. 40 No. 2, bars 7–9, with reduction

On occasion the musical surface is so overlaid by polyphonic details that they disguise the harmony, preventing the simultaneous statement of chord members. That is what happens in bars 7–8 of the C minor Polonaise Op. 40 No. 2. If my reading of the chordal structure of Example 8.11a is correct, the underlying pattern is a succession of inverted triads as in Example 8.11b.

It is not always easy to discern such an outline. In the E minor Mazurka Op. 17 No. 2, bars 39–49 elaborate V of the submediant C, by means of sevenths and ninths which move back and forth through one another, creating neighbours to the prevailing G. They arise polyphonically and seem superficially to serve no functional purpose; yet from bar 43 on the alternation of A♮ and A♭ permits one eventually to hear a V/ii–ii–♭VI–V progression (in the key of C) over the pedal on G. And in bars 49–51 the neighbours are transformed into passing chords which prepare for a modulation to the original tonic, E minor (Example 8.12).

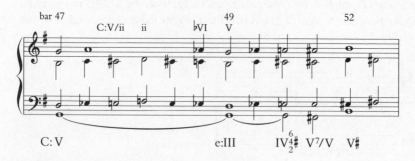

Example 8.12   Mazurka Op. 17 No. 2, bars 47–52, reduction

Occasionally voice-leading dissolves into pure parallelism, as in the impressionistic succession of sevenths leading to the final cadence of the Mazurka Op. 30 No. 4 (bars 129–32). Here one ceases to search even for ambiguity; one merely waits for functionality to reassert itself after the sequence is over. More often, though, Chopin's kaleidoscopic effects are the result of multiplicity rather than suppression of function. When we hear bars 81–9 of the Mazurka Op. 59 No. 2, we may again give up the search for ambiguity – but this time because the bewildering rapidity of harmonic change would necessitate a corresponding speed of reinterpretation impossible for us, as listeners, to sustain: the music would far outrun us.

The third type of local ambiguity, cadential reorientation, enhances continuity by mitigating the effect of obvious articulation between phrases. It destabilises a cadence by calling into question its rhythmic weight and its harmonic significance. The use of the technique is often signalled by phrase markings which blur cadential points. Of one such passage, bars 41–9 in the Mazurka Op. 17 No. 3, William Rothstein remarks, 'No composer so frequently slurred against the phrase structure of his music rather than in support of that structure.'[6]

Reorientation is at work in the opening phrase of the C♯ minor Nocturne Op. 27 No. 1. Over an arpeggio built on a tonic pedal, the first phrase deploys a melody which seems to cadence on the tonic in its fourth bar (bar 6). The melody does not pause here, however; under a new slur it moves on to an even stronger cadence in the next bar, this time supported by the first real motion of the bass: i–V⁷/III–III. Perhaps, then, the phrase is really one of five bars. But the bass immediately passes downward

---

[6]   William Rothstein, *Phrase Rhythm in Tonal Music* (New York 1989), p. 220.

to the tonic as the melody begins anew, and the resulting elision supports four-bar periodicity. This second version of the phrase seems to have lost its cadential tonic, which is replaced by a melodically empty bar. Actually the tonic has been postponed to open a third, contrasting phrase. At that point (bar 11) the second phrase is belatedly resolved; meanwhile the empty bar has preserved the periodicity.

The vacillation between i and III is extended still further in the C minor Nocturne Op. 48 No. 1, at the point where the central section of the first theme prepares for the return of the opening. At bar 16 a V^7/III points towards the mediant, but that tendency is defeated by a shift to the true dominant: $V^7/III–V^6_5$. When the next phrase introduces the reprise, however, the tonic is altered by V^7/iv, and a new harmonisation of the phrase leads back to III by a circle of fifths: $V^7/iv–iv^7–V^7/III–III$. In the short run, then, the initial direction of bar 16 has prevailed; but the circle of fifths does not stop there. It continues through VI^7, ii^{o7} and V^7, where an interrupted cadence only temporarily deflects the inexorable motion towards i.

On a more detailed level, the phrase overlaps characteristic of cadential reorientation can alleviate the threatening monotony of motivic repetition, as in the principal theme of the first Ballade. The entrance of the Moderato solves the harmonic problem of the introduction only to pose rhythmic questions. Its opening figure is both a resolution and a new beginning. Does it function the same way at each recurrence? Is its arpeggiation to be taken as melodic or as the more explicit spelling of a broken chord like that of bar 7? The two ambiguities are connected, for it is easier to hear a melodic motif as anacrustic, an arpeggiation as cadential. The latter interpretation is supported by the chordal effect of the double stems, but the upbeat reading is favoured by the significant modification of bar 14 as well as by the seventh added to the tonic of bar 21. That note undermines the cadential reading just at the point where the music takes leave of the motif. In contrast to this initial statement, the two reprises of the theme are persistently anacrustic. Starting afresh each time after an extended rallentando, and each time supported by a dominant pedal which inhibits any cadential inclination, the entire theme is turned into a huge upbeat.

Exceptionally, restatements may transform the role of an entire phrase, not merely of a motif. The opening phrase of the Nocturne Op. 55 No. 2 presents an anacrustic dominant bar followed by three which expand the tonic E♭ – together forming the antecedent of a four-bar consequent cadencing on iii. But cadential reorientation (iii–V^4_3–I) converts this second phrase into a new antecedent which in turn spawns its own consequent (bars 9–12) – which proves to be a modified restatement of the original antecedent! In this version the opening bar, no longer an anacrustic dominant, receives the tonic downbeat previously postponed until bar 2. The next appearance of the phrase is an abbreviated reference to its first two bars only (25–6) – now as the V–I cadence of an extended fourteen-bar period. Finally, at the climactic reprise of bar 35, a variant of the whole phrase in its second form serves as the sole representative of the original three-phrase theme.

III

An important effect of cadential reorientation is its alleviation of the uniformity produced by Chopin's propensity for four-bar metrical groups. A related technique, which I call rhythmic dislocation, disguises the hypermetre by shifting the boundaries of entire phrases. Again, such shifts may be signalled by slurs which oppose the obvious periodicity, but this time their function is not purely local. Rather, the markings are symptomatic of a deep-lying conflict between a free melodic-rhythmic phraseology and the regular harmonic-metrical pattern.

The contrasting D♭ major section of the [Fantasy-]Impromptu Op. 66 is a simple and familiar example. Its forty bars (after a two-bar introduction) fall into ten hyper-metrical groups of four bars each, twice 4 + 4 followed by twice 4 + 4 + 4; but the melodic design requires a division of twice 3½ + 4½ followed by twice 3½ + 4 + 4½ bars. Even the one apparently regular four-bar group (62–6, repeated at 74–8) begins with a half-bar and thus straddles the barlines. Here Chopin emphasises the ambiguity by slurs which divide the phrase in such a way as to contradict its previous articulation – as well as its derivation from the opening theme of the piece.[7]

A conflict of this kind sometimes drives a basic hypermetrical pattern of fours and eights so far underground that it is all but inaudible until its sway is once more established by an eventual realignment. For a sensitive listener the hypermetre, even during such passages, may still exert its control – not, however, by regularly recurring patterns of stress but by temporal spans of equal length. Thus in the Mazurka Op. 56 No. 3, the balanced grouping by fours is broken in bars 89–120 by the irregularity of 7 + 10 + 4 + 11 bars. But those phrases exactly span eight of the fours that control the rest of the piece, and their 32 bars are exactly framed by a sixteen-bar theme and its repetition.

The same principle governs the entire statement of the main theme of the Polonaise-Fantasy Op. 61. It begins conventionally enough (bar 24) with 4 + 4 bars. The ingeniously expanded third phrase forecasts what is to come: despite its apparent difficulties it manages to return to the opening after exactly 12 bars. That is what happens, on a larger scale, as the section develops. The second phrase of the restatement opens out into a huge group of 18 (or 8 + 10) bars (48–66). Its cadence, detached from what precedes by a fermata, and linked to what follows by an elision, might also represent a new beginning – on a hypermetrical downbeat (bar 64). But even if it is bar 66 instead which initiates the new phrase, six bars restore the hypermetrical pattern, which is easily perceptible until bar 92. That is a harmonic downbeat; but the original theme, entering two bars later, crosses the hypermetre, as does its sequential repetition. That is the composer's way of indicating that those are false reprises; the true reprise, in bar 108, restores both the key and the metre of the original statement. That metre is now in unambiguous command, and the B major cadence that heralds the quasi-trio arrives in bar 152 on a structural downbeat after thirty-two remarkable hypermeasures.

In his quest for rhythmic variety against metrical regularity Chopin also adopts more conventional techniques, as when he calls upon the time-honoured devices of

---

[7]   See the autograph version of the [Fantasy-]Impromptu in the Henle edition of the Impromptus, ed. Ewald Zimmermann (Munich n.d.), pp. 28–38.

hemiola and other cross-rhythms. In the waltzes, the three-crotchet pulse and the four-bar periodicity are usually so strong as to brook no real opposition; thus neither the thematic hemiola in Op. 64 No. 1 nor the persistently duple subject of Op. 42 presents more than the amusing elaboration of a familiar metrical pattern. More subtle in this regard are the thematic hemiolas of Op. 34 No. 3, which operate on two levels simultaneously (♩♩♩ and ♩ ♩ ♩).

Occasional passages are more problematic, such as the Più lento section of Op. 64 No. 2. Should the left hand in bars 65–72 be construed as in 3/2? If so, it is opposed by a counter-hemiola in the right hand, bars 70–1. In bars 73–7 the comparative regularity of the left hand is balanced by an overlap of hemiolas in the right (Example 8.13). Not until the climax of the section, at bars 92–3, do the two hands coalesce in an overt hemiola.

Example 8.13   Waltz Op. 64 No. 2, bars 73–7, overlapping hemiolas

In such cases the role of the performer is crucial. That is equally true of the cadential formulas of the polonaises, to which, owing to the very nature of the polonaise rhythm, the hemiola may offer only one of several possible interpretations. I have discussed elsewhere the availability of multiple readings for the principal cadence of Op. 40 No. 1 and their usefulness in varying the six appearances of a single perfect cadence.[8] Other cadential hemiolas may be found in the trios of Op. 26 Nos. 1 and 2, and in the coda of Op. 53. In Op. 44, syncopations obscure the hemiolas of bars 25–6; the same hemiola (bars 310–11) is buried by the expanded conclusion of the reprise.

The multiplication of obvious four-bar units, particularly in the waltzes, raises another question. Should those units be interpreted strictly according to a hypermetrical pattern of alternating strong and weak bars? Or do they embody a more flexible scheme, such as one distinguishing between initial and terminal downbeats?[9] In either case, what principles guide the determination of strong and weak bars? That distinction is by no means easy. A V–I cadence which one analyst may hear as a point of firm demarcation, rhythmically weak–strong, another may construe as just the opposite. Some see the position of a six-four as confirming a strong beat; others allow the six-four to precede a strong dominant.[10] Significantly, Chopin underlines this very ambiguity in his Waltz Op. 34 No. 3. A sixteen-bar period, bars 49–64, consists of two similar phrases. In the first I_4^6 enters in the fifth bar (53), resolving to V^7 in the seventh. In the second phrase, I is delayed until the sixth bar (62) but again resolves in the seventh.

8   See Edward T. Cone, *Musical Form and Musical Performance* (New York 1968), pp. 45–6, 49.
9   See ibid., pp. 26–31.
10 For a discussion of these possibilities, see Joel Lester, *The Rhythms of Tonal Music* (Carbondale and Edwardsville, Illinois 1986), pp. 177–81.

Even more striking is the notorious irregularity of the principal theme of the fourth Ballade. Because of an extra half-bar inserted after the first phrase (bar 12), its consequent is displaced by three quavers. After a third phrase of six bars, the first two are repeated, but their metrical roles are reversed; when the third recurs, it too is displaced. What is the 'real' metrical position of the theme? The registral placement of the bass, the occasional cross-rhythms in the melody (3/4 against 6/8) and the dynamic markings (at odds between the two hands) – all these suggest that Chopin was constantly rethinking and reinterpreting the relation of his theme to its prevailing 6/8 metre.

That flexibility of reinterpretation, transferred to the performance of some of the waltzes, might alleviate their rhythmic uniformity, not to say monotony. The refrain of Op. 64 No. 2 need not conform to the same pattern, hypermetrical or otherwise, on each of its occurrences. With the exception of the implied hemiola of bars 45–6, probably every bar can be read as either strong or weak. When one considers also the possibility of a cross-metre of 6/8 within the melodic motif itself (Example 8.14), one realises why Chopin was not afraid to call for six almost identical statements of an already repetitive theme.

Example 8.14   Waltz Op. 64 No. 2, bars 33–4, possible cross-rhythm

IV

The formal ambiguities characteristic of Chopin's longer works have been frequently discussed. So have the enigmatic aspects of certain well-known shorter puzzles. My treatment of overall design here will focus on certain compositions, mostly small-scale, whose patterns, while apparently promising adherence to formal convention, depart from the norm by deviant additions or omissions. Some of those, I believe, throw unexpected light on Chopin's stubbornest locus of ambiguity: the so-called bitonal compositions.

The simplest examples are such mazurkas as Op. 7 No. 3 and Op. 30 No. 3. Almost identical in pattern, they postpone the expected return of the main theme through a multiplication of contrasting sections: introduction – ABCD – transition – A – coda. Indeed, the form suggests a mere chain of dances until the transition reminds us that the first theme demands its right of return.

That simple explanation is not available for the more tightly organised Mazurka Op. 24 No. 4. Its initial song form is complete, even with repetitions; but the central section that follows, instead of conforming to the normal trio pattern, presents two contrasting ideas. Is the first (*sotto voce*) an appendage to the opening section, a parenthesis, an independent theme or a transition to the second (*con anima*)? Although sensitive performance could make a case for each possibility, two points favour the first: the tonal and motivic connections of the *sotto voce* with the principal theme (Example 8.15) and its correlation with the similarly placed coda.

Example 8.15   Mazurka Op. 24 No. 4, bars 50³–6

The grand example of ambiguity occasioned by the proliferation of contrast is, of course, the F♯ minor Polonaise Op. 44. When we first hear the drumming that succeeds the principal dance, we assume that it will be introductory to a trio (like, say, the famous octaves in the later A♭ Polonaise). But as the beats continue we wonder whether they may not function differently. And when a contrasting section derived from the original dance breaks the uniformity, only to yield to renewed drumming, we decide that what we are hearing is actually the trio itself. Wrong: despite its regular ABA pattern, this hypothetical trio dies away, becoming as it does so the transition we once suspected. The Tempo di Mazurka that follows is the real trio – in expression, although not in form. For it consists of a lengthy section in the relative major, A, almost exactly repeated in its dominant, E. It thus partially reflects the internal structure of each of its internal divisions. Those likewise contain a statement in the tonic followed by one in the dominant – but both times followed by a third, new period returning to the tonic. Does the entire trio call for a similar return – a third, tonic-seeking section, expected but precluded by the gradually insinuated transition to the reprise?

A: I V V–I   E: I V V–I

A: I   V   ?

The question of 'missing sections' is also raised by the anomalous forms of certain mazurkas. Op. 33 No. 4 may be roughly sketched as AABAABC – transition – A – coda. The length and internal organisation of section C are those of a two-part trio; its key and its position suggest that it has replaced an omitted return of A. Thus the final statement can serve both as the reprise after the trio and as the postponed answer to B. A similar argument applies to Op. 63 No. 1 ($A_1A_2BC_1C_2$ – transition – A_1A_3 – coda).

No section of the C♯ minor Mazurka Op. 50 No. 3 is lacking, but the initial three-part song form is elliptically shortened. Its opening section elaborates a V–i progression, both in the small (bars 1–5) and in the large (bars 1–16). When it returns after the digression of bars 17–32, it is incomplete, resting on an extended V (bars 33–44). The missing phrase of resolution is replaced by an interpolation in VII (B major). The ternary expansion of that section, however, offers an alternative perspective: it is a trio, to which the partial reprise was a transition. But the trio, too, is denied a final cadence, for its last phrase prepares for a recapitulation of the original song form. That is now complete – indeed, over-complete, for it includes three codas (bars 143–57, 157–81, 181–92), as if to make up for the former ellipsis.

On occasion Chopin even more obviously calls attention to ellipsis – witness the humorously 'unfinished' ending of the Mazurka Op. 41 No. 3. Especially germane to my purpose is the problematic conclusion of the Nocturne Op. 15 No. 3, which fails to deliver the reprise of an apparently promised ternary form. The ostensible middle section is a chorale whose F major replaces both the G minor tonic of the opening theme and the abortive F♯ major of the ensuing transition, and whose four balanced sixteen-bar groups contrast with the previous irregular phrases. Such a section might end with closure on its own temporary tonic, or lead into a retransition towards the original key. This one does neither: its final four bars modulate abruptly to G minor and the piece is over. My impression that the Nocturne is incomplete – that the final cadence replaces an expected reprise – is confirmed by an autograph sketch proving that at some stage Chopin had intended just such a return.[11]

Does the truncated Nocturne really end in G? The listener is given no time to absorb the modulation, and the melodic line remains stubbornly on d^1. Play the Nocturne, substituting at the end the previous F major cadence (bars 133–6) and the result is a bitonal piece. If Chopin set out to realise a ternary form, he may have found, as the chorale developed with the slow descent of its tolling bells, that, from an expressive point of view, no reprise was possible. Nevertheless, not yet willing to forsake conventional tonal principles, he tacked on the G minor ending.

He was more adventurous in the Prelude Op. 28 No. 2, perhaps because it was to take its place as a member of a series, or perhaps because in this case the composition ended in its original but unstated tonic. For I believe that this piece, too, is incomplete: what it lacks is an opening phrase. That would have been one in A minor, from which the present opening in E minor would have been sequentially derived (Example 8.16a). In defence of this somewhat bizarre proposition, I can point out that both the hypothetical phrase and the preceding Prelude cadence in C major on a melodic e^1; there are concealed motivic connections as well (Example 8.16b). Did the second Prelude begin imperceptibly during the course of the first?

Example 8.16   Prelude Op. 28 No. 2, hypothetical theme derived from Op. 28 No. 1, bars 27–9

[11] See Jeffrey Kallberg, 'The Rhetoric of Genre: Chopin's Nocturne in G minor', *19th-Century Music*, 11/3 (1988), pp. 238–61. Besides reproducing the sketch, this essay contains an excellent discussion of the formal and expressive ambiguities of the Nocturne.

Op. 30 No. 2 is unique among the mazurkas, for its concluding section refers neither to the opening subject nor to its key. Its thematic pattern, ABCB, and its tonal scheme, b–f♯–A–f♯, conspire to make it sound oddly incomplete. Either a return to section A, or AB with the refrain transposed to the tonic, would seem to be demanded. But the tendency of both sections A and C to turn B minor into a subdominant, as in bars 3–4 and 33–4, combined with the relentless nature of the refrain, may have suggested to the composer an experimental solution – a two-stanza form in F♯ minor: iv–i, III–i.

One's lingering sense of discomfort suggests that Chopin was not entirely successful in fusing the two perspectives, or in subordinating the one to the other.[12] He was triumphantly successful, however, when he combined two incomplete forms to achieve the remarkable unity of the second Scherzo. Neither the formal ambiguity nor the consequent dramatic suspense of this extraordinary work can be captured by an analysis such as Schenker's, which, reducing B♭ minor to submediant status beneath a prolonged D♭ tonic, predetermines the outcome from the start.[13]

Intentional analysis finds instead a sonata exposition in B♭ minor, with second and cadential themes in III. Although it is duly repeated, it is followed, not by a development, but by what at first sounds like a trio in A (B♭♭) major. As the new section proceeds, however, it too turns out to be a sonata exposition, likewise repeated, moving I–iii–V in the new key. How are those two expositions, in incompatible keys, to be reconciled? The ensuing development (bar 468) is at first based on material from the second exposition; but it is interrupted by an outburst from the first (bar 517), which progresses to a climactic dominant – of B♭ minor. The expansion of that harmony (bars 540–83) now prepares, both tonally and motivically, for a recapitulation of the opening.

The development has thus thematically fused the two sonata forms, but their tonal incompatibility is yet to be resolved. A diagram explains Chopin's strategy.

$$\text{I: A}$$
$$\text{i: b♭—— III: [D♭ – c♯] —— V: F}$$
$$\text{V: E}$$

Completing neither sonata form, he honours neither tonic; instead he promotes the mediant common to both. A reprise of the first exposition moves once again from B♭ minor to D♭ major – this time with an extension (bars 697–708) confirming the latter. The two earlier tonics do not accept their subordination without a struggle. With the outbreak that inaugurates the coda (bar 716), both A (B♭♭) major and B♭ minor try to reassert themselves, but they are forced to accept their roles as submediants

---

12 Schenker finds that 'the uncertainty which arises about the tonality . . . almost prevents us from calling this Mazurka a composition'. Heinrich Schenker, *Free Composition (Der freie Satz)*, trans. and ed. Ernst Oster (New York and London 1979), p. 131.

13 Ibid., Fig. 102[6].

(Example 8.17). In the end, D♭ is so firmly established that it can tolerate a momentary excursion to V/vi just before the final cadence.[14]

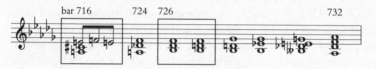

Example 8.17   Scherzo Op. 31, bars 716–32, reduction

A similar ambiguity of key permeates the Fantasy Op. 49. An unprejudiced ear must accept the introduction as stating and confirming a tonic F minor-major. The ensuing sonata exposition progresses through a cycle of thirds: f–A♭–c–E♭. An intentional analysis of this section finds two interlocked expositions, in contending keys: f:i–A♭:I–f:V–A♭:V. And although the subsequent B major theme makes sense only as being in C♭, ♭III of A♭, the reprise returns to the original interlock: f:iv–A♭:IV–f:i–A♭:I. Thus I cannot accept Carl Schachter's conclusion that 'there is a governing tonal centre, and it is A♭ major, the closing key, rather than F minor, the opening one'.[15] Despite his brilliant linear analysis,[16] I hear the ambiguity as powerful enough to raise grave doubt as to the outcome after the interrupted cadence of bar 310. Had the ensuing coda continued as it began, by following the parallel passage after the exposition (bars 143–55), it would have arrived at f:V. Even with the present version, it would still be easy, by a slight alteration of bar 319, to introduce the Adagio sostenuto on F:I$^6_4$ and to continue the cadence accordingly (Example 8.18). The Fantasy, as I hear it, maintains its tonal ambiguity until the last possible moment.[17]

My hypothetical version may not be entirely fanciful, for Chopin evidently changed his mind about the outcome of another bitonal work. According to Schumann, the famous struggle between two keys in the second Ballade was originally won by F major instead of A minor: 'Its impassioned episodes seem to have been inserted afterwards. I recollect very well that when Chopin played the Ballade here, it ended in F major; now it closes in A minor.'[18] Was Schumann describing a primitive version based solely

---

[14]   For a fuller discussion of the Scherzo, including an excellent critique of Schenker's analysis, see Harald Krebs, 'Tonal and Formal Dualism in Chopin's Scherzo, Op. 31', *Music Theory Spectrum*, 13/1 (1991), pp. 48–60. Krebs emphasises the role of the first sonata exposition but seems not to recognise the second.
    It is interesting to compare the Scherzo with Beethoven's experiment in bitonality. The finale of the Quartet Op. 59 No. 2, like the Scherzo, introduces in its opening phrases two contending keys a third apart, in this case C major and E minor. Unlike the Scherzo, the finale exhibits a completely worked out, unitary form (a modified sonata-rondo) whose thematic-tonal pattern clearly favours the second key. Moreover, the chances of the pretender, C major, are foredoomed from the start by the force of three previous movements in E minor.

[15]   Carl Schachter, 'Chopin's Fantasy Op. 49: The Two-Key Scheme', in *Chopin Studies*, ed. Jim Samson (Cambridge 1988), p. 222.

[16]   Ibid., pp. 221–53, especially p. 226.

[17]   It is true that my alternate version does not bring the *Urlinie* down to the tonic, only to the third. But that is just the way I hear the present cadence in A♭ as well. I do not find Schachter's reading of a linear descent to a♭^{2} convincing.

[18]   'Die leidenschaftlichen Zwischensätze scheinen erst später hinzukommen zu sein; ich erinnere mich sehr gut, als Chopin die Ballade hier spielte und in F-dur schloß; jetzt schließt sie in A-moll.' Robert

Example 8.18   Fantasy Op. 49, bars 319–22, hypothetical alternative ending

on the opening Andantino? Hardly: if what Chopin played had lacked the Presto passages, Schumann would have stated that they *were* added later, not that they seemed to have been. The locution thus reflects either an inference (from the score, or from Chopin's remarks?) or a critical opinion ('they strike me as having been added'). We shall never know what Schumann actually heard, but I shall hazard a guess. As the opening Andantino approaches its final phase it is interrupted (bars 32–3 in Henle) by a strange interrupted cadence, V^7–iii^6, which temporarily deflects the theme into A minor before it closes in F. The first reprise of the Andantino (bar 82) takes up the same passage; but this time the interruption becomes a gap, as if two-and-a-half bars had been replaced by silence. Bars 33–4 return, compressed, as bar 88, and the theme proceeds to its cadence, although that turns deceptive (bar 95). In just the same way the theme is taken up for the last time in the present coda – again after a break. Now the pause is represented by a composed fermata in bars 196–7: a climactic French sixth sustained by the pedal while reiterated As adumbrate the theme to come. Could we not be approaching the F major cadence of the Andantino once again, after the most startling interruption of all, but this time completed and satisfactorily extended? That is what I suggest Schumann heard.[19] Yet it could not have been satisfactory to Chopin, who must have come to realise what had happened during the course of the piece: F major had been replaced as the tonic. That was probably not his original intention; for, as Harald Krebs puts it, 'Only gradually does the A-minor triad assume the role of an independent tonality; it becomes more prominent with each appearance, while the F-major triad undergoes a decline.'[20]

The tonal ambiguity is matched by a formal one, for the pattern of the Ballade, like the key, shifts according to the listener's perspective. At the outset the Andantino presents what is heard as the principal theme, perhaps of a rondo. A familiar pattern appears to take shape: ABA–development–BA (and/or coda). But Theme B (Presto con fuoco) increasingly gains control. Eventually, just before the *agitato* coda, Theme A

Schumann, *Gesammelte Schriften über Musik und Musiker,* 5th edn, ed. Martin Kreisig, 2 vols. (Leipzig 1914), vol. II, p. 32. English translation from Robert Schumann, *On Music and Musicians*, ed. Konrad Wolff, trans. Paul Rosenfeld (New York 1946), p. 143.
19 The integral reprise proposed by Abraham seems to me improbably difficult to realise. See Gerald Abraham, *Chopin's Musical Style* (London 1939), pp. 56–7.
20 Harald Krebs, 'Alternatives to Monotonality in Early Nineteenth-Century Music', *Journal of Music Theory*, 25/1 (1981), p. 13. His linear analysis is based on two *Kopftöne*.

is forced into the bass, where it sacrifices its tempo and its register; its final brief recovery of both is only an ironic memory. In retrospect it is the Presto that predominates; the Andantino seems to have assumed the subordinate roles of introduction and interlude. Chopin's interruption of its concluding statement after a minimal reference and his transformation of its original A minor deviation into a permanent cadence confirm the reinterpretation of both the tonal content and the formal outline of his most ambiguous composition.

9 The Prelude in E minor Op. 28 No. 4: autograph sources and interpretation

CARL SCHACHTER

Introduction

In a characteristically bleak footnote to the opening chapter of *Free Composition*, Heinrich Schenker describes the reaction of musicians to the facsimiles of composers' autographs in the photographic archive of the Austrian National Library: 'this invaluable treasure is appreciated least of all by the musicians. They gaze at the prints as they would at locks of hair, watches, writing desks and the like, which are shown at exhibits that honor the memory of the great dead. I have often stressed that information of the greatest significance regarding the principles of art, the creation of musical coherence, the individual style of notation, etc., is to be derived from autographs as well as from sketches.'[1] In this essay on Chopin's Prelude in E minor Op. 28 No. 4, I shall explore (among other things) the significant information that musicians might gain through a careful perusal of its autograph sources – specifically from the calligraphically expressive manuscript in the complete autograph of Op. 28 (now in the Biblioteka Narodowa in Warsaw) and from Chopin's earlier draft, which is on a page that also contains a draft of the Mazurka Op. 41 No. 1 (part of the former collection of the late Gregor Piatigorsky, now owned by Mrs Daniel Drachman, Stevenson, Maryland).[2] I shall refer to the autographs as the 'Warsaw' and 'Maryland' autographs, respectively. I shall not present an exhaustive description of these documents, but shall concentrate on information which might benefit performers and analysts of Chopin's music – and I do not necessarily assume that they are different people. I should perhaps also mention that my conception of performers' needs is not a utilitarian one. Insights into 'the principles of art, the creation of musical coherence and the individual style of notation' can help shape an interpretation without always telling us whether to play louder or softer, faster or slower. And my discussion will not confine itself to the

[1] Heinrich Schenker, *Free Composition (Der freie Satz)*, trans. and ed. Ernst Oster (New York and London 1979), p. 7 n. 11. The archive he refers to was established at Schenker's instigation by Anthony van Hoboken.

[2] A facsimile edition of the Op. 28 autograph was published as *Fryderyk Chopin: 24 Preludia*, ed. Władysław Hordyński (Cracow 1951). Incidentally, the numbering of the Mazurka as Op. 41 No. 1 stems from the French first edition; in the German edition (and later ones based on it), the C♯ minor Mazurka of Op. 41 was (probably incorrectly) printed as No. 1 and our E minor Mazurka as No. 2.

161

autographs but will include my thoughts about the tonal structure, form and motivic design of the Prelude.

The autographs

The Maryland autograph (Plate 1) bears the heading 'E moll' (the key of both pieces) followed by 'Palma 28 9bre [= 28 November]'. The year (omitted from the heading) was 1838; Chopin spent the late autumn and early winter of 1838–9 on Majorca with George Sand, and these drafts were products of his sojourn there. Since the Mazurka begins at the top of this page directly under the heading, it is conceivable that the date applies only to it and that the Prelude was sketched later.[3] It could not have been very much later, however, for Chopin wrote to Julian Fontana on 22 January 1839 that he was sending him the manuscript of the complete set of preludes.[4] The draft seems almost certainly to be the first written version of the Prelude. The beautiful right-hand upbeat at the beginning of the completed piece was originally missing from the draft and added subsequently, as we can see from the extremely crowded space it occupies. The omission of this characteristic and important feature bespeaks a very early stage of the compositional process. Once Chopin had made his additions and corrections, however, the draft became very close to the eventual printed version of the Prelude. The intricate chromatic counterpoint of the left-hand part seems to have been written at once in abbreviated notation (without the repeated pitches), but already in its final form and without a single correction, except for the last few bars. The lines appear to be improvised on the page, and I should imagine that they were in fact improvised, or at least worked out, at the piano before Chopin wrote them down. The apparently simple right-hand melody has more corrections, some of which I shall discuss later on.

In the Warsaw autograph (Plate 2), the right-hand upbeat is written with the utmost breadth, as if to make up for its cramped presentation in the earlier draft. On the assumption that the expressive gestures of the composer's hand relate at times to the expressive character of the music he is writing, we should do well to play the upbeat with commensurate breadth. In any case, taking time for the octave leap (as a singer would do) fits the melody's vocal character and makes its large span a more effective foil for the almost monotone line that follows. This autograph has many more expression marks than the Maryland draft, and it contains a fair number of corrections. Some of these, however, seem to be routine revisions – striking out superfluous accidentals (bars 6 and 12), cancelling an accent and adding a crescendo sign (bars 20–1), and the like. There are only a few substantive changes, by far the most striking being the left-hand octave added to the downbeat of bar 17, a change which produces a far more powerful climax. Chopin frequently carried the process of composition well into the writing of his *Stichvorlagen* and beyond: many of his autographs are filled with alterations; his first editions often contain discrepancies which reflect

---

[3]   The other side of the page contains a draft of the A minor Prelude Op. 28 No. 2, and fragmentary sketches for an unidentified piece or pieces.

[4]   *Selected Correspondence of Fryderyk Chopin*, trans. and ed. Arthur Hedley (London 1962), p. 167.

Plate 1 Chopin's drafts of the Mazurka Op. 41 No. 1 and the Prelude Op. 28 No. 4, 28
November 1838. Collection of Mrs Daniel Drachman (former collection of Gregor Piatigorsky),
Stevenson, Maryland, USA

variants by Chopin himself; and further additions and corrections might find their
way into the printed copies he used for teaching. For the Prelude, however, we can
regard the Warsaw autograph as a definitive source.[5] The shaping of this extraordinary
piece, as rich in content and feeling as it is slender in size, seems to have taken place
quickly and without the need for extensive revision.

[5] George Sand copied the Prelude into an album possibly with some supervision by Chopin. A facsimile
of this copy is reproduced in the Polish edition of the Kobylańska catalogue: Krystyna Kobylańska,
Rękopisy utworów Chopina, 2 vols. (Cracow 1977), vol. II, p. 45. This copy differs in a few details from
the Warsaw autograph, mostly through omission. I view it as distinctly inferior to Chopin's autograph.
      A more important source is the manuscript copy of the Warsaw autograph, prepared by Julian
Fontana to serve as the basis for the German first edition. Fontana's copy is quite faithful, but the
notational style diverges from Chopin's in certain details, most significantly in the appoggiaturas of bars
11 and 19. I shall discuss this point later on. The Fontana copy (no. 391 in Kobylańska) was mistakenly
thought to be in Chopin's own hand; as such it was reproduced in lithographic facsimile in Moritz
Karasowski, *Friedrich Chopin: Sein Leben, seine Werke und Briefe*, 2 vols. (Dresden 1877), vol. II. The facsimile is bound in at the end of the volume without page number. I should like to thank Professor Jean-
Jacques Eigeldinger for drawing this facsimile to my attention.

Plate 2   Chopin's autograph of the Preludes Op. 28 Nos. 3 and 4. Biblioteka Narodowa, Warsaw

The form

Like many of the preludes, this one forms a period of two large phrases in a kind of antecedent–consequent relation. The two parts begin similarly, but only the consequent ends with a perfect cadence on the tonic. Period form is typical of closed thematic components within larger forms – for example, the first A sections in small ABA song forms (think of bars 1–8 of the 'Ode to Joy'). Using this schema for a whole short piece gives that piece something of the character of a fragment, for its form evokes the impression of a part of something larger. Such an impression is of course highly appropriate for pieces, like the preludes, which sound like brief, improvisatory flights of fancy. These preludes, however, are stylised rather than true fragments, for Chopin departs from normal antecedent–consequent construction in ways which give unusual weight to the tonic harmony of the final cadence and allow it to form a convincing structural close.[6] Since the two phrases of a period are normally of equal length, one way to emphasise the closing tonic is to expand the consequent phrase far beyond the length of the antecedent. Delaying the advent of the goal tonic enhances the effect of resolution that it conveys, and drawing it out in a coda adds further emphasis. This, in fact, is what Chopin mostly does in his period-form preludes. In Op. 28 No. 6, for example, the antecedent occupies eight bars while the consequent and coda take up eighteen; in Op. 28 No. 1 the dimensions are eight bars versus twenty-six. The inequality creates a kind of musical *contrapposto* – a balance achieved through the asymmetrical disposition of two inherently equal parts. The consequent phrase is like the engaged leg of a counterposed statue, the final tonic supporting the 'weight' of the structure and removing any need to go on further.

In Op. 28 No. 4, however, the consequent phrase is hardly longer than the antecedent – thirteen bars as against twelve – and there is no coda.[7] Here the *contrapposto* results not from the greater length of the second part but from its greater emotional range and structural density, and from the accelerated and then broadened pacing of its events, most obviously in the bass. Example 9.1 compares the bass lines of the two parts. For one-and-a-half bars, the phrases move at the same rate, but the consequent soon begins to race ahead, even abandoning stepwise progression in its haste. At the end of its fourth bar, it has already arrived at C, a note which the antecedent had reached only at bar 9. Whereas B forms the lowpoint of the antecedent (bar 10), the consequent reaches further down, to A in bar 18 (the contra B in bar 17 is a doubling for reinforcement). In its first bars, then, the consequent phrase has descended to a lower point than the antecedent had reached during its entire twelve-bar course. Thus the stretto that Chopin indicates is embodied in the composition itself, and not only in its manner of performance. With the *piano* of bar 19 we have clearly arrived at a V equivalent to the one in bars 10–12, and we still have seven bars to go. The interrupted cadence of bar 21, the dying away into the 4/2 chord of bar 23, the rest with

---

6   I discuss this procedure in connection with Op. 28 No. 3 in my article 'Rhythm and Linear Analysis: Durational Reduction', *The Music Forum*, vol. V, ed. Felix Salzer (New York 1980), p. 204.

7   The thirteen bars divide into three groups of four, four and five; and the last of these might properly be heard as a four-bar group expanded to five through a composed ritardando, bars 23–4 counting as one bar stretched to two.

fermata that follows – all of these create a composed allargando which stretches the approach to the final tonic, especially for listeners who hear (and performers who project) the passage in its contrast to the earlier stretto.

Example 9.1   Prelude Op. 28 No. 4: pacing of bass line

The fundamental line

The near-equality in the lengths of its two phrases is not the only feature that sets this Prelude apart from its companion pieces; the large-scale melodic structure is also far from typical. Most pieces in period form (and most antecedent–consequent phrase groups within larger pieces) show the kind of harmonic and linear segmentation that Schenker called 'Interruption'.[8] That is, the basic I–V–I is 'interrupted' at the V and split into two interdependent progressions: I–V ‖ I–V–I; the first of these progressions forms the harmonic structure of the antecedent, and the second one underlies the consequent. The descending melodic line is similarly arrested on $\hat{2}$, so that the structures $\hat{3}$–$\hat{2}$–$\hat{1}$ and $\hat{5}$–$\hat{4}$–$\hat{3}$–$\hat{2}$–$\hat{1}$ become $\hat{3}$–$\hat{2}$ ‖ $\hat{3}$–$\hat{2}$–$\hat{1}$ and $\hat{5}$–$\hat{4}$–$\hat{3}$–$\hat{2}$ ‖ $\hat{5}$–$\hat{4}$–$\hat{3}$–$\hat{2}$–$\hat{1}$ respectively. The first eight bars of the 'Ode to Joy' again offer an excellent illustration of this structure, at least in its melodic aspect; harmonies are absent from the theme's first presentation, though structural tonics and dominants are clearly implied under its $\hat{3}$–$\hat{2}$ ‖ $\hat{3}$–$\hat{2}$–$\hat{1}$.

Interruption also underlies most of the period-form preludes of Op. 28: see Nos. 1, 3, 5, 16 and 19. A close look at No. 4, however, reveals that its melodic line moves differently, even though the halt on $\hat{2}$ (F♯, bars 10–12) simulates the effect of interruption. Example 9.2a shows in simplified form the contour of the upper part; it reveals a gap between the A and the F♯ both in the antecedent and in the consequent. (The G at the head of bar 12 – not shown in the example – does not really fill the structural gap, for it appears on the scene after the arrival of F♯ in bar 10 and counts as foreground diminution.) The resulting contour has a strongly pentatonic character, a not uncommon feature of Chopin's melodic lines, though seldom deployed over such broad musical spans. As Example 9.2b shows, the Mazurka Op. 41 No. 1 begins with a very similar gapped line compressed into four bars: the main notes of bars 1–4 are B–A–F♯–E; the B is embellished by its upper neighbour C and then dips down to G♯ (decorating the resolution of a suspension) before reaching A as a main note – very much the contour of the Prelude only on a smaller scale. Thus these two pieces, written

8   Schenker, *Free Composition*, pp. 36–40.

in the same key and sketched on the same page (and possibly on the same day), contain two quite different realisations of a single compositional idea.

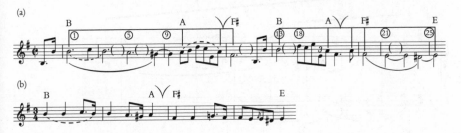

Example 9.2   (a) Prelude Op. 28 No. 4: gapped right-hand line
              (b) Mazurka Op. 41 No. 1: gapped line

The omission of $\hat{3}$ as a structural note in the right-hand part conflicts with a basic feature of large-scale tonal melody: a descending stepwise progression resolving into the tonic note as its goal. In the Prelude this conflict between pentatonic (gapped) contour and diatonic (stepwise) structure is mediated by the left-hand part. As Example 9.3 shows, the right-hand A, unresolved in its original register, is continued by its octave doubling in the left hand (V^7, bar 12), where it moves into the bass G at the beginning of the consequent part. In true contrapuntal style, Chopin overlaps the two halves of the piece by having the consequent phrase take up the unfinished business left over at the end of the antecedent. The dissonant A over V^7 resolves into the bass of the consequent's i^6, producing a large descending third B–A–G which bridges the division between the two phrases while arching downward from top voice through middle voice to bass. At the end of the piece the situation is different,

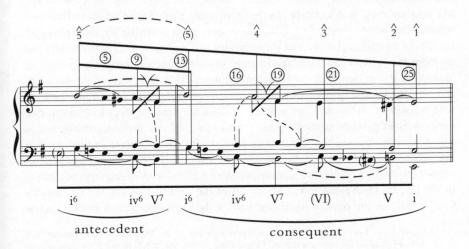

Example 9.3   Prelude Op. 28 No. 4: stepwise structure transferred to lower octave

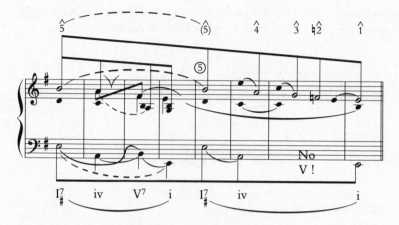

Example 9.4   Mazurka Op. 41 No. 1: bars 1–8, reduction

but related. The A once again resolves to G in the left-hand part (bar 21), over the VI chord of the interrupted cadence. The G remains in the left-hand part up to bar 23. It then resolves to F♯, still in the left hand, before proceeding to E at the very end. Thus the stretch 3̂–2̂–1̂ of the Prelude's fundamental line unfolds in the lower octave. (The 1̂ also occurs as a doubling in the higher octave.) Although the structure is fulfilled, the sense of melodic resolution is made somewhat obscure, adding to the improvisatory, quasi-fragmentary character of the piece. (Inner-voice resolutions of the *Urlinie* occur in several of the preludes; see Nos. 5, 15 and 18.)

In the Mazurka, an inner part also takes up the thread of diatonic continuity. The pitches are the same as in the Prelude, but the time scale is very much smaller: the 'soprano' A (over iv) in bar 2 prepares the seventh over V in bar 3, but the A switches to a lower octave in the 'tenor', where it resolves (Example 9.4).[9] Bars 5–8 of the Mazurka are roughly comparable to the consequent part of the Prelude in that they traverse the whole descending fifth 5̂–4̂–3̂–2̂–1̂, though with a strongly phrygian resolution which involves ♮2̂ and the omission of a cadential V. These connections between the Prelude and the Mazurka constitute a particularly intriguing instance of 'intertextuality' in two works of the same composer. That two pieces in the same key and with such striking similarities were conceived around the same time (perhaps within hours of each other) and written on the same sheet of paper must mean that they represent two products of a single creative process, two flowers growing out of a single branch. And yet how different they are, despite the similarities. In the Mazurka, each statement of the gapped 'pentatonic' line spans only four bars out of a total of sixty-eight. In the Prelude, the gapped lines stretch all the way through the two halves of the piece – twelve and thirteen bars out of the twenty-five. On the one hand a small detail, on the other a significant part of the large structure. Schenker's view

---

[9]   In Figure 75 of *Free Composition*, Schenker shows bars 1–4 of the Mazurka as traversing the fifth B–A–G–F♯–E all in the uppermost part. This reading implies that the G of bar 3 is a passing note between A and F♯ rather than a neighbour of F♯ – an untenable interpretation, I think.

that structure and detail connect with each other through what he calls *Fühlungnahme* (contact or rapport between levels) receives a strange sort of confirmation on this page, where the rapport reaches across the boundaries of the individual pieces. That the Prelude was written on the bottom of the page suggests that its inspiration was generated by work on the Mazurka, a supposition confirmed by the initially absent upbeat at the beginning, which makes the Prelude resemble the Mazurka even more. One might say that the whole Prelude composes out and transforms the deep middleground structure implicit in the Mazurka's first eight bars.

The neighbour-note motif

Yet another point of resemblance between the Prelude and Mazurka – indeed the most obvious of all – is the use of the neighbour-note figure B–C–B as a primary motif in both pieces. In the Prelude the motif sometimes occurs as the complete three-note figure; sometimes it is abbreviated to its most striking component, C–B, whose two-note semitonal descent winds through the piece like a chorus of sighs. (Even in the three-note version, the C is linked more closely to the second than to the first B.) In its two forms, the motif is the centrepiece of one of the most remarkable musical designs in the entire literature. Far from confining itself to the right-hand part, the motif permeates all the strands of the musical fabric and penetrates to deep levels of tonal structure. Example 9.5 shows the motif as it occurs throughout the piece. As soon as the right-hand line moves down from B to A (bar 5), the highest note of the left-hand part takes over the C. This C, which picks up the register of the opening upbeat's low B, persists as long as possible, resolving to B at the end of bar 8. The sketchy Maryland autograph gives a particularly expressive visual presentation of this long, drawn-out C, whose duration dwarfs that of any other sound in the descending left-hand chords. I attribute this emphasis on C to its motivic importance; without at all changing the large outlines, Chopin could easily have moved C to B at the beginning of bar 8 rather than at the end.

With the resolution of the middle-voice C to B accomplished, the descending bass arrives at C. This note supports a cadential subdominant which forms the first goal of the linear descent and which resolves to an even more important goal – the dominant – in the following bar. The bass line supporting this resolution of iv^6 to V^7 is, of course, C–B: the motif now participates in the harmonic structure. After the arrival on B, Chopin embellishes the V by twice repeating the iv^6–V^7 resolution; the repetition allows the motif to resume its original three-note form.

Perhaps the most remarkable manifestation of the neighbour-note motif is in bar 12. At the downbeat, the bass's B marks its final statement of the figure during the antecedent half of the Prelude. Immediately thereafter, the right hand takes up the two-note form of the figure, its motivic importance underscored by Chopin's accent sign. (The sign's placement in the Warsaw autograph, between C and B, embodies graphically the motivic unit formed by the two pitches, and suggests not only the accent but also an expressive diminuendo into the B.) In Jane Stirling's copy, Chopin pencilled in a silent change of fingers, 1–2, on the C, a fingering which furthers a

Example 9.5   Prelude Op. 28 No. 4: neighbour-note motif

legato performance of the rising arpeggio, but which also almost inevitably leads to an extra amount of time on the C.[10] After the arpeggio, the triplet D♯–C–B at the end of the bar is an embellished statement of the same C–B figure. The D♮ is an appoggiatura resolving into C, its ornamental function made unmistakably clear by its dissonance against the D♯ of the harmony. Thus the motif, which had slowly fallen from octave to octave during the course of the antecedent phrase, now rises through the same octaves to prepare the beginning of the consequent.

The portion of this rise belonging to the right hand has another meaning as well: it forms a fantastic recomposition of the opening upbeat's octave leap, the two Bs now embellished by the neighbour-note figure and broadened in duration by the connective arpeggio. But the rising line that starts on the second beat is still an upbeat formation, and it even reflects the dotted rhythm of the opening in the temporal relation between the lower and upper notes of the octave. The Maryland draft offers no clue as to when Chopin added the opening upbeat. I suspect that it was soon after he began writing the Prelude, but it could have been conceived more or less at the

10   See Jean-Jacques Eigeldinger and Jean-Michel Nectoux, *Frédéric Chopin: Oeuvres pour piano. Fac-similé de l'exemplaire de Jane W. Stirling avec annotations et corrections de l'auteur* (Paris 1982), p. 151.

same time as this transformation. Whatever the chronology of composition, with one inspired stroke Chopin brings his motif back to its original high register and incorporates his upbeat into the return in a more intense realisation which joins the phrases together and prepares for the emotional outburst of the stretto passage. Thus the Prelude's two parts are doubly overlapped: through the middleground line B–A–G that arrives at its goal in the bass at the beginning of the consequent; and through this expanded upbeat, which is linked to the melodic line of the consequent, but which occupies the time-frame of the antecedent.

The climax of the consequent (bar 17) explodes the motif into two fragments which are juxtaposed without any registral or syntactic connection: the octave B of the bass at the head of the bar, and the quaver C of the right hand on the second beat. This C is the Prelude's highest pitch and the lower note of the octave B its lowest thus far. The high C remains unresolved in its register, but the following bars bring C down, octave by octave, until it resolves (in the bass!) to B as structural V in bar 19. A curious correction in the Warsaw autograph indicates that Chopin might first have written in a B immediately after the high C of bar 17 (it could only have been a B or an A). In all probability, however, that corrected note represents a slip of the pen rather than an intentional change from the Maryland draft, which is the same as the final version. At the interrupted cadence of bar 21, C enters in the bass with greater emphasis than in any previous statement. Its resolution back to B is delayed by the 4/2 chord and the ensuing pause in bar 23.

Harmonic and contrapuntal structure

Example 9.6 is a foreground sketch of the Prelude which attempts to relate the details of its linear and harmonic organisation to the larger structure. In the discussion that follows, I shall supplement this example with others that concentrate on general features or specific details, but the reader should refer back from these supplementary graphs to Example 9.6 in order to relate detail to structure and structure to detail.[11]

Example 9.7a concentrates on the antecedent half of the Prelude. It shows that the organising principle of the left-hand part is the familiar and age-old technique of parallel 6/3 chords, here elaborated almost beyond recognition by suspensions, chromatic inflections and anticipations. But a conjunct passing motion in 6/3s fills the space between the opening i⁶ and the iv⁶ of bar 9, and these sonorities form the thread of Ariadne that guides the listener through this contrapuntal labyrinth. (In Example 9.6, the left-hand 6/3 chords appear in large notation.) Meanwhile the right hand is also moving down, but at a slower rate and with sounds that make dissonances (4/3 formations) against all of the left hand's 6/3s except the beginning tonic and the goal iv. These two structural pillars form the only consonant sounds in nine bars of music, and it is indeed their consonance as well as their position in the temporal flow that makes them stand out. In Example 9.7, I have tried to depict the time element

---

11 In my review/article 'Schenker's Counterpoint', *The Musical Times*, 129/1748 (1988), pp. 524–9, I discuss the voice-leading of the Prelude's antecedent phrase in its relation to strict counterpoint. I have drawn upon aspects of that discussion in this portion of the present chapter.

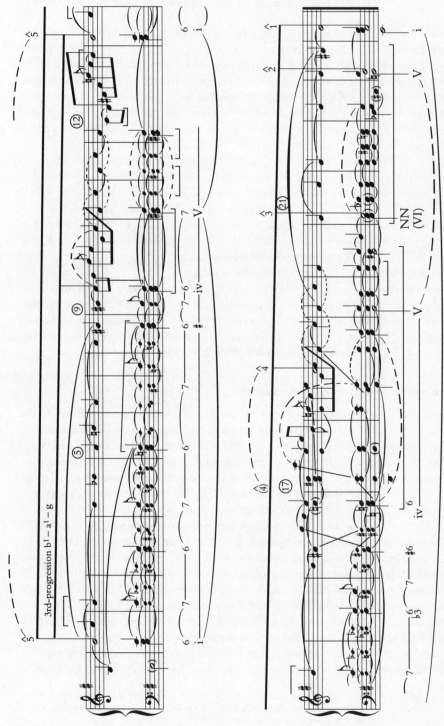

Example 9.6 Prelude Op. 28 No. 4: voice-leading sketch

by means of a durational reduction. Each 4/4 bar of the example stands for a four-bar group, and the ensemble of three bars stands for the twelve-bar phrase, subdivided into four, four and four. The proportions are not mathematically exact, but are rounded off to the nearest large value.

Just before the arrival on iv, the right hand reaches G♯. This note combines with the left-hand chord to form a diminished seventh (in 4/3 position) applied to iv. It also marks the end of the initial tonic prolongation. That is, the passing 6/3s of the left hand and the B–A–G♯ motion of the right are deployed within a harmonic framework of i moving to iv, the i inflected to tonicise the iv (Example 9.7b). Chopin signals the importance of this turning point in the harmony by syncopating the G♯ across the bar. The only dynamic mark in the Maryland draft, by the way, is the boldly written accent on G♯, a mark Chopin retained in the finished piece.[12] Important as it is, the G♯ is not the only preparatory sound for the tonicised iv. It coincides with an F♮ in the left-hand chord, and F♮ had already occurred as the bass note of the second 6/3 chord as early as bar 3. This emphasis on iv by means of F♮ (the 'phrygian' note in E) may also relate the Prelude to the Mazurka, whose characteristic phrygian sound results in part from a tendency to gravitate to the subdominant.

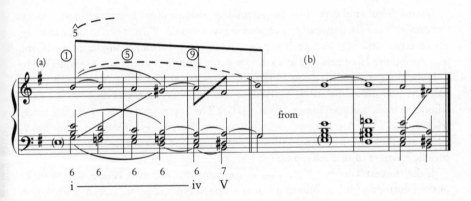

Example 9.7   Prelude Op. 28 No. 4, antecedent: parallel 6/3s

In the Prelude, each of the parallel sixths (except the first) is preceded by a suspended seventh over the same bass note or a chromatic inflection of it; in Example 9.6, the sevenths are provided with quaver flags. The resultant series of 7–6 resolutions is reminiscent of the fourth species of Fuxian counterpoint, though these resolutions are not confined to a strong–weak metrical framework. In particular, the 7–6 on bass E (bars 4–5) resolves on a doubly strong pulse – a downbeat which also comes at the head of a four-bar group. Holding over the bass note from fourth bar to first binds

---

12   This important marking does not occur in the George Sand copy referred to in note 5 above, although it does appear in Fontana's copy.

the four-bar groups together and prevents any effect of excessive segmentation. The alternation of sixths and sevenths culminates in the iv⁶–V⁷ progression that ends the antecedent. Example 9.8 shows the passage in a durational reduction (to the same scale as Example 9.7) which leaves out the chromatic inflections; comparison with Example 9.6 will show how the chromatics fit into this larger frame.

durational reduction

Example 9.8   Prelude Op. 28 No. 4, antecedent: 7–6 series

To my mind (and ear), this contrapuntal approach to bars 1–8 reveals more about the music than a harmonically orientated analysis would. That is not to deny that the ear receives some signals which it might interpret as harmonic implications. If one understood the E♭ of bars 2–3 as a D♯, one could read the chords as a 4/3 inflected to a 'French' augmented sixth on F♮ ultimately resolving to a V⁷ of A minor in bar 4. (At least two influential editions, Karl Klindworth's and the so-called 'Paderewski' edition, actually notate Chopin's E♭ as a D♯.[13]) The augmented sixth would ultimately resolve to a V⁷ of A minor (iv), which would eventually resolve to the iv⁶ in bar 9. There is a problem, however, with the 'ultimately' and 'eventually' that are an inextricable element of this interpretation.

If the downbeat of bar 3 contains an augmented sixth, what is one then to make of the D minor 6/3 that follows it? Does it not negate the impression of a resolution into a dominant seventh? And if that seventh on E is really a V of A minor, what is the meaning of the left hand's immediate move to G♮ and the C major sound in the bottom part at the next downbeat? In other words, the chord-by-chord successions fit most uncomfortably into this framework; the putative inferences receive inadequate confirmation from the subsequent course of events. And, of course, the series of 7–6 resolutions that does form a coherent path disappears in the 'harmonic' analysis. I do not invoke this analysis, however, only to reject it, for I feel that it plays a supporting role in our hearing of the Prelude. First of all, the signals it sends, though not integrated into a coherent discourse, do lead in the right direction: to the tonicised subdominant

13   *Frédéric Chopin, Oeuvres Complètes*, vol. II, ed. Karl Klindworth (Berlin 1880), p. 164, and *Fryderyk Chopin Complete Works*, vol. I, ed. Ludwik Bronarski, Józef Turczyński and Ignacy Jan Paderewski (Warsaw 1949), p. 19. Both editions also use D♯ in the corresponding passage of the consequent part (bars 14–15), and 'Paderewski' supplies a harmonic analysis in the Commentary (p. 74) to account for the notational changes.

as first main goal. And secondly, the inference of rising semitonal progressions with leading-note effect (D♯ to E and G♯ to A) intensifies the falling progressions that actually ensue, for the falling lines struggle against the ascending impulse evoked by that inference. Thus the steady downward movement – for me, emblematic of death – gains in poignancy. If I take the contrapuntal interpretation as primary here, I can perhaps claim the support of Chopin himself. On 7 April 1849, shortly before his own death, he expressed some of his views on the fundamental importance of counterpoint to his friend, the painter Eugène Delacroix, who recorded them in his journal. Noting a remark obviously critical of current music pedagogy, Delacroix writes: '[Chopin] told me that the custom was to learn the harmonies before coming to counterpoint, that is to say, the succession of the notes which leads to the harmonies. The harmonies in the music of Berlioz are laid on as a veneer; he fills in the intervals as best he can.'[14]

With its semitonal sighs, descending lines, throbbing repeated chords and pervasive dissonance, the antecedent conveys a pathos of unsurpassed intensity, but its grief is as controlled as it is intense: the feeling is one of tragic resignation. The left-hand part, for example, moves with the utmost deliberation, only one note at a time from the beginning of bar 2 all the way through bar 8, and that motion always by semitone. The rising upbeat figure of bar 12, with its accelerated motivic permeation and its crescendo, would seem to foretell an end to this restraint, but the consequent begins exactly like the antecedent. The sudden storm that builds up in the next few bars is all the more gripping in its contrast to the phrase's beginning, like a violent outburst of tears from a person not given to demonstrations of feeling. As I mentioned earlier, the initial phase of the consequent is a composed stretto. In the left-hand part, the antecedent's orderly progression of 6/3s gives way to a distorted variant, whose relation to its model is first disguised and then, for a moment, almost obliterated; and the right hand's music is similarly compressed. Example 9.9a contains a reduction of bars 13–16; the stave above the graph relates its contents to their equivalents in the antecedent.

Only the first and last of the left-hand 6/3s – the tonic and subdominant – remain intact. The 6/3s on F and E both occur as chromatically altered diminished chords, and the one on D (not shown in 9.9a) is omitted altogether. The 6/3 on F (bar 15) has A♭ as its inner note, anticipating enharmonically the G♯ of the next chord.[15] The one on E (bar 16) is equivalent to the passing diminished chord at the end of bar 4, but with A♯ instead of B♭ in the right-hand part. The earlier diminished seventh resolved in the left hand into a C major 6/3 still on E (bar 5), but this one abandons stepwise progression, transfers C♯ into the bass through an arpeggiation and then resolves into the 6/3 on C♮ at the end of the bar. As the graph suggests, this resolution compresses into a single event elements of both bars 5 and 9 of the antecedent. This time, the approach to the A minor chord lacks any tendency to tonicise it, so

---

14   *The Journal of Eugene Delacroix*, trans. Walter Pach (New York 1937), p. 195.
15   The Klindworth and 'Paderewski' editions change the A♭ to a G♯, clouding the chord's relation to the D minor 6/3 of the antecedent. This change, for presumed reasons of harmonic propriety, follows from the earlier substitution of D♯ for E♭, as described in note 13. See the Commentary of the 'Paderewski' editors, p. 74.

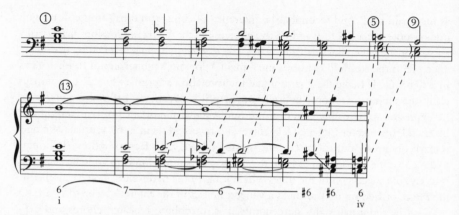

Example 9.9   (a) Prelude Op. 28 No 4, consequent: bars 13–16 compared with antecedent

Example 9.9   (b) Prelude Op. 28 No. 4, consequent: bars 13–25, durational reduction

that a 'harmonic' interpretation, such as reading the E seventh chord (bar 15) as V^7 of iv, has less validity than it had in the antecedent. In Example 9.9b, I present a durational reduction of the entire consequent part, with almost all chromatics removed, and to the same scale (bar becomes crotchet beat) as in Examples 9.7 and 9.8. Comparing 9.9b with 9.8 gives a vivid picture of the consequent's composed stretto in the approach to iv and composed smorzando in the final V–i cadence.

Examples 9.6 and 9.9 show that I read a prolongation of iv from the last beat of bar 16 to bar 18. In other words, I connect the A minor 6/3 with the 5/3 that comes a bar or so later. This interpretation may seem implausible in view of the strongly articulated octave B at the head of bar 17, which would normally signal the beginning of a dominant prolongation rather than a passing-note formation in the midst of an expanded subdominant. Here, however, the parallelism between antecedent and consequent speaks for the less obvious reading (Example 9.10). The 'tenor' A of the iv (bar 16) is retained as an octave above the bass's B; the higher A seems at first to be left hanging, but it is, in fact, continued by the right hand's B (last note in bar 17). The resultant line replicates almost note for note the melodic diminution that composed out the antecedent's iv⁶, but this time emerging out of the obscurity of the inner parts only as the music gradually recovers its repose (see the quotation of bar 9 in the upper stave). This beautiful and fascinating parallelism is weakened if we read a structural V in bar 17, before the advent of the melodic idea that had accompanied the iv⁶ in bar 9.[16] Incidentally, the unusual doubled seventh of the left-hand part did not occur in the Maryland draft; there is only the lower A, enclosed within an F♯ octave, and thus no audible continuation into the right-hand melody. In the Warsaw autograph, an obliterated F♯, originally at the downbeat, is perhaps a vestige of this earlier voicing, removed when the low B was added.

Example 9.10 Prelude Op. 28 No. 4: bars 16–19

It is obvious from the Warsaw autograph that Chopin had first written a single B in the bass, perhaps with that F♯, adding the octave only later. Of course we can never know what went on in his mind when he made this (or any other) correction, but we can attempt to compare the effects of the two versions. The single-note B of the first version forms a clear connection from the preceding C to A in the next bar; despite its metrical strength and dynamic emphasis, we can easily hear it as passing – as an accented passing note. In Chopin's revision, the textural disruption produced by the sudden octave doubling makes it much harder to perceive the event within a framing subdominant harmony. Our first reaction would almost certainly be to mark out the downbeat as the beginning of a new (dominant) prolongation. The immediate return of a subdominant-function chord together with a resumption of the melodic design of the antecedent, however, calls this initial reaction into legitimate question, especially since the later V that appears in bar 19 is so clearly equivalent to the earlier one in bar 10. (The right-hand part, still participating in the stretto, reaches the melody of bar 10 in the second half of bar 18, but the harmony lands on V only at the next downbeat; the bass B in bar 18 is a passing note.)

---

16 This reading of bars 16–19 is the late Ernst Oster's and is typical of his subtle and profound musical thinking. He explained this passage to me many years ago when I told him that it baffled me.

With this reinterpretation, the structural pillars are those equivalent to the iv and V of the antecedent; they frame a passage in which the music seems to have lost itself in an almost frenzied access of emotion. The momentary disorientation produced by these contradictory signals is itself an important part of the composition, and its emotional impact is palpable to all sensitive listeners and not only those with analytical skills. Anyone with musical ears can feel that the music breaks out of its restraint to enter upon a new and violent phase, but that the new phase carries forward a thread of the earlier discourse as it subsides into a resolution. That resolution, in turn, is called into question by the interrupted cadence of bar 21, where resistance flares up again for an instant with the bass line's C; but the energy behind that resistance ebbs, and the music comes to rest in the final cadence.

Performers who wish to project the sense of a prolonged subdominant in bars 16–18 need not at all minimise the climactic octave B of bar 17 or the intense melodic line that goes with it. Giving the B extra time, however, would make it sound like a goal of motion, and thus a structural V; this should be avoided. In other words, Chopin's stretto marking should be followed to the letter. In the Warsaw autograph, the dashes that indicate the extent of the stretto continue to the fourth beat of bar 18 rather than to the next downbeat. This notation suggests that the fourth beat should approximate the original tempo, which will now sound quite slow, following the stretto. The agogic nuance will emphasise both the iv^6 and the structural V that follows it and will thus help to clarify the harmonic structure.

In the right-hand part, the original melodic line seems to break off with the A♯ of bar 16; instead of the continued descent, the melody now 'reaches over' into the higher register of the stretto passage. But the A♯ (the counterpart of bar 4's B♭) is taken over by the left hand, where it resolves to A♮ on the last beat of bar 16 (see again Example 9.10). The A♮ is retained structurally through the prolonged iv, returns as a seventh at the end of the subsequent V and then resolves to G in the 'tenor' of bar 21. This A, then, represents a compression into a single prolonged pitch of the two As (bars 5–8 and bar 9) of the antecedent, where they were not connected structurally but occurred as parts of two different linear progressions on two different levels. Again this reflects the composed stretto.

Notation

Chromatics

In the Maryland autograph, there is no flat before the B, but the natural sign in the next bar proves that the flat was certainly intended. In place of the flat there is a blotch before the note, whose position on the stave suggests that Chopin must first have written an A♯, or at least the sharp sign; no other possibility seems in the least plausible. If I am right, it follows that Chopin's choice was a considered, not an impulsive, one. I mention this because unconventional chromatic spelling is often characteristic of Chopin's notational style, and it has moved some of his editors to frequent use of the blue pencil. I indicated earlier that the Klindworth and 'Paderewski' editions change Chopin's E♭ (bar 2) to a D♯; it should come as no surprise that

Klindworth also substitutes for this B♭ the very A♯ that Chopin had considered and rejected. The 'Paderewski' editors, to their credit, leave this first B♭ alone, but they cannot keep their hands off several other chromatics, including the bass B♭ of bar 23.[17]

Do these notational details matter? They most certainly do, perhaps most importantly where they contradict conventional procedures.[18] Usually, for example, ♯4̂ is preferred over ♭5̂, even in descending lines. In E minor, Chopin himself would normally use A♯ rather than B♭ unless the context suggests some particular tonal implication – tonicisation of ♮II, for instance – which demands the B♭. Such a tonal implication is not present here, so the A♯ that Chopin first wrote would certainly have been possible. Chopin's eventual choice of B♭, however, reflects the inexorable downward pull that governs the melodic line, and is thus far more expressive than the A♯. The bass B♭ of bar 23 presents an even more striking example of expressive notation. First of all, it certainly recalls the one in bar 4, although its eventual resolution after the pause and fermata is up to B♮ rather than down to A. The 'Paderewski' editors are perfectly right in maintaining that this bass note functions as ♯IV, that is as A♯.[19] But this function becomes clear only in retrospect: the B♭ could have gone down to A as the bass of a Neapolitan sixth (F major) chord. How much more artistic it is to hear – and play – the B♭ as if the music had become exhausted and lost, as if one did not know where it might go, than to give it a sharp focus and clear sense of forward motion. Often enough an 'incorrect' notation is truer to the passage than a 'correct' one, especially where the sense of the music becomes evident to the listener only after the fact.

In the stretto passage of bar 16, Chopin writes A♯ instead of B♭, even though its sound is unquestionably equivalent to the B♭ of bar 4. But this is the very spot where the music breaks out of its resigned lament, characterised by steady downward movement, into a brief but impassioned protest. Although the A♯ is taken over by the left hand, where it resolves to A♮ (exactly like the earlier B♭), the right-hand part resists the downward pull and tries to move into a higher register. This registral change marks the great dramatic turning point of the Prelude, and the notated sharp embodies the melody's upward drive, which succeeds for a moment only to sink back as if

---

17 It would be tedious to detail all the other notational changes made by Klindworth in his edition – the 'seule édition authentique', as the title page modestly calls it. Few pianists use Klindworth these days, but the 'Paderewski' is widely circulated, and almost as arbitrary at least with respect to the notation of chromatics. Except for the B♭ of bar 4, its editors adopt all of Klindworth's respellings for Op. 28 No. 4, possibly as a result of his influence (his edition is one of those they cite as sources).

18 I am not trying to maintain that the orthography always conveys an important musical message, but that it often does so and that the performer has the right in all cases to see what the composer actually wrote rather than an editor's notion of what he 'ought' to have written. Brahms addressed himself to this very issue when he worked on the Breitkopf edition of Chopin. In a letter to Ernst Rudorff (1 November 1877), he wrote, 'I wish very much that Bargiel would agree with us in not attempting to improve on Chopin's orthography! From here it would be only a small step to attack his texture as well.' See *Johannes Brahms im Briefwechsel mit Karl Reinthaler, Max Bruch, Hermann Deiters, Friedrich Heimfoeth, Karl Reinecke, Ernst Rudorff, Reinhard und Luise Scholz*, ed. Wilhelm Altmann, 2nd edn (Berlin 1912), p. 173. This letter is cited in a fascinating article by Oswald Jonas, 'On the Study of Chopin's Manuscripts', in *Chopin-Jahrbuch 1956*, ed. Franz Zagiba (Vienna 1956), pp. 142–55. I have used Jonas's translation of the Brahms letter; it appears in his article on p. 143.

19 See the editors' Commentary, p. 74.

exhausted. Viewed in this larger context, the pattern of related enharmonics B♭ (bar 4), A♯ (bar 16) and B♭ (bar 23, foreshadowed in 21) encapsulates almost iconographically the Prelude's form, its falling and rising contours, and its emotional history.

Appoggiaturas

In the Warsaw autograph, Chopin writes the appoggiaturas in bars 11 and 19 as small quavers, as if they were the long appoggiaturas of eighteenth-century practice. This notation was taken over in the French first edition, which follows the autograph quite faithfully. It also occurs in most of the standard recent editions, though not in 'Paderewski', which follows the German first edition (and many others) in adding a stroke across the quaver's flag as if to show a short appoggiatura. (The 'short' notation of the appoggiaturas appears in Julian Fontana's manuscript copy, from which the German edition was engraved; see note 5 above.) The Maryland draft may shed some light on the performance of the appoggiaturas in our Prelude. In bars 10 and 18, Chopin writes out the ornaments in large notes as ordinary quavers; oddly enough he placed the ornamented As before the plain ones (which appear in 11 and 19). This suggests to me that a long or an 'expressive short' appoggiatura (perhaps a semiquaver, as Cortot suggests) may well be what he had in mind here even in the final version with its small notation.[20] But since these very bars went through several revisions, one cannot know, in the absence of explicit notation, how much of his earlier intention was preserved at the end. He may well have used the less explicit notation to give the performer more freedom of choice in the declamation of these notes. (In the last section of the essay, I discuss the revisions of bars 10–12 and 18–20; Example 9.11 shows how the appoggiaturas occur in the three successive versions.)

Direction of stems

In his autographs Chopin frequently tends to maintain the upward or downward direction of his stems throughout a musical continuity, even where convention demands a change of direction. He also, it seems to me, tends to prefer downward stems. Both of these tendencies are visible in our two autographs, which are remarkably consistent in the stemming of the right-hand part. In the Warsaw source, the initial anacrusis gets upward stems, but the rest of the antecedent is stemmed down until bar 12, which is where the anacrusis returns in disguise.[21] The consequent resumes the downward stems, giving them up only in bar 20, where the right-hand part enters its final phase and the 'tenor' begins to take over the structural line. Chopin's calligraphy conveys the continuity of the long melodic line far better than any of the printed editions with their alternating up and down stems. The melodic line of bars 1–11 makes a particularly instructive comparison; pianists would do well to project that visual continuity in a long, legato, *espressivo* line.

---

[20]   Chopin, *24 Préludes, Édition de travail*, ed. Alfred Cortot (Paris 1926), p. 12.
[21]   In the Maryland draft, the first upbeat gets downward stems, but then continues exactly as in the Warsaw autograph. In any case, there would have been no room for ascending stems when Chopin added the upbeat to the draft.

Various revisions

In this last section of the paper, I shall discuss a few of the more important and interesting changes revealed by the two autographs.

Tempo The Warsaw autograph's original tempo mark is almost completely obliterated, but a reasonable guess is that it was 'Lento'. The upper loop of a capital L seems to project above the blotch, and the shape and size would fit. 'Largo' is, of course, generally considered to be a slower tempo than 'Lento'.

Upbeat The Maryland draft shows that Chopin added some left-hand notes below the opening upbeat. One cannot know for sure what they might have been: E and G underneath the right hand's B would be a possibility, or even a 6/4 chord with Great B as bass note. Curiously enough the Warsaw autograph also has something scratched out in the lower stave; it looks as though it might have been Great B, an octave below the right hand.

Bars 10–12 and 18–20 The right-hand part gave Chopin some difficulty here, and these parallel passages went through several versions. Fortunately, Chopin failed to obliterate what he had written in the later passage, so a plausible reconstruction of the first attempt is possible. (I assume that the two passages were more or less the same.) Example 9.11 illustrates.

Example 9.11   Prelude Op. 28 No. 4: bars 10–12 and 18–20, three versions

Bars 20–3 Reconstruction is much more problematic for the passage that encompasses the interrupted cadence near the end. I think, however, that Example 9.12 shows something fairly close to what Chopin had originally written. This hypothetical version harks back to the 7–6 resolutions of the opening bars, but it affords a much less convincing resolution of the structural line. In particular, the progression of $\hat{4}$ to $\hat{3}$, so beautifully combined with the interrupted cadence in the final version, is dwarfed by the 'tenor's' emphasised B♭. Chopin's revision here may strike the ear with less impact than the octave reinforcement he added to bar 17, but it shapes the composition in a more profound and fundamental way.

[crossed
out]

Example 9.12   Prelude Op. 28 No. 4: bars 20–3, hypothetical first version

10 Performing the F♯ minor Prelude Op. 28 No. 8

L. HENRY SHAFFER

I

Over the past few years I have been examining computer recordings of piano performance as a means of answering certain questions about pianistic skill. The advantage of capturing performance as a numerical sequence, as well as a sound recording, is that it is easy to create from it a graphic representation of the sound pattern, allowing both the fleeting moments and the large-scale organisation in a performance to be inspected at leisure. The timing and intensity of every note and the articulation of note sequences can be measured with precision, and just as the analyst can produce reductions of a score, it is possible to produce reductions of a performance, in order to observe the movements of its parameters over both small and large time spans. It should be said that the graphic method is a matter of convenience, and what I attempt to extract from the graphs is only what a perceptive listener could hear in the original sound, though it would require great concentration and probably many listenings to distil the equivalent information. It would also be possible to examine subliminal patterning in the constituent parameters, but the information this yields belongs more to the realm of physiology than to music. Among the recordings I have obtained are two performances by a concert pianist, PB, of Chopin's F♯ minor Prelude Op. 28 No. 8, and these will be the focus of the present study.

Given the precision in the recordings, the research lends itself most readily to tackling matters of technique, that is the degree of control pianists have over their expression, but sooner or later in discussing the research the question is raised whether it is possible to discern quality of performance from the graphs. Can they be used to tell a good from an indifferent or poor performance? The answer is that in principle they can, provided that one can satisfactorily define what is meant by a 'good' performance. Clearly it is something over and above technical fluency and is separate from athleticism on the keyboard, which can result in 'bad' performance. I am looking for that rarer artistic entity, a 'musical' performance.

It is an interesting problem, and a useful first step in tackling it is to posit a clear, workable definition of a musical performance. The exercise may founder at this step if musicians believe that musicality is ineffable, or if they strongly disagree on what is

musical. Some musicians may even be of the opinion that the exercise of trying to evaluate performances in this way is a matter of dull pedantry, and that we should instead
regard every performance as unique and look for its particular merits. This position is
generous to the performer but it is ultimately unhelpful, because it offers little general
guidance and it ignores the evidence that performers themselves seek out masters to
learn how to improve their musicianship.

If we listen to what is said about musical performance, then at least two quite distinct
criteria emerge. The first has to do with a refinement of touch which can impart a
special subtlety of phrasing or a quality of sound appropriate to the music, whether a
limpid legato for a Chopin nocturne or a springing percussiveness for a Bartók dance-
piece. The second has to do with whether the performance conveys an insight into the
musical meaning. These may not be wholly independent, but it is certainly possible
to satisfy one criterion and not the other, though they sometimes get confused. Both
these qualities deserve special study, but I shall concentrate here on the second one.

Before doing so, let us briefly consider the concept of an inspired performance,
which refers to the rare occasions when a performer is lifted to a different level of
playing. On these occasions the performer may feel in special communion with the
music or the composer, but I suggest that this is a benign illusion. In a heightened
mood of confidence, he or she may achieve an increased level of motor control which
confers a subtly increased command of the instrument. If there is a special communion, it is with the instrument. Moods come and go, but special insights would
not be subsequently lost so easily. The concept of inspired performance makes an
appeal to the first criterion rather than the second, to touch rather than understanding.
However, such inspiration can have a profound effect on the performance. It is
sometimes thought that great works have a spirituality which is fully brought out only
in the finest performances. The performer combining a heightened refinement of
touch with a full understanding of the music may on these occasions achieve this. The
refinement of touch would be apparent in the computer recordings, but a visual
representation cannot capture the spiritual quality conveyed in the sound.

A different kind of inspiration can be found in a performance which aims to
entertain an audience by its virtuosity. This may be a virtuosity of improvising skill
or of instrumental technique, requiring a thorough grasp of the musical idiom or
the resources of the instrument. Many of the great composer-performers, including
Beethoven and Chopin, possessed both these skills, and sometimes found it congenial
to give brilliant improvisations on their own works. Though such performances take
risks with the music, they can in their own way be intensely musical. We can nowadays
hear the spirit of these captured in the more inventive cadenzas in concertos and in
the jazz of such musicians as Art Tatum and Charlie Parker. It would be interesting
to study improvised performance both as a phenomenon in social dynamics and as an
exercise in spontaneous creativity.

As soon as we try to apply the concept of musical insight, we discover that it is
deeply ambiguous. It can be made to reflect the very different attitudes that musicians
bring to playing and listening to composed music. A survey of these suggests that it is
possible to reduce the variety to a few dimensions, of which two may be basic. These

involve attitudes towards the textual status of a score and towards the meaning of music, and we need to consider both in turn.

In terms of musical hermeneutics, a score can be viewed as a sacred writ or as a stimulus for creative interpretation. According to one view, there is an 'authentic' performance, the one intended by the composer, and any performance can be evaluated as an approximation to it. Opposed to this is the view that aiming at a fixed interpretation would ossify the work and turn the concert hall into a museum. The way to keep music alive is to reinterpret it each time it is performed. Thus musical insight can be either the discovery of the composer's fixed intention or the discovery of a generative potential in the music for different performances. If we examine composers' attitudes to their own music, we see that the concept of an ideal performance is scarcely tenable, though it can be useful as a counterweight to an assumption that the performer has unlimited interpretative freedom. We need look no further than Chopin's work and practice to expose the futility of a platonic ideal, and his practice is by no means exceptional among the musical masters. He continually reworked his pieces over the years, altered publishers' proofs and students' copies, and even published differing editions.[1] Thus it is apparent that he seldom regarded a score as a definitive statement of the piece. In performing his own works he would often improvise changes to the written version, and his students indicated that he would sometimes play a piece several times, expressing it differently each time.[2] Nor did he limit spontaneity to the teaching session: Charles Hallé commented that in a performance of the Barcarolle Op. 60 at his 1848 Paris recital, he played the final return of the opening theme *pianissimo* instead of increasing momentum and dynamic to reach the climax as marked in the score.[3] On the other hand, there is the evidence of a fastidious crafting in his work, which should convince us that he had a fairly definite conception of the sound he was aiming at. If he saw a generative potential, we can suppose that this was firmly bounded within a clear aesthetic perspective, and it seems desirable that a performer should understand this perspective and interpret the music within its bounds.

Sometimes associated with the creative view of performance is the idea that music can be decontextualised and treated as an abstract structure, without reference to its historical background or to the composer's expressive intentions. Again, this counterbalances a rigid insistence on authenticity, but it risks losing an important part of

---

1 See Jeffrey Kallberg, 'The Problem of Repetition and Return in Chopin's Mazurkas', in *Chopin Studies*, ed. Jim Samson (Cambridge 1988), pp. 1–23.

2 See Jean-Jacques Eigeldinger, *Chopin: Pianist and Teacher as Seen by His Pupils* (hereafter *CPT*), trans. Naomi Shohet with Krysia Osostowicz and Roy Howat, ed. Roy Howat (Cambridge 1986), p. 55.

3 *Life and Letters of Sir Charles Hallé*, ed. C. E. Hallé and Marie Hallé (London 1896), p. 36. Chopin's declining strength could of course have necessitated a less robust performance on this occasion. [It is relevant to note Liszt's comments (as reported in Anton Strelezki [Arthur Bransby Burnand], *Personal Recollections of Chats with Liszt* (London [1887]), pp. 12–13) about Chopin's performance of Op. 28 No. 8: '[Chopin] played for me in succession some eight or ten of his latest works, in a style which was a "revelation" of him, both as a virtuoso and composer. Especially beautiful was the Prelude in F♯ minor, a work replete with enormous difficulties, which he *wove* intricately under his fingers, [so] that at times a wailing melody was unravelled, and then again completely absorbed by wonderful arabesques and chromatic progressions. It was so enchanting that he complied with my earnest entreaty, and repeated it *twice*. Each time it seemed more beautiful, and each time he played it more ravishingly.' Quoted from *CPT*, pp. 273–4. Eds.]

aesthetic experience, a feeling of continuity with a cultural history. In the spirit of creative licence, a performer may reinterpret the music in a way which departs from the score or from its historical context but which produces something musically interesting in its own right. It then depends on our attitude whether we consider the performance to be insightful or only interestingly eccentric. Glenn Gould used to play the Aria of the 'Goldberg Variations' so slowly that it almost lost its pulse. Whether this was to create a sense of timelessness or to fit his theory of tempo relationships among the movements, the Aria performed this way bore little resemblance to a sarabande: one could certainly not dance to it. We can admire the experiment or be dismayed by its abuse of a classic. At the same time we can recognise that Gould had a marvellous understanding and technical control of polyphony, and in this sense his performances were highly musical. They illustrate very well the distinction made here between musicality of touch and insight into musical meaning.

Music means different things to different people, and we can encounter a spectrum of attitudes which seem to polarise on the relative importance they attach to the structure of the music and to the music's ability to convey a character, in terms of mood or narrative. At one extreme, music is regarded as mathematical structure in sound, having its aesthetic in the formal unity of its structure;[4] at the other extreme, it is a direct medium for conveying affect, with structure serving only to facilitate this. Thus music allows us to commune with the heavenly spheres or with the most intimate feelings of the composer, perhaps with both in the case of Beethoven's last piano sonata, Op. 111. These disparate attitudes can lead to very different expectations of how music should be expressed, ranging from an emphasis on clarity and precision to an emphasis on feeling. Expressive feeling does not itself preclude clarity and precision, only its excess. The accounts of Chopin's playing of his own music suggest that he was able to combine these qualities. It relied on a special discipline of playing which arose from his preference for modelling the piano sound on *bel canto* singing, employing a light touch and making sparing use of loud dynamics and of *tempo rubato*. He could thus convey feeling in a 'natural' way without impairing the clarity of the musical argument, allowing a fluidity of timing in the melody while maintaining a more steady pulse in the accompaniment.[5] Such control of dynamic and timing combined with a sparing use of the sustaining pedal allowed him to convey transparently the polyphonic textures of his music. It is worth noting too that he preferred the lighter acoustics of Graf and Pleyel pianos to the more resonant sound of the Erard or Broadwood.

The concepts of character and mood seem equivalent in a musical context, and I shall distinguish them only by making the former more inclusive, including narrative as well as mood. Otherwise they give rise to much the same metaphors for describing certain qualities of the musical surface. These qualities are the province of expressive markings in a score. Character has some degree of independence of structure, and this can be demonstrated by playing the same piece with different tempos, different levels

[4]   See Douglas Hofstadter, *Gödel, Escher, Bach: An Eternal Golden Braid* (New York 1979).
[5]   See *CPT*, pp. 49–51.

of dynamic and different kinds of legato–staccato articulation: changing these parameters alters the perceived character of the music though the perceived structure remains invariant, except that choosing very different tempos may lead to the pulse of the music being heard at different metrical levels, affecting the perceived rhythms. Thus character can be only partly intrinsic to a piece of music, the rest being contributed by the performer's choice of expression. On the other hand, it seems generally true that melody, rhythm, harmony and texture combine to limit the scope of an appropriate characterisation.

Put another way, a performer can choose different ways of characterising a piece, but only some of these will fit the music naturally, the others seeming contrived. If this claim is valid, then whatever attitude we take on the structure–affect issue of musical meaning should not alter the conclusion that structure provides the proper basis for character, and so should take logical precedence in acquiring an understanding of the music. The idea that we can intuitively determine character before understanding structure seems misconceived: at best it implies that we already have an intuitive though not yet explicit understanding of structure, and at worst it allows the assignment of character to become whimsical. Despite these conclusions, it remains an open question how one goes about determining the options of character from a structural analysis of the piece. Wallace Berry[6] offers some remarks on this in his fuller discussion of analysis and expression, but his suggestions for getting from one to the other have still to be taken beyond a tentative stage.

Mood and narrative have long been common metaphors for describing the character of music. It is easy enough to trace a narrative in song, opera and overtly descriptive music, but it seems less obvious that we can do this in absolute music. Janet Schmalfeldt[7] has found it useful to consider a variant of this concept, the dramatic idea, as an entity mediating between an analysis and the choice of an expressive form. Thus she sees Beethoven's Bagatelle Op. 126 No. 2 as the particular working-out of a conflict between two themes introduced in the opening phrase. In general, the dramatic idea determines the inner logic of a piece, and the concept is an attempt to provide a basis for the structures described by thematic, motivic and harmonic analyses. Perhaps the main use of the dramatic metaphor is as a guide to an appropriate mode of expression, and Schmalfeldt sketches these implications of the concept in a thesis engagingly presented as a dialogue with herself in the successive roles of analyst and performer.

It has been convenient so far to assume that musical structure is a well-defined concept, and that analysts and performers would have little difficulty agreeing on the structure of a piece. The reality is less simple, since structure arises from a combination of melodic, harmonic and rhythmic processes operating on different levels, interacting within and perhaps across levels. An analysis provides at best a partial description of structure, and so there are many possible descriptions, which may sometimes come into conflict because of ambiguities in the music. It is even possible that the theoretical goals of analysis and the pragmatic goals of performance diverge enough to require

---

6   Wallace Berry, *Musical Structure and Performance* (New Haven 1989).
7   Janet Schmalfeldt, 'On the Relation of Analysis to Performance: Beethoven's Bagatelles Op. 126, Nos. 2 and 5', *Journal of Music Theory*, 29/1 (1985), pp. 1–31.

different descriptions; this has been suggested by Jonathan Dunsby[8] and others, though the arguments are not convincing. It seems preferable to suppose that analysts and performers should be able to agree on what considerations are relevant to a performance. An analysis driven by theory might come into conflict with musical considerations and so be of little use to the performer, but arguably it would be a poor analysis which took theory so far from its empirical and pragmatic roots.

In short, it should be feasible to evaluate a performance not only in terms of technical control and quality of phrasing, but also in terms of conveying a grasp of the music's structure and character, which entails an expressive form natural to the structure and to the historical context of the work. I shall use these ideas as a framework for the following exercise of examining performances of the F♯ minor Prelude.

This Prelude can be regarded as a complete piece of music, or, as the name implies, as a preface to something else, or as part of a cycle of preludes. The set of twenty-four Preludes Op. 28 forms a cycle because it is published as a sequence which completes a tour of the relative major and minor keys in the dominant direction around the circle of fifths. The impression of a linked sequence is reinforced by the sense that Nos. 1 and 24 sound distinctly like an introduction and a finale respectively. We know that Chopin himself played individual pieces as preludes to something else, but it is not clear how often he continued to do so after he had completed the set (which took him several years) and if he ever played them as a cycle. Attempts by scholars to find musical coherence in the set, apart from the fact that their keys form a cyclic group, have not been altogether convincing. Jean-Jacques Eigeldinger,[9] for instance, has claimed to discover a motivic cell which runs through the entire set. It is made up of an ascending sixth falling back to a fifth, which is a note sequence used in tuning the piano in equal temperament. The set of preludes could thus be seen as an elaborate lesson in the temperament of Chopin's piano. This would be an exciting discovery were it not the case that in many of the preludes the three notes forming the putative motif can only be found dispersed within a phrase, and one has to ask how often the motivic cell so defined would occur in almost any piece of tonal music. Since, however, the preludes are most often played nowadays as a cycle, we can ask whether the context has expressive implications for playing the individual pieces. Paradoxically, what they can contribute to the context is their diversity of harmony, rhythm and texture, and perhaps the most effective way to convey this is with a restrained use of expression which allows the structural contrasts to emerge in an unforced way, also perhaps by pacing the pauses between preludes.

II

The performances described here were obtained on a Bechstein grand piano connected to a computer. The recording was based on information about the movements of the

---

8   Jonathan Dunsby, 'Guest Editorial: Performance and Analysis of Music', *Music Analysis*, 8/1–2 (1989), pp. 5–20.

9   Jean-Jacques Eigeldinger, 'Twenty-four Preludes Op. 28: Genre, Structure, Significance', in *Chopin Studies*, ed. Jim Samson (Cambridge 1988), pp. 167–93.

hammers in the piano action. Thus it is possible to identify which notes were played and to reconstruct the attack moments of successive notes, their duration and articulation, and their dynamic, estimated from the hammer velocity at the moment it hits the string. This information can then be used to construct performance graphs of the kind shown in Figure 1. The figure shows two performances, P1 and P2, of the F♯ minor Prelude, played in fairly close succession by the pianist PB, who had recently performed the entire cycle as part of a Chopin recital. The upper graphs show the played duration, in milliseconds, of each beat and so give an inverted picture of tempo variation. The lower graphs show an estimate of dynamic of each beat in some arbitrary unit relative to a true zero. Since many notes were played in each beat, its dynamic is represented by the most intensely played of these. We can project these graphs into more musical terms by noting that the upper graphs indicate a basic tempo of about ♩ = 80, and the lower ones indicate a dynamic range roughly between *p* and *ff*. The Prelude is thirty-four bars long, the last two bars containing only chords. These two bars were played in a broad allargando and have been omitted from the graphs. The axis counts the successive bars and the piece has a 4/4 time signature, so it is easy to trace timing and dynamic beat by beat.

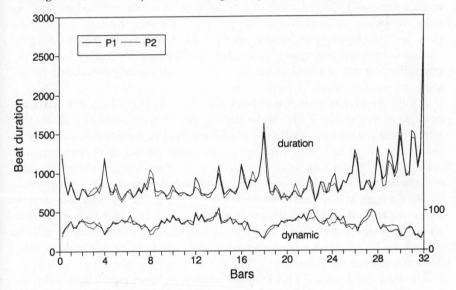

Figure 1   Graphs of timing and dynamic for two performances, P1 and P2, of the F♯ minor Prelude by the pianist PB. The axis counts the bars; there are four beats per bar. The left ordinate calibrates played beat duration in milliseconds; the right ordinate calibrates played beat dynamic in arbitrary units with a true zero.

Two things are immediately apparent in the graphs. The first is the repeated use of a typical phrasing gesture which gives temporal shape and coherence to a musical unit by accelerating into it and slowing at its boundary; at the same time, there is often a rise in dynamic followed by a fall at the boundary. This expressive gesture can be applied recursively in a hierarchy of units. It requires little effort to see that the performer has used the gesture to divide the piece into two sections, the first ending at bar 18. We can also see in the timing graphs the division of each section into phrases varying in length. Within a phrase a separation of bars is often made apparent, each with its own acceleration and slowing. It is not difficult to analyse a metrical hierarchy in the Prelude, but as we shall see this may not coincide altogether with the hierarchy implied by the expressive timing observed here. Dynamic on the other hand shows a rather flatter hierarchy, indicating mainly the larger groupings of phrases and sections, though it may be more responsive to local processes within the music.

The second thing we can observe in the figure is that the graphs for the two performances are very similar, differing at only a few isolated points. The observation of such precision has now become commonplace in the study of highly skilled musical performance, and it occurs particularly in the playing of well practised pieces. It tells us in the case of PB that she was in full technical control of her performance, and we can also infer that she had for the most part a precise mental representation of an expressive form for the piece. Musicians can seldom describe their interpretation or choices of expression in this detail, and without the evidence of such recordings we might suppose that they improvise much of it as the spirit moves them, as indeed they can if they so wish or when playing at sight. It seems, however, that having practised a piece and developed an interpretation, they are more conservative in changing expression from one performance to another. We can see a few small changes in the graphs. For instance, PB used slightly less rubato in her second performance, particularly towards the end of the piece.

A third observation arises from a fuller inspection of the graphs, and it makes the study more interesting. If indeed the Prelude can be represented structurally as a hierarchy of phrase units, and if the pianist had applied the phrasing gesture in a mechanical fashion to each of these in turn, we would observe much more regularity of shape in the graphs than in fact appears. In his 1968 monograph, Cone[10] discusses the importance of using phrase structure to introduce breathing spaces in a performance, but does not go on to consider the ways in which the phrasing gesture may itself be responsive to the nature of the processes forming the phrases. It is evident that PB's use of expression went beyond simply conveying phrase grouping, and in order to understand her expressive intentions more fully we need to undertake a more detailed analysis of the Prelude.[11]

A conspicuous feature of the F♯ minor Prelude is its highly regular surface rhythm. Except for the last two bars, which contain solid chords, a rhythmic figure is repeated in each beat of the four-beat bar. In this figure the first and seventh of a group of eight notes in the right hand form a melody played by the thumb in a dotted quaver-semiquaver rhythm, while the rest form a background figuration. At the same time a four-note group in the left hand divides the beat in half and contains a triplet rhythm in the first half, producing a polyrhythm between the two hands.

---

[10]   Edward T. Cone, *Musical Form and Musical Performance* (New York 1968).
[11]   I would like to thank Jim Samson and John Rink for helping me understand the F♯ minor Prelude, but should make it clear that any errors and infelicities are entirely my own.

The melody notes in the right hand are immediately followed by an octave leap. Chopin has cleverly exploited a well-known auditory illusion in which a sequence of notes alternating between different pitch regions will be perceived to split into distinct melodies if it is played fast enough. The upper notes become part of the figuration and the remaining notes following the octave leap attach themselves to this through their temporal proximity, even though the later ones come close in pitch to the melody. Thus when the Prelude is played at a fast tempo there is no need to accent the melody notes: this can be shown by synthesising a deadpan performance on a computer. In fact PB may have attempted but did not achieve consistent accenting of the melody notes in her performances. Similarly, the left-hand figuration remains distinct from the melody because of its downward leap following the first note and its different rhythm. Thus the control of touch in performance is simplified at a fast tempo. If the pianist slows down and does not compensate by accenting the melody notes, then these merge with the right-hand figuration and a single melody line is heard against a rhythmically contrasting left-hand figuration. This occurred when PB slowed the music at the end of a phrase, producing a striking effect resembling a clockwork toy running down.

In the same spirit, the pianist has to do little more than play at a fast tempo to imbue the music with an agitated character. This alone will give a sense of urgency to the obsessively repeated dotted rhythm of the melody against a complex poly-rhythmic figuration, which is in turn set within a restlessly moving melody line and rapidly changing and often dissonant harmonies. In particular there is no need to play with exaggerated rubato or an insistently loud dynamic, thus freeing the expressive use of the parameters of timing and dynamic to give shape to the large-scale structures that define the rise and fall of tension in the music.

The Prelude falls into four-bar phrases, except that there are two 'extra' bars, bars 13–14, disturbing an overall symmetry, which can be heard as an extension of the third phrase or as an added short phrase. The rhythmic asymmetry created in this way contributes to a climax which is built at that point in the music. This analysis of metrical structure agrees in many respects with one we would be led to infer from the performance graphs, but if we take the degree of slowing at a boundary to reflect the degree of closure at that point, then there are important discrepancies between what the graphs suggest and what we would expect on analytical grounds. These will be examined later.

The opening bars establish the tonality of F♯ minor by twice stating a theme which ascends C♯–F♯–G♯ in a basically i–V progression, the couplet on the last beat being syncopated by the A♮ appoggiatura to G♯ over a dominant seventh harmony. The melody completes an octave ascent but then moves downward stepwise in a sequence which returns it to its initial register. The linear motion of voices in the sequence creates dissonances of mainly seventh and diminished harmonies in paired fifth-progressions. The tonality becomes unstable in this motion but the phrase ends in bar 4 on the dominant seventh, preparing a return to the tonic.

The second phrase is an imitation of the first, but midway it ascends a third higher than before, giving rise to an expectation that it might move into the relative major.

This possibility is enhanced by the bass E♮ (suggesting V^7/III) on the last beat of bar 6, but the sequence that follows dissipates tonal direction and is more tonally unstable than before. The melodic descent in the sequence does not complete an octave as before but is arrested in the final beats, ending on a repeated B♭ above the dominant seventh harmony of C♭ major (bar 8). Thus it prepares enharmonically to move to the subdominant of F♯ major, but what follows instead is a musical pun which Chopin often uses, in which B♭ major can be heard both as the tonicised major mediant (literally A♯ major in the context of F♯ major) and as the dominant of the relative minor, in this case enharmonically equivalent to E♭ minor.

This ambiguity provides the intensifying dynamic for the following ten bars, in which there is at the same time an inversion of the theme, so that it falls and rises instead of rising and falling, giving it a questioning intonation appropriate to the continual shifts of harmony. Furthermore, the first six of these bars have the feel of a series of interrupted sequences, with imitations occurring first at one-bar then at two-bar intervals. The sequence starting at bar 9 appears to begin in B♭ major, initially stated by its tonic (in second inversion) and then maintained for two bars by an F pedal, during which time it is undermined by linear processes which pose V–i progressions in C minor and D minor. Bar 11 initiates a melodic expansion of the preceding sequence. It begins by reaffirming B♭ major in a V–I progression but ends with a similar progression in G minor. However, in bar 12 B♭ becomes more firmly identified as the dominant of E♭ minor, with a more sustained V–i progression in that key seeming to resolve the earlier ambiguity.

Bar 13 begins as if to imitate the previous melody and so extend the preceding phrase in an altered harmony, but this is interrupted on the second beat, when the melody descends abruptly to its lowest point and then ascends for the remainder of bars 13–14, the harmony resolving with a V–I progression in C♭ major, which was adumbrated and then abandoned in bar 8. This concludes a harmonic descent in thirds, B♭ major – G minor – E♭ minor – C♭ major, and restores the ambiguity. The climax of this passage is reached in the following bars, in which the melody reverts to a more compact version of the original theme, while the harmony returns to E♭ minor in a repeated ii^7–V progression, as if finally to confirm the dominant function of B♭. The climax is played out over a four-bar phrase forming an antecedent–consequent pair of subphrases, each in the form of a theme and imitation. In the antecedent the melody ends in an upward leap to B♭, but, ironically, in the consequent it descends on the last beat to C♯ while the harmony shifts back to the dominant of F♯, abruptly preparing a return to the tonic and a possible recapitulation.

In bar 19 the music indeed returns to its beginning, but it skips the first phrase and goes directly to the second phrase, in which the theme had extended its upward movement. Unlike its earlier counterpart, the ascent continues in the following sequence, taking all the voices to the highest point in the Prelude. The combination of this registral shift with a sequence of continually shifting diminished sevenths and dominant sevenths creates an explosive rise of intensity leading to the climax in bar 22. The melody in this bar repeatedly states the couplet G♯–A, in which G♯ is an appoggiatura, reversing the roles of these notes in the original theme. The loss of tonal direction over the sequence is recovered only in bar 22^3, when the flattening of D♯ (literally E♭) to D♮ provides an enharmonic augmented sixth preparing a dominant return to F♯ minor.

In the following phrase, the melody descends over two bars (23–4) to reach C♯ in its initial register. There it becomes static for the rest of the phrase, though the top voice in the left hand provides a tenor countermelody which continues a stepwise, closing descent to E♯. The harmony is mainly the dominant of F♯ minor, forming a strong V–i cadence in bars 26–7. There is a compelling sense of the music winding down, and by the end of the phrase the restlessness implied by the Molto agitato e stretto marked at bar 19 is sustained only by the repeating rhythm. The remaining eight bars of the piece contain essentially a coda in the tonic harmony, in which the penultimate phrase has the form of a theme and imitation. That theme is a rhythmically expanded version of the original theme, a sustained C♯ followed by a sustained D rising briefly to F♯ in a i–iv progression. In the imitation, the sharpening of A in the left hand and of D in the right gently lifts the melody into the parallel major, as though conferring a state of grace on the music. The melody persists in major for one bar of the final phrase and then gives way again to the minor. The simplifying process of the closing phrases is taken to its logical conclusion in the last two bars, with a progression via the Neapolitan sixth to a perfect cadence in sustained chords.

III

Let us briefly consider the overall shape of the Prelude relevant to its performance. It seems to be based on a drama which unfolds continuously, in which after an early loss of tonal centre, already threatened in the first phrase, the music follows a series of false trails seeking its recovery. These trails include an extended digression in the remote tonal region of E♭ minor. The appearance of a reprise following this at bar 19 is deceptive, since the music returns only to the unstable version of the opening theme and loses its direction more quickly and fully than before. Furthermore the digression itself achieves only an incomplete resolution, and the sudden last-minute shift to a dominant seventh in F♯ minor, obtained with an enharmonic change of the melody note, can be heard as an upbeat to bar 19. Thus we can trace a single trajectory of tension over the piece which builds up in successive waves to reach its peak in bar 22, with a secondary peak earlier in bar 15, and is then quickly dissipated. The respite between these climaxes is brief, with the marking of *poco ritenuto* at the end of bar 18 compensated by the marking of *stretto* at bar 19, as if the relaxation is only to gather momentum. The dynamic markings in the score support this picture, and suggest that despite the Molto agitato marking and dynamic markings *ff* at the climaxes, the drama is a fairly contained one. Given that the first crescendo, starting at bar 9, takes the dynamic to *f* at bar 13, we can suppose that the piece begins quietly, with a dynamic no more than *p*. Furthermore, in the long coda the dynamic is marked first *p* then *pp*. What is indicated is a piece which builds from an initial mild restlessness to an intermediate fury – intense but fairly shortlived – and then subsides into relative calm. The challenge to the pianist is to shape a pyramid of intensity over the Prelude while maintaining control of the repeating rhythmic figure played at speed, so that the melody can emerge in an unforced way, yet an overall clarity of the complex texture is achieved.

Returning to PB's performances, we can now examine them more fully in the light of this description, using it to elucidate her expression and to comment on it. I have also listened to six gramophone recordings of the piece and can later make brief comparative comments on these. The recordings are by Artur Rubinstein,[12] Nikita Magaloff,[13] Martha Argerich,[14] Vladimir Ashkenazy,[15] Maurizio Pollini[16] and Livia Rev.[17]

PB starts fairly slowly and quietly and quickly accelerates within the first bar to a tempo around $\bf J$ = 80, pausing at the end of each statement of the theme. At the same time she increases the dynamic to f on each ascent to the appoggiatura A. There is a gradual decline of tempo and dynamic over the sequence with a rapid fall in both at the end of the four-bar phrase. Thus PB quickly establishes a fairly dramatic character for the piece, favouring a high dynamic level and a heavy use of rubato, presumably to emphasise its agitated quality. She attempts to foreground the melody notes in the right hand by accenting them, but succeeds as often as not in accenting the neighbouring pitches around the short note. Accenting the short notes enhances the restless feel of the music, and we can note here that the gramophone artists also tended to perform the Prelude in this way.

PB begins the imitation phrase similarly, and in the sequence she accents the E♮ in bar 7^1 (in the first performance only), a response to the highest point so far in the melody, and perhaps to express surprise at not reaching the expected A major. The slowing in the sequence is more hesitant than in the first phrase and the pause at the phrase boundary briefer, though still greater than we might expect given the nominal degree of closure in the music. We might also expect a greater expressive intensity than in the previous phrase on several grounds. There is a greater tonal displacement and more frequent dissonance in this phrase, and not only does the melody ascend further, with the hint of a shift to the relative major, but there is also a fairly steep ascent of the bass. However, PB does not increase the dynamic beyond the level of the first phrase, except to accent the E♮ at the beginning of the sequence.

PB appears to treat the next ten bars as a sustained passage with some internal phrase grouping. It is the passage in which the tonal digression around E♭ minor is played out. She produces basically a single rising and falling gesture of dynamic over it and a slight, gradual slowing of underlying tempo. There is also a tendency to pause at two-bar intervals, corresponding to a patterning of the melody and to the V–I progressions in transitional keys, and these pauses are themselves graded. Thus there is a pause following the V–i progression in E♭ minor in bar 12; a larger one following the C♭ major cadence in bar 14; another large one in bar 16 to separate the

[12] RCA Victor 60047.
[13] Philips 6768 067.
[14] Deutsche Grammophon 431 584–4.
[15] Decca 417476–2.
[16] Deutsche Grammophon 3300 550.
[17] Hyperion 66324.

antecedent and consequent subphrases, each with its ii^7–V progression in E♭ minor; and a more massive pause following the arrival of the dominant seventh of F♯ minor in bar 184, which in effect splits the Prelude into two sections.

The score marks a crescendo from bar 9 which reaches *f* in bar 13 and builds further to *ff* in bar 15. The rising tension in the music is evident from the harmonic restlessness up to that point: the harmonies pose a series of dominant sevenths which either fail to resolve or change harmonic direction immediately following a resolution. PB builds local peaks of dynamic in bars 9 and 10, accenting successive paired fifth-progressions, but she allows dynamic to decline for the next two bars, corresponding to a melodic descent in these bars, with a sudden rise to a new peak at the end of bar 12. Thus she appears to anticipate the change of the melodic G♭ from being the mediant of E♭ minor to the dominant of C♭ major. However, combined with the pause at this point, she is perhaps anticipating the steeper melodic descent in the opening beats of bar 13. She allows the dynamic to fall in this bar, except for an accent on the sudden melodic descent to A♭, and then builds to the biggest climax so far at the end of bar 14 by steadily increasing dynamic and slowing the tempo. Again, as in bar 12, she anticipates the climax marked in the score, when this time the melodic E♭ changes from being the mediant of C♭ major to the tonic of E♭ minor. If C♭ major displaces a briefly adumbrated E♭ minor, it is in turn dismissed in bar 15 by a return to the earlier key, now established in repeated dominant harmony. At the same time the shape of the original theme is suddenly restored, supporting a sense of affirmation that the harmonic conflict in this intermediate passage has been resolved. Instead of conveying this, PB produces a marked lowering of intensity at this point.

The antecedent–consequent subphrases of bars 15–18 are marked *ff* and *p* respectively in the score. The repetition of a ii^7–V progression in these renders them harmonically static, and so the dynamic contrast seems designed to create a statement–echo effect. If the antecedent serves to close the sustained tonal digression, the consequent is able to anticipate a return to the original tonic. Instead of this contrast, PB produces a diminuendo to *p* over the four-bar phrase, and marks the boundary between the antecedent and the consequent by a pause. This seems to miss the changing significance of the subphrases, supported by the melodic-harmonic contrast between their endings. Furthermore, the massive ritardando at the end of the phrase destroys the continuity that would take the rising curve of intensity to its true climax in bar 22, where the sustained process of tonal disruption finally founders and the original tonality is allowed to prevail once and for all. Thus the marking of *poco ritenuto* at the end of bar 18 seems best interpreted as a brief respite in an increasingly urgent search for tonal resolution.

PB accelerates to a slightly faster tempo in bar 19, complying with the Molto agitato e stretto marking, and builds the dynamic to a climax in bar 23. The score places the climax on the first G♯–A couplet in bar 22, where all the voices reach their highest point, at the same time that tonal direction founders on a sequence of diminished chords, and the repeated melodic couplet seems to mock by its reversal the A–G♯ couplet that rounds off the original theme. The tension begins to release on the third of these couplets, when the harmony changes, with the flattening of D♯ (E♭)

to D♮, from a diminished seventh to an effective augmented sixth, preparing a return to dominant harmony in F♯ minor. Again PB does it differently from what this analysis leads us to expect, and she is different in each performance. Having built the dynamic progressively up to bar 21^2, she cuts back slightly in bar 21^3 and then in one performance increases again to reach a peak on A at bar 23^1, the note on which the melodic descent begins, whereas in the other performance there is a much smaller increase up to G♯ in bar 23^2. She pauses at the end of bar 22, to emphasise a phrase boundary and perhaps to mark the transition between melodic ascent and descent. The expressive difference between the two performances suggests that PB did not have a consistent conceptual basis for interpreting this passage. It also seems that she understood the main climax of the Prelude to occur in bar 14, rather than in bar 22, since that receives greater emphasis.

What she does from then on is also a little unexpected. Following the climax the structural tension in the music ebbs away, leaving a relative tranquillity from bar 27 onward in a coda which offers only brief swells of intensity. Indeed, PB steadily slows the tempo but allows it to fluctuate in increasingly large swings, which become more and more frequent, until they occur in each bar. It was perhaps her understanding that the work should maintain an agitated character throughout, and so she used heavy rubato to sustain a feeling of restlessness, or perhaps as an affective response to the aftermath of tension. The result in any event is a loss of the simplicity suggested by the structure. A further unexpected touch comes in her shaping of the implied diminuendo to the end of the piece. In bars 27–8 she builds a large crescendo accenting the melodic couplet C♯–D, even though the score indicates only a slight crescendo to F♯ in this subphrase and the following one. Perhaps she wanted to bring out the contrast between the passage in minor and its imitation in major, and consistent with this she makes a similar gesture on a smaller scale in bar 31. It is musically valid to underline the major–minor contrast, but the scale of her gesture in bars 27–8 misses the significance of the contrast in the context of minimal melodic and harmonic movement, and seems wholly out of place in the coda. Finally, she draws out the final bars in a massive ritardando, whereas the progressive simplicity of the musical structure, reducing the last two bars to a series of chords, suggests that a slighter allargando, allowing the final spread chord to fade into silence, would be more appropriate.

In summary, PB has chosen a fairly dramatic reading of the Prelude, interpreting Molto agitato as an instruction to be heavily expressive, rather than as a recommendation to play at a fast tempo a piece which is intrinsically restless but not dramatically so. Thus, rather than allow the intensity to increase gradually in cumulative waves from a quiet beginning, as the score suggests, she raises it early on and maintains it except for moments of respite until near the end. By making a distinct break in the middle of the piece, she loses the sense of a continuous impulse, only briefly subdued, which takes the melody to its later climax. And instead of the subsequent descent to tranquillity which the music offers as a contrast to the earlier tension, she allows the drama to decline more grudgingly. In opting for a spirited rendering of the Prelude, she loses much of its subtlety. Thus if anyone asks me I would say that these are enjoyable but not good performances, as they are not sufficiently sensitive to the music's intrinsic shape and character.

Turning briefly to the gramophone recordings for comparison, PB's rendition lies within a spectrum which extends from Martha Argerich to Livia Rev. Argerich gives a demon-ridden performance which is very fast with a massive use of rubato, and relentlessly loud with only some concessions to the dynamic markings in the coda. It is in every way a more extreme version of PB's reading. Rubinstein achieves greater contrast in tonal colour, but his too is a dramatic interpretation similar to PB's. Ashkenazy gives a spirited reading, which still tends to the dramatic and employs a great deal of rubato, but also makes a more varied use of dynamic (although not always related to the score markings). His florid ending includes a broad spreading of the III chord at bar 33^1. The other three, Magaloff, Pollini and Rev, give fairly straight readings which stay close to the score markings, though Magaloff misses the climax at bar 15 and becomes unexpectedly heavy in bars 25–6, where the melody completes its descent and settles on C♯. Rev's performance opts for a medium tempo which misses the urgency the music seems to require, making it slightly ponderous. It is Pollini whose performance comes closest to that suggested by the analytical description. His playing of the coda is beautifully judged, allowing the music to fade to a whisper in a graceful allargando. He like Rev builds essentially a single dynamic arch over the piece, but whereas Rev and Ashkenazy allow the tempo to relax in the melodic descent in bars 23–4, in order to release the tension after the climax, Pollini if anything accelerates slightly. He and Rev alone properly place the climaxes at bars 15 and 22 as the score indicates; Argerich and Rubinstein actually relax the tension at bar 15, while Ashkenazy and Magaloff produce an ebb and flow of tension over the middle passage leading to the return of the tonic in bar 19. All of these performers, like PB, lower the intensity at bar 8 by slowing and lowering the dynamic, responding more to a structural symmetry between the first and second phrases than to the differences of closure in their endings.

PB's performances stand up fairly well in this company. None of these artists fully responds to the patterning of harmonic tension that gives the piece its character, though they are considered among the best modern exponents of Chopin's music. Several of them, Argerich in particular, seem to have taken the tempo marking of Molto agitato so literally as to override other expressive markings in the score, which indicates a more subtly exciting composition than the one they end up playing.

IV

The goal of this study has been to explore how far one can go towards reaching evaluative judgements on a performance from its numerical recordings. In order to make this possible, I have placed considerable emphasis on a criterion that the primary responsibility of a performance is to convey the music's meaning, which I have described in terms of structure and character. It is a flexible criterion which does not require us to suppose that there is an ideal performance, because it is understood that any complex work can be interpreted in different ways, and any interpretation can be realised in a number of expressive variants. Yet the criterion still offers sufficient constraint for us to be able to test the compatibility of a performance with an analytical description of the work.

In the exercise I have exposed a number of features in PB's performances which depart from the recommended markings in the score, in ways which suggest that she may not have fully understood its structure beyond its broad metrical grouping, missing even essentially foreground features of structure. She seems instead to have responded mainly to the affective implications of the tempo marking. There is of course little intrinsic value in describing and evaluating a particular performance of a particular piece, and so I have broadened the perspective slightly by comparing it with other recorded performances of the Prelude.

One of the uses of this kind of exercise is that it provides a context in which to examine an assumption that performers may intuitively understand a piece of music more directly and perhaps more comprehensively than the music analyst. There is undoubtedly an element of romantic fiction in this belief, but it may capture a half-truth which is worth exploring. It is fairly common among cognitive skills that we can solve a problem and remain unaware of the mental processes that led to the solution. Subjectively the solution appears to come as a 'direct' or 'intuitive' insight. What the fiction misses is that intuitive problem-solving works well only when we have implicitly learned appropriate problem-solving techniques through practice. Thus the performer seeking to understand a piece of music needs to have developed analytical skills, whether implicitly through practice or explicitly through abstract study. Without these skills the performer can only respond haphazardly to the musical surface, exploring the expressive possibilities of the piece until one is found which 'sounds right'. Of course, even with such skills the schedules of concert performance may not allow the time to obtain a full understanding of a complex piece.

In principle the analyst should have an advantage over the performer in interpreting a piece of music, but this is not guaranteed. Explicit analytical techniques may fail to capture the insights afforded by the analytical knowledge developed implicitly through experience. This is likely to happen the more the analyst relies on theoretical preconceptions rather than empirical evidence. Thus the musical cause may be better served by combining the incisiveness of analytical theory with a pragmatic perspective on the music, and we should expect the insightful interpretations of music to come most often from the performer-analyst. The dialogue that Schmalfeldt[18] sets up between the performer and the analyst, jointly searching for both the structure and the character of a work, seems a productive strategy. This does not preempt the performer's task of finding a suitable expressive form which can realise the interpretation in performance.

These remarks apply acutely to interpreting the works of a composer like Chopin, who on the one hand could create a musical surface so poetic that the performer might feel it sufficient to respond to it intuitively in a poetic spirit, and on the other hand could provide such an elegant structure for this surface that the analyst immersed in its abstract study might lose sight of the music's broader meaning.

---

[18]   'On the Relation of Analysis to Performance'.

11 *Chopin's* tempo rubato *in context*

DAVID ROWLAND

Tempo rubato has been defined in many different ways during the last two hundred and fifty years. Its broadest definition concerns the practice of speeding up and slowing down within a passage. Riemann, for example, specifies that '*Tempo rubato* is the free treatment of passages of marked expression and passion, which forcibly brings out the *stringendo–calando* in the shading of phrases, a feature which, as a rule, remains unnoticed.'[1] Some definitions such as Fuller-Maitland's restrict the rhythmic ebb and flow in order to give each bar exactly the same length:

RUBATO, lit. 'robbed' or 'stolen', referring to the values of the notes, which are diminished in one place and increased in another. The word is used, chiefly in instrumental music, to indicate a particular kind of licence allowed in order to emphasise the expression. This consists of a slight *ad libitum* slackening or quickening of the time in any passage, in accordance with the unchangeable rule that in all such passages any bar in which this licence is taken must be of exactly the same length as the other bars in the movement, so that if the first part of the bar be played slowly, the other part must be taken quicker than the ordinary time of the movement to make up for it; and *vice versa*, if the bar is hurried at the beginning, there must be a *rallentando* at the end.[2]

Others go further still, insisting that the accompanying part should keep strict time while the melody anticipates, or lags behind, the beat, causing non-synchronisation between the two parts. This technique, vitally important to a discussion of Chopin's rubato, was described in a number of eighteenth- and nineteenth-century sources: the English translation (1742) of Tosi's singing treatise (1723) is a frequently quoted example which refers to the use of this type of rubato in both instrumental and vocal music ('Mr G', the eighteenth-century translator, glosses Tosi's comments):

The stealing of time, in the pathetic, is an honourable theft in one that sings better than others, provided he makes a restitution with ingenuity.

---

[1] Hugo Riemann, *Musik-Lexicon* (Leipzig 1882), trans. John Shedlock as *Dictionary of Music* (London 1893–7), s.v. 'Rubato'.
      When published translations are cited as well as original titles, the text and page (or dictionary article) references pertain to the translation.
[2] J. A. Fuller-Maitland, 'Rubato', in *A Dictionary of Music and Musicians*, ed. George Grove (London 1883), vol. III, p. 188.

Mr. G. Our Author has often mentioned time; the regard to it, the strictness of it, and how much it is neglected and unobserved. In this place, speaking of stealing the time, it regards particularly the vocal, or the performance on a single instrument in the pathetic and tender; when the bass goes an exactly regular pace, the other part retards or anticipates in a singular manner for the sake of expression, but after that returns to its exactness, to be guided by the bass.[3]

Recent literature on performance practice uses these categories to distinguish the rhythmic flexibility of different performers,[4] and two important conclusions emerge from this approach. First, certain types of rhythmic flexibility have gone in and out of fashion at different stages of performance history. A striking example of this is the decline in the use of the non-synchronised type of rubato in our own century, at least in the 'classical' instrumental repertoire.[5] Secondly, amongst performers of the same generation, but perhaps from different performing traditions, there are conflicting opinions concerning the appropriateness of one or other type of rubato. As Niecks observed: 'Above all . . . we have to keep in mind that the *tempo rubato* is a genus which comprehends numerous species. In short, the *tempo rubato* of Chopin is not that of Liszt, that of Liszt is not that of Henselt, and so on.'[6]

In the light of these two conclusions, it is important to evaluate the various accounts of Chopin's rubato in the context of the performing traditions in which he was schooled, the different styles of playing current in his mature years and performance trends during the lifetimes of his commentators.

Rhythmic flexibility in eighteenth-century performance styles

Rhythmic flexibility of various kinds was intrinsic to eighteenth-century performance. C. P. E. Bach's *Versuch*, for example, mentions a number of instances where the performer should not play in strict time:

Figure 178 [see Example 11.1] contains several examples in which certain notes and rests should be extended beyond their written length, for affective reasons. In places, I have written out these broadened values; elsewhere they are indicated by a small cross. Example *a* shows how a retard may be applied opportunely to a melody with two different accompaniments. In general the retard fits slow or more moderate tempos better than very fast ones. There are more examples in the opening allegro and the following adagio of the B minor Sonata, No. 6, of my second engraved work [the Württemberg Sonatas]; especially in the adagio, where a melody in octaves is transposed three times against rapid notes in the left hand. Each transposition can be effectively performed by gradually and gently accelerating and immediately thereafter retarding. In affettuoso

---

[3]   Pier Francesco Tosi, *Opinioni de' cantori antichi e moderni* (Bologna 1723), trans., with additions, by John Ernest Galliard as *Observations on the Florid Song* (London 1742; ed. Michael Pilkington, London 1987), pp. 70–1 (1987 edn).

[4]   See, for example, Sandra P. Rosenblum, *Performance Practices in Classic Piano Music* (Bloomington 1988), chapter 10, and Robert Philip, *Early Recordings and Musical Style* (Cambridge 1992), part 1. Jean-Jacques Eigeldinger adopts these categories in his discussion of Chopin's rubato in *Chopin: Pianist and Teacher as Seen by His Pupils* (hereafter *CPT*), trans. Naomi Shohet with Krysia Osostowicz and Roy Howat, ed. Roy Howat (Cambridge 1986), p. 120.

[5]   See Philip, *Early Recordings*, part 1, chapter 2. Non-synchronised rubato remains common in jazz and 'popular' styles.

[6]   Frederick Niecks, *Frederick Chopin as a Man and Musician*, 3rd edn, 2 vols. (London 1902), vol. II, p. 101.

Figure 178

Example 11.1   Figure 178 from C. P. E. Bach's *Versuch* (Eng. trans., p. 162)

playing, the performer must avoid frequent and excessive retards, which tend to make the tempo drag. The affect itself readily leads to this fault. Hence every effort must be made despite the beauty of detail to keep the tempo at the end of a piece exactly the same as at the beginning, an extremely difficult assignment . . . Passages in a piece in the major mode which are repeated in the minor may be broadened somewhat on their repetition in order to heighten the affect. On entering a fermata expressive of languidness, tenderness, or sadness, it is customary to broaden slightly. This brings us to the tempo rubato. Its indication is simply the presence of more or fewer notes than are contained in the normal division of the bar. A whole bar, part of one, or several bars may be, so to speak, distorted in this manner.[7]

Bach's words are echoed in a number of sources, notably Türk's *Klavierschule* of 1789,[8] which belongs to a similar performing tradition (Türk was associated in various ways with the Bach family). Other eighteenth-century authors are more guarded, however. Leopold Mozart, for example, takes pains to stress a strictly rhythmic manner of performance,[9] and his son, Wolfgang, seems to have followed suit, allowing for a non-synchronised type of rubato but otherwise stressing the need for strict time in performance. A letter dated 24 October 1777, written in Augsburg,

7   Carl Philipp Emanuel Bach, *Versuch über die wahre Art das Clavier zu spielen*, 2 vols. (Berlin 1753, 1762), trans. William J. Mitchell as *Essay on the True Art of Playing Keyboard Instruments* (New York 1949), pp. 160–1.
8   Daniel Gottlob Türk, *Klavierschule* (Leipzig and Halle 1789; 2nd edn, 1802), trans. Raymond H. Haggh as *School of Clavier Playing* (Lincoln, Nebraska and London 1982), esp. chapter 6, part 5.
9   Leopold Mozart, *Versuch einer gründlichen Violinschule* (Augsburg 1756, with several subsequent editions), trans. Editha Knocker as *A Treatise on the Fundamental Principles of Violin Playing* (London 1951), pp. 223–4.

describes Wolfgang's encounter with the daughter of the piano maker Stein and the pianist Beecke, both of whom were regarded as accomplished performers. Wolfgang's cutting remarks about their playing may reflect certain technical deficiencies, but perhaps they also reveal his feelings about a school of playing with which he had little sympathy:

She rolls her eyes and smirks. When a passage is repeated, she plays it more slowly the second time. If it has to be played a third time, then she plays it even more slowly . . . Further, she will never acquire the most essential, the most difficult and the chief requisite in music, which is, time, because from her earliest years she has done her utmost not to play in time. Herr Stein and I discussed this point for two hours at least and I have almost converted him, for he now asks my advice on everything. He used to be quite crazy about Beecke; but now he sees and hears that I am the better player, that I do not make grimaces, and yet *play with such expression* that, as he himself confesses, no one up to the present has been able to get such good results out of his pianofortes. Everyone is amazed that *I can always keep strict time*. What these people cannot grasp is that in tempo rubato in an Adagio, the left hand should go on playing in strict time. With them the left hand always follows suit.[10]

The non-synchronised rubato that Mozart described was referred to in a number of eighteenth-century treatises, many of them (such as Leopold Mozart's) discussing the performance of soloists accompanied by an orchestra. The precise extent of its use by solo keyboard players is uncertain, however. Some performers evidently did employ this style, such as the Countess von Hatzfeld ('one often hears her tempo rubato, which is not at all unsteady in its time'[11]). But the rhythmic independence of the two hands in this manner is considerably more demanding on the performer than the rhythmic independence of a soloist and orchestra, suggesting that its use may have been unusual in solo keyboard performance, and perhaps explaining why the audience was apparently so 'amazed' at Mozart's performance.

Non-synchronised rubato after 1800

There are some indications that the non-synchronised style of rubato practised by the Mozarts and others was declining in popularity by the beginning of the nineteenth century, possibly in favour of other types of rubato. In 1808 Koch described

that manner of performance of this or that cantabile passage of a solo part, in which the player intentionally digressed from the assumed movement of the tempo and from the usual distribution of note values, and executed the melodic line as if without any fixed division of time, while the accompaniment played on absolutely strictly in tempo. Among others, Franz Benda often made use of this manner of performance as a special means of expression in the Adagio movements of his concertos and sonatas. Although there are . . . virtuosos who . . . occasionally make use of a similar manner of performance . . . still there is usually only a far less noticeable deviation from the tempo than previously, so that one can maintain that kind of execution . . .

---

[10]   *The Letters of Mozart and his Family*, ed. Emily Anderson, 3rd edn (London 1985), pp. 339–40, my emphases.

[11]   Carl Friedrich Cramer, *Magazin der Musik* (Hamburg 1783), pp. 387–8, trans. Rosenblum, *Performance Practices*, p. 380.

to be obsolete nowadays. The neglect . . . may well be far more advantageous than detrimental for the art . . . in part because modern composers work out fully the melody of the Adagio movements of their concertos . . .[12]

With the growth in the music publishing industry, there was indeed a tendency for composers to write out ornamented melodic lines in full, yet Koch may be drawing exaggerated conclusions from music notation when he suggests that non-synchronised rubato was a dying art: several sources indicate that the tradition continued into the nineteenth century, albeit among a limited number of performers. At about the same time that Koch was writing, Dussek, one of the most influential pianists in Paris, evidently used a non-synchronised style of rubato:

Dussek greatly liked Rubato, although he never wrote the word in his music; Dussek had tried to render it visibly by means of syncopations; but if one were to render these syncopations exactly, one would be far from playing in his sweet and delightful manner. He did away with them, and contented himself with writing espressivo. Lucky those who heard him play his music like that! Even more lucky those who could imitate it![13]

Some of Dussek's pupils in Paris cultivated this tradition. One of them, Hélène Montgeroult, wrote a three-volume piano treatise in 1822 which includes studies for various aspects of piano technique. One of these has a simple right-hand melody without complex sub-divisions of the beat, accompanied by the left hand. Part of the preface to the piece reads:

The left hand should be completely independent of the right. There are moments when the expression demands that the top part lengthen the value of certain notes a little; the accompaniment should never have to be altered. The anticipation or slackening within the bar often serves the expression; but it only produces a disagreeable ensemble problem if one hand fails to maintain a constant poise. This anticipation is what is known in Italy as TEMPO ROBATO.[14]

Just over a decade later, a similar technique was described in Baillot's violin treatise.[15] It was also mentioned outside Paris in, for example, Hummel's pianoforte tutor, which appeared simultaneously in Vienna, Paris and London in 1828. Unlike Montgeroult's example, however, in which the right-hand part has relatively long note values, and where the effect of non-synchronisation will therefore be pronounced, Hummel's examples contain embellishments using faster note values with complex subdivisions of the bar or the beat (groups of fifteen, seventeen, nineteen, etc.) above a simple left-hand accompaniment in triplets. The rubato, in other words, will be less immediately obvious to the listener. Nevertheless, the general principles of independence of the hands and strict time in the accompanying part are spelled out:

Observations. In such passages it must be remarked:
1. that each hand must act independently

12 Heinrich Christoph Koch, 'Über den technischen Ausdruck: Tempo rubato', *Allgemeine musikalische Zeitung*, 10/33 (1808), cols. 518–19, trans. Rosenblum, *Performance Practices*, p. 376.
13 *Le Pianiste*, 1/5 (1834), p. 78, my translation.
14 Hélène Montgeroult, *Cours complet pour l'enseignement du fortepiano*, 2 vols. (Paris ca 1825), vol. II, p. 92, my translation.
15 Pierre Baillot, *L'art du violon* (Paris 1834), pp. 136–7.

2. that the left hand must keep the time strictly; for it is here the firm basis, on which are founded the notes of embellishment, grouped in various numbers, and without any regular distribution as to measure.[16]

The non-synchronised rubato described by Hummel, which depends on fast note values irregularly grouped, appears to have been more widely practised than the type that occurs in Montgeroult's tutor, judging by the number of composers who notated textures similar to Hummel's, in contrast to the relatively rare indications of the more extreme form.

It is interesting to compare Czerny's comments with Hummel's. Czerny discusses passages like those in Hummel's tutor (with florid but irregularly grouped right-hand parts), and implies that there will be a degree of non-synchronisation within the main beats of the bar. But he also discusses instances where the left-hand accompaniment should follow the right-hand part in accelerating or slowing down, so that the two parts coincide on the important beats.[17] In so doing, he was arguing for a style of playing which was fundamentally different from Mozart's or Dussek's, but which was almost certainly more representative of the pianism of his time.

The non-synchronised form of rubato was often described as an extremely difficult technique which was highly challenging to the solo performer. In its most extreme form it was practised by a very select group of pianists, but it lived on through the nineteenth century into the twentieth in the playing of pianists such as Paderewski, Pachmann and Rosenthal.[18] Only relatively recently has it seemed to fall into disfavour.

The development of rhythmic flexibility in the nineteenth century

Whilst non-synchronised rubato continued to be popular with at least a few pianists from the late eighteenth century onwards, significant changes in performers' approaches to rhythm in general were occurring around 1800, especially, but not exclusively, in France.

Paris at the beginning of the nineteenth century was becoming an important centre of pianistic activity. Developments in performance and in the writing of keyboard textures happened there which were only later adopted by pianists elsewhere in Europe.[19] One of the new trends in performance was an 'expressive' mode of performance in which a strict beat was not adhered to. Louis Adam, an important but somewhat conservative figure during these years, spoke out against these developments in his highly influential tutor of 1804:

[16] Johann Nepomuk Hummel, *Ausführliche theoretisch-practische Anweisung zum Piano-forte Spiel* (Vienna 1828), trans. as *A Complete Theoretical and Practical Course of Instructions on the Art of Playing the Pianoforte* (London 1828), part 3, p. 53.

[17] Carl Czerny, *Vollständige theoretisch-praktische Pianoforteschule Op. 500* (Vienna 1838–9), trans. James Alexander Hamilton as *Complete Theoretical and Practical Pianoforte School* (London 1838–9), part 3, pp. 31–50.

[18] Philip, *Early Recordings*, part 1, p. 47.

[19] See, for example, David Rowland, 'The Nocturne: Development of a New Style', in *The Cambridge Companion to Chopin*, ed. Jim Samson (Cambridge 1992), pp. 32–49.

Some people have tried to start a trend of playing out of time, playing all genres of music like a fantasy, prelude or capriccio. It is thought to enhance the expression of a piece, while serving in effect to distort it beyond recognition. Naturally, expressivity requires certain notes of the melody to be slowed or quickened; however, these fluctuations must not be used continually throughout the piece, but only in places where the expression of a languorous melody or the passion of an agitated one demands a slower or a more animated pace. In this case it is the melody that should be altered, while the bass should strictly maintain the beat.[20]

The trend that Adam described was not altogether confined to Paris: hints of a similar approach can be found, for example, in Beethoven's playing at about the same time. Ferdinand Ries recalled that around 1800 Beethoven 'in general . . . played his own compositions most capriciously, though he usually kept a very steady rhythm and only occasionally, indeed, very rarely, speeded up the tempo somewhat. At times he restrained the tempo in his crescendo with a ritardando, which had a beautiful and most striking effect.'[21] Newman argues that the tendency to vary the tempo increased in Beethoven's later style.[22] Weber also seems to have espoused a flexible approach to tempo: 'the beat, the tempo, must not be a controlling tyrant nor a mechanical, driving hammer; it should be to a piece of music what the pulse beat is to the life of a man'.[23]

Amongst pianists of the Viennese school, however, there were many who remained conservative in their approach to tempo flexibility. Chief among these was Hummel, who had much to say on the subject:

In the present day, many performers endeavour to supply the absence of natural inward feeling by an appearance of it; for example,
1. by distortions of the body and unnatural elevations of the arms;
2. by a perpetual gingle [*sic*], produced by the constant use of the Pedals:
3. by the capricious dragging or slackening of the time, (*tempo rubato*), introduced at every instant and to satiety . . .[24]

Nevertheless, even Hummel advocated some flexibility, within certain limits:

The *Allegro* requires brilliancy, power, precision in the delivery, and sparkling elasticity in the fingers. Singing passages which occur in it . . . may be played with some little relaxation as to time, in order to give them the necessary effect; but we must not deviate too strikingly from the predominating movement, because, by so doing, the unity of the whole will suffer, and the piece degenerate into a mere rhapsody . . .

The player must not waver in the time in every bar; but whether in passages of melody or of mere execution, even from the first bar, he must catch firmly hold of, and preserve equably the precise time . . .[25]

20 Louis Adam, *Méthode de piano du Conservatoire* (Paris 1804), p. 160, translated in *CPT*, p. 119.
21 Franz Gerhard Wegeler and Ferdinand Ries, *Biographische Notizen über Ludwig van Beethoven* (Koblenz 1838), trans. Frederick Noonan as *Remembering Beethoven*, with foreword by Christopher Hogwood and introduction by Eva Badura-Skoda (London 1988), p. 94.
22 William S. Newman, *Beethoven on Beethoven* (London and New York 1988), chapter 4.
23 Carl Maria von Weber, 'Tempo-Bezeichnungen nach Mälzl's Metronom zur Oper Euryanthe', *Allgemeine musikalische Zeitung*, 50/8 (1848), col. 127, trans. Newman, *Beethoven*, p. 112.
24 Hummel, *Instructions*, part 3, p. 40.
25 Ibid., part 3, p. 41.

All relaxation of the time in single bars, and in short passages of melody, in pleasing and intermediate ideas, must take place almost imperceptibly . . .[26]

Czerny underlined Hummel's conservative performing style by remarking that 'Hummel himself performed his compositions in such strict time, that we might nearly always have let the metronome beat to his playing'.[27]

Meanwhile, Paris continued to become the centre of a more 'expressive' and liberal school, following the trend at the beginning of the century observed by Louis Adam. Kalkbrenner was one of the most influential performers and teachers in Paris during the 1820s and his keyboard tutor suggests that he was in sympathy with these developments. The text of his treatise mentions that 'all terminations of *cantabile* phrases should be retarded . . . when a frequent change of harmony occurs, or modulations succeed each other rapidly, the movement must be retarded',[28] and the musical examples that conclude the tutor contain several instances within each piece. Significantly, however, these musical examples contain no indications to accelerate the tempo – a notational feature which was to emerge, but never to the same extent as markings for slackening the speed.

Of all the virtuosos from the second quarter of the nineteenth century who established themselves in Paris while continuing to tour Europe, Liszt was the pianist most noted for his flexible approach to rhythm. In 1842, for example, he played to a large audience in St Petersburg which included Glinka, who proclaimed that 'Liszt sometimes played superlatively, like no one else in the world, but at other times intolerably, falsifying the expression, stretching the tempi, and adding to the works of others . . .'[29]

Flexibility of tempo formed an important part of Liszt's teaching, and hence shaped the performing styles of many pianists from the following generation. Hans von Bülow reported to his mother:

After frequently hearing Liszt, I have now made a special study of what was particularly defective in my playing, namely, a certain amateurish uncertainty, a certain angular want of freedom in conception, of which I must completely cure myself; in modern pieces especially I must cultivate more *abandon*, and, when I have conquered the technical difficulties of a piece, I must *let myself go* more, according to how I feel at the moment . . .[30]

Bülow made a similar point in correspondence to his father a few years later: 'My piano-playing has latterly made substantial progress; I have gained in elasticity and a certain virtuoso *chic*, which was formerly entirely wanting.'[31] Another pianist, William Mason, observed:

Evidently I had been playing ahead in a steady, uniform way. He [Liszt] sat down, and gave the same phrases with an accentuated, elastic movement, which let in a flood of light upon me.

[26] Ibid., part 3, p. 47.
[27] See note 42 below.
[28] Friedrich Kalkbrenner, *Méthode pour apprendre le pianoforte* (Paris 1830), trans. Sabilla Novello as *Method of Learning the Pianoforte* (London 1862), p. 12.
[29] Vladimir Stasov, *List, Shuman i Berlioz v Rossii* [*Liszt, Schumann and Berlioz in Russia*] (St Petersburg 1896), p. 11, trans. Adrian Williams, *Portrait of Liszt* (Oxford 1990), p. 187.
[30] Hans von Bülow, *The Early Correspondence*, trans. and ed. Constance Bache (London 1896), p. 35.
[31] Ibid., p. 116.

From that one experience I learned to bring out the same effect, where it was appropriate, in almost every piece that I played. It eradicated much that was mechanical, stilted, and unmusical in my playing, and developed an elasticity of touch which has lasted all my life . . .[32]

So concerned was Liszt to ensure flexibility of tempo in performance that he struggled to find a means of notating it. In 1870 he wrote:

With regard to the deceptive *Tempo rubato* I have settled the matter provisionally in a brief note (in the finale of Weber's A♭ major Sonata); other occurrences of the *rubato* may be left to the taste and momentary feeling of gifted players. Metronomical performance is certainly tiresome and nonsensical; time and rhythm must be adapted to and identified with the melody, the harmony, the accent and the poetry . . . But how [to] indicate all this? I shudder at the thought of it.[33]

Yet as early as the *Album d'un voyageur* (composed 1835–6), Liszt had invented symbols to indicate subtle, rhetorical pauses, slight slackenings of the tempo and (much less frequently) small increases in tempo. His influence can also be seen in the flexible approach to rhythm in, for example, Bülow's heavily marked edition of Beethoven's piano sonatas.

Not everyone adopted Liszt's style of playing. Mendelssohn is reported to have had 'the greatest dislike to any modification of the time that he had not specifically marked',[34] and he disparaged 'the Parisian tendency of overdoing passion and despair'.[35] Another German, Friedrich Wieck, was perhaps the most outspoken critic of the modern, fluid, approach to rhythm. In *Clavier und Gesang* he ridicules the latest pianistic fashions from Paris – namely, the virtuoso who lacks all good taste and restraint, who over-pedals and gesticulates wildly in performance. An essential part of this histrionic performance style as condemned by Wieck was flexibility of tempo. In a particularly sarcastic passage, he asks of one such virtuoso (the hypothetical Herr Forte), 'where did he learn to play?', to which he replies:

he didn't learn at all. He is a genius. It all comes naturally. Instruction would have chained his genius, and he would then play distinctly, correctly, naturally, and in time. That would be dilettantish. This unrhythmical and indisciplined hubbub is what is called 'inspired pianistic genius'.

(Herr Forte thunders through a sequence of exotic chords at top speed with sustaining pedal down and, without pausing, goes into the Mazurka in F♯ minor, accentuating heavily. He stretches one measure out by two quarters, robbing another measure of a quarter, and so he proceeds until, highly pleased with himself, he comes to the end . . .)[36]

Elsewhere, Wieck criticises another imaginary pianist who uses 'this affected and sweetly languishing manner, this *rubato* and distortion of musical phrases, this rhythmic license, this vacuous sentimentality'.[37]

32 William Mason, *Memories of a Musical Life* (New York 1901), pp. 99–100.
33 *Letters of Franz Liszt*, ed. La Mara, trans. Constance Bache, 2 vols. (London 1984), vol. II, p. 194.
34 Fuller-Maitland, 'Rubato', p. 188.
35 Felix Mendelssohn-Bartholdy, *Briefe aus den Jahren 1830 bis 1847*, ed. Paul Mendelssohn-Bartholdy, 9th edn (Leipzig 1882), vol. II, p. 41, translated in *CPT*, p. 267.
36 Friedrich Wieck, *Clavier und Gesang* (Leipzig 1853), trans. and ed. Henry Pleasants as *Piano and Song* (New York 1988), p. 140.
37 Ibid., p. 100.

Wieck was by no means the only critic of this growing rhythmic 'anarchy'. In 1856, three years after *Clavier und Gesang* appeared, Hanslick reviewed a performance by Wieck's daughter, Clara: 'As compared with *the common misuse of rubato*, she maintains, almost without exception, a strict conformity of measure.'[38]

It would be unfair, however, to portray Wieck and others as pianists who allowed no rhythmic flexibility whatsoever. Like Hummel, Wieck permitted it within strict limits, criticising yet another hypothetical pianist who was 'too pedantically concerned with technic and strict time'.[39] Elsewhere he recommends: 'This passage I would play a bit hesitantly, but without any conspicuous ritard, that passage a bit faster.'[40] In this respect, Wieck's teaching was similar to Czerny's, who detailed a number of circumstances where the tempo might be slackened,[41] but who nevertheless had harsh words for those whose performance he considered unruly:

we have almost entirely forgotten the strict keeping of time, as the *tempo rubato* (that is, the arbitrary retardation or quickening of the degree of movement) is now often employed even to caricature. For instance, how frequently are we constrained to hear, in modern days, even the first movement of HUMMEL'S Concertos (which should consist but of one time) played thus: the first few lines *Allegro*, the middle subject *Andante*, the ensuing passage *Presto*, and then again single passages needlessly protracted, – whilst HUMMEL himself performed his compositions in such strict time, that we might nearly always have let the metronome beat to his playing.[42]

Despite his cautious approach, however, Czerny could not quite bring himself to criticise Liszt: 'The very frequent application of each kind of *tempo rubato* is so well directed in LISZT'S playing, that, like an excellent declaimer, he always remains intelligible to every hearer.'[43] As Liszt's former teacher, Czerny was unlikely to fault his illustrious pupil; yet there is more in these remarks than mere deferential politeness. Czerny clearly indicates that Liszt's use of rubato was appropriate to the *rhetoric* of the music being played. Similar concerns had been voiced by earlier authors in both the eighteenth and nineteenth centuries, and they are summed up well in Georges Mathias's comments on rubato: 'its essence is fluctuation of movement, one of the two principal means of expression in music, namely the modification of tone and of tempo, as in the art of oration, whereby the speaker, moved by this or that emotion, raises or lowers his voice, and accelerates or draws out his diction'.[44] It was those pianists who could be accused of 'empty rhetoric' who were most harshly judged by the likes of Czerny and Wieck.

Chopin's rubato

The performing milieu in Paris that Chopin entered in 1831 was one in which rhythmic licence was increasingly cultivated. This trend inevitably spread throughout

---

[38] Eduard Hanslick, *Music Criticisms 1846–99*, trans. and ed. Henry Pleasants (Baltimore 1950), p. 50, my emphasis.

[39] Wieck, *Piano and Song*, p. 100.

[40] Ibid., p. 133.

[41] Czerny, *Pianoforte School*, part 3, pp. 33–4.

[42] Carl Czerny, *Supplement (oder vierter Theil) zum großen Pianoforte Schule* (Vienna ca 1845), trans. as *Supplement to Czerny's Royal Pianoforte School* (London ca 1845), p. 29.

[43] Ibid., p. 28.

[44] Georges Mathias, Preface to Isidore Philipp, *Exercices quotidiens tirés des œuvres de Chopin* (Paris [1897]), p. 5, translated in *CPT*, p. 49.

Europe, and by the middle of the century a performance style in which rhythm was treated with considerable flexibility was by far the most common style amongst pianists. Yet Chopin had grown up in a more conservative environment, and it is clear from numerous sources that certain rhythmic aspects of his playing remained distinct from those of his contemporaries. Moscheles observed, for example, that 'the *ad libitum* playing, which in the hands of other interpreters of his music degenerates into a constant uncertainty of rhythm, is with him an element of exquisite originality'.[45] But precisely which rhythmic features of his playing were different from those of his contemporaries, and to what extent? In order to answer these questions, we need to discuss the different sorts of rubato in Chopin's performance. Eigeldinger distinguishes three types:

The first type of rubato [equivalent to the non-synchronised rubato defined above] descended from the Italian Baroque tradition . . . [and] occurs principally in works with broad cantilenas. The second, more common type consists of fleeting changes of pace relative to the basic tempo; these agogic modifications may affect a whole section, period or phrase, slowing down or accelerating the flow depending on the direction of the music . . . [T]he third component of Chopinian rubato is derived from the mobile rhythm of the Mazur.[46]

We shall examine these three types, though in a different order, beginning with the general practice of slowing down or accelerating over a few bars in order to give a phrase a particular character or a moment of structural importance greater emphasis.

It appears that Chopin's playing was indeed flexible in this manner, though perhaps not so much as that of many contemporaries. In the music itself, Chopin specifies many instances of ritardando, accelerando and their equivalents – more so than in the works of some particularly conservative composers such as Mendelssohn. Mikuli recalled Chopin's flexible approach in a passage reminiscent of Czerny's comments quoted on p. 208 above, on the playing of Liszt ('an excellent declaimer . . . intelligible to every listener'[47]):

Chopin was far from being a partisan to metric rigour and frequently used rubato in his playing, accelerating or slowing down this or that theme. But Chopin's rubato possessed an unshakeable emotional logic. It always justified itself by a strengthening or weakening of the melodic line, by harmonic details, by the figurative structure. It was fluid, natural; it never degenerated into exaggeration or affectation.[48]

These remarks seem to contradict others by the same author, however. In the preface to his edition of Chopin's works, for example, Mikuli stated that: 'In keeping time Chopin was inflexible, and many will be surprised to learn that the metronome never left his piano.'[49] Here, however, Mikuli was endeavouring to correct what he saw as a disturbing trend. A 'false' tradition of Chopin playing had evidently grown out of

45 *Aus Moscheles' Leben*, ed. Charlotte Moscheles, 2 vols. (Leipzig 1872–3), trans. and adapted by Arthur Duke Coleridge as *Life of Moscheles*, 2 vols. (London 1873), vol. II, p. 52.
46 Eigeldinger, *CPT*, pp. 120 and 121.
47 See note 43 above.
48 Quoted in Aleksander Michałowski, 'Jak grał Fryderyk Szopen?', *Muzyka*, 9/7–9 (1932), pp. 74–5, translated in *CPT*, p. 50.
49 Carl Mikuli, *Vorwort* to his edition of Chopin's works (Leipzig 1880), trans. as *Introductory Note* in Schirmer's edition (London 1949), p. i.

the more 'progressive' style of the mid nineteenth century, characterised above all by a high degree of rhythmic licence:

According to a tradition – and, be it said, an erroneous one – Chopin's playing was like that of one dreaming rather than awake – scarcely audible in its continual *pianissimos* and *una cordas*, with feebly developed technique and quite lacking in confidence, or at least indistinct, and distorted out of all rhythmic form by an incessant *tempo rubato!*[50]

References to this tradition can be found in earlier sources, for example, Hanslick's review of Clara Schumann's performance in 1856:

Some may have been surprised by her metronomical playing of the middle movement of Chopin's Db [sic] Impromptu, sharply marked even in the bass. Nobody can object to it, but whether Chopin's music gains by the dispersal of its misty nostalgia is open to question.[51]

Exaggerated affectation in performance was clearly something which Chopin himself avoided, however: '[Chopin] required adherence to the strictest rhythm, hated all lingering and dragging, misplaced rubatos, as well as exaggerated *ritardandos*. "Je vous prie de vous asseoir" [Pray do take a seat] he said on such an occasion with gentle mockery.'[52] What exactly did 'the strictest rhythm' mean to Chopin? The answer appears to have varied according to the music's genre. In the mazurkas, the length of the bar was uniform, but within those confines, a considerable degree of distortion took place, as Chorley noted:

the delicacy of M. Chopin's tone and the elasticity of his passages are delicious to the ear. He makes a free use of *tempo rubato*; leaning about within his bars more than any player we recollect, but still subject to a presiding sentiment of measure, such as presently habituates the ear to the liberties taken. In music not his own we happen to know he can be as staid as a metronome; while his Mazurkas, etc. lose half their characteristic wildness if played without a certain freak and licence, – impossible to imitate, but irresistible if the player at all feels the music. This we have always fancied while reading M. Chopin's works; – we are now sure of it after *hearing* him perform them himself.[53]

Chorley states that Chopin's distortion of the rhythm in the mazurkas was more extreme than any other pianist's of the time, a claim which is reinforced in the writings of others. Lenz compared Chopin's playing to Henselt's: 'Henselt's priority when playing the Mazurkas is the beat and the barline . . . His rubato is not Chopin's: it is a shifting of accents within a maintained tempo, rather than a radical readjustment of the whole field of vision to view the piece in its entirety as if seen through reversed opera glasses.'[54] So extreme was this 'radical readjustment' that Hallé and Meyerbeer thought that Chopin was playing his mazurkas not in the 'correct' 3/4 but (respectively) in 4/4 and 2/4, much to Chopin's consternation.[55]

[50] Ibid., p. i.
[51] Hanslick, *Music Criticisms*, p. 50.
[52] Friederike Streicher's comments, related in Niecks, *Chopin*, vol. II, p. 341.
[53] Henry Chorley, *The Athenaeum*, no. 1079 (1 July 1848), p. 660.
[54] Wilhelm von Lenz, *Die großen Pianoforte-Virtuosen unserer Zeit* (Berlin 1872), p. 102, translated in *CPT*, p. 72.
[55] See *CPT*, pp. 72–3.

The mazurkas were a special case, however: Chopin was not normally so rhythmically pliant. In certain circumstances he was very strict in his adherence not only to the length of the bar, but also to the beat, which brings us to the third sort of tempo rubato – the rubato in which the accompanying part keeps strict time while the melodic line anticipates or drags behind the beat, causing non-synchronisation of the hands. Mikuli described this in the following terms: 'the hand responsible for the accompaniment would keep strict time, while the other hand, singing the melody, would free the essence of the musical thought from all rhythmic fetters, either by lingering hesitantly or by eagerly anticipating the movement with a certain impatient vehemence akin to passionate speech'.[56] This was the rhythmic characteristic of Chopin's playing that seems to have attracted most attention, presumably because of its rarity among other pianists of the time, or because in Chopin's hands it was used in an extreme form, or both.

We have already seen how some eighteenth-century pianists used non-synchronised rubato, and that there existed an unbroken tradition of this among pianists in the nineteenth century before Chopin. Non-synchronisation in passages with simple melodic lines (i.e. with relatively long note values) was a particularly specialised technique, and its use seems never to have become widespread. This was emphasised in earlier accounts, but was also noted in some of those associated with Chopin:

This way of playing is very difficult since it requires complete independence of the two hands; and those lacking this give both themselves and others the illusion of it by playing the melody in time and dislocating the accompaniment so that it falls beside the beat; or else – worst of all – content themselves with simply playing one hand after the other. It would be a hundred times better just to play in time, with both hands together.[57]

It was not just the difficulty of the technique that dissuaded pianists from using it, however. Even those who undoubtedly had sufficient technical ability to perform in this way chose not to, such as Liszt:

On this occasion [Liszt gave us] an important insight into the Lisztian rubato, consisting of subtle variations of tempo and expression within a free declamation, entirely different from Chopin's give-and-take system [*Eilen und Zögern*]. Liszt's rubato is more a sudden, light suspension of the rhythm on this or that significant note, so that the phrasing will above all be clearly and convincingly brought out. While playing, Liszt seemed barely preoccupied with keeping in time, and yet neither the aesthetic symmetry nor the rhythm was affected.[58]

The non-synchronised type of rubato in Chopin's playing is described as appropriate in textures with both a melodic line and an accompaniment. It follows, therefore, that it has limited application, a point made by Kleczyński, who adapted Liszt's metaphor for Chopin's rubato ('the wind plays in the leaves, stirs up life among them, the tree remains the same'[59]):

56 Mikuli, *Vorwort*, translated in *CPT*, p. 49.
57 Pauline Viardot's comments, related in Camille Saint-Saëns, 'Quelques mots sur l'exécution des œuvres de Chopin', *Le courrier musical*, 13/10 (1910), pp. 386–7, translated in *CPT*, p. 49.
58 Carl von Lachmund, *Mein Leben mit Franz Liszt* (Eschwege 1970), p. 62, translated in *CPT*, p. 122. This description is reminiscent of Czerny's remarks – see note 17.
59 Niecks, *Chopin*, vol. II, p. 101.

Some of Chopin's students have assured me that in the rubato the left hand ought to keep perfect time, whilst the right indulges its fancy; and that in such a case Chopin would say, 'The left hand is the conductor of the orchestra' . . . It is, nevertheless, my belief that this means can only be employed in certain particular cases . . . There are passages in the works of Chopin, in which not only do the leaves tremble (to continue the comparison of Liszt), but the trunk totters. For instance: the Polonaise in C♯ minor (Op. 26 No. 1), 3rd part, measures 9–14 [=58–63]; Nocturne in A♭ (Op. 32 No. 2), the middle part [bars 27–50]. We may quote also the Impromptu in A♭ [Op. 29]; here everything totters from foundation to summit, and everything is nevertheless so beautiful and clear![60]

The term 'rubato' was specified by Chopin in only a limited number of passages, all of which are detailed by Eigeldinger.[61] These markings occur in works first published in the years 1832–6 with the exception of the G♯ minor Polonaise and the Mazurka Op. 67 No. 3, both of which appeared posthumously. After 1836 Chopin abandoned the term, evidently because it was not understood by his contemporaries, as Liszt noted: 'as the term taught nothing to whoever already knew, and said nothing to those who did not know, understand, and feel, Chopin later ceased to add this explanation to his music'.[62] Perhaps we should not be surprised, therefore, that recent commentators have found it difficult to agree on its meaning.[63] Despite the difficulties in interpreting Chopin's use of the term, however, a number of important points can be made, and questions asked, even if the answers are more tentative than we might wish.

Eigeldinger argues that in the Nocturne Op. 15 No. 3 and the Mazurkas Op. 24 No. 1 and Op. 67 No. 3, where the term 'rubato' occurs in the first bar, an 'agogic' rubato is intended, which is characterised by 'fleeting changes of pace relative to the basic tempo'. In the case of the Nocturne Op. 9 No. 2, the Trio Op. 8, the Rondo Op. 16 and the Concerto Op. 21, however, he argues for the non-synchronised type of rubato described first by Tosi, and used by pianists such as Mozart and Dussek.[64] In addition, Eigeldinger notes that out of all the works in which the term occurs, 'a good three-quarters . . . are genres connected with Polish folk music', in almost all cases the mazurka. In such instances, the kind of rubato which maintains a regular bar-length, but in which certain beats of the bar are 'stretched', seems appropriate. Eigeldinger also admits the likelihood of some overlap between the various types of rubato.

Most of Eigeldinger's observations are well made. On occasion, however, the evidence seems a little strained. This is particularly so in the case of the Nocturne Op. 15 No. 3 and the Mazurkas Op. 24 No. 1 and Op. 67 No. 3, where Eigeldinger argues for 'fleeting changes of pace'. Chopin was in the habit at the time of indicating minor tempo fluctuations in his music by other means such as the terms 'stretto', 'ritenuto', 'più mosso', etc. Indeed, terms like these occur in the nocturne and mazurkas in question. Why should Chopin wish to duplicate his instructions by including 'rubato' in bar 1, and why should he use the term in this manner in just *three* works when it is clear from performance indications in other pieces, as well as from

[60] Jean [Jan] Kleczyński, *How to Play Chopin*, trans. Alfred Whittingham, 6th edn (London [1913]), p. 57.
[61] *CPT*, p. 121.
[62] Franz Liszt, *F. Chopin*, 6th edn (Leipzig 1923), p. 115, translated in *CPT*, p. 51.
[63] Some of the arguments are outlined by Eigeldinger in *CPT*, p. 121.
[64] Ibid., p. 121. See also notes 3 and 14 above.

contemporary accounts of his playing, that he frequently required a flexible approach to tempo in common with almost all pianists of his day? Other factors suggest that the term rubato may mean something else in these three works. In particular, in all the passages in which Chopin specified rubato, including the three mentioned above, the configuration of parts could be described as 'treble melody with accompaniment lower in the texture'. (In all cases, the melody is in single notes, with the exception of the Rondo Op. 16, where it is doubled, predominantly in sixths.) Moreover, in all these instances, the melody comprises simple note values: Chopin never applies the term rubato to passages of decorated melody which use irregular groups of faster notes. In each case, therefore, at least an element of non-synchronised rubato is almost certainly intended. Eigeldinger is nevertheless correct to draw attention to the high instance of the term in genres connected with Polish folk music. Where this is so, it seems likely that the non-synchronised style of rubato should be combined with that which keeps the bar-length regular, but stretches certain beats – a possibility suggested by Eigeldinger.

Another important point is raised by Eigeldinger's categorisation of the instances of the term rubato in Chopin's music: by far the most common use of the term is at the repetition of a phrase or half-phrase. This suggests that Chopin thought of rubato as an aspect of ornamentation, according to the principle whereby the repetition of a melodic phrase is amended in some way. By implication, earlier renderings of the phrase should be played 'straight', without any such rhythmic distortion.

Finally, do the markings for rubato in the years 1832–6 represent the sum total of occasions in music from this period on which one or other of the rhythmic effects described above should be used? This is, of course, impossible to ascertain. Yet the extent to which Chopin's commentators remarked on the use of rubato in his playing suggests that it might have been a more widespread feature of his performance than the markings alone imply. Perhaps these early indications relate to passages where a particularly extreme form of rubato was intended.

Conclusion

Chopin belonged to an era in which excesses of all sorts were becoming fashionable in performance, especially in Paris. To a certain extent, he followed this trend, keeping abreast of the latest developments. As far as rhythm is concerned, it seems that he was content to modify the tempo in the middle of a performance for expressive effect, and in common with most of his contemporaries he notated some of these changes in his music. Many of his Parisian contemporaries went much further than he did, however: it is clear from the literature that many pianists developed a style which lingered over certain notes and upset the regular length of the bar. This tendency persisted into the later nineteenth century and beyond, and at its most extreme, in the hands of lesser pianists, it degenerated into performances which to some observers seemed rhythmically chaotic. It was against this trend that Chopin's playing stood out. In particular, his ability to create an impression of rhythmic flexibility within the framework of a strict bar-length or beat was a rare quality which prevented his critics from labelling him rigid or austere, and guaranteed his unique place in the history of performance.

12   Authentic Chopin: history, analysis and intuition in performance

JOHN RINK

Finding one's 'voice' as a performer is becoming increasingly difficult in this age of historically and analytically informed interpretation. The stringent demands now imposed on musicians by scholars, critics and listeners threaten the pursuit of individual artistic convictions to an unprecedented extent: on the one hand, historical performance specialists tell us to play the music as the composer intended, to strive for stylistically 'accurate' performances, while theorists and analysts insist that systematic dissection of the score must lie behind our interpretations, that we 'can never plumb the aesthetic depth of a great work without an intense scrutiny of its parametric elements'.[1] These new requirements, along with the circumscribed tastes and exaggerated expectations of a listening public accustomed to 'flawless' recordings, greatly inhibit interpretative freedom and undermine the performer's confidence that a given interpretation does justice to him- or herself as well as to the music.

Yet it is this very sense of conviction in one's interpretation, not the achievement of historical accuracy, analytical rigour or technical expertise in and of itself, that ultimately matters to the artistically minded performer and that underlies truly 'authentic' performance. The latter results not only from the thorough musical understanding obtained when one knows a work as one knows a close friend or relation (prolonged contact yielding an almost intuitive 'feel' for the other's character), but also from the ability to project the piece as a coherent dramatic statement, in which all its elements, however mutually contradictory, are somehow linked to a central 'spine', a 'single, uni-fied interpretative vision'[2] joining parts within the whole. When such a vision is lacking, the interpretation will itself lack cogency and commitment: effective perfor-mance cannot be achieved unless the interpreter, in Erwin Stein's words, has 'a whole

---

[1]   Eugene Narmour, 'On the Relationship of Analytical Theory to Performance and Interpretation', in
    Explorations in Music, the Arts, and Ideas, ed. E. Narmour and R. A. Solie (Stuyvesant 1988), p. 340. See
    John Rink, review of Wallace Berry, *Musical Structure and Performance*, in *Music Analysis*, 9/3 (1990),
    pp. 319–39 for discussion of the literature on analysis and performance. The historical performance
    and 'authenticity' movements are outlined in *Authenticity and Early Music*, ed. Nicholas Kenyon (Oxford
    1988).
[2]   Christopher Wintle's phrase, applied to Webern ('Analysis and Performance: Webern's Concerto Op.
    24/II', *Music Analysis*, 1/1 (1982), p. 75). The reference to a work's 'spine' derives from Stanislavsky.

214

piece of music in a nutshell' in his or her mind.[3] It is how that vision can be gained in performing Chopin's music that concerns me here: how, despite the many constraints currently placed on the performer, convincing interpretation – 'authentic' performance – might be achieved.

In claiming 'authentic' interpretation as my goal, I do not of course mean that so-called 'authenticity' born simply of a chimerical desire to recreate an original performing style, which has been the aim of much self-styled 'historical performance', but rather a far less restrictive – indeed, liberating – authenticity determined largely by self-knowledge and conviction, by the artistic imperative to express oneself. In Richard Taruskin's words, this amounts to 'knowing what you mean and whence comes that knowledge', and 'having . . . a "sentiment of being" that is independent of the values, opinions and demands of others'.[4] An 'authentic' performance in this sense will certainly take historical evidence into account when appropriate (it would be foolish to ignore the full fruits of musicological research, as certain aspects of the music's 'meaning' can perhaps be understood only in terms of the composer's original intentions); it will be analytically defensible (there should be at least some audible relation between the music's structure, however that may be manifested, and the structure of the performance); and it will display technical control, but it will also reflect, and ultimately be shaped by, the performer's individual artistic perspective, which determines the very *musical statement* to be articulated by the interpreter, in an inspired act transcending the sterility of the merely 'correct'. This definition of 'authenticity' is the one to which the title of my essay refers and which is the basis of the following study.

It is relevant to note the comments of Chopin's pupil Georges Mathias on his teacher's playing: 'Chopin, performer of genius, interpreted Mozart, Beethoven *with the feeling of Chopin*, and it was extremely beautiful, it was sublime. He was not of the category of critical or historic performers, which is not to say that the latter are unworthy: for not everybody can possess genius.'[5] Even when playing the works of other masters, Chopin could remain true to his own stylistic principles yet still achieve a supremely *musical* result: Chopin, 'performer of genius', thus practised the 'authentic' interpretation I have been describing. His performance aesthetic was based on obtaining 'the most beautiful quality of sound', on nuance, *l'art du toucher*, suppleness, simplicity and colouristic variety.[6] With the aid of innovative fingering and intensive listening, Chopin produced a legato *cantabile*, an 'inimitable sense of line and phrasing'[7] which rivalled that of the *bel canto* singers he so admired, whose style he translated into a unique keyboard idiom. This placed particular emphasis on principles

---

3 *Form and Performance* (London 1962), p. 71. For further discussion of the knowledge structures used in performance, see Eric Clarke, 'Generative Principles in Music Performance', in *Generative Processes in Music*, ed. John A. Sloboda (Oxford 1988), pp. 1–26.

4 Richard Taruskin, 'The Limits of Authenticity: A Discussion', *Early Music*, 12 (1984), p. 3.

5 Quoted in Jean-Jacques Eigeldinger, *Chopin: Pianist and Teacher as Seen by His Pupils* (hereafter *CPT*), trans. Naomi Shohet with Krysia Osostowicz and Roy Howat, ed. Roy Howat (Cambridge 1986), p. 277 (my emphasis). This book is one of the central reference sources for my study and an indispensable aid to the Chopin performer in general.

6 These features are discussed in *CPT* and in Eigeldinger's edition of Chopin's *Esquisses pour une Méthode de Piano* (Paris 1993).

7 *CPT*, p. 15.

of declamation, with the aim of moving and convincing the listener 'by means of intonation and accentuation appropriate to the meaning of the text'.[8] According to Mikuli, 'under his fingers each musical phrase sounded like song, and with such clarity that each note took the meaning of a syllable, each bar that of a word, each phrase that of a thought'.[9] In essence, Chopin, 'the only musical genius of the nineteenth century whose pianism does not emulate the orchestra of his era, . . . lies at the heart of a *tradition of vocal inspiration*, with its prime emphasis on refinement of touch'.[10]

Defending Chopin's interpretative legacy within late-nineteenth-century performance traditions was the passionate aim of one of his students, Princess Marcelina Czartoryska, who was widely considered the most faithful heir to Chopin's performance style, particularly with regard to phrasing and accentuation.[11] An 1892 article[12] by Czartoryska's pupil Cecylia Działyńska, based on the Princess's sentiments and derived in part from one of her letters, was published at a time when Chopin's historical position, although secured through the publication of monographs and collected critical editions as well as the music's place in the concert repertoire, was under threat from what Czartoryska and others perceived as a 'pseudo-tradition' developing in Chopin performance, characterised by unwarranted agogic distortions ('rubato') and other stylistic solecisms affecting dynamics, pedalling, tempo and even the notes themselves, all perpetrated in Chopin's name but unfaithful to his original intentions.[13] As Eigeldinger comments, Czartoryska's testament to how Chopin *should* be played 'amounts to a confession of faith: on the basis of an accomplished pianistic technique, love of Chopin's music and scrupulous fidelity to the score, one can attain a sort of second sight, an exact comprehension – an "intuition" – of Chopin's intentions, able to challenge any claims of tradition'.[14] For Czartoryska, intuition based on thorough assimilation of the music allowed the pianist (in her words) to 'breathe the air of Chopin' – to resurrect the music in the true Chopin manner.

Although reliance on intuition in and of itself is often an extremely dubious if not downright risky interpretative strategy,[15] the situation is altogether different when

---

8   Ibid., p. 14.

9   Quoted in *CPT*, p. 42.

10   *CPT*, p. 21; my emphasis.

11   See the comments of Albert Sowiński, quoted in ibid., p. 163.

12   Originally published in the *Kurier Poznański* (No. 270 (November 1892), pp. 2–3) and entitled 'Jak grać Chopina [How to Play Chopin]', this is reprinted in Adam Czartkowski and Zofia Jeżewska, *Chopin żywy* (Warsaw 1958), pp. 471–8, and is translated into French in Eigeldinger, *Esquisses*, pp. 124–32. I am grateful to Professor Eigeldinger for drawing this article to my attention and for providing a copy of the Polish original.

13   Gradual erosion of the 'true' Chopin performance tradition prompted Wilhelm von Lenz to write: 'Chopin's compositions . . . run the risk of being misunderstood if one has not known the master's way of playing, his intentions and his conception of the instrument – since their result on paper is quite different from that of the sound world in which they really live.' Quoted in *CPT*, p. 65.

14   Eigeldinger, *Esquisses*, p. 110, my translation. Compare Lenz's comments (quoted in Anne Swartz's chapter in this volume, p. 47 above) that 'one can sense [how to play] Chopin, one cannot learn it'.

15   Henry Shaffer outlines some of the problems associated with 'intuitive' performance in his chapter in the present volume. Compare Wallace Berry, *Musical Structure and Performance* (New Haven 1989), passim, and my review thereof (especially p. 324), where, in contrast, I define the term 'informed intuition' to denote that 'intuitive' response to music which 'accrues with a broad range of experience and which may exploit theoretical and analytical knowledge at the "submerged level of consciousness" referred to by Berry [p. xi]'.

one's 'intuition' has resulted from an utter familiarity with the composer's style and performance aesthetic, as well as prolonged immersion in the music itself. The 'second sight' obtained from such an intimate understanding of the music and its stylistic context is in fact an essential goal for the performer. Without it, the 'unified interpretative vision' necessary for convincing performance remains elusive: the performer will almost inevitably 'distort' the work, yielding to concerns of relative insignificance while playing, without regard – without a 'feel' – for the demands of the whole, or possibly offering a historically 'accurate' or analytically rigorous interpretation which at heart is musically impoverished.

The stylistic basis of this 'second sight' will be investigated in the following case studies. These derive from my own experiences in performing the music, in private and in public. The issues broached here were explicitly considered *after* the performances had occurred, and thus the three studies retrospectively examine the very 'intuitions' that guided my interpretations: in short, they show how historical evidence and analytical insight *as part of one's general stylistic awareness* can influence the decision-making process guiding an interpretation without exerting ultimate authority over it, instead indirectly helping to shape the mental representation, or 'aural image', that one constructs of the piece to be played. I shall demonstrate how the performer determines what lies behind the notes in one of Chopin's large-scale works (C♯ minor Scherzo Op. 39), in a 'small form' (D major Prelude Op. 28 No. 5) and in a passage from the Concerto Op. 21, the score in each case serving as an incomplete version of the music it attempts to represent.[16]

Expressive form in the C♯ minor Scherzo Op. 39

Contemporary accounts reveal Chopin's insistence that his students 'analyse' the music they were learning to play. It is worth speculating about the nature of that 'analysis'. Mikuli records Chopin's view that 'any work selected for study should be carefully analysed for its formal structure, as well as for the feelings and psychological processes which it evokes', while the anonymous Scottish lady who had lessons with Chopin in the late 1840s observes:

> he called my attention to its structure [that of Beethoven's Sonata Op. 26], to the intentions of the composer throughout; showing me the great variety of touch and treatment demanded . . . He would sit patiently while I tried to thread my way through mazes of intricate and unaccustomed modulations [in his own music], which I could never have understood had he not invariably played to me each composition . . . letting me hear the framework . . . around which these beautiful and strange harmonies were grouped.[17]

At least as important to Chopin as 'technical' dissection of the music was description of its expressive content: for this (Eigeldinger comments) he 'readily resorted to

16   See Roy Howat, 'What Do We Perform?', in *The Practice of Performance: Studies in Musical Interpretation*, ed. John Rink (Cambridge, forthcoming) for discussion of this point.
17   Quoted in *CPT*, p. 59. Lenz's description of the E♭ Nocturne Op. 9 No. 2, quoted in *CPT*, p. 77, also demonstrates this sort of analysis.

images or analogies to evoke the mood of a piece and to arouse the right musical impulse in the pupil'; a 'single, concise image' often sufficed, 'so intensively was he imbued with the reality of his vision even as he translated it into words'.[18] In Weber's A♭ Sonata, for instance, Chopin heard 'an angel . . . passing over the sky',[19] whereas the *sotto voce* opening of his Scherzo Op. 31 'must be a question . . . It must be a house of the dead.'[20]

The latter statement could also be applied to parts of the C♯ minor Scherzo Op. 39, composed in 1839. This astonishingly powerful work reveals the composer at his most masterful, uniting form and content, structure and expression, syntactic and semantic process. Like his other scherzos, Op. 39 draws upon but transcends the symmetrical ternary plan (scherzo–trio–scherzo) characteristic of the classical archetype, as well as the principle of contrast (both large- and small-scale, formal and figurative) at work in Beethoven's scherzos.[21] From the performer's perspective, the piece hinges on an eventual opening-out of the symmetrical formal model, whereupon Chopin invests the music with a momentum-generating impulse leading to almost overwhelming climax. Herein lies the essence of the work's 'expressive form' – its 'plot archetype' – to be defined in detail in the following discussion.

Example 12.1 depicts the Scherzo's essential components: tonal structure (initially 'static', or symmetrical, later to become 'dynamic',[22] or hierarchical), operative formal paradigm (ternary/closed, then goal-directed/open), principal sections and subsections, and expressive function thereof. Chopin subverts the listener's expectations (created in part by the genre title) of a succession of closed, self-contained scherzo and trio sections. Within the scherzo (itself ternary in design), a' is an abbreviated variant of a, its final bars functioning as a brief reorientation towards the trio. The latter is also asymmetrical, as the concluding cadential gesture from c (bars 187^2–99 and 231^2–42) is omitted from c', the trio suddenly abandoned as the music heads

---

18   CPT, pp. 12 and 13.

19   Georges Mathias, quoted in CPT, p. 12.

20   Lenz, quoted in CPT, p. 85. According to Lenz (see CPT, p. 85), Chopin considered the opening bar 'the key to the whole piece'. In a similar vein, Adolf Gutmann recorded Chopin's view that the middle section of the F♯ minor Nocturne Op. 48 No. 2 'should be played as a recitative. "A tyrant commands" (the first two chords), he said, "and the other asks for mercy".' Quoted in CPT, p. 81.

The use of extramusical imagery can be of enormous evocative value to the performer, and I shall not avoid it in this study, even though my subjective language will offend some analysts; nor shall I refrain, in the interests of 'authenticist' criticism, from using technical vocabulary or diagrams as necessary, for although these would not have been available to Chopin, they might well express, albeit differently, what he would have said about his music. (Delacroix's April 1849 conversation with Chopin indicates the composer's sensitivity to 'technical' matters (see note 64 below), as does the anonymous Scottish lady's account, quoted above.)

21   The scherzo genre is discussed in Jim Samson, 'Extended Forms: The Ballades, Scherzos and Fantasies', in *The Cambridge Companion to Chopin*, ed. Jim Samson (Cambridge 1992), pp. 103–11.

22   These terms are defined in John Rink, 'Tonal Architecture in the Early Music', in *The Cambridge Companion to Chopin*, ed. Jim Samson (Cambridge 1992), pp. 78–97; see also John Rink, 'The Evolution of Chopin's "Structural Style" and its Relation to Improvisation' (Dissertation, University of Cambridge 1989).

It is useful to regard Example 12.1's depiction of Op. 39's tonal structure as 'metaphorically' representing fundamental progression towards closure; in this sense, it is of particular relevance to the performer. Note that C♯ major and D♭ major are treated as enharmonic equals for the purpose of notational convenience and clarity, and in keeping with Chopin's own enharmonic flexibility.

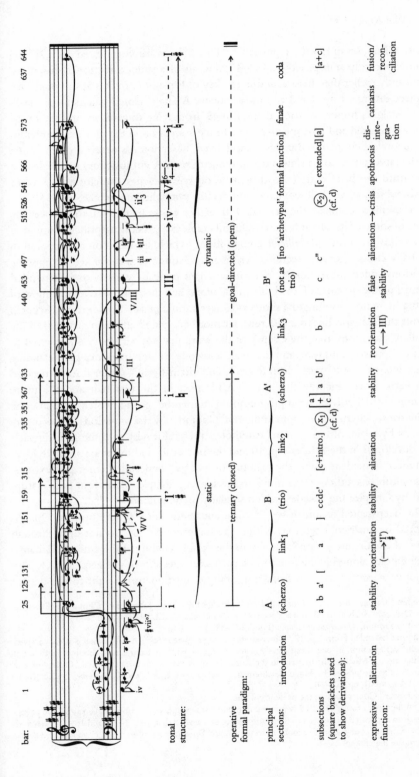

Example 12.1 Scherzo Op. 39: tonal structure, form, expression

back to C# minor and to the reprise of A. This A' is similarly truncated: bars 91–105 are unexpectedly transposed in 433–47, and all of a sudden section B re-enters, significantly earlier than before, and in the key of E major (III). It is at this point that the piece diverges from standard formal models. A single, closed statement of c leads to a 'nostalgic', minor variation thereof in 497ff. moving towards iv, and the music becomes tortured and introspective, only to blossom again in the glorious apotheosis of c's chorale-like theme. But this is short-lived, as section A's octaves return in 566 and the rapturous mood disintegrates into one of rage. A virtuosic fury permeates the finale until the brief coda (also driven by octaves) reaches the closing C# major chords, which, as we shall see, have considerable symbolic importance.

It is useful to compare the Scherzo with earlier works by Chopin to discover the source of some of its salient features. Op. 39 employs a structuring principle found in many of his pre-1832 *stile brillante* compositions, which are based on a succession of essentially closed thematic sections, lyrical and virtuosic in turn, linked by episodic transitions added subsequently; the formal chain typically ends with an extended cadential phrase (to close off the body of the work) and then a finale overflowing with bravura figuration, leading to a short coda over a tonic pedal. The C# minor Scherzo exploits this scenario but to a different, far more integrated effect: in fact, it is in the so-called 'transitions' that the essence of the work lies; any virtuosity is harnessed to specific expressive purposes; and the finale and coda are not gratuitous grandstanding but are integral to the work, both formally and 'dramatically'. Other features derived from early works include the 'static' ABA' plan in the first half and the more 'dynamic' i → III → iv → V → i progression spanning the second, which juxtapose the symmetrical schemes found in much of Chopin's Warsaw-period music (characterised by a lack of momentum at remote structural levels) with the goal-directed ones developed in the Etudes Op. 10 and the nocturnes and mazurkas from 1830–2. On a more immediate plane, the manipulation of two opposing themes and textures, whose ultimate synthesis owes much to the sonata principle, recalls four fully mature works by Chopin: the ballades, which similarly invoke the sonata dialectic.[23]

The deep-seated fusion of symmetrical and hierarchical progressions in Op. 39, mirrored by analogous tensions within the foreground,[24] occurs not only through organic thematic integration[25] but also in the skilful handling of the emotional drama, which unfolds alongside the tonal and formal structures shown in Example 12.1. This expressive narrative extends from the 'oblique' introduction[26] right to the defiant

---

[23] See Jim Samson, *Chopin: The Four Ballades* (Cambridge 1992); also, John Rink, 'Chopin's Ballades and the Dialectic: Analysis in Historical Perspective', *Music Analysis*, 13/1 (1994), pp. 99–115.

[24] See Jim Samson, *The Music of Chopin* (London 1985), p. 168.

[25] Samson ('Extended Forms', p. 109) observes that 'a single "parent cell" (A–G#) which is already implicit in the introduction, is spelled out clearly in the main scherzo theme and is used to effect a subtle link to the trio . . . Much of the material in the work may be derived from this parent cell.' Other 'organic' connections are posited by Hugo Leichtentritt (*Analyse der Chopin'schen Klavierwerke*, 2 vols. (Berlin 1921–2), vol. II, pp. 57–69).

[26] See Edward Cone's essay in the present volume.
    Although in Example 12.1 I depict the introduction's expressive function as 'alienating', the passage acts as an expressive microcosm of the entire work: the chords in bars 6–8, 14–16 and 18–20 respectively project moods of *confidence* (like much of sections A and B), *anxiety* (compare link$_2$, c" and x$_2$) and *defiance* (compare the ending).

ending in C♯ major, played out largely within the passages surrounding the thematic blocks (the 'transitions'), especially the introduction, link$_2$ and bars 497–540, which are joined by a network of subtle references traversing huge musical spans. As Example 12.1 indicates, these intermediate passages possess structural similarities: they are each built on descending bass motions, accompanied by more or less chromatic progressions in the treble which temporarily suspend diatonic affiliation (as does the succession of parallel dominant sevenths in 271–6, just before c' begins, which resembles the 'showers of chromatic particles'[27] found in the early 'brilliant' repertoire). There are expressive similarities as well: the music from bars 1ff., 320ff. and 497ff. (the last derived from c, but here in the minor for the first time) has an alienating as opposed to stabilising effect, in the first and second instances anticipating the barely repressed violence of the octave theme to follow in A and A'. Implicit in all three passages is an almost desperate quality, which peaks in two places: bars 336–51 (x$_1$ in Example 12.1 – compare Example 12.2a) and 526–40 (x$_2$ – see Example 12.2b), where the music virtually grinds to a halt, as if losing its will to carry on, with silences punctuating the futile ascending gestures in 336–9, 344–7, 530–3 and, to particularly striking effect, 538–9, where the shape is abbreviated, like a dying gasp.

The power of these passages derives partly from their 'ironic' restatement of material first heard in a different setting. Example 12.2c shows the start of the trio's middle section, d, where a light-hearted ascending quaver arpeggio in both hands launches a six-bar response to section c's descending sprays, presented earlier in alternation with the chorale-like theme. Here the quaver motion is articulated three times (moving from V/V to V, then V/IV to IV), a fourth, incomplete statement giving rise to the descending chromatic 'shower' in 271–6 that prompts d's ecstatic finish in 279–86, itself initially based on the upward quaver arpeggio. This playful, even frivolous episode, at the very heart of the work, is something of an anomaly, resembling invocations of the world of 'popular' pianism in the four ballades (compare, for instance, the central waltz episodes within Op. 23 and Op. 47).[28]

When the figure returns in x$_1$ and x$_2$ (importantly, the only other statements of the distinctive ascending arpeggio figuration), it is but a shadow of its former self: what had once been so unburdened now conveys anguish. Indeed, I would venture to describe x$_2$ as among the darkest moments in all of Chopin – a passage projecting musically the sense of loss conveyed in his pathetic letter of 30 October 1848 to Wojciech Grzymała, where he mused to himself, 'what has become of my art?'[29] This expression of utter futility is preceded by a striking repetition of the descending quaver pattern one octave lower in the previous bars, the only time in the piece that it occurs twice in succession, and thus a sign to the listener that something uniquely important is about to happen.

Rightly or wrongly, the feeling of crisis (in the etymological sense of a *decision*, or turning point) engendered at this point guides my performance of the entire Scherzo. This for me is its emotional focus: the poignancy of the registrally contracted, *pianissimo*,

27   Gerald Abraham, *Chopin's Musical Style* (London 1939), p. 18.
28   This issue is investigated in Samson, *Chopin: The Four Ballades*.
29   *Selected Correspondence of Fryderyk Chopin*, trans. and ed. Arthur Hedley (London 1962), p. 349.

Example 12.2   (a) Scherzo Op. 39, bars 336–51 ('x₁')

Example 12.2   (b) Scherzo Op. 39, bars 526–41 ('x₂')

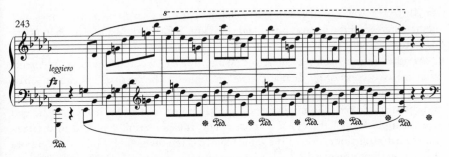

Example 12.2   (c) Scherzo Op. 39, bars 243–50

sotto voce chords (which are a pale reflection of the trio's rich sonority) and the gasping arpeggios (recalling both the untroubled d section – whose meaning is retrospectively made clear by its negation in this context – and the relatively potent x_1, which is grounded by a dominant pedal versus the 'detached' ii_3^4 of 526ff.) is without equal in the work. In this light, the apotheosis (literally, 'elevation') of c that follows seems all the more miraculous, the sense of aspiration building as the melody soars beyond its normal four-bar span in a rhapsodic sweep climbing higher and higher until the music shatters with the octave interruption in 566. For a while, however, there is a hint of optimism – a promise of redemption – projected in the right hand's 'choral' theme,[30] the low dominant-pedal G♯s in the left-hand accompaniment all the while articulating a tension-building ostinato rhythm (♩. | ♩ ♩ ♩) which, like the knocking of fate, foreshadows what inevitably will follow.

The crisis precipitated at this point can be traced back to the transposed sequence in $link_3$. When B' enters thereafter in 453, the music enters a world entirely removed from the stable formal framework operative hitherto (indeed, the only challenges to formal equilibrium thus far occur in the introduction and in $link_2$, which, as noted earlier, alienate rather than stabilise). Transposed to III, the former trio loses all predictable function: its stability is false, and (once again) could even be called ironic.[31] The strong closing gesture some forty bars later – one of the most definitive thus far – is also ironic, for it is followed by the crisis of alienation as well as the extraordinarily swift and itself destabilising succession through apotheosis and disintegration to catharsis, or purgation, in the finale.[32] It is thus when the form opens out and the 'dynamic'

[30] I hear and play it as a polyphonic, not homophonic texture, so that each note is connected melodically to its counterpart in the next. In a similar vein, Leichtentritt (*Analyse*, vol. II, p. 66) calls the texture 'symphonic'.

[31] Had $link_1$ reappeared at its original pitch in bars 433–47, the main body of the piece would probably have ended after A', with the finale/coda to follow – that is, the music would have progressed from the (slightly revised) counterpart of bar 106 directly to bar 573. This reveals just how much structural weight the actual 'extension' is made to bear.

James Huneker (*Chopin: The Man and His Music* (New York 1900), p. 213) also observes the role of irony in the work, in somewhat different terms: 'Opus 39 . . . is the most dramatic of the set . . . irony lurks in its bars and there is fever in its glance - a glance full of enigmatic and luring scorn.'

[32] Such rapid juxtapositions of opposing expressive states recall the eighteenth-century free fantasy, in which the improviser would move 'audaciously from one affect to another', 'constantly varying the passions' (C. P. E. Bach, *Essay on the True Art of Playing Keyboard Instruments*, trans. William J. Mitchell

i → III → iv → V → i progression is launched at bar 453 that the Scherzo's emotional drama enters its most intense phase and the music's form and expressive content are masterfully fused.

Another fusion occurs at the close, when, for the second time only, elements from the two contrasting thematic areas are united. The first such occasion – bars 352–9, part of the retransition to A' – is explicit, in that variants of the scherzo theme and the trio's dotted-minim chords are superimposed in the two hands. At the end (see Example 12.3a), the effect is more subtle and powerful, captured in the last-minute harmonic inflection to the tonic major via the tierce de Picardie E♯, a gesture at once recalling the tonal setting of the contrasting trio section. This 'startling last-moment victory'[33] for the parallel C♯ major tonic comes as a shock – perfectly logical in retrospect, but unexpected given the seemingly inexorable octave descent crashing chromatically downward towards C♯ *minor* and surging in an exciting hemiola (reinforced by Chopin's pedalling) to reach *fff*[34] in 644.[35]

Having now reached the Scherzo's conclusion, we can assess how the preceding study relates to my performance of Op. 39. Virtually every aspect of this discussion contributes in some way to – or, to be more precise, *has been dictated by* – my interpretative vision of the music. In short, my fundamental aim in playing this work is to create a coherent expressive and dramatic statement so that the alienating effect of the introduction is reinvoked when we reach link$_2$, along with remembrance of the

(New York 1949), pp. 153 and 152). Bach writes that in the unbarred fantasy, as in the accompanied recitative, 'tempo and meter must be frequently changed in order to rouse and still the *rapidly alternating affects*' (p. 153; my emphasis).

[33] This is how Cone regards the arrival of C♯ minor at the end of the introduction (see his essay in this volume, p. 143). Compare Huneker's description (*Chopin*, p. 214): 'There is a coda of frenetic movement and the end is in major, a surprising conclusion when considering all that has gone before.'

[34] Triple *forte* is the fullest dynamic employed by the composer. See *CPT*, p. 126 n. 114.

Observe the *timbral* resemblance of the D♭ major chord in bar 159 *et seq.* and the C♯ major chord in 644–5 – yet another facet of the last-minute fusion.

[35] It is worth noting in passing the striking similarities between this ending and the last few bars of the G minor Ballade Op. 23 (see Example 12.3b), which also employ an octave descent in both hands (after the breathtakingly dissonant 'upbeat' in 258^2–9) leading to three 'chords' rhythmically and registrally analogous to those in Op. 39. This parallel is one of many between Op. 39 and the ballades; others include the blend of 'popular' and serious elements, the metamorphosis and fusion of themes via the sonata dialectic, and the presence of a strong 'narrative' impulse to guide the unfolding drama.

To interpret the Scherzo (and likewise the ballades), the performer must somehow make sense of that 'narrative' content: it is his or her task to decide what musical 'message' to convey and how it should be recounted. As I have written elsewhere ('Chopin's Ballades', p. 112), this is achieved 'by following indications in the score as to "plot", and, as in the enactment of any "plot archetype", by shaping the unfolding tale on the spur of the moment in an expressively appropriate manner. Certainly in the act of performance one is conscious of communicating *something* to an audience – not of course a story or programme in the usual sense, but some sort of emotional message, however that may be manifested or conceived, which, like an imagined, sublimated "voice", speaks to one through the music while playing.'

It is perhaps ideas such as these which inspired the following comments: 'notes are mere notes, but music lives by whoever reads the notes, and you can hear at once if someone is just spelling out ABC or really speaking' (Teofil Lenartowicz referring to the playing of Chopin's friend Julian Fontana, quoted in *CPT*, p. 154); and, concerning the third movement of Chopin's Sonata Op. 35: 'this trio is a touchstone for recognizing whether the performer is a poet or merely a pianist; whether he can tell a story or merely play the piano' (Lenz, quoted in *CPT*, p. 86).

See Samson, *Chopin: The Four Ballades* for discussion of music and narrativity and its related literature; also Anthony Newcomb's chapter in this volume.

Example 12.3   (a) Scherzo Op. 39, bars 637–49

Example 12.3   (b) Ballade Op. 23, bars 257–64

happier mood left only moments earlier in section d; then, with B's transposition to E major, when the music enters an unknown realm (what will happen next? what *can* happen next?), an even greater sense of uncertainty is projected as ambiguity reaches crisis point; and finally, in the brief respite that follows, redemption is glimpsed, overwhelmed by the irrepressible octaves but resurrected at the very end by the defiant C♯ major inflection.

There are of course many other details in one's mind – for instance, obtaining different colours for the C♯ minor and D♭ major themes (the 'affective' contrast between these keys exploited in numerous Chopin works, e.g. Op. 27 Nos. 1 and 2, Op. 28 No. 15, Op. 64 No. 2 and Op. 66), in part by using a heavier touch for the octaves, a full *cantabile* for the trio's chorale-like theme and a weightless brushing of the keys for the consequent quavers. And certainly there are more mundane technical matters to contend with – just getting the notes right is challenging enough. But what *essentially* guides my performance is an awareness of the underlying expressive plot and a concern to project this above all.

That this plot is not grasped by everyone who comes in contact with Op. 39 can be seen in the literature and heard in many commercial recordings. For instance, one author refers to Chopin's ostensible 'reversal of typical sonata procedures' (that is, use of a i–I–i–III tonal scheme rather than the 'more orthodox' i–III–i–I),[36] which in my view shows little appreciation of the work's unique closed–open formal succession and its potency in precipitating emotional crisis. Were the former viewpoint to guide my performance, the result would, I think, lack cohesion: at least, my ability to relate the interpretation to a 'spine', a 'unified vision' (defined by both form and expressive content), would be severely compromised.

Rhythmic shape in the D major Prelude Op. 28 No. 5

Music's two fundamental properties are pitch and rhythm. The latter, notoriously difficult to systematise in the act of analysis, is even more elusive when describing performance, where its normative state is largely one of irregularity. Partly for this reason, the rhythmic properties of Chopin's performance aesthetic (apart from his idiosyncratic *tempo rubato*)[37] were discussed by his contemporaries far less often than sonority and articulation, which are much easier to write about than the shaping of time.

Those few accounts that do address rhythm are therefore of special interest. These range from general comments ('his interpretation [of the mazurkas] is shot through with a thousand nuances of movement of which he alone holds the secret, and which are impossible to convey by instructions'[38]) to more detailed observations based on Chopin's playing ('In the national dances . . ., the main rhythmic notes should be strongly accentuated, followed by a gentle release of the rhythmic impulse wherever the accent (or long-held accented note) is omitted or displaced. But this must never degenerate into mere lack of rhythm.'[39]). Of particular interest are the composer's 'rules' for musical punctuation and elocution as recorded retrospectively by Kleczyński,[40]

---

[36]   See Anatoly Leikin, 'The Sonatas', in *The Cambridge Companion to Chopin*, ed. Jim Samson (Cambridge 1992), p. 166.

[37]   For discussion see David Rowland's chapter in this volume.

[38]   Hector Berlioz, quoted in *CPT*, p. 71.

[39]   Mikuli, quoted in *CPT*, p. 71.

[40]   For instance, the final bar of an eight-bar phrase 'will generally mark the termination of the thought', so the pianist should pause slightly and 'lower the voice'; shorter pauses, like commas or semicolons, are inserted after four-bar units. See *CPT*, pp. 42–4 (but note Eigeldinger's caveat about Kleczyński (*CPT*, pp. 102–3 n. 34)).

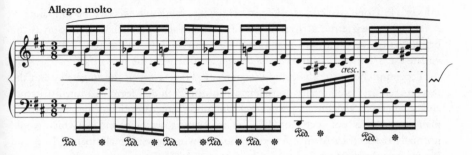

Example 12.4   Prelude Op. 28 No. 5, bars 1–6, 12–14 and 32–9

which reveal an implicitly hierarchical approach to phrasing and thus to rhythmic structure in general. On the basis of these principles, 'Chopin arrived at the following conclusion, to which he attached much importance: *do not play by too short phrases*'. Karasowski corroborates this conclusion: '[Chopin] advised his pupils not to fragment the musical idea, but rather to carry it to the listener in one long breath.'[41]

Both of these comments apply with uncanny accuracy to the D major Prelude Op. 28 No. 5, a fleeting thirty-nine-bar work of which all but the last two-and-a-half bars (a coda within a coda) lie under a single slur. Determining the slur's function is an important first step in defining the Prelude's 'rhythmic shape', this being (in

---
[41]   Quoted in *CPT*, p. 44.

Edward T. Cone's words) the key to achieving 'valid and effective performance'.[42] At the other extreme, a rhythmic detail of relevance to such a definition is the bracketed quaver figures in bars 1–4, 17–20 and 33–6 (see Example 12.4),[43] which violate the 3/8 metre and thus invite special treatment by the performer.

To comprehend the rhythmic hierarchy that lies between the huge slur and the quavers requires preliminary consideration of the Prelude's form and tonal structure and of certain motivic details pertinent to the music's interpretation. One of the work's main features is a 'pun' between A♯ (which is biased towards B) and B♭ (which would normally descend to A) manifested in the following ways: the alternating B–A and B♭–A appoggiaturas in 1–4 and 17–20;[44] the A–A♯–B motion (itself of motivic importance) in 5 and 21; the A♯s in 13–16, part of F♯ major (immediately followed by A♮ and F♯ minor); and the B♭–A and B♭–A–G–F♯ motions in 29–36. The pun also gives rise to the 'motivic' role of major/minor mixture, in 1–4, 13–16, 17–20 and 29–36 (also compare 6^2–7 and 22^2–3). A final motif of interpretative importance is the three-note melodic line heard in 13–16 (F♯–G♯–A♯/A♮), 29–32 (D–E–F♯) and 37–9 (F♯–E–D), where at the last moment it restates in miniature the Prelude's underlying tonal structure.

This is depicted in Example 12.5, along with other essential structural features, including the upbeat–downbeat shape created by the massive slur (level 1), which defines the body of the Prelude as a single gesture directed towards the principal structural downbeat at bar 37.[45] Within this span pulses an extraordinarily regular harmonic rhythm (shown in a four-bar-per-crotchet reduction on level 4), reflecting the steady succession of four-bar sections (level 7)[46] and the clear-cut middleground

---

[42] Cone (*Musical Form and Musical Performance* (New York 1968), pp. 49 and 31) is referring here to *all* rhythmic aspects of a work: phrase rhythm, harmonic rhythm, formal rhythm, etc. – in short, the unfolding temporal profile of every active parameter, the composite of which could be thought to constitute the music's 'rhythmic shape'. My discussion of the Prelude will focus on rhythm in the narrower sense, although my observations also relate to the work's rhythmic contour more broadly conceived.

   Concerning the thirty-six-bar slur in Op. 28 No. 5, note Pauline Viardot's comment (quoted in *CPT*, p. 54): 'when huge slurs extend over entire musical periods [in Chopin's works], they indicate this *spianato* [levelled] playing, without nuances or discontinuities in the rhythm – impossible for those whose hands are not graced with perfect suppleness.' (See also *CPT*, pp. 124–5 n. 18.)

[43] Bars 17–20 (a slightly altered repeat of 1–4) do not appear in Example 12.4.

   In the autograph manuscript (KK 397, held by the Biblioteka Narodowa, a facsimile of which was published in 1951 by PWM, edited by Władysław Hordyński), Chopin originally grouped the third and fifth right-hand semiquavers in bars 13–16 and 29–32 using supplementary quaver beams, but later crossed these out (possibly because of the unwieldy intervals created when sustaining this 'middle part').

[44] I hear these B–A and B♭–A appoggiaturas as a response to the neighbour-note motifs in the E minor Prelude (see Carl Schachter's chapter in the present volume). This relationship could be explained by the close composition dates of the two preludes: Eigeldinger ('L'achèvement des *Préludes* op. 28 de Chopin', *Revue de musicologie*, 75/2 (1989), p. 240) writes that Nos. 4 and 5 were composed in Majorca after 28 November 1838 along with five other preludes, roughly in the order 4, 9 and 5, then 7, 10, 14, 16 and 18. Another explanation is the role of 6̂–5̂ motions as an *Urmotiv* in Chopin's music generally.

[45] This gesture recalls Momigny's *levé-frappé* concept, also the rhythmic theory of Hugo Riemann. See Cone, *Musical Form and Musical Performance*, chapter 1, for discussion of this concept's relation to performance.

[46] It is instructive to view the form 'paradigmatically':

   A   B₁
          B₂   C
   A'   B₁'
          B₂'   C'
   A"   D

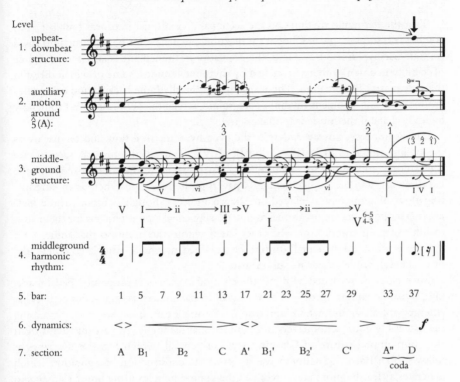

Example 12.5   Prelude Op. 28 No. 5: structural and formal components

structure (level 3), which reveals an ascending-fifths sequence in B_1/B_2 and B_1'/B_2' (I–V–ii–vi), leading respectively to III#–V (sections C and A') and to V–I (C' and A"/D, the latter serving as a coda). The harmonic-rhythm diagram demonstrates the anacrustic function of A, A' and A", with 'downbeats' on bars 5, 21 and (especially) 37, where the slur from bar 1 reaches the most important stress of all, on the registral peak f#[3] (with the ensuing *forte* the Prelude's loudest explicit dynamic level, the dynamics otherwise contained within the wave shapes shown on the example, which are not unlike wave patterns in the figuration), and it is the high F# that precipitates the coda's $\hat{3}$–$\hat{2}$–$\hat{1}$ descent. In addition to the middleground voice-leading, Chopin decorates the fifth scale degree A with the auxiliary progression shown on level 2, this pitch being prolonged throughout the work as the anacrusis element of the fundamental upbeat–downbeat gesture.[47]

---

[47]   Note that the Prelude composes out a massive A–F# ascending sixth, the archetypal anacrusis pattern employed by Chopin (as in the E♭ major Nocturne Op. 9 No. 2 and the C# minor Waltz Op. 64 No. 2). In conjunction with the linear descent that follows, this upbeat–downbeat structure articulates a large-scale $\hat{5}$–$\hat{3}$–$\hat{2}$–$\hat{1}$ motif, in other words, 'motif Y' in Eigeldinger's study of cyclic unity in Op. 28 ('Twenty-four Preludes Op. 28: Genre, Structure, Significance', in *Chopin Studies*, ed. Jim Samson (Cambridge 1988), p. 182). This strikes me as a more profound manifestation of the motif than those actually cited by Eigeldinger in No. 5.

That the harmonic rhythm and the sectional divisions fall into neat four-bar units comes as no surprise, given Chopin's well-known penchant for phrase structures based on four-bar hypermeasures. Here, the regularity of the scheme is an essential source of stability in a work otherwise racked by rhythmic tensions, some of which threaten the very metrical foundation. These arise not in the rhythmic background or middle-ground[48] but the turbulent rhythmic foreground, which the performer must somehow logically shape if the music is to make sense.

This is not easy, however, despite the even hypermetrical flow and regular over-the-barline impulses in $B_1/B_2/C$ and $B_1'/B_2'/C'$. Indeed, the three A sections are rhythmically ambiguous to an almost Brahmsian extent; furthermore, except for the last three bars and the 'supplementary' quavers in the A sections, there is an unremitting flow of semiquavers played at Allegro molto. Though constant, these *moto perpetuo* semiquavers are by no means functionally equal, and it remains for the pianist to infer shaping criteria from the clues latent within the music so that some notes emerge as more 'fundamental' (thus to be sustained, accented, articulated differently, or whatever), while others are subordinate.

Such clues are provided by the Prelude's motifs, harmonic properties, pedal markings, dynamics and so forth – in short, by all its parameters, acting in concert. What emerges, at least in my own interpretation, is a complex *rhythmic counterpoint* organising the ostensibly equal semiquavers into a functional hierarchy. In part this stems from the contrapuntal nature of Chopin's style in general, which Samson describes as follows: 'like Bach . . . Chopin was adept at the construction of figuration which generates a clear harmonic flow while at the same time permitting linear elements to emerge through the pattern'. This counterpoint 'is often at the kernel of the musical idea in Chopin, and usually a counterpoint which starts from the capacity of the piano to "layer" voices through shaded dynamics, allowing voices to emerge and recede from the texture'.[49]

It is my contention that by responding to both this general characteristic of the composer's style and certain innate properties of the figuration here, the performer

[48]   A fragment of this rhythmic middleground (sections $B_1/B_2/C$ and $B_1'/B_2'/C'$) is shown in Example 12.6, where, despite their different rhythmic groupings, basic and subsidiary harmonic progressions form a pattern of lilting, over-the-barline impulses, with occasional realignments of the underlying pattern as in bars 11^3-13^1 and 27^3-9^1. The layers of tension arising between the different groupings provide considerable rhythmic variety within the stabilising gestural pattern. As we shall see, the rhythmic middleground of A, A' and A" is by no means as regular.

Example 12.6   Prelude Op. 28 No. 5: rhythmic middleground, bars 5–15 and 21–31

[49]   Samson, *The Music of Chopin*, pp. 73–4. Compare Schachter's discussion of counterpoint in Op. 28 No. 4 as well as Eigeldinger's chapter in this book.

'intuitively' constructs a rhythmic counterpoint which shapes the steady semiquaver pulse into layered textures. Turning first to the figuration, note that in A, A' and A" the music pivots around certain pitches: in A and A', G in the left hand (played with the second finger) and B–A/B♭–A in the right (fingered 3–2); in A", A in the bass (played with 3) and the descending B♭–A–G–F♯ line in the treble (articulated 3–2, 3–2). These are in each case the centre of wave shapes oscillating between the outer reaches of each hand, rolling figures which perfectly exploit the natural properties of the second and third fingers as defined in Chopin's unfinished piano method: 'the pivot is the index finger, which divides the hand in half when it spreads open'; and, the third finger is 'the middle and the pivot [*point d'appui*]'.[50] As for the figuration in the B and C sections, this presents itself to the 'intuitive' performer as a *four-voiced texture* (not *two* semiquaver strata, as it appears on the printed page), exploiting the hand's division into the subordinate mechanisms also alluded to in Chopin's method: 'the two hands together will give four, five, six parts'.[51]

Processing this information at an entirely subconscious level, my 'ear'[52] reworked the music into the version shown in Example 12.7. It must be stressed that *this diagram is not the product of an independent rhythmic analysis*. Rather, it represents the rhythmic basis of my interpretation in notated form: it is an 'aural image' of the Prelude committed to paper *after* the piece had been prepared and publicly performed. The durations represent note-lengths as sustained on the keyboard or, given that the tempo is very fast, those I sustain in my 'inner ear' but not in actuality, all the while maintaining the forward momentum of a steady semiquaver flow.

This interpretative 'map' or 'mental script' (of which only excerpts appear in Example 12.7) shows first of all how I treat the quaver groupings in the anacrustic introduction. Unlike Leichtentritt and Chomiński (both of whom renotate section A according to unconvincing criteria),[53] my reading reflects the inner tensions that drive A and A'. In each section, the first bar is heard in 3/8: bar 1's initial B–A semiquavers establish the 3/8 metre (they are *not* upbeats, as Chomiński maintains), which lasts until the start of bar 2 (compare the similar 3/8 in A', bar 17). Thereafter, a 2/8 metre sets in for three four-semiquaver groups, extended by a quaver at the end of the section to propel us towards the strong downbeats that kick off the B sections in bars 5 and 21 (compare Example 12.5). The beamed semiquaver groupings, which possess an implied hemiola function, *treat the B–A/B♭–A appoggiaturas as syncopations*

50 Quoted in *CPT*, pp. 29 and 32. Compare Eigeldinger, *Esquisses*, pp. 78 and 74.
51 Quoted in *CPT*, p. 25. This comment is made regarding double notes in two parts (thirds, sixths and octaves) but applies equally well to other, more explicitly linear textures.
52 Note Schoenberg's comment: 'Das Ohr ist eines Musikers ganzer Verstand' (quoted in Stein, *Form and Performance*, p. 23).
53 Both of Leichtentritt's rebarrings (*Analyse*, vol. II, pp. 137–8) overemphasise the right-hand a¹ (see Example 12.8a): the first treats the quaver shape as an extended neighbour-note motion centred on a¹; the second makes a¹ a downbeat in each of three bars (arranged in a complicated metrical succession), while the left hand pivots around g in an unsynchronised 2/4. Józef Chomiński (*Preludia Chopina* (Cracow 1950), pp. 101–15 – see Example 12.8b) hears a 2/4 beginning in both hands after a three-semiquaver upbeat; after two bars, the metre is abbreviated to 2/8 + 1/16 whereupon 3/8 enters. While this makes sense *visually* (at least more so than Leichtentritt's reading), it betrays little understanding of the music *as played*.

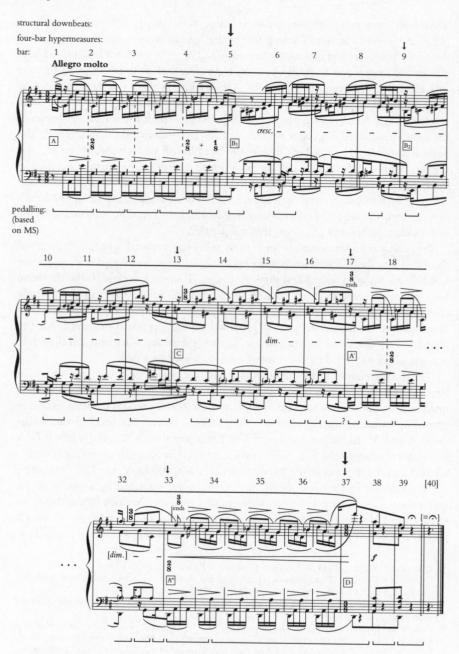

Example 12.7   Prelude Op. 28 No. 5: foreground rhythmic counterpoint, bars 1–18 and 32–[40]

Example 12.8   Prelude Op. 28 No. 5: renotated versions of bars 1–4
(a) Leichtentritt, *Analyse*, vol. II, pp. 137–8
(b) Chomiński, *Preludia Chopina*, p. 105

(not as falling on accented downbeats), the pivotal quaver shape thus serving as a rhythmically enlivening rather than accentually stultifying force. This driving force is enhanced by the analogous left-hand groupings, which are synchronised with the right and which complement the syncopated treble by slurrings *against* the four-note grouping, extending from the low A in each group (separated from the preceding upper G by a slight 'breath', that is, raising/dropping of the wrist (discussed below)) to the first note in the next. The syncopated undercurrents are also reinforced by the pedalling (which shapes the music with a sort of foot-tapping effect)[54] and by the

---

[54]   Both the Henle and Universal *Urtext* editions specify pedal indications in A' different from those in A, whereas the 'Paderewski' repeats the pedalling. For once, the latter's policy of consistency is not misguided. The discrepancy in the 'Urtexts' (which results in curious, even nonsensical pedalling) arises from the confusing state of Chopin's manuscript at this point. At first glance, the pedalling specified in A' seems to be that of the *Urtext* editions; but on closer inspection it is clear that Chopin's

'long accents' that one instinctively imposes on the right-hand appoggiaturas and the lower part. Notwithstanding the tensions thus created in A and A', the original 3/8 is not entirely supplanted[55] (thanks to its presence in bars 1 and 17), meaning that complete rebarrings like Leichtentritt's and Chomiński's oversimplify the music's metrical flow. In A", however, which has a closing as well as an anacrustic function, the situation is different. Here, without the 'grounding' 3/8 bar at first, the implied 2/8 prevails from the start, articulated by the rolling contrary-motion shapes in both hands and by the outer Ds, the inner lines in quavers now sounding even more syncopated than their appoggiatura counterparts in A and A'. The terrific momentum generated by this surging duple (which 'summarises' all the conflicting metrical implications) catapults the music towards the structural downbeat on f♯³, in the same way as a hemiola – which is what A" amounts to, spread over four bars – precedes a cadence point in much baroque and classical repertoire.[56] The effect in performance, when the huge slur finally reaches its goal after thirty-six bars, is electrifying.

Whereas hemiola effects are exploited in A, A' and (especially) A", the propulsive device used by Chopin in C and C' is metric shift, as the 3/8 metre is retained but starting at a different point in the bar. Both C sections follow eight bars of relative metrical tranquillity, this being necessary given the processive, more discursive sequential activity in B_1/B_2 and B_1'/B_2' (versus the 'static', though rhythmically energised, repetition structures in the highly contrasting A and C sections). Once the 'correct' 3/8 pulse has been well and truly established in bars 5–12 and 21–8, Chopin enlivens the rhythm by the three-note melody in the uppermost part of C and C', which is shifted out of phase by a semiquaver to pull against the foundation below, almost prevailing by the time C and C' draw to a close.

It is in the B and C sections that the four-part SATB texture referred to earlier emerges. Here too the music is riddled with syncopations (indeed, the Prelude is almost a study in syncopation), and it is one of the pianist's greatest challenges to invest the bass line with the breathless forward energy it requires, given the way Chopin delays and hence abbreviates pitches which ordinarily would attract emphasis

'ped' markings, which were written in subsequent to the notes themselves, do not apply to the *left-hand* pitches but to those in the *right hand*, which *are not synchronised with the lower part's semiquavers* in bars 18 and 19. By matching the 'ped' signs to the right-hand notes and ignoring the left hand, the emergent pedalling is exactly that of section A: Chopin wants the pedal depressed and released in conjunction with the right-hand appoggiaturas. This hypothesis is confirmed by the presence of 'correct' (i.e. consistent) pedalling in the French first edition, which was based on this manuscript, whereas the German first edition, prepared from a copy (now lost, but photographed before its disappearance) by Julian Fontana (who either misunderstood Chopin's intentions or simply transcribed the erroneous indications without reflection), has pedalling like that in Henle and Universal, which follow the 1839 Breitkopf edition. The pedalling in Wessel's first English edition, published after the German and French, is even more bizarre here.

See Debussy's comment (quoted in *CPT*, p. 129) on the pedal as 'a kind of *respiration*'. Compare note 70 below.

55   Compare Meyerbeer's accusation that Chopin played his Mazurka Op. 33 No. 3 in 2/4 rather than the notated 3/4, despite his insistence to the contrary. According to Lenz, who was present at the time, '[Chopin] was right . . . for though the third beat loses some of its value, submerged . . . in the flow of the melody, still *it does not cease to exist*.' (Quoted in *CPT*, p. 73; my emphasis.)

56   See Edward T. Cone, '*Musical Form and Musical Performance* Reconsidered', *Music Theory Spectrum*, 7 (1985), pp. 149–58.

as bearer of the harmonic foundation. Note for instance the delayed left-hand downbeats in bars 6, 7, 9, 10, 11 and 12, and the elided A in bar 8: all of these need to be hastened onwards rather than held back. It is interesting to observe extensions and contractions in the rhythmic motifs that 'naturally' arise here: for instance, the tenor rhythms in bars 5 and 6 are doubled in length in 7–9, impelling the music towards the second harmony in the underlying I–ii–III♯ ascent; similarly, the bass is extended in 11–13, leading to the start of section C, whereas the soprano is cut off in bar 12, the alto then stepping in to guide us to the new section.

Given that all the information conveyed in this example was realised without any explicit attempt to analyse the music beyond what one 'instinctively' does in learning to play the work (it is, after all, no more and no less than a notated version of my performance), the value of 'informed intuition' as a guide to the performer seems self-evident. I am not arguing that the interpretation emerging from this notated mental picture is necessarily a 'good' one or that no plausible alternatives exist, but I do maintain that the 'aural image' in Example 12.7 reveals the inner ear's power to devise a performance strategy even for the extraordinarily subtle rhythmic complexities that make up this Prelude. That this 'intuitive' interpretation is corroborated by Chopin's view of piano technique (that is, his conception of the hand as divided into two parts and of the fingers' different functions) and his approach to the projection of rhythm in performance, as well as evidence about his style in general, supports my belief that the performance sketched here goes some way towards achieving the sort of authenticity defined earlier in the essay.

Musical language in the F minor Concerto Op. 21

Chopin often taught his students seated at the piano, demonstrating rather than describing. Emilie von Gretsch recalled that 'during one lesson, Chopin played as I never heard him play before. He seemed to want to attain the ideal of his poetic soul; the first time he played me his Nocturnes, he apologized for *not having "said it"* in the way he wanted me to hear it, and he repeated them with even more perfection.'[57]

Chopin's use of the expression *dire un morceau de musique* – to 'tell' a piece of music[58] – is highly revealing. It is a notion implicit in some of the definitions of music proposed in his unfinished piano treatise: 'thought expressed through sounds', 'the manifestation of our feelings through sounds', 'the expression of our perceptions through sounds', 'the indefinite (indeterminate) language [*parole*] of men' and 'the indefinite language [*langue*]'. Also, 'we use sounds to make music just as we use words to make a language'.[59]

Chopin's observation of the close relation between language and music was of course nothing new, but the way in which his compositions exploit that relation is uniquely his own. The 'vocal' quality in Chopin's music to which I alluded before developed at an early stage in his career and can easily be discerned in the two piano

---

57 Quoted in *CPT*, p. 77; my emphasis.
58 Eigeldinger writes that this expression was 'current in French musical circles of the last century' (*CPT*, p. 14 n. 23).
59 Quoted in *CPT*, p. 195; compare Eigeldinger, *Esquisses*, p. 48.

concertos, written in 1829–30. Among the many sophisticated stylistic attributes[60] of these pieces are subtle contrapuntal textures governing certain expressive passages, defined, as noted above, by a pianistic layering of parts. Eigeldinger sees in this 'super-imposition of lines' 'the transfigured imprint of Bach', although Chopin's inventive 'polymelodic texture' is 'a very long way from the neo-Baroque counterpoint prac-tised at this same period by Mendelssohn or Schumann'.[61] As Carl Dahlhaus observes, Bach's influence on Chopin 'emerged from an idea that was central to nineteenth-century musical thought: the idea that expressivity and counterpoint need not be mutu-ally exclusive, but may complement each other, or even bring each other into being'.[62]

I have already suggested that one of the performer's chief responsibilities is to infer the expressive message implicit in the work being played;[63] to the extent, therefore, that counterpoint is an important agent of expression in Chopin's music, it is to coun-terpoint that we must look for a clue to the music's latent message. This requires us first to reconsider the vocal origins of Chopin's keyboard aesthetic. In enlightening Eugène Delacroix on the nature of musical logic, Chopin states that in the fugue (the 'element of all reason and consistency in music') 'each of the parts has its own move-ment which, while still according with the others, *keeps on with its own song* and follows it perfectly; there is your counterpoint, "*punto contrapunto*"'.[64] For Chopin, counter-point was literally the superimposition of 'voices', hence its capacity to convey such profound poetic meaning.

I shall show how this stylistic principle is put into practice by examining a passage from the F minor Concerto Op. 21 which on close inspection reveals an expressive message pronounced by layered 'voices' of this sort. The excerpt appears in Example 12.9: bars 143–51 of the first movement, which follow the lyrical second theme (a nocturne-like[65] statement invoking Chopin's *bel canto* keyboard idiom) and precede a

---

[60] It is regrettable that the two concertos have been so widely criticised in this century despite these sophisticated features. My book *Chopin's Piano Concertos* (Cambridge, forthcoming) redresses the balance in favour of these early masterpieces.

[61] Eigeldinger, 'Twenty-four Preludes', p. 175. The comment refers to Op. 28.

[62] *Nineteenth-Century Music*, trans. J. Bradford Robinson (Berkeley 1989), p. 31.

[63] I recognise that this statement is contentious, but assessing the role (functional and/or expressive) of compositional features *within a given stylistic context* is legitimate when that context has been defined as the background or framework for the determination of meaning. It is only when meaning is inferred with reference to uncertain criteria, or when a critical paradigm is assumed to be universally valid, that such attributions are suspect. In cases where the music was conceived with regard to a distinct expressive vocabulary, as was certainly true of Chopin, the critic/performer/analyst/historian should not wilfully ignore that context in interpreting the work's meaning. I do not however favour the 'authenticist' criticism practised in some recent publications, which shun the critical apparatus that has evolved since a work was composed in an attempt to view the music strictly on the terms of its creator. This approach strikes me as no less chimerical a goal than 'authentic' (i.e. historically accurate) performance. A more fruitful approach is to consider the full range of historically validated approaches as part of the critical/interpretative/analytical/historical tradition impinging on the work, and to strike a new stance somehow accounting for but advancing beyond all of these.

[64] *The Journal of Eugene Delacroix*, trans. Walter Pach (New York 1937), p. 195; my emphasis. Compare the chapters by Eigeldinger, Schachter and Berger in this volume.

[65] In 'Understanding Genre: A Reinterpretation of the Early Piano Nocturne' (*Atti del XIV Congresso della Società Internazionale di Musicologia*, 3 vols. (Turin 1990), vol. III, pp. 775–9), Jeffrey Kallberg traces the vocal origins of piano nocturnes, which, he demonstrates, are essentially songs without words or serenades 'sung' at the keyboard. This partly explains why the listener perceives a potent expressive message intoned in these works, or in nocturne-like passages such as Op. 21's second theme.

Example 12.9   Concerto Op. 21, I, bars 142–51

section ending the first solo and leading to the second tutti (this concluding section begins and ends in the minor dominant, but moves temporarily to A♭ in bars 161–70). The first thing to note is the unexpected nature of the passage: the listener anticipates a full cadence in A♭ in 142–3 to close off the section, possibly with a virtuosic 'Spielepisode' to follow. This expectation arises in part from Theme 2's regular phrase structure: four-bar antecedent (a, 125–8); four-bar consequent (b, 129–32); varied restatement of a (a', 133–6); and abbreviated, two-bar variant of b (b', 137–8), which propels the music towards the closing four-bar phrase shown in Example 12.10

(c, 139–42). Here the phrase ends as anticipated, with a hypothetical continuation in Ab adapted from bars 161ff. In the event, however, the bass ascends by semitone to E♮ on the last beat of 142 (see Example 12.9) so that the harmony can progress to F minor, or iv of C minor (bar 143^1). This direction-changing chord on E – ♮vii°^{7} of F minor (heard earlier in a similar progression, at the end of the piano's introductory statement in 81^4–2^1) – is transformed into an extraordinary dissonance through Chopin's contrapuntal handling of the cadence. The soprano's appoggiatura c^2, itself quite dissonant, is doubled by the tenor's c^1 implicitly prolonged from beat 3 (I actually sustain this note on the piano to highlight the clash!), which resolves fractionally earlier than the soprano on the second quaver of beat 4. The crunch on this beat and the staggered resolutions that follow are enormously potent:[66] after this moment of unforeseen crisis (again in the sense of turning point), we are wrenched into turmoil.

Example 12.10   Concerto Op. 21, I, hypothetical version of bars 139ff.

[66] Play the fourth-beat chord rearticulating the tenor c^1 to appreciate the cluster's dissonance and the expressiveness of the two-phased resolutions.

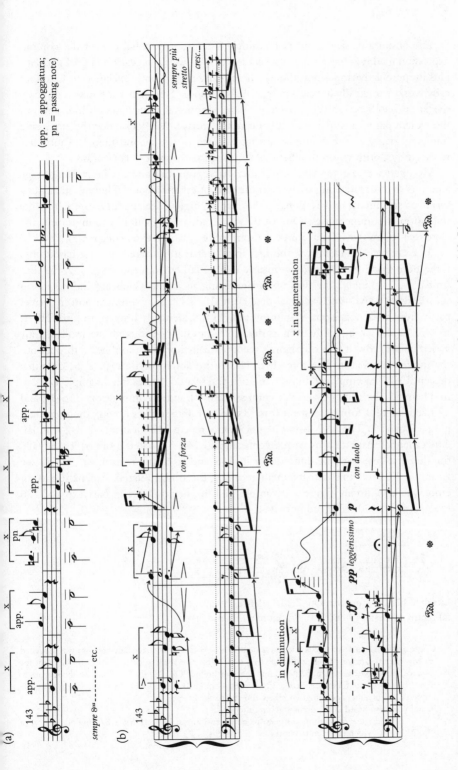

Example 12.11   Concerto Op. 21, I (a) rhythmic profile, bars 143–51   (b) gestural reduction, bars 143–51

The ensuing passage is overwhelmingly intense, in part because of the copious expression markings (*con forza*, *sempre più stretto*, *leggierissimo*, *con duolo* and finally *risoluto*, plus numerous dynamic indications), these being meticulously specified in Chopin's early works particularly in places of special significance. This eight-bar phrase is certainly special: it stands out in the movement as an emotional climax and an indication of the violent passions contained just beneath the surface. All of a sudden the expressive 'message' darkens: the gentle, yearning lyricism of the second theme evaporates, replaced by a grim vision prophetic of some of the composer's later music.

My reference to a 'message' is not just a lapse into metaphor: at heart, the passage amounts to a recitative improvised on the spur of the moment.[67] Chopin articulates a series of statements and responses, the former highly declamatory, the latter like impassioned commentaries. One of these, a 'cadenza', reaches breaking point; the close that follows (*con duolo*) conveys a spirit of resignation, even collapse.

As Example 12.11a shows, the first four declamatory statements are based on a three-note shape (x), descending linearly in a dotted-rhythm pattern ♩. ♪ ♩; the fifth (in bar 147) is kinked, the final upturn initiating an ascent which suspends x; this in turn leads to a five-note cadential descent to 151's C. X's expressive power derives partly from its appoggiatura–resolution pattern (momentarily broken, to great effect, in 145; see the score), partly from its rhythmic consistency (although this too is slightly varied in 145). But it is in the figure's recontextualisation of a motif heard throughout the movement that its true force lies. This is the dotted-rhythm (♩. ♪ ♩) cadential descent C–B♭–A♭ employed in both the first and second themes (see Example 12.12a): in Theme 1 (bars 84, 86 and 92; compare also 94 and, in diminution, 116–17 and 120, left hand) it forms a descent from 5̂ to 3̂ in F minor, thus leaving the preceding phrase 'open'; in Theme 2 (bars 126 and 134; compare 142⁴) it descends 3̂–2̂–1̂ in III. The cadential shape returns with a vengeance in 143–51, stated more or less literally for the first five bars, in diminution in 148 and in augmentation in 150–1 (see Example 12.11b), this last statement recalling the other, related, cadential pattern employed by Chopin, figure y (Example 12.12b), heard earlier in bars 128 and 136 (compare also 130, 132) and here in 150⁴–1¹.[68]

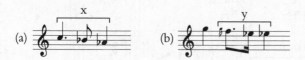

(a)   (b)

Example 12.12   Concerto Op. 21, I: cadence patterns
(a) figure x (Themes 1 and 2)   (b) figure y (Theme 2)

---

[67] Compare the recitative in the second movement, whose parallel-octave recitative texture was modelled on Moscheles' G minor Concerto. The same stylised texture appears in later works by Chopin: for instance, in the Nocturne Op. 32 No. 1 and F minor Prelude Op. 28 No. 18. Note also the recitative-like 'cadenzas' in the C♯ minor Prelude Op. 45 and F minor Ballade Op. 52. In each of these cases, the impression is of a message being 'vocalised' directly to the listener.

[68] X and y are also heard in the orchestral introduction.

A similar use of rhythmic ostinato to build tension can be seen in the 3/4 middle section of Op. 27 No. 1, which is driven to climax by an insistent ♩. ♪♩ figure.

It is not really necessary for the performer to 'bring out' these motivic connections: they should sound 'natural', as if they happen of their own accord. But what is imperative is that the pianist sense the enormous expressive potential conveyed by x's ostinato-like repetitions, the starting/stopping quality and seeming inevitability of these creating expectations which Chopin almost cruelly exploits to destroy Theme 2's lyrical mood. The performer need also be aware of the unusually refined manipulation of register, contour and texture. This is implicit in Example 12.11b, where the arrows ('vectors') show directional impulses, representing, in a quite literal sense, the *musical gestures articulated by the performer*, either as lines or, in the case of the responding flourishes, as curves. Note the essential four-part texture, which again derives from the division of each hand into two (occasionally, three) voices. The minim bass moves steadily until the breaking-point in 148 is approached, whereupon the pace accelerates and the intervallic spans widen. Above this lies a 'tenor' accompaniment, which moulds the left-hand part in a variety of figurations: insistent pedals on C (143–4); rhapsodic sweeps (145) which highlight x's passing-note motion in the soprano; more registrally confined chords from which emerges a staggered doubling of the soprano melody (146–8), this doubling becoming particularly poignant (in part through suspensions, also found in the left hand's inner lines) as climax is reached; and, finally, broken-chord patterns articulating a countermelody (149–51), with the appoggiaturas in 150 underscoring the treble's pathetic descent.

The right hand also boasts enormously varied figuration, spread over different registral levels. At first the alto is in contrary motion to the soprano's descending line, but in 144 in reinforces x in octaves. Disappearing for the next four bars (the soprano left to 'speak' for itself), the alto returns in 149 again to double the top part in octaves, though here it is ingeniously manipulated so that it sometimes follows, sometimes precedes the upper line. By acting in concert with the soprano when the cadential close (y) is reached, the alto imbues the *con duolo* with an even stronger sense of dejection. The soprano, jumping desperately between registers (it spans three-and-a-half octaves in just six bars), alternates between x and the connecting flourishes. The latter are best thought of as sweeps of notes joined in a perfect legato, like a vocal *portamento* or *strascino*, rather than in terms of separate attacks; hence their portrayal in Example 12.11b as undulating curves. In playing these, I employ what I term an 'accelerando principle' – which in my view is an essential part of Chopin's performance aesthetic – whereby the notes of an ornamental shape are rendered not equally but more slowly at first and faster towards the end.[69] It is also appropriate to use a Chopinesque rubato in the right-hand runs while the left maintains the quaver pulse, both hands 'breathing' with the wrist (as Chopin would say) to give the music life.[70]

[69] Kleczyński cites numerous examples (from Op. 9 No. 2, bars 16 and 24, and Op. 21, II, bars 26, 28, 30, 40, 75 and 77) of 'ornamental passages which should be played more slowly at the commencement and accelerated towards the end' (quoted in *CPT*, p. 53). To some extent this 'accelerando principle' compensates for the piano's inability to sustain a note at a constant or increasing volume, which the voice can of course easily manage.

[70] In his piano method Chopin describes the wrist as 'respiration in the voice' (quoted in *CPT*, p. 45; compare Eigeldinger, *Esquisses*, p. 76). See Emilie von Gretsch's revealing comments on this point, quoted in *CPT*, p. 45.

242   *John Rink*

These flourishes, which inhale and exhale in turn, range from bar 143's smooth arpeggiation; the tortured turn in 145 surrounding x (played with terrifying energy – *con forza* – at its suddenly higher register); the highly dissonant, convoluted descent that follows in 145; the ascending gestures in 146 and 147 (the first effecting registral change, the second climbing more deliberately towards the climactic breaking point); and the cascading 'cadenza' in 148, played in a state of shocked exhaustion (*pp*, *leggierissimo*) after the stabbing *ff* leap not to the expected melodic a♭^{3} (compare the tenor doubling underneath, as well as the broken octave earlier in 144^4) but a third higher, to c^4, with great impact on the listener. The cadenza's vertiginous descent shatters the tension, and the music winds down in the state of resignation already described (effected by the descent's registral containment and its slow articulation in octaves – two voices conveying the same expressive message at once).[71]

The 'meaning' of this passage can best be grasped, I believe, by comparing it to a 'narrative' work of J. S. Bach: the Chromatic Fantasy, specifically its *Recitativo* in bars 49–74 (which is preceded by a toccata-like section and followed by a coda). This harmonically ambitious passage was of central importance in the history of improvisation, serving as a source of inspiration for numerous later improvisers and composers, not least C. P. E. Bach. Indeed, it is likely that Emanuel Bach modelled his improvisatory style directly on the Chromatic Fantasy's recitative, as the following comments from the *Versuch* indicate:

it is especially in fantasias . . . that the keyboardist more than any other executant can practice the *declamatory style*, and move audaciously *from one affect to another* . . . Unbarred free fantasias seem especially adept at the expression of affects, for each meter carries a kind of compulsion within itself. At least it can be seen in accompanied recitatives that tempo and meter must be frequently changed in order to rouse and still the *rapidly alternating affects* . . . It is a distinct merit of the fantasia that, unhampered by such trappings, *it can accomplish the aims of the recitative at the keyboard* with complete, unmeasured freedom.[72]

Although neither the Chromatic Fantasy nor the F minor Concerto is an unbarred free fantasy, both contrive to 'accomplish the aims of the recitative at the keyboard'. Bach achieves a recitative effect in the Chromatic Fantasy by punctuating the soprano's speech-like discourse in bars 49–74 with impassioned chords, and by employing an evocative appoggiatura motif throughout this section (in different rhythmic positions within the bar) and in the coda (on alternate beats). Excerpts of both are shown in Example 12.14. The bracketed figures are accompanied by the chords and connected by flourishes which 'comment' on the deeply felt lament voiced by the appoggiaturas, which variously project defiance, remorse, resignation, suffering and so on. The effect

71   To my ear, this poignant close is strikingly similar to a cadential pattern in the G minor Ballade Op. 23 (see Example 12.13a). It too follows a *fioritura* (although a joyous, not an enervated one), leading to a harmonic and melodic progression like that in Op. 21 in which even the tenor countermelody is preserved. Compare also the syncopated left-hand minim line in bars 22–3 of the Ballade (Example 12.13b), which I hear as analogous to the repeated left-hand Cs on the second and sixth quavers in bars 143–4 of the concerto movement, stemmed as syncopated crotchets in 144. These close 'intertextual' references suggest that the *expressive content* of the respective passages may in some way be related.

72   *Essay*, p. 153 (my emphases). For further discussion of Bach's improvisatory practices, see John Rink, 'Schenker and Improvisation', *Journal of Music Theory*, 37/1 (1993), pp. 1–54 passim. See also note 32 above.

Example 12.13   Ballade Op. 23 (a) bars 33–6 (b) bars 22–3

is particularly strong in the coda, where the appoggiatura-flourish pattern is strictly maintained (although the flourishes themselves are varied: no two are identical).

Even though Chopin's musical language differs in many respects from Bach's, the passage from Op. 21 under discussion here employs the same 'vocabulary', 'grammar' and declamatory procedures as the Chromatic Fantasy to project a similar expressive message. This is not wholly surprising, as Chopin's style was shaped not only by Bach's but also, in a more general sense, by the practice of improvisation[73] – both the way in which the music was conceived and its essential 'spirit'. What is perhaps more astonishing is that an improvisatory passage – a 'keyboard recitative' – of such overwhelming power should appear at this early stage in Chopin's career, a passage whose intensity, whose 'rapidly changing affects' and 'abrupt contrasts and unexpected

---

[73] See Rink, 'The Evolution of Chopin's "Structural Style"'.

(a)

(b)

Example 12.14　J. S. Bach, Chromatic Fantasy
(a) recitative (upper parts), bars 49–53　(b) coda (upper parts), bars 75²–6

outbursts'[74] foreshadow one of his most improvisatory, and masterful, works, the
F minor Ballade Op. 52.[75]

Although these comments may seem distant from the realm of performance, they
have in every particular shaped or been shaped by my interpretation of Op. 21, which
is not to say that I was always conscious of the stylistic resonances with the Chromatic
Fantasy or even the recitative-like alternation between motif x and the sweeping
flourishes, although, if only 'intuitively', I certainly stressed that alternation in
performance. In short, the interpretative strategy I had crafted for this music – a
strategy determined long before these words were written or the ideas behind them
fully articulated – depended on a sense, a 'feel', for what I have been discussing, this
'second sight' stemming from a 'familiarity with the composer's style and performance
aesthetic, as well as prolonged immersion in the music itself', such as I referred to earlier.

To summarise, I do not propose that before playing a composition the performer
must produce complex analytical diagrams (mine were drafted well after the fact), nor
must he or she carry out extensive historical research on the music or its style. But if at
some stage the particular knowledge that can accrue through continued exposure to a
composer's works – with the aid of 'an accomplished technique, love of the music
and scrupulous fidelity to the score' – has been assimilated by the performer so that it
operates at a 'submerged level of consciousness', it may well guide the intuitive
understanding of the music that alone can inspire authentic interpretation.

---

[74]　Samson's description (*The Music of Chopin*, p. 48) of fantasies by C. P. E. Bach and Beethoven; it
applies to Chopin's music by extension.

[75]　Samson (*Chopin: The Four Ballades*, p. 19) notes Op. 52's resonances with contemporary improvisation.
It was one of Chopin's great achievements to shape entire works such as the Ballade by using
improvisatory procedures like those in this passage from Op. 21.

Appendix

Encounters with Chopin: Fanny Erskine's Paris diary, 1847–8

JEREMY BARLOW

As a young woman Fanny Erskine[1] (1825–70) kept a series of twelve diaries or journals between 1839 and 1852;[2] the seventh of these covers a two-month stay in Paris from December 1847 to January 1848. Fanny was a keen amateur singer, and one of her principal aims in visiting Paris was to have lessons with the renowned teacher Manuel Garcia (1805–1906). In the diary, interspersed between passages of religious introspection and accounts of sightseeing, shopping and social engagements, are descriptions not only of the thirteen lessons she received from Garcia, but also of four meetings with Chopin. The names of Jane Stirling and her sister Mrs Katherine Erskine[3] appear on almost every page, and there are references to concerts, operas and domestic music-making. The diary, while not remarkable for any great insights or original outlook, helps to fill the gap in Chopin biographies between his departure from Nohant in November 1846 and his final Paris concert in February 1848.

Fanny arrived in Paris on Wednesday 1 December 1847, along with her widowed aunt Mrs Mary Rich; the two were received as guests of the Schwabe family, who had rented part of a house on the Champs-Elysées. The name Schwabe immediately brings us into known Chopin territory, and also provides a link with a Chopin manuscript dedicated to Fanny and bequeathed by her daughter[4] to the Fitzwilliam Museum, Cambridge. During his Anglo-Scottish tour in 1848, Chopin stayed at the Schwabes' substantial English residence, Crumpsall House (near Manchester, where he performed

---

[1] Fanny Erskine (great-great-grandmother of the present author) was born in Edinburgh, the ninth child of William and Maitland (née Mackintosh) Erskine. Her father was a civil servant and the family travelled widely. At the time of her Paris visit, she was living with her parents in Bonn. In 1854 she married Thomas Henry Farrer (1819–99), created Baron Farrer in 1893.

[2] The diaries were passed down through the family to Fanny's granddaughter, the Hon. Anne Farrer (1908–92), who kindly allowed me to examine and bring to light the diary under discussion. Permission to publish the excerpts in this appendix has graciously been provided by the present owner, who retains the copyright.

[3] Fanny Erskine and Katherine Erskine were related by marriage: Katherine's brother-in-law Thomas Erskine appears to have been a rather distant cousin of Fanny's father.

[4] Emma (Ida) Farrer (1854–1946), who married Charles Darwin's youngest son in 1880.

on 28 August).⁵ It seems that Fanny Erskine was there as well, because the manuscript (a single-stave transcription of the song 'Wiosna') is inscribed 'souvenir de Crumpsal [*sic*] House / à Mademoiselle Fanny Erskine / F Chopin / 1. Sept. 1848'.⁶ The Schwabes emerge from the diary as cultured and musical, and together with Mary Rich appear to have had many acquaintances in Parisian artistic and intellectual society.

On her second day in Paris (2 December), Fanny encountered Chopin's Norwegian pupil, Thomas Tellefsen, at the Schwabes' house: 'a wild looking genius, quite devoted to Chopin. I thought him like the pictures of Schiller and he evidently found a likeness to me, for I caught him scrutinizing me once or twice & at last he asked if he [had] not seen me somewhere before, bolting out of the room looking rather confused and awkward . . .' The following day at dinner Fanny was introduced to Katherine Erskine and Jane Stirling, 'energetic and earnest as I had expected'.⁷ Later that evening, Tellefsen again visited the Schwabes 'and enchanted us all. He played principally Chopin, so wild & touching & was delighted with my Jenny Lind songs . . . His music was a great treat.'

The first meeting with Chopin took place three days later, on Monday 6 December:

Aunt M. & I dined at Mrs. James [Katherine] Erskine's the only other company Chopin of whom Miss Jane Stirling made much. He is such an interesting looking man but Oh! so suffering, & so much younger than I had expected. He exerted himself to talk at dinner & seemed so interested in Mendelssohn⁸ & the honors paid to his memory in London but said there was something almost enviable in his fate dying in the midst of his family surrounded by love – & with his wife beside him – & having lived so purely happy a life – & he looked so sad. I felt for him for they say he is so lonely & obliged even to go out for his Breakfast & suffering dreadfully from asthma. He asked me about the Beethoven Fest. & was so happy to see Aunt Mary again, he grew quite playful & seemed to forget his suffering[.] I was in a dreadful fright about singing & felt my hands quite cold but the moment at length came & I commenced, he was so encouraging & while I was still playing the accompaniment [she was evidently accompanying her own singing] said – 'Ah that will do[,] she is a musician – I will speak to Garcia myself about her' – wh[ich] I was delighted at from him & after I had sung several things he came to me & told me to be sure & go on with my music, and that as to my voice he was sure I had twice as much as I shewed. So my first great alarm is over! – And then he sat down to try Miss Jane S's new Erard – and how can I

5   In a letter from Johnston Castle, Scotland, to Wojciech Grzymała in Paris, started on 4 September 1848, Chopin mentions staying with 'my good friend Schwabe', and also the presence of 'that dear Mrs Rich' (*Selected Correspondence of Fryderyk Chopin*, trans. and ed. Arthur Hedley (London 1962), p. 340).

6   The dedication was by no means exclusive: several other copies by Chopin survive, including one written about two months earlier in an album belonging to Mendelssohn's friend Sophie Horsley. See Krystyna Kobylańska, *Rękopisy utworów Chopina: Katalog*, 2 vols. (Cracow 1977); vol. I, pp. 434–40.

7   Chopin biographers have typically devoted more attention to Jane Stirling than Katherine Erskine: she was, after all, his pupil, later assuming the role of his 'widow'. One gains the impression from the diary, however, that as friends to the composer the sisters were more or less equals. (In letters from England and Scotland, Chopin would refer jointly to them as his 'Scottish ladies'. See *Selected Correspondence*, pp. 319–53 passim.) Fanny does not mention Jane Stirling as part of the company on the three occasions she met Chopin at Katherine Erskine's house, although, as the two sisters seem to have shared the house (the 'new Erard' that Chopin played there was Jane's – see below), it may be that Fanny simply took her presence for granted.

8   Fanny had also met Mendelssohn, who (like Chopin) dedicated a copy of one of his songs to her ('Des Mädchens Klage').

describe his playing – Anything so pure & heavenly, & delicate I never heard – & so mournful; his music is so like himself – & so original in its sadness. The feeling awakened in my heart listening to him was like that inspired by Jenny Lind, so soothing & with nothing to grate or jar on the feelings. His preludes & his nocturnes composed at the moment were so delicious I could have jumped up with joy! & he played us a Mazurka after. He is a Pole & seems very fond of his country. I was quite sorry to come away but had his exquisite harmonies in my heart for long.

So it appears that at least one purpose of the meeting was for Chopin to screen Fanny as a potential pupil for Garcia. She learnt that she had been accepted a few days later, on Friday 10 December, when Katherine Erskine and Jane Stirling came to dinner: 'Miss S– brought with her a summons to me to attend Garcia tomorrow at 2 oc. [o'clock] wh[ich] which puts me in a great fright. It was very kind of Chopin to manage it all so nicely & quickly for me.' Fanny then began a course of lessons, held twice a week until 22 January, the last entry in the diary.

Ten days later, on Thursday 16 December, Fanny had her second encounter with Chopin, over dinner at Katherine Erskine's:

Chopin did not come till late & looking Oh! so suffering but so kind[.] Much interested in Garcia. He spoke so pleasantly all dinner & seems so simply true, with a keen sense of the good & beautiful & full of imagination. He told us his first remembrances of hearing Catalani[9] in her glory & seeing her set up Tableaux which made a strong impression on his musical excitable soul. When Mr. & Mrs. S– [Schwabe] came he talked more generally & pretty late played – Oh! so exquisitely[.] Such bursts of feeling & passion. Such shakes! I was so sorry to come away & shall always be interested in him, there is something so uncommon in him altogether & so oppressedly suffering yet patient & uncomplaining – God be with him & grant him the rest & happiness good for him!

Before her fourth meeting with Chopin on 13 January, exactly four weeks later, various Chopin-related incidents are briefly recounted. On Tuesday 28 December following her singing lesson Fanny was joined by Jane Stirling and Katherine Erskine: 'We drove after to Chopin's where Aunt M. & Miss S[tirling] got out. We waited for a long time for them & found they had been detained by finding the concierge's little child dying – & they were most active after going to Dr. Petrus & the Trotters & prescribing for it.'[10] The entry for the following day describes Miss Trotter's commission of a *croquis* of Chopin by Winterhalter[11] as a New Year's Day present for Jane Stirling ('great will be her joy!') 'for whatever it might cost. This she had done for 800 francs – Chopin helping her', although he 'was shocked at the price'. On Tuesday 4 January Fanny was accompanied by her aunt and Jane Stirling to her singing lesson with Garcia: 'Miss S. was delighted with him! We called to enquire for the Trotters &

---

9   Angelica Catalani (1780–1849), the celebrated soprano who in 1820 presented Chopin with a gold watch on her visit to Warsaw.

10   Chopin's concierge Mme Etienne crops up again in 1849, when she allegedly failed to pass on a packet containing Jane Stirling's gift of 25,000 francs to the ailing composer; its non-delivery was discovered four months later.

11   Franz Xaver Winterhalter (1805–73); for a reproduction of the sketch (dated 'Paris 1847') see Mieczysław Tomaszewski and Bożena Weber, *Fryderyk Chopin: A Diary in Images*, trans. Rosemary Hunt (Cracow and Warsaw 1990), p. 224. (Tomaszewski and Weber claim that the drawing was commissioned by Jane Stirling; Fanny's diary indicates otherwise.)

Chopin who had all been ill but were better & then they brought me home.' A week later, after her singing lesson, she accompanied 'the others . . . to different places for a present to give Chopin'. The next day (Wednesday 12 January) Fanny's third meeting with Chopin took place, when she heard him give a piano lesson, presumably to Jane Stirling: 'I was driving over this forenoon early, to fetch Miss Stirling & Miss Hall to convey to Chopin's . . . such a bijou of a room & such a lesson I envied it – every now & then if it did not go quite he played away on another piano – & was so good about it.'

The entry for Thursday 13 January begins: 'I pattered over through the mud to Mrs. E[rskine]'s to hear Franchomme accompany Miss S. [Stirling] on the violincello [*sic*] & was not disappointed. It comes quite up to what I had expected, & how richly & fully he made it sing out!' Later that evening, after dinner, Fanny returned to Katherine Erskine's house for the final encounter with Chopin during her stay in Paris:

A little select party there[.] Richmond[12] – Chopin – Miss Trotter, Tellephson [*sic*] & ourselves – Richmond was so pleasant & talking of the benefit to the character of trial & having to wait & expect what we earnestly desire to obtain & of the way in wh[ich] it is doubly prized after . . . Chopin played for a long long time so splendidly & was quite frisky after[,] making rabbits on the wall & shewing off his various accomplishments[.] Tellephson & I had a long argument about taste in music – he arguing it could not properly be there unchangeably before the age of 22 [Fanny's age that year] – Chopin alarmed him by taking my part & insisting on it a little sooner! They were all very much at home & merry.

The diary ends on Saturday 22 January, when Fanny received a letter from her mother summoning her home. In her final lesson that day with Garcia she had 'a very melancholy hour & touching parting . . . I was quite sorry to see the last of him.'

---

[12]   George Richmond (1809–96), the Victorian portrait painter, for whom Fanny sat on at least three occasions.

Index

Abraham, G., 92
Adam, L., 204–6
Adorno, T., 1, 17
Alard, D., 121–2
Alekseevna, E., 36
Alexander I, 36–7
Alexander II, 49
Alexander III, 49
Alkan, C.-V., 105, 121
Anonymous Scottish lady, 217
Argerich, M., 194, 197
Aristophanes, 65
Arnold, M., 10
Ashkenazy, V., 194, 197
Auber, D.-F.-E., 106

Baader, F. von, 58
Bach, C. P. E., 200–1, 223, 242
Bach, J. S., 6, 36, 103–4, 107–11, 113, 119–22, 124–7, 129, 138–9, 230, 236, 242–4
Bądarzewska, T., 29
Baillot, P., 120, 122, 203
Balakirev, M., 8–9, 42, 44, 49
Ballanche, P.-S., 58
Ballstaedt, A., 6
Balmont, K., 40
Balzac, H. de, 47, 52, 58, 61
Bartók, B., 184
Becker, J., 37
Beecke, I. von, 202
Beethoven, L. van, 6, 25, 29, 36, 45, 47, 72, 78–9, 85–6, 103, 111, 122, 124–6, 136–7, 140, 142, 184, 186, 205, 207, 215, 217–18, 246
Bellini, V., 104–6
Benedict, J., 123
Benjamin, W., 24, 83
Berlioz, H., 40, 51, 83, 105–6, 124–6
Bernard, M., 38–9, 44
Berry, W., 187
Blanchard, H., 53

Bloch, E., 80
Blok, A., 40
Boccherini, L., 122
Borodin, A., 44
Bourges, M., 120
Brahms, J., 6, 120, 179, 230
Broadwood, J., 5, 38
Brodziński, K., 8
Broeckx, J., 16
Bronarski, L., 44, 108, 174, 178–80
Bruch, M., 6
Bruner, J., 84, 87, 89, 98
Bülow, H. von, 45–6, 206–7
Busst, A. J. L., 58
Butler, J., 61–2

Carew, D., 10
Catalani, A., 247
Catherine II, 37
Chenavard, P., 58
Cherubini, L., 103–4, 122
Chomiński, J., 232–4
Chopin, F., works
    Variations on 'Là ci darem la mano' Op. 2, 107, 111–15, 119
    Sonata Op. 4, 107–10, 114, 119
    Five Mazurkas Op. 7, 44
        No. 3, 154
    Trio Op. 8, 212
    Three Nocturnes Op. 9, 44
        No. 1, 46, 147–8
        No. 2, 212
    Twelve Etudes Op. 10, 38, 45, 105, 220
        No. 9, 131
    Concerto Op. 11, 42, 47, 112–15, 117, 119, 129–30, 137, 235–6
    Fantasy on Polish Airs Op. 13, 114, 116
    Rondo à la Krakowiak Op. 14, 128–9
    Three Nocturnes Op. 15
        No. 2, 132
        No. 3, 156, 212

Rondo Op. 16, 212–13
Four Mazurkas Op. 17
  No. 2, 150
  No. 3, 150
  No. 4, 144
Waltz Op. 18, 19, 38, 44
Bolero Op. 19, 19
Scherzo Op. 20, 45
Concerto Op. 21, 42, 47, 112–14, 119, 129,
  212, 217, 235–44
Andante spianato and Grande Polonaise brillante
  Op. 22, 46, 131
Ballade Op. 23, 10, 72–83, 85–6, 89, 144,
  146, 151, 221, 224–5
Four Mazurkas Op. 24
  No. 1, 212
  No. 4, 134–5, 154–5
Twelve Etudes Op. 25, 38, 45
  No. 1, 131–2
Two Polonaises Op. 26, 153
  No. 1, 148–9, 212
Two Nocturnes Op. 27, 135, 226
  No. 1, 136, 150
  No. 2, 148
Twenty-four Preludes Op. 28, 45, 119, 129,
  188
  No. 1, 166
  No. 2, 14, 156
  No. 3, 166
  No. 4, 110–11, 161–82
  No. 5, 166, 217, 226–35
  No. 8, 183, 188–98
  No. 15, 226
  No. 16, 132, 166
  No. 19, 166
  No. 20, 113
  No. 21, 127
  No. 23, 148
Impromptu Op. 29, 212
Four Mazurkas Op. 30
  No. 2, 157
  No. 3, 154
  No. 4, 150
Scherzo Op. 31, 45, 157–8, 218
Two Nocturnes Op. 32, 44
  No. 2, 212
Mazurka Op. 33 No. 4, 155
Three Waltzes Op. 34
  No. 2, 44
  No. 3, 153
Sonata Op. 35, 14, 45, 47
Nocturne Op. 37 No. 2, 45
Ballade Op. 38, 14, 85–6, 131, 158–60
Scherzo Op. 39, 143–4, 217–26
Two Polonaises Op. 40
  No. 1, 91, 153
  No. 2, 95, 145, 149
Four Mazurkas Op. 41, 38

  No. 1, 142, 161, 166–9, 173
  No. 3, 140, 156
Waltz Op. 42, 28, 153
Polonaise Op. 44, 95, 153, 155
Prelude Op. 45, 129, 144
Allegro de concert Op. 46, 46
Ballade Op. 47, 28, 85–6, 94, 99, 108–9, 131,
  142, 221
Nocturne Op. 48 No. 1, 151
Fantasy Op. 49, 14, 85–6, 90–1, 95, 131,
  158–9
Three Mazurkas Op. 50, 104
  No. 3, 155
Ballade Op. 52, 13, 45, 85–6, 94, 98, 140–1,
  153, 244
Polonaise Op. 53, 91, 153, 155
Scherzo Op. 54, 95, 134
Two Nocturnes Op. 55, 44
  No. 1, 130–1
  No. 2, 151
Three Mazurkas Op. 56, 104
  No. 1, 146
  No. 3, 109, 143, 152
Berceuse Op. 57, 114–16, 118–19
Sonata Op. 58, 45, 47, 112, 114, 144
Three Mazurkas Op. 59, 104
  No. 1, 146–7
  No. 2, 150
Barcarolle Op. 60, 98, 114, 116–17, 132,
  134–5
Polonaise-Fantasy Op. 61, 84–101, 152
Two Nocturnes Op. 62, 114
  No. 1, 118, 137–8
Three Mazurkas Op. 63, 38, 104
Three Waltzes Op. 64, 5
  No. 1, 27, 153
  No. 2, 44, 153–4, 226
Cello Sonata Op. 65, 99, 113–14, 123
[Fantasy-]Impromptu Op. 66, 152, 226
Four Mazurkas Op. 67
  No. 2, 104
  No. 3, 212
Mazurka Op. 68 No. 4, 104, 110–11
Waltz Op. 70 No. 3, 44
Nocturne Op. 72 No. 1, 44
Trois Nouvelles Etudes No. 2, 135
Polonaise in G♯ minor, 212
Grand Duo concertant, 28, 33
Lento con gran espressione, 9
Chorley, H., 85
Cimarosa, D., 107, 123
Clementi, M., 104–5, 107, 120
Cone, E. T., 98, 190, 228
Cook, N., 13, 98, 100
Corelli, A., 120
Couperin, F., 121
Courty, Mme de, 132
Custine, A. de, 52, 55, 65, 69

Czartoryska, M., 75, 103, 106, 123, 216
Czartoryski, A., 75
Czerny, C., 107, 120–1, 204, 206, 208

Dahlhaus, C., 236
Damke, B., 39
Dante, 81
David, F., 106
Davison, J. W., 54
Debussy, C., 110, 114, 118–19, 125–30, 133–7, 139
Debussy-Bardac, E., 134
Delacroix, E., 77, 79, 81, 106, 121–7, 129, 138–9, 175, 236
Delsarte, F., 121
Diederichs, T., 37
Döhler, T., 31, 38, 42, 105
Donizetti, G., 106
Drachman, Mrs D., 161, 163
Dreyschock, A., 36, 42
Dubois-O'Meara, C., 123
Dudevant-Sand, S., 64–5, 106
Dunsby, J., 188
Durand, J., 135–6
Dussek, J., 203–4, 212
Działyńska, C., 216
Dziewanowski, D., 76

Eberlin, J. E., 122
Eichtal, Baron, 51
Eigeldinger, J.-J., 188, 209, 212–13, 216–17, 236
Ellis, K., 4
Elsner, J., 102, 104, 107, 113, 124
Empson, W., 140
Enfantin, P., 58
Erard, S., 5, 22, 38
Erskine, F., 245–8
Erskine, K., 245–8
Eschmann, J. C., 31
Escudier, L., 52
Ezdinli, L., 62

Fauré, G., 5
Feodorovna, M., 36
Fet, A., 40
Fétis, F.-J., 41, 121
Field, J., 28, 36, 46–7, 114
Fink, G. W., 85
Fish, S., 1, 15
Fontana, J., 75–7, 105, 162–3, 180, 234
Foucault, M., 63, 67
Frackmann, V., 38
Franchomme, A., 103, 121–3, 248
Fuller-Maitland, J. A., 199

Gadamer, H.-G., 16
Gajewski, F., 99
Ganche, E., 56
Garcia, M., 245–8

Gautier, T., 58
Geoffroy Saint-Hilaire, I., 67–9
Gładkowska, K., 102, 104
Glinka, M. I., 48–9, 206
Gluck, C. W., 110, 121
Godowsky, L., 12–13
Goethe, J. W. von, 29, 90
Gottschalk, L. M., 41
Gould, G., 186
Gounod, C., 123
Gretsch, E. von, 235
Grimm, Baron, 22
Grzymała, W., 56, 221
Gubert, *see* Hubert, N. A.

Habeneck, F.-A., 122
Halévy, F., 106
Hallé, C., 10, 12, 51, 134, 185, 210
Handel, G. F., 6, 104, 107, 120–1, 124
Hanslick, E., 18, 79–80, 208, 210
Hatzfeld, Countess von, 202
Haweis, H. R., 55, 68
Haydn, J., 85, 103, 110, 122
Henselt, A., 30–1, 36, 38, 105, 200, 210
Herz, H., 22
Hiller, F., 38, 121
Hipkins, A. J., 122
Hubert, N. A., 43–4
Hummel, J. N., 46–7, 104, 114, 121–2, 203–6, 208
Huneker, J., 223

Ingres, J.-A.-D., 78, 138
Ippolitov-Ivanov, M. M., 44

Janin, J., 53
Janion, M., 82
Jarociński, S., 134
Jurgenson, P., 43–5, 57

Kahlert, A., 6
Kalkbrenner, F., 22, 31, 105, 206
Kallberg, J., 3, 12, 81, 90–1, 93–7, 101, 104
Kamieński, M., 104
Karasowski, M., 163, 227
Kirnberger, J. P., 121
Kistner, F., 5
Kleczyński, J., 132, 210, 212, 226
Klengel, A., 107, 124
Klindworth, K., 43, 174, 178–9
Koch, H. C., 202–3
Koczalski, R., 126
Köhler, L., 30, 33
Krasiński, Z., 82–3
Kulakov, A., 38
Kurpiński, K., 104

Lamartine, A. de, 3
Lassus, O., 126

Latouche, H. de, 58
Launer, The Widow, 120
Laurens, J.-J.-B., 121
Leichtentritt, H., 7, 87, 90, 92, 97, 232–4
Lenz, W. von, 45–7, 80, 103, 119–20, 136–7,
     210, 216
Léo, A., 105
Leppert, R., 9
Leroux, P., 58
Leverkühn, A., 55
Lichtenthal, H., 37
Lieven, Countess, 22
Lind, J., 246–7
Liszt, F., 4, 22–4, 27–8, 30, 32–3, 36, 38, 40,
     42–6, 51, 54, 86, 101–2, 105, 119, 121,
     139, 200, 206–7, 209, 211–12
Long, M., 133
Louis-Philippe, 105, 107, 134
Lully, J.-B., 121

Magaloff, N., 194, 197
Mahler, G., 14, 83, 86, 97
Mallarmé, S., 137
Mallefille, F., 81–3
Mann, T., 55, 69
Marcello, B., 104, 121
Marliani, C., 56
Marmontel, A.-F., 54, 70, 130
Marx, A. B., 13
Mason, W., 206
Mathias, G., 208, 215
Mauté, Mme, 136
Mayer, C., 36
Mendelssohn, F., 6, 29, 38, 44–5, 121, 207, 209, 236
Meyer, L. B., 8
Meyerbeer, G., 106, 210
Michelangelo, 126
Mickiewicz, A., 74–6, 81–2
Mikuli, K., 121, 126, 209, 211, 216–17
Monet, C., 131
Moniuszko, S., 39
Montgeroult, H., 203–4
Moreau, G., 58
Moscheles, I., 12, 27, 38, 104–5, 121, 209
Mozart, L., 201–2
Mozart, W. A., 6, 29, 36, 47, 78, 85, 103–4, 106,
     110, 119, 121–6, 139–40, 201–2, 204,
     212, 215
Müller, F., 120
Musorgsky, M., 44

Namier, L., 73–4, 76
Napravnik, E., 44
Neefe, C. G., 103
Neukomm, S., 105
Nicholas I, 35–7, 39, 41–2
Niecks, F., 200
Nietzsche, F. W., 7

Nodier, C., 51, 58
Novalis (Friedrich von Hardenberg), 58
Nowik, W., 104

Olivet, A. F. d', 58
Onslow, G., 85, 107
Oster, E., 177
Oury de Belleville, C., 122
Ovid, 64

Pachmann, V. de, 204
Paderewski, I. J., 44, 174, 178–80, 204
Palestrina, G. P. da, 6, 126
Pape, J. H., 22
Parakilas, J., 89–90, 94, 97
Parker, C., 184
Pavlovna, E., 42
Pergolesi, G. B., 104, 121
Piatigorsky, G., 161, 163
Pixis, J. P., 107
Plato, 58, 64–5
Pleyel, C., 20, 22, 52, 122
Pleyel, I., 122
Poizat, M., 61
Pollini, M., 194, 197
Potocka, D., 104
Poussin, N., 126
Probst, H. A., 81
Proust, M., 4, 114

Rachmaninoff, S., 44
Rameau, J.-P., 121
Raphael, 126
Ravel, M., 5
Reber, H., 121
Récamier, Mme, 22
Rellstab, L., 6
Rev, L., 194, 197
Rich, M., 245–6
Richmond, G., 248
Ricoeur, P., 84, 87
Riemann, H., 7, 33–4, 199
Ries, F., 85, 205
Rimsky-Korsakov, N., 44, 48
Rink, J., 97, 224
Roland, Mme, 22
Rosen, C., 139
Rosenthal, M., 204
Rossini, G., 104, 106, 114, 123
Rostislav (F. M. Tolstoi), 41–2, 46–8
Rothschild, J. de, 21
Rothstein, W., 150
Rozmyslov, P., 38
Rubens, P. P., 126
Rubinstein, Anton, 12, 42, 44–6, 48
Rubinstein, Artur, 194, 197
Rubinstein, N., 43–4, 46–7, 49
Ruthardt, A., 31

Said, E., 12
Samson, J., 90, 94, 97, 99, 230
Sand, G., 25–6, 47, 56–62, 64, 68, 70, 77–81,
    106, 119, 121, 123, 138–9, 162–3
Sand, M., 78
Satie, E., 129
Sauzay, E., 120–1
Scarlatti, D., 120–2
Schachter, C., 86, 158
Scharlitt, B., 7
Schenker, H., 7–8, 157, 161, 166, 168
Schiller, J. C. F. von, 29
Schlegel, F., 58
Schlesinger, M., 4, 22, 120
Schloezer, B. de, 126
Schmalfeldt, J., 187, 198
Schoenberg, A., 125
Schopenhauer, A., 3, 7
Schreder, J. F., 38
Schubert, F., 6, 25, 29, 36, 44
Schulhoff, J., 39
Schumann, C., 19, 208, 210
Schumann, R., 6, 18–19, 28–9, 44–5, 80–1, 83,
    85, 97, 131, 140, 158–9, 236
Schwabe, Mr and Mrs S., 245–6
Scott, W., 58
Scruton, R., 79
Serov, A., 42, 48
Shakespeare, W., 52, 58, 123
Shelley, P. B., 55
Signac, P., 126
Słowacki, J., 82
Sobański, I., 75
Soliva, C., 104
Spontini, G., 107
Staël, Mme de, 22
Stein, E., 214
Stein, N., 202
Stirling, J., 132, 169–70, 245–8
Stradella, A., 104
Straus, J., 8
Strauss, R., 83
Streicher, N., *see* Stein, N.
Subotnik, R., 4
Sutherland, Duchess of, 122
Swartz, A., 9
Szymanowska, M., 36
Szymanowski, K., 9

Tallien, Mme, 22
Tarasti, E., 91, 97
Tartini, G., 120
Taruskin, R., 215
Tatum, A., 184
Tchaikowsky, P., 37, 44, 48–9
Tellefsen, T., 121, 123, 246, 249
Thalberg, S., 22–4, 36, 38, 42
Timanov, Miss, 46
Todorov, T., 87
Tolstoi, F. M., *see* Rostislav
Tomlinson, G., 71
Tosi, P. F., 199–200, 212
Towiański, A., 75
Turczyński, J., 44, 174, 178–80
Türk, D. G., 201

Urhan, C., 120

Vaudemont, Princesse de, 22
Verdi, G., 106
Verlaine, P., 131, 134
Veronese, P., 123, 126
Viardot-Garcia, P., 121, 228
Victoria, T. L. de, 126
Viotti, G. B., 120
Voltaire (François Marie Arouet), 103–4

Wagner, R., 14, 42–3, 86, 119
Walicki, A., 74
Walton, K. L., 79
Weber, C. M. von, 47, 104, 123, 205, 207, 218
Weil, K., 64–5
Weissmann, A., 7
Wessel, C. R., 77
White, H., 88
Wieck, C., *see* Schumann, C.
Wieck, F., 207–8
Winterhalter, F. X., 247
Witwicki, S., 75
Wollheim, R., 79
Woyciechowski, T., 105

Zeitblom, S., 55
Zimmermann, P., 121
Żmigrodzka, M., 82
Żywny, W., 102–3, 113